Building a Global Zion

David O. McKay

Building a Global Zion

THE LIFE AND VISION OF DAVID O. MCKAY

Brian Q. Cannon

SIGNATURE BOOKS | 2025 | SALT LAKE CITY

Join our mailing list at signaturebooks.com for details on events and related titles we think you'll enjoy.

FIRST EDITION | 2025

Paperback ISBN: 978-1-56085-526-2
Ebook ISBN: 978-1-56085-506-4

Contents

Preface

"If ever a man of modern history left his world better for having lived in it, that man was David Oman McKay. Wherever his influence was felt, man and God became closer in purpose and in action." So editorialized Joseph Lundstrom in the *Deseret News* on the day following McKay's passing, expressing the sentiments of many devoted Latter-day Saints. Secular organs also acknowledged McKay's influence, particularly upon the Church of Jesus Christ of Latter-day Saints. *Time* magazine speculated that as church president McKay "had done more in his 19-year tenure to change the image and direction of the Mormon church than any president since Brigham Young." He had "expanded his church's horizons and involvement" and "tempered" Young's legacy of "exclusivism ... with his own remarkable vision of a much wider, friendlier world."[1]

Had he not been called to general church leadership in his thirty-third year in 1906, McKay might have lived out his life as an effective educator, local church leader, and dedicated citizen. His private family life would have been more focused and rewarding as he spent more time at home with his wife and children. Instead, that pivotal moment in 1906 reoriented McKay's trajectory, enormously broadening his reach and influence while linking his life to the scope and demands of the church. When he died in 1970, roughly 60 percent of the church's membership had known no other church president and prophet. Some Saints (members of the LDS Church) wept upon hearing the news, and many experienced for the first time the transition from one church president to the next.[2]

Given McKay's long tenure as an apostle and prophet, his historical importance, and members' affection and outsiders' respect, it is not surprising that multiple biographers have traced facets of his life. At the outset of this new biography, I acknowledge the work of others. In so doing, I point readers to sources they might consult for additional insights beyond my work, and I also bring into relief some of the distinctive contributions of this biography.

Each biography of McKay confers valuable perspectives. Devotional biographies and life sketches appeared in McKay's own lifetime, written by his son

1. Joseph Lundstrom, "Dignitaries, Church Members Join in President McKay Tribute," *Deseret News*, Jan. 22, 1970, 1; "Prophet, Seer and Innovator," *Time*, Feb. 2, 1970, 49–50.

2. "Statistical Report—1950," delivered Apr. 6, 1951, *Conference Reports*, 9; Joseph Anderson, address of Apr. 6, 1970, *Conference Reports*, 115.

Llewelyn, and his sister Jeanette Morrell. Nearly two decades after McKay's death, another son, Lawrence, published *My Father, David O. McKay.* Like the work of previous family members, his is an admiring portrait from a devoted relative. By his own admission it is "neither analytical, complete, nor interpretive," but these works by family members provide intimate, familial perspectives unavailable elsewhere.[3]

Three major biographies have been published since McKay's death.[4] In 1986, Deseret Book published Francis M. Gibbons's *David O. McKay: Apostle to the World, Prophet of God.* A lawyer by professional training, Gibbons left his practice shortly after McKay died in 1970 to begin work as secretary to the First Presidency, a position that he held until his retirement in 1986. Gibbons was granted unprecedented, unrestricted access to all of McKay's diaries, correspondence, and scrapbooks, and he drank deeply from the sources as he wrote his devotional biography. His book remains the most thorough account of McKay's life and career prior to McKay's tenure as church president.[5]

In 2004, Covenant Communications published Mary Jane Woodger's *David O. McKay: Beloved Prophet.* As a doctoral student in Brigham Young University's College of Education, Woodger studied McKay's educational ideas. She interviewed many of his family members and associates. Her research was integral to

3. McKay, *Home Memories*; Morrell, *Highlights*; McKay, *My Father*, x. Llewelyn sought to make readers "more intimately acquainted with [my] father … because *to know him is to love him*" (preface). Morrell acknowledged that her work is "by no means a complete biography" but instead an intimate portrait that she was specially qualified to provide, having shared in "many of his joys and sorrows." Morrell undertook the work, she wrote, "because I know he is a powerful witness of the divinity of Jesus Christ, and is a true emissary of the living God." Her object was, in her words, to "share with others some highlights in my brother's life as I have viewed them" (x). Lawrence largely focused on McKay's life as it was shared and observed by his wife and children.

4. Additionally, a lyrical narrative biography, comprising thirty-three vignettes, *David O. McKay: Prophet of Love*, was self-published by Keith Terry via Butterfly Publishing in 1980. A devotee of McKay who largely observed him from afar, Terry interviewed the prophet for two hours in 1965 and subsequently interviewed over twenty of McKay's family members, friends, and coworkers. His is the first footnoted overview of McKay's life and was inspired by his admiration for the prophet and his memory of McKay's "magnetism" (preface).

5. Gibbons, *David O. McKay.* From a historian's standpoint, Gibbons's book possesses two key drawbacks: a lack of detailed documentation in footnotes and insufficient critical evaluation of sources. Gibbons takes the McKay diaries compiled by McKay's secretary, Clare Middlemiss, at face value as McKay's words, which he assumes Middlemiss transcribed from McKay's dictations (ix). At times Gibbons takes unwarranted liberties with limited evidence. For instance, in treating the calling of J. Reuben Clark, an outsider, to the First Presidency in 1933, Gibbons notes that McKay's diaries say nothing about the appointment. He infers, "It was almost as if President Clark's call was a matter of indifference to him, an attitude the other members of his quorum seemed to share." Actually, McKay's sparse diary record for 1932 does not record many significant events. There are no entries for several months, and there is no extant diary for 1933, the year that Clark's call was publicly announced. Gibbons improperly uses the absence of any commentary in a diary as a springboard to a devotional point he desires to make: "those called to the apostleship are obligated by covenant and personal disposition to follow the direction of the Prophet without hesitation" (149–50).

BYU's McKay research project that preceded the college's rebranding as the David O. McKay School of Education. For her biography, Woodger drew upon her interviews, along with McKay's personal correspondence and conference notebooks, which had recently become available for research, as well as the scrapbooks Middlemiss compiled. Rather than providing a "fuller, more critical treatment of his life," Woodger selected facets of his life in order to convey "the personality, character, and ideals for which he is so lovingly remembered." McKay was "the ideal example to be followed for Church members in the twentieth century," she posits, and she identifies the prophet's "high ideals" as the "dominant theme" of her work. Having previously edited McKay's correspondence with his wife, Ray, she felicitously conveys the richness and nuance of their courtship and marriage in her biography.[6]

In 2005, Gregory A. Prince and William Robert Wright's magisterial *David O. McKay and the Rise of Modern Mormonism* was published. The book's mainstay, a source unavailable to Woodger, was the daily record made by Middlemiss over the course of her career, a copy of which she retained and bequeathed to her nephew Wright.[7] Prince and Wright left few available stones unturned in their research, although they acknowledged that a more complete study of McKay's presidency could have been written using the corpus of official minutes and general authority diaries that are unavailable to researchers. The two authors conducted over two hundred interviews with McKay's family and associates—a vast resource. Focusing almost exclusively upon McKay's presidential administration, their meticulously documented book treats the final nineteen years of McKay's life topically.

Prince and Wright paint a largely admiring but balanced portrait of McKay as prophet. They note his "deep, authentic spirituality" and admire his charisma and his grasp of the "importance of image." He "set a tone of tolerance that has not since been equaled," giving associates free rein in their assignments and trusting their creativity unless they abused his trust. He "democratized Mormonism" through his focus on member involvement in missionary work and by assuring "members of all stripes that he welcomed them to join him and build the Church within it." Chief among his weaknesses were his stubbornness and his limited administrative skills. He was "not a conventional leader," and he "often frustrated subordinates" by changing his mind midstream in the face of "humane factors." As Boyd Petersen observes in a trenchant review of the book, most of it is an institutional history of the church; McKay's thoughts and

6. Woodger, *David O. McKay*, preface; McKay and McKay, *Heart Petals*.

7. Prince and Wright, *David O. McKay*. As a young man visiting her home, Wright observed firsthand that Middlemiss "dedicated her evenings, weekends, and holidays" to the record. Often when he visited, he found her "laboring over numerous stacks of articles, pictures, and other information that she painstakingly organized into diaries, discourses, and scrapbooks" (ix).

feelings recede into the background in most chapters. As Douglas Alder observes in another review, the authors' "proclivity for controversy" shapes their approach: "many policy disputes [comprise] the bulk of the book."[8]

This book was commissioned as part of the Signature Books brief biography series. Due to the series design and the meticulous coverage by Prince and Wright of many administrative issues McKay confronted as church president, I do not attempt to duplicate their extensive treatment of many significant administrative issues documented in the Middlemiss record. For instance, I choose not to treat the development of the church's radio and television broadcasting ventures, the rise of correlation, management of many facets of the Church Educational System, or the church's extensive political dealings during the McKay presidency. Despite their limitations in capturing McKay's thoughts and words, I rely heavily upon the McKay/Middlemiss "diaries" bequeathed by Wright to the University of Utah, including those compiled when McKay was a counselor in the First Presidency. Aside from Gibbons, biographers have made little use of the record for those years, and they are vital to understanding McKay's activities from the 1930s onward. Although I studied each volume of the Middlemiss record in manuscript form, I benefit greatly from Harvard Heath's superbly edited and footnoted excerpts from the diaries from 1951 onward, *Confidence amid Change*.[9]

For information on the early years of McKay's life, I primarily draw upon his daybooks and diaries from his mission to Scotland, his world tour, and his stint as European mission president—records that reflect his own views most closely. McKay's mission diary is particularly impressive, revealing his flair even at a relatively young age for crisp narrative, keen observation, and acute assessment of character. McKay's mission diary was expertly edited for publication by Stan and Patricia Larson.[10] Lamentably, in the years immediately following his mission, McKay did not keep a journal. He resumed journaling abruptly following his call to the Quorum of the Twelve, leaving space at the outset to describe his call to the apostleship but never managing to fill in the blank pages. Over the next three years, he kept a fairly detailed record. Diaries were either not kept or have not survived for about half of the time between May 1909 and December 1920, when he embarked upon his world tour. Some diaries from that period contain fairly rich detail; two are merely appointment books or daybooks with intermittent entries. On his world tour, McKay kept a handwritten, detailed diary for much of the time. It was then typed, and in some cases augmented, by his traveling companion, Hugh Cannon, who also typed his own record of the

8. Prince and Wright, *David O. McKay*, 2–3, 13, 18, 21, 25, 43, 404; Petersen, review of *David O. McKay*, by Prince and Wright, 270–71; Alder, review of *David O. McKay*, by Prince and Wright, 388.

9. McKay, *Confidence amid Change*.

10. McKay, *What E'er Thou Art*.

tour. These detailed accounts have been carefully edited for publication by Reid Nielson and Carson Teuscher and provide a rich record of McKay's months abroad.[11] Following his return from his world tour in 1922, McKay reverted to more skeletal journaling, briefly recording places and people he visited in entries such as "Ogden 7th ward at 2 p.m., memorial service for a missionary" and "Accusation against High council; Huntsville; Conference with John Farr."[12] It is possible to trace McKay's travels and activities during his two years as European mission president in fairly good detail. Following his return from Europe at the end of 1923, diaries, some of them only pocket daybooks, survive for only portions of four years over the next decade of McKay's life. The best documented year is 1932, but even in that year he left off writing for months at a time. Following his sustaining as a member of the First Presidency in October 1934, McKay began writing brief notes about his activities on most days.

As Prince and Wright observe, "the title 'diaries'" as applied to the record kept by Clare Middlemiss is "something of a misnomer" because first-person dictations compose "only a small part of the record" she compiled. McKay ceased keeping his own handwritten diary midway through 1937, when Middlemiss began keeping a daily account of his activities. Thereafter he scribbled brief notes in appointment books. Eventually the Middlemiss record extended to tens of thousands of pages. On some days McKay dictated information for the diary. In many other instances, Middlemiss cobbled together a record of McKay's activities from minutes of meetings, McKay's appointment calendar (which she kept), written and oral reports from others, and what she heard and observed. Lola Timmins, who worked under Middlemiss's direction and often typed final drafts of the Middlemiss record, explained that Middlemiss "would actually make the draft of his day's work, and go over minutes of meetings he attended and take excerpts from it where President McKay had made a decision or said something noteworthy." When McKay was ill or hospitalized, Middlemiss filled in the details, sometimes referring to McKay in the third person. In many instances, though, it is unclear if first-person statements in the diary are direct quotations or Middlemiss's own rendering of the information in a first-person tone. For instance, did McKay dictate that "by unanimous vote last week at Council Meeting, the brethren decided that I should not attend Council Meeting until my lung is healed. Have come to the conclusion that I shall have to leave this cold weather for a short time in order to let the affected lung heal, and also to overcome an attack of the 'flu,'" or was this Middlemiss's reporting of events? Ultimately, one must bear in mind, as Gary Bergera pointed out, that despite the first-person writing, "Middlemiss was the actual author." Harvard Heath, who edited about 10 percent of McKay's presidential diaries for publication,

11. McKay, *Pacific Apostle*; Neilson, *To the Peripheries*.

12. David O. McKay, diary, hereafter cited as DOMD, Jul. 30 and Sep. 25, 1922.

surmised that "much of it was dictated to his secretary," but there is no way to ascertain how much, if anywhere near half, of the material in Middlemiss's voluminous record was dictated. As a record of daily church administration, the McKay presidential diaries are indispensable, but they also promise more than they deliver as a window into McKay's heart and mind. The diary entries grow more prolix as McKay's health wanes, serving as a record of decisions rendered. Although one cannot be certain, given McKay's poor health, garbled speech, and waning attention to detail, I suspect that McKay dictated a relatively small portion of the diary entries for the final five years of his life.[13]

To a greater degree than previous biographers, I plumb McKay's missionary diary. The mission profoundly shaped McKay, awakening and expanding spiritual sensitivities and honing his administrative and leadership skills. Reflecting my historical training, I pay particular attention to the historical backdrop of key developments that affected McKay and the church, including Prohibition, the Great Depression, World War II, the Cold War, the Civil Rights Movement, and the sexual revolution. As a social historian who is drawn to the experiences of common people, I also highlight McKay's interactions with individual rank-and-file members and local church leaders. Although he was revered as a man of the people, his personal ministry, measured by his interpersonal interactions, has not received the attention it deserves in previous biographies. I also highlight McKay's moral crusading, ranging from his battle against "Demon Rum" to his attempts to investigate and expose municipal corruption. By exploring key themes in his teachings, I supplement the valuable work of Mary Jane Woodger in seeking to explain his powerful, motivating appeal as a religious leader, an appeal that resonates with me as a believer in McKay's prophetic calling. Information and quotations I have drawn from unpublished excerpts of interviews conducted by Greg Prince and Robert Wright illuminate facets of McKay's personality, health, and administrative decisions. Finally, although Gary Bergera wrote a detailed article on the subject, McKay's biographers have paid insufficient attention to challenges and tensions that arose in the 1960s as faithful, well-meaning individuals in McKay's orbit sought to safeguard the church and represent the will of an aging and increasingly infirm church president. These vital, challenging matters arising from the inevitable arc of mortality confronted McKay and his colleagues as well-meaning humans with finite judgments. Channels of authority that functioned well with McKay in control when he was physically strong and mentally astute atrophied as his

13. Prince and Wright, *David O. McKay*, xv; excerpt from Lola Timmins to Greg Prince, Aug. 4, 2000, box 22, folder 24, Gregory A. Prince Papers, hereafter cited as Prince Papers. McKay clearly dictated the entry in DOMD for Mar. 10, 1938, for instance, but Middlemiss refers to McKay in the third person on Dec. 31, 1939. The entry regarding the flu is from Mar. 14, 1940. The diary shifts to Middlemiss's hand by Jun. 28, 1937. Bergera, "Tensions," 209; Heath in McKay, *Confidence amid Change*, xi.

declining health fanned his own sense of vulnerability and abetted suspicion, distrust, and opportunism among his associates, despite their deep commitments to sustaining McKay and safeguarding the church.

Acknowledgments

In 2018, Gary Bergera, editor of Signature Books, invited me to write a brief biography of David O. McKay. I'm grateful that he did. McKay's diaries, housed in the special collections division of the J. Willard Marriott Library at the University of Utah, provide the foundation for my research, and I'm grateful to the archivists there who accommodated my research requests, especially as the world gradually reopened following the COVID-19 pandemic. I'm grateful to Brigham Young University, my employer, for giving me the opportunity to research and to write; to the College of Family, Home, and Social Sciences and its Deans Ben Ogles and Laura Padilla-Walker for their support; and to my colleagues in the history department for their congeniality and encouragement.

One of the great pleasures of teaching at BYU is the opportunity to interact with and mentor talented, dependable students. Over the years that I've worked on this project, my undergraduate research assistants have conducted archival research, critiqued and proofread drafts, and edited my notes and bibliography. I'm enormously grateful to Jared Cluff, Michael Dew, Ariana Feichko, Miranda Jessop, Josh Stevenson, Hayden Weenig, Hunter Westbrook, and Caitlin Zollinger for working with me.

I owe much of my interest in history to my father, Don Cannon, and I'm grateful to him for reading and critiquing drafts of my chapters in manuscript form. Finally, I'm grateful to my wife, Anna Lea, for taking time from her own projects to critique my writing and listen to my ideas. I am especially grateful for her encouragement and love.

1: Taking Root

On Monday, September 8, 1873, the *Salt Lake Tribune* asserted, "Mormonism as a missionary power abroad is dead." Referring to Brigham Young's network of cooperative stores and industries, the writer speculated, "As a grand Mercantile Co-operative Institution, it may yet astonish the world, but its mission as a church of spiritualities is concluded." The next day in Huntsville, a small farming community in the mountains east of Ogden, a Welsh immigrant, Jennette Evans McKay, gave birth to a son in a modest rock home. She and the boy's father, David, a Scotsman, named their son David Oman McKay. Over the course of his life, their baby boy would confound the *Tribune*'s prediction, expanding the international reach of Mormonism and enhancing its spiritual appeal. The baby joined two older sisters in the family, four-year-old Margaret and two-year-old Ellena. Two years later, Thomas was born, followed by Jeanette in 1879. Although the family escaped the ravages of diphtheria, which took the lives of sixty-four children under the age of ten in the community in the winter of 1877–78, a crushing blow walloped the family in 1880 when David was only seven. Within a week, both Margaret and Ellena died of rheumatic fever and pneumonia. The loss haunted the parents for the rest of their lives, but over the next thirteen years the birth of three more daughters and two more sons furnished some consolation. Ann was born in 1881, Elizabeth in 1884, William in 1887, Katherine in 1891, and Morgan in 1893. David was particularly close to his proximate siblings, Jeanette and Thomas, the latter being his best friend and confidant. Jeanette described the McKay siblings' childhood as "happy." David developed an enduring compassion and love for animals and had many pets—a dog, a pony, pigeons, rabbits, and even a magpie that he tamed. His days were filled with work on the farm and at school, but he also found time for diversions including "swimming, horseback riding, reading, baseball, dancing, and singing in the glee club," as well as gathering wildflowers and playing parlor games and croquet.[1]

Huntsville was a small, predominantly agricultural community. The picturesque mountain valley was marginal farm country; the winters were "severe,"

1. "Is Mormonism Declining as a Missionary Power?," *Salt Lake Tribune,* Sep. 7, 1873, 3; Morrell, *Highlights*, 22–23, 30; "Huntsville," *Ogden Junction*, July 2, 1880, 4.

with several feet of snow blanketing the valley most years until mid-April and "occasional light frosts each month" in the summer. In 1880, when David was six years old, the census taker enumerated 170 households and 819 residents in the precinct. Sixty-three percent of the heads of households were farmers, farm laborers, stock herders, or dairymen. The remaining adults included an assortment of carpenters, blacksmiths, shoemakers, masons, weavers, tinsmiths, teachers, and teamsters along with a sawmill operator, a miller, and a butcher. Eighty-three percent of the heads of households were immigrants: Scandinavians predominated with 79 Danes (40 percent of all household heads), 36 Swedes (18 percent), and 2 Norwegians. As was the case elsewhere in the territory, native English speakers tended to be socially and economically advantaged. Seventeen percent of the heads of households were born in the United States. Thirteen percent, including David's father, hailed from the British Isles. Most of the Scotsmen belonged to the McKay clan.[2]

A large public square ringed by two rows of shade trees hosted Huntsville's community activities. Children studied in a large rock building near the center of town. Two hundred sixty-six pupils between the ages of six and eighteen were eligible to attend, but only about half that number, including David, attended the school regularly. By 1880 a handsome brick church measuring forty by seventy feet, designed with pillars, gothic windows, a tower, and a steeple, was under construction.[3]

The McKays grew their own fruit and vegetables to the extent possible in their mountain valley, raised their own livestock and poultry, and harvested grain and hay for their own use and for sale. When David was four, the inhabitants of Huntsville were organized into a Latter-day Saint ward. The church bell rang at 9:30 on Sunday mornings, summoning youth and their teachers to the 10:00 Sunday school opening exercises. The Sabbath school enrolled about 200, including teachers and officers, and unlike most Latter-day Saint households in Utah while McKay was a child, the McKay family attended consistently. In addition to morning Sunday school exercises designed primarily for children, Latter-day Saints attended afternoon worship services where the sacrament was administered, and members sometimes gathered for evening preaching meetings. Priesthood quorums met in Huntsville on Monday evenings, and Relief Society as well as auxiliary meetings for young adults met during the week. Above the pulpit in Huntsville's meeting house hung a portrait of John Taylor, the prophet, with the words "The Kingdom of God or Nothing." As he gazed each week at the portrait and caption, David gave "little thought if any to its implication," he recalled, but the message made a deep, subconscious impression.[4]

2. "Huntsville," *Ogden Junction*, July 2, 1880, 4; Huntsville Precinct, United States Census, 1880.
3. "Huntsville," *Ogden Junction*, July 2, 1880, 4.
4. Morrell, *Highlights*, 17; "Huntsville," *Ogden Junction*, July 2, 1880, 4; David O. McKay,

As a young child, David developed a simple faith in God. Years later he related that he became "fearful at night" after dreaming that "two Indians came into the yard ... and one of them shot an arrow and hit me in the back." Then one of the Indians barged into the home and "sneered and frightened mother." The threat was entirely imaginary; the Shoshone in northern Utah had struggled to survive ever since hundreds in their band had been slaughtered by United States soldiers in 1863, and many had embraced Mormonism for spiritual relief and self-preservation. Nevertheless, the images and anxieties of that dream repeatedly haunted him, as did his mother's fear of burglars and other intruders while her husband was away. Unable to sleep one night, he "fancied [he] heard noises around the house" and decided to pray. "I thought I could pray only by getting out of bed and kneeling, and that was a terrible test. But I did finally bring myself to get out of bed and kneel and pray to God to protect mother and the family." As he prayed, "a voice as clearly to me as mine is to you, said, 'Don't be afraid. Nothing will hurt you.' ... To me it was a direct answer, and there came an assurance that I should never be hurt in bed."[5]

At the age of eight he was baptized along the willow-lined section of Spring Creek running through the town. Eighty-two years later, he reminisced about the people who attended and were baptized and the counsel he received. "I was instructed not to swear or use bad words; that if I had spoken harshly to my mother, I was not to do it anymore; that I was never to be disobedient."[6]

David and Jennette's devotion to the Church of Jesus Christ of Latter-day Saints was palpable. David Sr. believed that "home was the place to begin to preach the Gospel by our actions." When he was in his seventies, their son David reflected, "They lived the gospel. Father used to preach it, particularly to visitors who came, more than to us boys and girls; but both Father and Mother lived the gospel.... My parents' teachings and their examples led me to the absolute knowledge that God is my Father." In 1877, David Sr. accepted the call to serve as branch president for a congregation in Eden, northwest of Huntsville. For the next twenty-eight years, he served as either a bishop or branch president during all but the two years he was a missionary in Scotland and a few months following his return. Jennette labored in the church's auxiliaries, first as secretary of the ward Relief Society and later as a counselor in the Young Ladies Mutual Improvement Association. While serving as a missionary, David's father received an epiphany that he often recounted for his children. Discouraged after several hours of unsuccessfully approaching people about Mormonism,

address of Oct. 2, 1953, *Conference Reports*, 8; Heber R. McBride, diary, June 18, 1876. On lax church attendance and the number of Sunday and weekday religious meetings see Walker, "'Going to Meeting,'" 154.

5. David O. McKay, address of Oct. 6, 1951, *Conference Reports*, 182; Parry, *Bear River Massacre*, 43–54, 68–69.

6. McKay, "Choose the Right," in *My Young Friends*, 41–42.

he retreated to a small cave to pray. There he heard a voice confirming Joseph Smith's prophetic calling. Hearing this experience so inspired young David that he sought a similar manifestation. As he related years later, while rounding up cattle "an intense desire came over me to receive a manifestation of the truth of the Restored Gospel." Kneeling by a serviceberry bush, he "prayed that God would declare to me the truth of his revelation to Joseph Smith." Although he prayed "with as much faith as a young boy could muster," when he climbed back into the saddle he admitted to himself, "No spiritual manifestation has come to me.... I am just the same 'old boy' that I was before I prayed." Despite his disappointment, David continued to attend church.[7]

When he was thirteen, McKay received his patriarchal blessing from Patriarch John Smith. McKay was an avid marbles player and bristled when the stodgy patriarch remarked, "My boy you have something to do beside playing marbles." The words of the blessing itself made little impression on him at the time, but in hindsight he recognized the patriarch's foresight. "The Lord has a work for thee to do, in which thou shalt see much of the world.... It shall be thy lot to sit in council with thy brethren and preside among the people and exhort the Saints to faithfulness," Smith foretold.[8]

In his teens, McKay worked in the summer as a courier, delivering mail and copies of the *Ogden Standard Examiner* to La Plata, a small mining community. Leaving home on horseback at seven in the morning, he picked up the mail and newspapers from a rider straight from Ogden, loaded his saddlebags, and threaded the trail up Middle Fork Canyon. "I arrived at the Camp at 11:30, fed my horse, and ... ate my lunch in a little cabin on the west side of Main Street," he remembered. After lunch, McKay circled back to Huntsville through Geertsen Canyon, arriving home around 5:30. "That was a ten-hour horseback ride for me every day until the road was built," he recalled.[9]

McKay liked to attend dances in Huntsville and played the piano in a dance band. No matter how late he stayed out, his father would awaken him at five to begin farm work. "Those who dance must pay the fiddler," his father insisted. David and his brother chafed under their parents' rules. "Youth sometimes think parents are old-fashioned. We boys in our teens thought so. It took us a long while, probably until we ourselves had children, to realize how wise our parents were," he recalled years later.[10]

---

7. McBride, diary, Jan. 7, 1884; David O. McKay, address of Oct. 6, 1951, *Conference Reports*, 182; David O. McKay, address of Oct. 5, 1968, *Conference Reports*, 85–86; David O. McKay, address of Apr. 5, 1948, *Conference Reports*, 172; Norcross, "Biographical Sketch," entry for Jennette Eveline Evans [McKay], KWZZ-KQW, Family Search, familysearch.org; McKay, *Gospel Ideals*, 21–22.

8. Morrell, *Highlights*, 26.

9. DOMD, July 5, 1957.

10. Interview of David O. McKay by Richard L. Evans, DOMD, July 25, 1963; McKay, "Safeguard Loyalty," in *My Young Friends*, 79.

The closest high school to Huntsville was in Ogden, so after McKay completed the eighth grade, he moved down the canyon to his maternal grandmother's home so he could study at Weber Stake Academy for two years. After graduating, he returned to Huntsville and taught grade school for a year. Drawing upon their mother's inheritance, a financial asset few possessed, David and three of his siblings rented a home in downtown Salt Lake and enrolled in the University of Utah in 1894. The young siblings traveled south to Salt Lake by horse and wagon with a cow in tow, the wagon stocked with bottles of home-canned fruit and sacks of flour. Few Utahns of McKay's generation enjoyed the opportunity to study at a university. Total enrollment in the territorial school that year was roughly 500, including those who were taking high school courses in the Preparatory division. On average, the university awarded only 5.4 bachelor's degrees per year between 1892 and 1900. Most students doing college work were, like McKay, enrolled in the Normal School and pursuing a teaching certificate. The first two years of the three-year Normal course had been administered by the Preparatory School until the year prior to McKay's enrollment. Even though McKay was enrolled in the Normal School proper, his course work for the first two years straddled the divide between high school and college.[11]

During his first semester in Salt Lake, McKay signed up for the football team. The Deseret Agricultural and Manufacturing Society had invited the university to field a team and play in a match at the territorial fair against a team from Salt Lake High School. The winner would receive a gold medal. Because the university had no team, the male students were canvassed, and eleven who showed "the most willingness" became the team. McKay was assigned to play right guard in the new and rough sport. Half the players reportedly had never seen a football before joining the team, and only three had ever played. The Fort Douglas Athletic Association lent the team uniforms, and volunteer coaches provided a crash course in the basics of the game. Not surprisingly, the neophytes lost their first contest against the more experienced team from Salt Lake High School, but they redeemed themselves in a rematch on Thanksgiving. McKay sprained his ankle in the team's first winning game. Lacking change for the streetcar fare, he walked several miles home from Wandamere Park in South Salt Lake on his swollen ankle.[12]

In his first year at school, David joined Zeta Gamma, a men's literary and debating society comprised primarily of students from the Normal and Preparatory Schools. Later that year he served as society vice president, and in 1896 he served as president alongside two good friends, George Q. Morris,

11. DOMD, June 8, 1964; *University Chronicle* (University of Utah), Oct. 2, 1894, 4; Chamberlin, *The University of Utah*, 182–83.

12. Chamberlin, *The University of Utah*, 224; *University Chronicle*, Oct. 12, 1894, 4; *University Chronicle* Dec. 4, 1894, 7; DOMD, Feb. 11, 1965.

the vice president, and Stephen L Richards, the secretary-treasurer. Little did they dream they would later serve together in the Quorum of Twelve Apostles. In his third year at the university, McKay was elected president of the senior class. At the graduation ceremonies, he delivered the class oration and received a three-year Normal School teaching certificate, as did twenty-five peers. His speech, "Ignorance of Ignorance," warned educated students against "sit[ting] complacently by and saying we have the whole truth." "Let us not be blind to our own ignorance," he urged. Already he was displaying a broadmindedness that would characterize his quotation-studded essays and speeches later in life. Religious zealots who closed their minds to science because they perceived a conflict between the forces needed to think harder and reconcile the two. God's laws, "whether revealed by science or religion … must be the same," he insisted. Three years of higher education had only whetted McKay's appetite for more learning. Speaking from his own experience, he encouraged his fellow graduates: "The glimpse into the wide field of geological thought has aroused you to a realization of the vastness of creation. Communion with a few great men in literature has made your heart-throbs quicken and has inspired you not only with a love of the beautiful but with a determination to associate with the leading writers of the ages."[13]

During his final year at school, David was offered a teaching position for the following year. His career path seemed bright. The salary would allow him to replenish his mother's depleted inheritance so that she could send the younger children to school. Shortly after receiving the job offer, the postman delivered an unwelcome letter from church headquarters, calling David to serve in the British Mission. His brother Thomas was writing a school assignment in their rented home in Salt Lake when the letter arrived. As Thomas remembered, "The mailman handed him a letter and as he read, I glanced up and saw that he was quite agitated. He threw the letter across the table in disgust and said, 'Isn't that [hell]?'" David's father and bishop, who had forwarded the letter, advised, "We'll leave it to you to decide whether you accept the call or not." David made an appointment with church president Wilford Woodruff to discuss the call, hoping to persuade the prophet to defer it for at least two years. Woodruff counseled, "Well, you finish your school. This is January and you graduate in June, and when you're ready to accept the call you let us know." In the coming weeks, McKay recalled, the words of a couplet came to mind: "Do your duty; that is best; Leave unto the Lord the rest." Ultimately, after McKay's father encouraged him to accept the call and pledged to support him financially, McKay agreed to serve. Still, he longed for a greater witness that the principles

13. *University Chronicle*, Apr. 9, 1895, 9; *University Chronicle*, Oct. 13, 1896, 1; *University Chronicle*, Dec. 16, 1896, 2; *University Chronicle* June 3, 1897, 3; *University Chronicle*, June 11, 1897, 13–15.

he would teach as a missionary were correct. "I still had that same desire that made me kneel on that hillside and out in the meadow across Spring Creek, the same thing, and I still knew that I would have to live in such a way as to merit the call and guidance," he later reflected.[14]

---

14. Thomas E. McKay, address of Apr. 4, 1952, *Conference Reports*, 25; couplet by Henry Wadsworth Longfellow, from "The Legend Beautiful," in *Tales of a Wayside Inn* (Tichnon and Fields, 1863); David O. McKay, testimony presented at a missionary conference of the North British Mission, Mar. 1, 1961, quoted in Terry, *David O. McKay*, 32.

2: A Mission to Scotland

After Elder Seymour Young set him apart, McKay left Utah on August 7, barely a month shy of his twenty-fourth birthday. He left behind not only his immediate family but also two young women vying for his affections. One, Ray Riggs, was the twenty-year-old daughter of his landlord, Emma Robbins Riggs, and a close friend of his sisters. Ray's parents were estranged, and her father, Obadiah Riggs, had moved east, where he became a medical doctor in Cincinnati and joined the Reorganized Church of Jesus Christ of Latter Day Saints (now called the Community of Christ).[1] David had invited Ray to his farewell party with a bit of verse composed for the occasion:

> This invitation is late, I know,
> But avoided it cannot be;
> With tardy people, it's always so—
> That's why it is so with me.
> But late is better than never: they say—
> I'm glad this saying was made
> So please overlook my tardiness, Ray,
> And accompany your true friend—Dade.[2]

On his last Sunday evening at home, McKay rode with Ray Riggs over the hills south of Huntsville where they "told each other secrets" and "held hands."[3] The second girlfriend was Claire Whitehead, a seventeen-year-old incoming freshman at the University of Utah. McKay spent his last evening in Utah with her rather than Ray. Over the next two years, David and Claire would exchange dozens of long, introspective letters that attested to the depth of their friendship.[4]

After traversing the country by train and sightseeing in Chicago, Washington, DC, and New York, McKay, in company with twenty-one fellow missionaries,

1. Bringhurst, "The Forgotten Odyssey of Obadiah H. Riggs," 48–64.
2. McKay and McKay, *Heart Petals*, 7.
3. McKay, *What E'er Thou Art*, 3 (Aug. 1, 1897); McKay, *My Father*, 2.
4. McKay, *What E'er Thou Art*, 4 (Aug. 6, 1897), 298. After graduating from Salt Lake High in 1896 (*Salt Lake Herald*, May 21, 1895), Claire and her sister Winnifred (Winnie) enrolled at the University of Utah Normal School, where Claire took an active role in student clubs and societies. "Home Happenings," *University Chronicle* (University of Utah), Oct. 13, 1896, 7; "Home Happenings," *University Chronicle*, Jan. 26, 1897, 6. Claire married Alexander Hardy Birrell Sr. on Aug. 21, 1900. Entry for Claire Jenny Whitehead, KWJC-2B4, Family Search, familysearch.org.

boarded the SS *Belgenland*, a four-masted steamer with sails capable of carrying over 1,000 passengers, on August 14, 1897, bound for Liverpool. The next morning, the missionaries participated in an ecumenical devotional that brought McKay up short with the painful realization that he "knew nothing about the Bible." After twelve days at sea, the missionaries arrived in Liverpool and received their assignments. McKay entrained for Glasgow, a city with a population of nearly 800,000 that cast a "gloomy" pall over him. "*Utah is dearer* than *ever* ... Glasgow is a rocky city—*rock* houses, *rocky* streets, and on Saturday night *rocky* people," the homesick elder wrote.[5]

He was assigned to labor roughly thirty miles southeast of Glasgow in the town of Lanark and its environs with Peter Johnston, a prosperous Scottish-born thirty-three-year-old sheep rancher who had emigrated to Idaho, and Joseph Mitchell, a Scottish convert also in his thirties. Extending outward from the River Clyde, the mill town of several thousand was described in an 1880s gazetteer as being situated in "singularly pleasant" environs near three "celebrated" waterfalls with "some good public buildings and many handsome well-appointed shops." The trio went to work promptly, knocking on doors and distributing tracts for three hours. Although most residents politely accepted their pamphlets, McKay could not shake his "gloomy" funk. "I sighed as I knocked at the door, breathed heavily as I gave the tract, and sighed again as I walked away. This was repeated about seventy-five times," he confided to Ray. Even an excursion later that day to a cave and the scenic waterfalls failed to lift his spirits.[6]

As he made the acquaintance of local members, McKay's spirits gradually improved. Among the members were Nellie Jack, a recent convert; her daughters; and Robert Orr, who sometimes preached with them. The members' hospitality and home-cooked food warmed McKay's heart and stomach. On September 5, McKay made a feeble attempt to speak in a street meeting. He had not been given to sustained scripture study, and he felt his deficiency keenly. Recognizing the need for gospel scholarship, he began studying the New Testament diligently. To refute the common Protestant belief of salvation by grace alone, he marked proof texts showing that "Christ redeemed us from the bonds of death, but we must work out our own salvation." The question of salvation through the atonement and the relationship between grace and works continued to engage the young missionary. He puzzled over the born-again experiences of devout non-Mormon Christians, wondering whether their convictions came from God or Satan. Would those who sincerely believed they had been saved be blessed or condemned by God? He believed in God's general beneficence vis-à-vis sincere seekers, but he had less hope for the ministers. After

5. *Belgenland* (1878), Wikipedia; McKay, *What E'er Thou Art*, 4–7 (Aug. 15, 1897), 11 (Aug. 27, 1897), 12 (Aug. 28, 1897).

6. Groome, *Ordnance Gazetteer of Scotland*, http://scottish-places.info; McKay, *What E'er Thou Art*, 13 (Aug. 31, 1897); McKay and McKay, *Heart Petals*, 13–14.

listening to one Protestant divine, McKay was disgusted. "He is one of these saved men, and a worse perverter of the true gospel cannot be found among men of even ordinary intelligence. Nothing to do but to say, 'I am saved.' O, it is abominable! I wonder why it is that such men cannot see their error. Surely they know that they are not teaching correct doctrine."

Although the Catholic understanding of salvation by rites and ordinances was more compatible with McKay's outlook, he distrusted Catholics even more than Protestant ministers. After walking twelve miles and distributing one hundred tracts, he noted that the only two who refused to take one were Catholics, memorializing that fact in verse: "All missionaries know this stubborn fact: / To offer a Catholic a gospel tract, / Is like pouring water down the small of your back. / Such a look does he get as the door goes 'smack.'" Although he disliked tracting (going from door to door to distribute pamphlets, or tracts), McKay was not one to shirk his duties. When his two companions suggested partway through a rainy day that they should quit until the weather improved, McKay insisted on continuing to work until they had distributed every pamphlet in their satchels.[7]

After McKay had served for only a month in Lanark, the presiding priesthood authority in Scotland, Mack McMillan, recalled him to Glasgow, where he would spend the next six months. McMillan assigned the university graduate to spend much of his time in the conference (or regional) office paying bills, reconciling accounts, mailing copies of the church periodical the *Millennial Star,* compiling reports, and answering correspondence. After McMillan wound up in the hospital on January 7, 1898, McKay managed much of the conference business for the next two months, a fate that drove him to complain that all he did was "write, write, write!"[8]

McKay's responsibilities in the office included facilitating the emigration of converts and the departure of missionaries. Occasionally, complications arose. When Edith Ellerby, a twenty-year-old recent convert, decided to emigrate, her parents were appalled. As the supervising elder, McKay faced the father's wrath and his accusation that the missionaries had hypnotized his daughter. The father swore that if he had a pistol he would "rather shoot" Edith than see her leave with the "Mormons." The Ellerbys' minister warned Edith that she was driving her mother to the grave by emigrating. Edith hesitated and asked her father if he would allow her to attend church with the Saints if she remained at home, but he stonily refused. The interchange reduced Edith to tears, and after her father and the minister stormed off, McKay had "a long talk" with her. After he assured Edith that her mother would survive, her resolve was steeled, and she boarded the ship.[9]

7. McKay, *What E'er Thou Art*, 23 (Sep. 20, 22, 1897); Joseph Mitchell diary, Sep. 22, 1897, quoted in McKay, *What E'er Thou Art*, n54.

8. McKay, *What E'er Thou Art*, 24 (Sep. 30, 1897), 51 (Jan. 7, 1898), 63 (Feb. 11, 1898).

9. McKay, *What E'er Thou Art*, 61–63 (Feb. 9–10, 1898). See also Leone Jacobs, "She Put Her Trust in God and Sailed for America," *Church News*, May 31, 1969, 11.

During the months he worked in the office, McKay became well acquainted with members of the small Glasgow branch as he visited and counseled with them, dined and taught in their humble homes, worshipped with them, and pronounced priesthood blessings when they were ill. As he witnessed the suffering and poverty of the members, McKay's maturity and capacity to love and sympathize swelled. In one hovel he ministered to a diseased woman in "intense agony . . . lying in a dirty bed" and trying to nurse a baby and care for an eighteen-month-old child. Witnessing the faith of twenty-three-year-old tubercular Mary Good, struggling for breath as she weakly sang, "Beautiful home of my Savior, bright beautiful home," he reevaluated his own commitment to God. "That scene I shall never forget," he recorded. "Her white countenance depicting the suffering she has endured; her dark hair streaming in striking contrast to her death-like face; that audible gurgle in her throat; the gloomy surrounding occasioned by the dull day; the dead silence broken only by the seeming knell of the kitchen clock; her feeble plaintive tones as she sang that heavenly hymn." In this "lovely maiden, full of faith and patience" he glimpsed the transformative power of intense faith.[10]

Occasionally the young, unmarried missionary mediated spousal arguments. George Taylor, a member in Rutherglen, was married to a non-member who was friendly toward the LDS Church and welcomed the missionaries in her home. McKay administered to the couple's infant, held cottage meetings in their home, and attended their baby's funeral. In the months following the baby's death, George drowned his sorrow in liquor, and after a bitter argument over his drinking that ended with Taylor driving his wife from their home, McKay was called upon to effect a reconciliation.[11]

The elders walked long distances to visit branches and preach at cottage meetings. One Sunday, McKay and his companion walked eight miles from Glasgow to Blantyre, held two meetings, and then walked back, much of the return journey being made through a cold, driving rain. They arrived home sore and exhausted at 11:30 p.m., fourteen and a half hours after they left home in the morning.[12]

In the course of his labors, the young missionary's testimony of the message he preached grew. One morning in Sunday school, pupils and their teacher struggled to comprehend a confusing passage in the book of Matthew. When a class member consulted Joseph Smith's translation of the chapter in the Pearl of Great Price, the revisions clarified the chapter and reinforced McKay's conviction of "the divinity of Joseph Smith's mission." On another occasion, McKay gave a priesthood blessing to Daniel Ferguson, who had been bedridden from a mining accident for eight years. A week later, Ferguson told him that following the blessing, his pain had abated for the first time in years. While preaching extemporaneously on the

10. McKay, *What E'er Thou Art*, 74 (Mar. 12, 1898), 30–31 (Oct. 23, 1897), 55 (Jan. 18, 1898).

11. McKay, *What E'er Thou Art*, 123 (Aug. 29, 1898), 125 (Aug. 24, 1898), 201–2 (Mar. 4, 1899).

12. McKay, *What E'er Thou Art*, 69 (Feb. 27, 1898).

atonement, McKay prepared to quote a scripture in Daniel but "could not recall a word of it." Instead, the words of Revelation 20:12–13 regarding the final judgment of "every man according to their works" came into his mind, and he recited the scripture as if he knew it by heart—"a peculiar experience" that filled him with reverent awe. Such experiences coexisted with nagging doubts and persistent feelings of inadequacy. Four months into his mission he taught Sunday school extemporaneously when the teacher failed to arrive on time and "felt [his] weakness." Six months into his mission, he was seized with homesickness; "it seems a *lifetime* before two years shall have passed," he despaired.[13]

To his delight, McKay's duties in the conference headquarters prevented him from tracting regularly, but they also limited his opportunities to teach non-members. He did manage to informally teach some of the unbaptized "strangers" who attended Latter-day Saint services. One of them was Miss Rennie, a young woman who regularly attended sacrament meetings. McKay often walked her home after meeting, conversing about theology and doctrine. After several weeks of casual conversation, she broached the subject of polygamy. McKay found her questions about the principle "intelligent" yet "amusing" and felt he succeeded in allaying some of her concerns. A week later, though, he wondered if she was more curious than sincerely interested. "I do not know whether she is a real *investigator* or not," he admitted. On Valentine's Day, he gave her a Book of Mormon, but from her response he judged that she was "not . . . very much interested in the gospel."[14]

Others who attended meetings were perpetual investigators, like a Mr. Anderson who admired the missionaries and their teachings but seemed unlikely to commit to baptism because he believed all religions were equally valid. Some non-members who listened to McKay, like the Thomsons, some of his favorite investigators in Glasgow, were related to members. Margaret, Duncan, and Thomas Thomson had been raised in the LDS Church after their mother joined in 1851, but their spouses were not members. In 1898, Margaret introduced McKay and his companion to Duncan, his wife Mary Ann, and her sister-in-law Mrs. Thomas Thomson, whose mannerisms reminded him of his own mother. From the outset, Thomas's wife stressed that she was not interested in joining a church that encouraged its members to move to America. The church should construct chapels in Glasgow instead of encouraging emigration, she maintained. "I am afraid it will be a long time before she joins the Church," McKay despaired to Ray. Mary Ann Thomson, on the other hand, was only waiting on her husband Duncan to become active in the church. "But I fear she will wait a long time," McKay confessed.[15]

---

13. McKay, *What E'er Thou Art*, 28 (Oct. 17–18, 1897), 31 (Oct. 24, 1897), 67 (Feb. 25, 1898).
14. McKay, *What E'er Thou Art*, 54 (Jan. 16, 1898), 56 (Jan. 23, 1898), 64 (Feb. 14, 1898).
15. McKay, *What E'er Thou Art*, 59 (Jan. 31, 1898), 75 (Mar. 16, 1898); McKay and McKay,

Occasionally, McKay found diversion in the theater or in visiting botanical gardens, cathedrals, and the magnificent Glasgow Art Gallery. In March, toward the end of President McMillan's mission, he invited McKay to accompany him to Ireland. In Belfast, they toured an art gallery, an immense rope factory, government buildings, and the anatomical museum at Queen's University, where nude cadavers, "some of them cut and slashed in the most inhuman manner conceivable," repulsed him.[16]

Late in March, after having served for nearly six months in the conference headquarters, McKay was transferred to Stirling, a gateway town to the Scottish Highlands located about twenty-six miles from Glasgow, where he labored with his former companion, Peter Johnston. There was no congregation in the town of roughly 17,000 residents, and missionaries had not been stationed there in four decades. The companions rented a room in a boardinghouse run by Elizabeth Sharp, who lived there with her husband and their three children, James, Annie, and Jeanie.[17]

After securing lodgings, the missionaries toured Stirling Castle, a picturesque royal residence dating from the fourteenth to sixteenth centuries and perched atop a volcanic crag with a commanding view of the city. Much later, McKay recalled an experience that he did not record at the time in his diary: "I was homesick, and we walked around the Stirling Castle, really not doing our duty," he remembered. As they walked back to town, McKay spied an oddly decorated stone with geometric shapes and an inscription that read, "What e'er thou art, act well thy part." The couplet reminded him of a custodian he had known during his football playing days at the university. "I realized then that I had just as great a respect for that man as I had for any professor in whose class I had sat.... I recalled how he helped us with the football suits, how he helped us with some of our lessons. He was unassuming, unostentatious, but did his duty well." The couplet also applied to two missionaries sightseeing rather than working, and McKay and his companion pondered its meaning for themselves.[18]

Neither McKay nor his companion liked to tract, but after visiting some elders and members in neighboring towns they could think of no other work to fill the time, so they decided to tract on their fourth day in the area. "Oh, I do dislike tracting; there is nothing pleasant about it," he wrote. "We both felt miserable." McKay also wrote, "Perhaps [we] did some little good—it is very

---

Heart Petals, 19. For information on the Thomson family that clarifies relationships see "1891 England, Scotland & Wales census," line 10, page 1, Glasgow Dennistoun Parish, Enumeration District 15.

16. McKay, *What E'er Thou Art*, 57 (Jan. 26, 1898), 71 (Mar. 30, 1898), 73 (Mar. 7, 1898).

17. McKay, *What E'er Thou Art*, 76–77 (Mar. 26, 1898).

18. McKay, *What E'er Thou Art*, 78 (Mar. 26, 1898). McKay's frequent narration of the reproof and instruction he gained from the message carved in stone is deftly reconstructed and evaluated by Stan and Patricia Larson in *What E'er Thou Art*, xxxiii-xxxvi. The saying may have originated as a Gaelic proverb.

doubtful, though." The next week, after reading that war would likely break out between Spain and the United States, he reflected, "I believe I would as like *fight* as *distribute tracts*." McKay was having doubts about the merits of acting well his part, if that meant tracting. The fact that locals had a difficult time understanding McKay's accent added to the displeasure. "The women can hardly understand me when I offer them a 'gospel tract.' Nearly everyone misunderstands me or asks me what I said," McKay complained. One woman thought he was trying to give her a gas bill. Another "haggard-looking creature" threw the tract back in his face, retorting, "I'm a lost sinner, and I dinna want yer blatherin' gospel." Many people on the street distrusted the missionaries. He heard a group of passing women whisper that he was recruiting women for his harem. "Poor deluded souls!" he reflected. "If they could only pass through Utah and see the hundreds of pretty young women there, I think such a foolish idea would leave them."[19]

McKay preferred preaching to tracting. On March 31, he and his companion preached to a small audience in a rented hall in Alva, eight miles from Stirling. They planned a similar meeting for the following week in Stirling, advertised it in the newspaper, and invited people they met while tracting to attend. The much-anticipated meeting attracted a congregation of eighteen, including their landlord, Mrs. Sharp, her daughter Annie, and their minister. The Sharps were receptive, and another young woman "expressed herself as believing that what we said was true." Feeling on top of the world, the elders celebrated their success by again visiting Stirling Castle and a historic battlefield. Unfortunately, a few days later they learned that the believing young woman's father had forbidden her from speaking further with them.[20]

McKay and his companion began collaborating with two other missionaries, Thomas Gilchrist and Joseph McKnight, who were laboring in nearby Alva. "Really, we have formed a fast friendship," McKay commented. They jointly planned and conducted meetings in rented halls, taught investigators, and rejoiced in the baptisms of a Mr. Sneddcn, his son Peter, and Mrs. Alex Thompson.[21]

McKay's favorite investigator in Stirling was Annie Sharp, his landlord's daughter. Relations between male LDS missionaries and female investigators in the 1890s were not circumscribed by rigid proscriptions against private visits and activities or by the requirement that missionary companions should always be within eyesight of each other, as they are today. Annie came into McKay's life at a lonely time, when he had determined to no longer write to Ray after learning she was seeing other men. For her part, Ray stopped writing, having discovered that McKay was also writing to Claire Whitehead. From the outset,

19. McKay, *What E'er Thou Art*, 81–82 (Mar. 29, 1898), 84–85 (Apr. 6, 1898), 93 (May 9, 1896).
20. McKay, *What E'er Thou Art*, 85 (Apr. 7–8, 1898), 87 (Apr. 13, 1898).
21. McKay, *What E'er Thou Art*, 86 (Apr. 10–11, 1898), 91 (Apr. 30, 1898), 102 (June 5, 1898).

Annie and McKay were drawn to each other. McKay described her as "a very pleasant, intelligent, young woman and quite *bonnie* too" and "*the gem of the household.*" "Miss Sharp is such a jewel! Just the touch of her hand puts everything in 'apple-pie order,'" he gushed. Often Annie visited with him about the gospel. On April 4, she had "a lengthy chat" with McKay and his companion in which they gave her some tracts to read. A few days later, McKay remained in the house while his companion was in Glasgow on business and conversed with Annie. When she asked about polygamy, McKay held his breath. "This principle is a stumbling block in the path of all of them," he wrote. At least Annie "was not very antagonistic," and McKay hoped that eventually she would "understand more fully the true situation."[22]

Later in the month, McKay again found himself alone with Miss Sharp, his companion having once again traveled to Glasgow on business. They spent "four of the happiest hours" he had known and "became mutually confidential." McKay steered the subject to the first principles of the gospel, including baptism by immersion. Annie was "astonished" that it was necessary to submerge the body, "head and all," but when McKay showed her the New Testament account of Jesus's baptism by immersion, Annie was persuaded. They discussed the church's early history, and "she seemed quite interested." On May 5 while his companion was again in Glasgow, McKay visited late into the evening with Annie. She said she disliked her minister and wanted to follow God. McKay expressed his "sincere hope" that she would continue studying the gospel. Later he wrote that "more pleasant hours, I fancy, have never passed." He added, "I cannot say that we talked all the time about 'repentance and baptism,' but *sincerity* was mentioned and thought of, by me at least, quite often." Perhaps he suspected that Annie was falling in love with him. The next day, after spending several more hours with Annie, he wrote that if people in town learned "how sociable we are one with another," they "would at once conclude that Miss Sharp will be going to Utah." But, he added, they would be mistaken.[23]

When McKay left Stirling on a genealogical research trip to Edinburgh in mid-May, Annie followed a few days later, ostensibly to visit her cousin. The two spent Saturday afternoon and evening hiking the massive basaltic Salisbury Crags and dining at a restaurant. On Sunday she accompanied McKay to church, and then they went for a pleasant walk. Monday evening they again visited before Annie boarded the train for home. "The time we spent together in Edinburgh shall always be remembered as some of the happiest hours in Scotland—and, in fact, anywhere else," the infatuated missionary wrote. After Annie left, McKay felt "lonesome," and a few days later he felt a "miserable" mixture of

22. McKay and McKay, *Heart Petals*, 22, 153n53; McKay, *What E'er Thou Art*, 79 (Mar. 26, 1898), 84 (Apr. 2, 4, 1898), 86 (Apr. 11, 1898), 85–86 (Apr. 9, 1898).

23. McKay, *What E'er Thou Art*, 89–90 (Apr. 23, 1898), 92–93 (May 5–6, 1898).

depression, "homesickness, lonesomeness," and "other unpleasant moods." Back in Stirling on June 8, he again spent a "pleasant evening" alone with Annie, who told him she had read the tracts he gave her and now believed in baptism by immersion. The mutual ardor might have overwhelmed the lonely missionary had it not been cut short by McKay's reassignment in early June to Glasgow to serve as president of the Scottish Conference, with its 434 members and 14 missionaries. Fearful that he would perform poorly in the assignment, he retreated to a wooded area below the grand national monument to Sir William Wallace in Stirling, where he rededicated himself to God and prayed for assistance. In his reply to mission president Rulon Wells, McKay told him he did not want the assignment but accepted it "since God, through his servants, has seen fit to place this duty upon me." Annie accompanied McKay to Glasgow on the train, and the two spent a final "pleasant yet somewhat sad evening" walking the streets and saying their goodbyes.[24]

The responsibilities of serving as presiding authority in Scotland, including supervising the fractious Glasgow Branch, weighed heavily upon McKay. Although he continued to write to Annie, he had little time to pine for her. Despite McKay's fond hopes, in his absence Annie never joined the Church. At the center of the rancor in the Glasgow Branch were two large families of long-time members, the Leggats and the Neilsons. Fifty-two-year-old Joseph Leggat, the patriarch of a family of eight living children, had grown up in the church and had been excommunicated repeatedly but each time had returned to fellowship in the church. John Neilson, born seven years after Leggat, had been a member for nearly two decades. He and his wife, Isabella, were the parents of nine living children. Neilson was the branch president; Leggat was his counselor; and McKay as conference president mediated. Until McKay censured him, Neilson was accustomed to rambling sermons, interspersed with pointed public criticism of the members and claims to visionary experiences. Often taking offense, he "borrow[ed] trouble," according to McKay. Leggat and Neilson were critical and jealous of each other. When McKay proposed calling Leggat's

24. McKay, *What E'er Thou Art*, 97 (May 21, 1898), 98 (May 22–23, 1898), 99 (May 28, 1898), 102 (June 8, 1898), 178 (Jan. 10, 1899), 103 (June 9, 11, 1898). McKay and Annie Sharp continued to correspond sporadically and met occasionally. In August, for instance, while visiting the elders in Stirling, McKay had "a good, social, confidential talk" with Annie for an hour and a half. In November Annie's mother telegraphed to inform McKay that Annie was near death. McKay came as quickly as he could and taught her about life after death. She wondered if she would be punished for not having joined the church, and McKay assured her that she would not. "She believes the gospel to be true," he wrote. Alone in the room with her, McKay knelt and prayed for her. She seemed to revive but the next day seemed worse again. "To see her suffering there and so desirous of living was heartrending," he wrote. Fortunately, Annie revived. Five months later, after visiting the Sharps again, McKay wrote, "I believe Annie will yet join the Church, but I am doubtful about the others." I have found no record that Annie joined the church. McKay, *What E'er Thou Art*, 121 (Aug. 13, 1898), 154–55 (Nov. 12, 1898), 222 (Apr. 15, 1899).

son as a Sunday school officer, Neilson objected. When Leggat accused Neilson of mismanaging branch funds, Neilson "went on the warpath." A few months later it was Leggat who was "at war with Neilson." "There is trouble all the time," McKay complained. Both were sensitive to personal slights and craved recognition and honor. In one protracted conference, President Neilson complained that "he has not enough power given him" while Leggat groused that the branch president acted unilaterally without consulting him. "How little do some men understand the true spirit of the gospel," McKay lamented. When McKay determined that he and his replacements as conference presidents would preside over the Glasgow Branch, with Leggat and Neilson as assistant presiding officers, Neilson refused to serve on an equal footing with Leggat.[25]

The general membership mirrored their leaders' unseemly coarseness. "Many of the members of our Church are very uncouth and uncultured, showing no refinement whatever," the missionary vented. "If one would judge our Church by the actions of some of the members in Glasgow, he would shun it as he would the hottest corner of H—l!" James Clark, the branch Sunday school teacher and a former volunteer preacher and shoemaker, often showed up Sunday morning with a hangover but complained that his talents were unappreciated. "Revels in drink Saturday night and then thinks he ought to preach to the saints on Sunday! Not much!" McKay commented. A few weeks later, after Clark lumbered home in a drunken stupor and walloped his wife, McKay dropped him from his calling. Many of the others were not much better. After Joseph Leggat's daughter-in-law Kate died, her husband, James, became engaged to a recent convert in the branch whom McKay had baptized, Georgina Ferguson. McKay warned Georgina that James had no money and advised her to look for a better mate, but she was determined to proceed. "If the bride had any love for her husband, the saying that 'love is blind' is truly verified," McKay reflected. "If she married him simply to 'get a man,' she will be sadly disappointed for she has not a *man* at all! His actions have been anything but *manly*."[26]

By contrast, a handful of the branch members earned McKay's unstinting praise. He loved Flora Gain and her seven children ranging in age from twenty-one-year-old Lizzie to four-year-old John. The children's father had gone to Australia, ostensibly to earn money for the family, but time would prove that he had abandoned them. "This is one of the best families in the branch," McKay wrote soon after arriving in Glasgow. He admired Flora's ability to overlook the petty jealousies and trifles that engulfed other members. Often the older

---

25. McKay, *What E'er Thou Art*, 103 (June 12, 1898), 104 (June 19, 1898), 110 (July 19, 1898), 139 (Sep. 25, 1898), 150 (Nov. 2, 1898), 154 (Nov. 10, 1898), 157 (Nov. 22, 1898), 168–69 (Dec. 24, 1898).

26. McKay, *What E'er Thou Art*, 194 (Feb. 17, 1899), 165 (Dec. 14, 1898), 217 (Apr. 2, 1899), 252 (June 13, 1899), 255 (June 25, 1899).

daughters, Lizzie, Maggie, and Jeanie, visited the elders in the conference headquarters to sing hymns, study their Sunday school lessons, and visit.[27]

The strapping young conference president's charisma sometimes got the best of young women in the branch, even married ones. At a surprise party sprung by two sisters on behalf of the elders, they flirted with McKay and his companion. On another occasion, he "had a few minutes private talk with sister [Annie] Carney, during which she expressed herself too freely for her own happiness," McKay wrote, as she reflected upon "what might have been" if she were not already married. He was "surprised" at this profession of admiration from the twenty-seven-year-old wife and mother and "told her [he] took the expression as coming from a sisterly feeling and nothing more." The awkward exchange left McKay shaken and "thankful" that nothing more unseemly had transpired. Six months later McKay blessed Carney's baby son at the request of the parents, who chose to name him David Oman McKay Carney. Another young woman in the branch assisted by McKay was twenty-seven-year-old Janet Lang, who requested his help in sizing up a marriage proposal she received. "Rendered some assistance!" wrote McKay. "Peculiar position!"[28]

As conference president, McKay spent much time visiting the members of nearby branches, ministering to them, counseling against excesses, and nurturing their faith. On September 4, after a forty-eight-hour fast, he joined with the elders in Newarthill in administering to Charlotte Duncan, a young girl believed to be possessed by evil spirits. On another occasion he was flummoxed when William Reid and Agnes Cook asked him to perform their wedding: "I have never even *seen* a couple married, not to mention *marrying* them!" he mused. He complained of the "many little *knotty* questions" regarding church administration that vexed him. "I often feel that the responsibility is too much!" he despaired. After traveling to Newarthill to resolve conflicts between the branch president and the missionaries, he returned home one evening "tired and worried." The misunderstandings in the branch persisted, with members criticizing the missionaries in public church meetings. "O, it is awful!" he deplored.[29]

As presiding authority, McKay planned what today would be called zone conferences. It was during one of these gatherings that one of the spiritual highlights of his mission, and indeed his life, occurred. In a "most remarkable priesthood meeting" where the missionaries reported their labors, "a peaceful

27. McKay, *What E'er Thou Art*, 168 (Dec. 23, 1898), 109 (July 15, 1898), 120 (Aug. 9, 1898), 111 (July 20, 1898), 143 (Oct. 10, 1898), 152 (Nov. 5, 1898). James remained in Australia, falsely claimed to be a widower, and remarried in 1911. See marriage certificate for James Gain and Mary McCarthy, Sep. 21, 1911, entry for James Gain, KWZV-8Q8, Family Search, familysearch.org.

28. McKay, *What E'er Thou Art*, 164 (Dec. 12, 1898), 165 (Dec. 13, 1898), 253 (June 18, 1899), 180 (Jan. 16, 1899).

29. McKay, *What E'er Thou Art*, 129–30 (Sep. 4, 1898), 141 (Oct. 3, 1898), 180 (Jan. 16, 1899), 171 (Dec. 31, 1898), 188 (Feb. 1, 1899), 193 (Feb. 16, 1899).

heavenly influence pervaded the room." The tender emotions moved several to tears. Charles Woofenden, visiting from the Leeds Conference, testified that he saw two angels. James McMurrin, the first counselor in the mission presidency, validated Woofenden's testimony and stated that the two angels were the guardians of Elders Eccles and Young and that "all your guardian angels are with you." McMurrin assured all the elders they were acceptable to God. Although neither he nor the others in the meeting recorded it at the time, decades later McKay recalled that McMurrin sternly warned him, "Let me say to you, Brother David, Satan hath desired you that he may sift you as wheat, but God is mindful of you. If you will keep thc faith you will yet sit in the leading councils of the Church." At the time McKay interpreted the statement "more [as] a caution than a promise." Into his mind came memories of previous close calls with temptation and a resolve to "keep the faith" more perfectly. McKay came to regard the experience as "the spiritual manifestation for which I had prayed as a boy in my teens."[30]

In his presiding role McKay supervised the fourteen missionaries in the conference and safeguarded their spiritual and physical well-being. His own companion, John T. Edward, fell seriously ill under his watch. McKay worried, fasted, and prayed for Edward's health and tried to care for him when he suffered from bronchitis. As conference president McKay also heard the confession of another elder, who arrived in Glasgow from America on March 14, confessed to serious transgressions on March 17, and left for home barely a week later.[31]

Elder McKay also officiated for the church in public relations matters. After a Glasgow newspaper reprinted an article from a Welsh paper alleging that missionaries were recruiting naïve British women for their harems, McKay wrote a letter refuting the allegations and sent it to the editor of the paper, who published it the next day. When James E. Talmage, a fellow of the Royal Society of Edinburgh and former president of the University of Utah, toured Great Britain lecturing on Utah and its people, McKay rented a spacious auditorium and coordinated advertising. He arranged for Samuel Taylor, the American consul in Glasgow, to introduce Talmage, sent invitations and complimentary tickets to seventy-five leading citizens, printed a thousand programs, and contracted with a prominent organist to provide music for the evening. Talmage held forth for two hours and was frequently interrupted by applause as he described Utah, its scenic and architectural wonders, and Mormon industry and culture. "He did not preach Mormonism, but praised the Mormons in many an eloquent

30. McKay, *What E'er Thou Art*, 161 (Dec. 4, 1898), 238–39 (May 28, 1899), 244n351; David O. McKay, "Two Significant Statements," *Deseret News* (Church Section), Oct. 27, 1934, 1, 8, quoted in McKay, *What E'er Thou Art*, xxxixn21; David O. McKay, address of Oct. 5, 1968, *Conference Reports*, 86.

31. McKay, *What E'er Thou Art*, 209 (Mar. 13, 1899), 210 (Mar. 14, 1899), 211 (Mar. 17, 1899), 214 (Mar. 25, 1899).

sentence....The doctor is worth hearing," a reporter for the *Glasgow Evening Times* gushed. McKay believed the lecture had done more to "allay prejudice than the efforts of all the elders could possibly do" in five years.[32]

Although administrative matters occupied much of his time, McKay still managed to visit and teach people who were interested in the church or in learning about the Saints' Great Basin home. One couple with little interest in doctrine but a great fascination with the American West encouraged the missionaries to "call again at any time." He felt that "more good is done by such visiting than can be done at several open-air meetings; and they are certainly more enjoyable." As he gained confidence as a missionary McKay came to relish gospel discussions and debate. Following a street meeting, a man well-versed in the Bible accompanied McKay to the missionaries' home to continue debating the apostasy. McKay reviewed scriptures from the Bible in an attempt to document the apostasy, but his pupil insisted that the scriptures proved nothing of the sort. One of the elders became so infuriated that he stormed out the door and went to bed, but McKay continued the verbal gymnastics until 2:30 in the morning. In another street meeting a drunken man repeatedly interjected, "That's the truth! Give it to 'em! Don't be 'fraied, mister!" When he cried, "We're not dumb," McKay retorted, "Well, I wish you were; perhaps we could get peace!"[33]

McKay's first opportunity to baptize someone he had taught came sixteen months into his mission when he performed the ordinance for Georgina Ferguson, the twenty-five-year-old daughter of the missionaries' housekeeper. He also subsequently witnessed the baptisms of Jane and Nancy Wallace, whom he had helped to teach, and he confirmed Nancy. McKay had hopes that their parents would also join, but over time their initially keen interest in the gospel waned.[34]

Near the end of his mission, McKay visited the branches in Glasgow, Edinburgh, and Aberdeen and bid farewell to friends and investigators. In a priesthood meeting two and a half weeks before his departure, McKay said he "had learned to love his brethren and sisters, which had indeed made his missionary labors the happiest time of his life." Many were sorry to see McKay depart but none more so than one sister missionary, Josephine Booth of Provo. McKay had greeted her at the train station upon her arrival from the States only a few weeks earlier. Over the next few weeks McKay accompanied Booth and her companion as they toured the Cyclorama, the art museum, and the Robert Burns home. On the night before his departure Booth helped McKay pack his

32. McKay, *What E'er Thou Art*, 164 (Dec. 12, 1898), 167–68 (Dec. 21, 1898), 108 (July 13, 1898), 111–12 (July 22, 1898), 112 (July 23, 1898), 113 (July 29, 1898), 115 (Aug. 1, 1898), 116–18 (Aug. 2, 1898).

33. McKay, *What E'er Thou Art*, 143 (Oct. 10, 1898), 228–29 (May 1, 1899), 140 (Sep. 28, 1898).

34. McKay, *What E'er Thou Art*, 170 (Dec. 27, 1898), 226 (Apr. 24, 1899), 234 (May 18, 1899).

trunk and danced the two-step with him at his farewell party. She was so ecstatic that sleep failed her. The next day, August 26, she and her companion saw McKay and the other returning missionaries off at the docks as they boarded the *City of Rome*, a four-masted steamer with a capacity of 1,300 passengers. She recorded that she "cried as 'usual' and still not as 'usual'" because of her feelings for the charismatic elder. Two days later, after she and her companion received a polite letter McKay had posted before he left, she felt emotions she dared only to allude to obliquely in her diary.

Meanwhile, McKay had other matters on his mind. A few days into the voyage, *City of Rome* struck an iceberg. Passengers lost their balance and fell to the floor, and dishes in the dining room shattered. "My heart seemed to jump to my throat as all the horrors of a shipwreck rushed before me," McKay wrote. Fortunately, the captain had seen the iceberg and reversed the engines before the collision occurred. The boat remained afloat, its engines unimpaired, and the passengers arrived safely in New York Harbor after ten days at sea. From New York the missionaries entrained for Utah. On September 10, 1899, the train rolled down Echo and Weber Canyons. He disembarked at the same station where he had said his goodbyes twenty-five months earlier. There he was greeted by his family.[35]

McKay's mission laid a vital foundation for his subsequent church work. The spiritual conviction he had long sought came as he labored and served in Scotland. Over his life McKay would repeatedly recount the call to responsibility and maturity he had sensed in Stirling as he read the words "What e'er thou art, act well thy part," and subsequent events would validate the unforgettable priesthood meeting where some had sensed an angelic presence and James McMurrin had foretold McKay's lofty future. McKay's persistence in unpleasant tasks from clerical work and administrative minutiae to tracting had honed his work ethic and discipline. McKay had developed a love of preaching and a sympathy borne of ministering—traits that would make him an indefatigable champion of missionary work. He had been forced to confront deep poverty, the ravages of alcoholism, crippling illness and death, and human turpitude and pettiness. In his friendships he had wrestled with betrayal and temptation and had learned much about the application of Christian virtues such as patience, forbearance, boldness, and charity. Although he could not imagine the weighty responsibilities the future held for him, McKay was much better prepared to shoulder them as a result of his mission.

---

35. McKay, *What E'er Thou Art*, xl, 267n393, 268; "*SS City of Rome*, Anchor Line," Norway Heritage, norwayheritage.com; DOMD, Dec. 8, 1960; Josephine D. Booth Woodruff, journal, Aug. 1–3, 9, 19, 25, 1899.

3: A Career and Marriage

Shortly before McKay completed his mission, Weber Stake Academy renewed the offer of a teaching position it had extended prior to his mission, and McKay accepted. Barely a week after he returned, McKay began teaching. That first year he taught pedagogy and literature, directed the school choir, and worked as registrar on the campus of just a little over two hundred students. The following year he added courses in history and theology. As he supervised student dances, outings, and sporting events, he became well acquainted with his students' lives beyond the classroom.[1]

Soon after he began teaching, McKay, now an experienced church administrator because of his mission, received a call to serve on the Weber Stake Sunday School Board. It was a calling well suited to a man trained in pedagogy. At a Sunday School convention in November 1900, McKay drew upon his training, urging teachers to select music with a "lively" tempo for their pupils to march to as they sang. The virtues of marching to and from classes included saving time, maintaining order, and instilling discipline, he advised.[2]

McKay's courtship with Ray Riggs proceeded over the following months. After breaking off their correspondence for over a year while McKay was in Scotland, Ray had resumed her letter writing the previous February. She had been under the impression, she wrote in her first letter after the hiatus, that David "cared not for further correspondence," but she decided to test the waters anyway. He assured her stiffly, "Your letters, as your company are appreciated and esteemed more highly than you evidently have thought." With a bachelor's degree in hand from the University of Utah—an honor that only a handful of Utahns could claim at the time—Ray had taken a teaching job at James Madison Elementary School in Ogden, and she joined his family to meet McKay at the train station when he disembarked following his mission. On and off that year the two schoolteachers visited. Over the same period, McKay wrote a handful of times to Josephine Booth in Scotland in response to her letters, inadvertently nurturing her hopes. After she received a letter in mid-October, she fancied herself "Bro. McKay's girl" because of "something" McKay's letter

1. Woodger, "Progressive Educational Ideas," 213–14; "Educational," *Salt Lake Herald*, Sep. 17, 1899, 7.

2. Gibbons, *David O. McKay*, 58; "Talked of Marriage," *Salt Lake Tribune*, Nov. 13, 1900, 5.

"said" to her. The day before Christmas she was depressed and cried. The next day her spirits soared when she received a note from McKay, the first in two months. She read it repeatedly, savoring the words and trying to conceal from others that she was "awfully glad." A few weeks later she dreamed of her imagined beau. Meanwhile, McKay had been thinking far more about Ray than Josephine for several months. At the end of the previous school year he had been uncertain of her affections. As they parted, she had said something about being "only friends" that puzzled him, and when she did not write immediately after she returned to Salt Lake for the summer, he became despondent. He signed his first letter that summer "Your loving friend." He did not have to wait long for an encouraging response, and they spent a pleasant day together at Saltair on the shores of the Great Salt Lake later that month. A few months later David proposed to her under a tree in Ogden's Lester Park. When the news of the engagement finally reached Booth two days before the wedding, she canceled her New Year's Eve plans and wept "for a long time." It was the "saddest day of the year," she wrote.[3]

On January 2, 1900, David and Ray were married by Apostle John Henry Smith in the Salt Lake Temple. As he remembered it, they were the first couple married in the temple in the new century. "Though it was crisp, zero weather, our hearts were warm and we didn't feel the cold," Ray nostalgically recalled decades later. That evening they greeted well-wishers at the home of Belle Barrett White, Ray's married cousin with whom she had lived following her mother's death. The bride and groom stood beneath a canopy of green leaves and pink flowers in the parlor. Among the guests were Apostles John Henry Smith and George Albert Smith. After honeymooning for a couple of weeks they set up housekeeping in a small home at 2247 Monroe Avenue in Ogden. A rough pregnancy beset with severe morning sickness ensued almost immediately after their honeymoon. A son, David Lawrence, was born nearly nine months to the day after their wedding on September 30.[4]

During McKay's second year at the academy, the Weber Stake presidency notified Principal Louis Moench that they intended to release him at the end of the school year, and they asked McKay to succeed him. When Moench was unable to find another position, the board permitted him to remain for one more year and deferred McKay's appointment. Meanwhile, William Terry, another faculty member who coveted Moench's position and its attendant salary, took offense. "He went so far as to say that he wouldn't let a young man with only a [teaching] *certificate* to preside over *him*, a *B.S*," McKay reported to his

3. McKay and McKay, *Heart Petals*, 22, 29; Woodruff, journal, Oct. 13, Dec. 24, 25, 31, 1899.

4. DOMD, Jan. 2, 1944, Feb. 23, 1967; McKay and McKay, *Heart Petals*, 47; "Social and Personal," *Salt Lake Tribune*, Jan. 3, 1901, 8; "In Society," *Salt Lake Tribune*, Jan. 6, 1901, 18; Ogletree, *No Other Success*, vi.

brother. Terry "needn't have worried," McKay quipped, because if McKay had taken charge, Terry "wouldn't have been asked to stay." Finally at the end of the 1901–02 school year, McKay succeeded Moench at the respectable yearly salary of $1,500. Although he was inclined to show Terry the door, McKay's temper had cooled, and he resisted the impulse.[5]

In the six years he served as principal, McKay proved to be an able leader of the faculty, which included his siblings Thomas and Jeanette. He continued to work in the trenches as a teacher, ran faculty meetings using an agenda, solicited faculty input in making policy, and instituted new practices to encourage students to be punctual. McKay promoted women's education by establishing a domestic science department; instituted athletic programs, including women's basketball; oversaw the establishment of a student newspaper; and instituted elections for student body officers. He lobbied the LDS Church Board of Education and local commercial and civic leaders for funds to expand the school's physical plant and recruited students by speaking in wards throughout the Weber Stake. When faculty members failed to measure up, he let them go. He summoned one "incompetent teacher" to his office, documented her poor performance, and fired her despite her pleas for clemency. "I was grieved by the condition, and especially when she pleaded, but the school, and her classes, will not succeed under her," he judged. A few weeks later when the woman demanded a full year's salary even though she had been let go, he stood firm. "Her incompetence necessitated her discharge, and the school is not responsible," he tartly informed her.[6]

As an assistant superintendent in the Weber Stake Sunday School, McKay devised a tiered system of meetings for training Sunday School officers and teachers: the stake Sunday School board met weekly for training in lesson planning and organization. Members of the board then presented the materials they had learned to the Sunday School teachers from the wards in monthly union meetings. As part of those meetings the stake board members coached teachers as they outlined lessons for the coming month and identified instructional materials. The ward Sunday School superintendency met in turn each week with their faculty to fine-tune the outlines the teachers had drafted in the monthly training meetings. At the invitation of Joseph F. Smith, church president and general superintendent of the Sunday School, McKay distilled his principles of lesson organization into an article that was published in the Sunday School's general magazine, the *Juvenile Instructor*, in April 1905. The Weber superintendency also instituted Sunday School classes for parents to complement the church-wide Sunday School classes for children. In these classes, devised by

5. Woodger, "Progressive Educational Ideas," 226–28; "Weber Stake Academy," *Salt Lake Herald-Republican*, Aug. 1, 1902, 7.

6. Woodger, "Progressive Educational Ideas," 226–42 (quotation 230); DOMD, Dec. 17, 1907.

McKay, parents learned how to teach their children gospel principles so that the Sunday School became a supplement to instruction in the home. A kickoff meeting for the weekly parents' Sunday School classes took place in a convention in the Ogden Tabernacle where Joseph F. Smith presided. A general board committee studied the Weber Stake innovation and recommended its adoption church-wide. Just a week before the church's April general conference, McKay traveled to Salt Lake to begin organizing parents' classes there. Little did he suspect that the ground beneath his feet was about to shift dramatically.[7]

7. McKay, *Home Memories*, 29; Gibbons, *David O. McKay*, 58–59, 64; "Meetings during Conference Week," *Deseret Evening News*, Apr. 9, 1906, 14; Morrell, *Highlights*, 62; "Weber Stake Academy Notes," *Ogden Daily Standard*, Apr. 7, 1906, 7.

4: Apostleship, 1906–1920

McKay's visionary efforts to extend Sunday School to parents brought the young church worker to the attention of President Smith. Impressed as he pondered that work, in 1906 Smith proposed McKay's name to fill a vacancy in the Quorum of Twelve Apostles, and on April 5, 1906, the First Presidency and Quorum of the Twelve approved. Church leaders had passed over more prominent individuals, the First Presidency informed Heber J. Grant by mail, because they were polygamists whose call might further inflame prejudice against the church in the nation's capital. According to family lore, McKay only learned of the calling between the Sunday morning and afternoon sessions of the general conference. The family was in Salt Lake for the conference, where McKay was scheduled to speak that evening at the Sunday School leadership session. They were dining with Ray's cousin Belle and her husband, Parley, when McKay was summoned to Elder Francis M. Lyman's office. When Lyman, as president of the Quorum of the Twelve, informed him that "the Lord wants you to be a member of the Quorum of Twelve Apostles," McKay stammered that he was "neither worthy nor able" to accept. He was morally worthy, he clarified, but unqualified. "Don't you have faith the Lord can make you able?" Lyman queried. McKay's affirmative response settled the matter.[1]

Contrary to family lore, the calling process occurred over a three-day period. The surprising lunchtime invitation occurred on Friday, April 6, the first day of the conference. In that meeting, Lyman made general inquiries regarding McKay's health and testimony. Lyman asked McKay to return the following day, and McKay came away from the interview thinking that he might be asked to serve on the Church Board of Education. On Saturday, Lyman, joined by Apostles John Henry Smith and George Albert Smith, met with David O. McKay, George F. Richards, and Orson F. Whitney, the three men who were to be called to the Quorum of the Twelve. Lyman issued the call, "asked for and received from each of us our views and feelings, and then enjoined us to strict secrecy regarding the whole matter," Whitney recorded. When the thirty-two-year-old McKay's name was read from the pulpit on Sunday afternoon,

1. Lund, *Danish Apostle*, 336; Joseph F. Smith to Heber J. Grant, Apr. 12, 1906, box 2, folder 2, Scott G. Kenney Research Materials; DOMD, June 23, 1967; McKay, *My Father*, 38–40.

near the end of the session, Ray, who was three months pregnant, burst into tears, knowing that she would now be alone on many evenings and weekends with four-year-old Lawrence, two-year-old Llewelyn, and the expected infant. According to her son Ed, "The first she knew about [the calling] was in the afternoon session, when they read the Apostles for the sustaining vote." From a seat behind, Ray heard someone whisper, "There's the wife of one of them. See, she's crying." The next day after Ray's father heard the news in Ohio, he wrote to David, "An old Patriarchal blessing on me stated that I would be an associate with apostles. It may be as that prediction has not been fulfilled in me, that satisfaction may come out in another member of the family."[2]

The newly sustained apostle soon found himself immersed in church work, performing weddings, speaking at funerals, visiting stake conferences, and attending weekly apostolic council meetings in the Salt Lake Temple. Stake conference visits on the weekends typically stretched over two days and entailed presiding and speaking at a general session, a priesthood meeting, a Sunday School session, a leadership training session, and a meeting with teenagers. Some conferences were stimulating and reinvigorating, but others were frustrating and discouraging. Occasionally the travel and accommodations were downright arduous. On a trip to the San Luis Valley in 1907, McKay slept in a stuffy attic bedroom in the home of the La Jara Ward bishop. "Spent a miserable night! I endured the heat, and fought mosquitos, but when a silent army of ravenous bedbugs fell upon me, I succumbed," he recorded. To make matters worse, he was scheduled to spend a second night in the same bedroom. Out of consideration for the bishop and his wife's feelings, he said nothing to them about the bedbugs and stayed up for most of the second night with the coal oil lamp burning so that he could dispatch any bugs that got too close. He was "quite sure," he wrote in jest, that "the persecutors and tormenters of Hell are not devils and brimstone; they are bedbugs!"[3]

As a neophyte in the Quorum of the Twelve, McKay entered a brotherhood of men who differed on many matters but shared a rock-ribbed faith. He respected his associates, whom he judged to be "pure and true." When Orson F. Whitney told him that Heber J. Grant had offered to assume Whitney's debt of $400 on his home, McKay was deeply touched. McKay knew how ominous that debt appeared to Whitney. "That is an expression of true friendship," McKay recorded in admiration. Although he esteemed and respected his associates, he did not always agree with them, even as a newcomer. "My feelings and will had to submit to those of the majority," the junior apostle recorded

2. Emma Ray Ashton, "Emma Ray Riggs McKay," *Relief Society Magazine*, June 1967, 412; McKay, *My Father*, 38–39; Whitney, *The Life of Orson F. Whitney*, 239–40; Edward McKay, excerpts from interview by Greg Prince, Feb. 16, 1995, box 23, folder 13, Prince Papers.

3. DOMD, July 21, 1907. McKay's diary entries for the first three months of his call provide a good overview of his new duties.

after a discussion in a quorum meeting nearly ten months after his call. Later that year he was amused by Hyrum M. Smith's objections to George Albert Smith's efforts on behalf of the church to purchase the Joseph Smith farm and the Sacred Grove in New York. "He does not believe in paying for sentiment. He does not care for the Past," McKay wrote incredulously. Traveling with senior members of the quorum on speaking assignments, McKay learned from them. In a hotel room in southwestern Colorado, John Henry Smith conveyed some treasured wisdom he had received from Brigham Young: "No man who had ever balked in this church [like Orson Pratt or Orson Hyde] could ever be its president," McKay recorded. Early in his apostolic career McKay attended a council meeting where Reed Smoot's desire to run for reelection to the US Senate was discussed. Francis M. Lyman was opposed to his doing so, and McKay was ready to add his voice to Lyman's. Usually, the prophet invited discussion from each apostle on important matters, and McKay was ready to speak his mind. Instead, Joseph F. Smith simply announced, "Brethren, we have a very important question before us—whether a member of our Council should run for the Senate. I want to tell you that it is the will of the Lord that he does." Lyman then said, "I move that be the sentiment of the Council."[4]

Sacred moments heightened the apostle's spirituality. Standing at the deathbed of his friend Stewart Eccles in the Ogden Hospital in 1914, McKay heard Eccles address an unseen presence: "Yes Father, I recognize you. Father, may I come back?" Shortly after, Eccles passed away. Recalling the incident years later, McKay summarized a lesson he learned from the experience: death was "an occasion for looking up to God rather than down to the mortal remains."[5]

As if his apostolic duties were light, McKay continued his work as principal of the Weber Stake Academy for two more years. He had raised funds for a new multipurpose academy building with an auditorium, labs, and classrooms, and he wanted to see that project through to completion. In the intervening years Apostle McKay organized and hosted eleven guest lectures at the academy for Ogden residents, including talks by the spellbinding orator and former presidential candidate William Jennings Bryan and renowned education professor S. H. Clarke of the University of Chicago. McKay also continued to profoundly influence students. One, Charles Owen, had been a student at the academy but dropped out when he was eighteen. His mother, a Huntsville native, made an appointment for her son to see McKay in Salt Lake during the October conference. Owen recalled, "When he saw me, he said, 'Charles, why weren't you in school last year?' I had no alibi, so he said for me to be in school Monday." McKay's influence kept him in school until he graduated in the spring of 1908.

4. DOMD, Oct. 4, 1907; DOMD, Jan. 28, July 14, 29, 1907; DOMD, Sep. 5, 1962.

5. McKay, *Confidence amid Change*, 318–19.

"He was a wonderful teacher. I thoroughly enjoyed being under the influence of his pleasing, spiritual personality," Owen wrote.[6]

McKay's day off each week was Monday unless he was still returning from a far-flung stake conference. His major teaching day was Tuesday. During the winter 1907 quarter, for instance, he taught advanced rhetoric at 7:30 a.m., conducted devotional at 8:45 a.m., and taught theology at 9:25 a.m., followed by English literature at 10:30 a.m. Generally he traveled by train to Salt Lake on Tuesday afternoon for committee meetings followed by a meeting with the General Sunday School Board in the later afternoon or evening. After returning to Ogden late at night, he reported to the academy for faculty meetings on Wednesday morning and then either traveled to Salt Lake in the afternoon for meetings or spent the time at home drafting or editing church lesson manuals or completing other church work. Thursdays were devoted to apostolic business in Salt Lake, including the Quorum of the Twelve's regular meeting in the temple. Fridays were generally devoted to academy business unless he had to begin traveling to a distant conference. McKay often used a bicycle as he traveled from his home to the train station en route to Salt Lake. Perched on the handlebars, Lawrence as a grade schooler sometimes accompanied his father to the train station and then pedaled the bike home after his father boarded the train.[7]

McKay struggled to balance work, church, and civic obligations, which consumed most of his waking hours, with his responsibilities to his young family at home. "I feel I am away from [my family] too often," McKay wrote ten months after his call. Returning from a five-day trip to the Teton Stake in Idaho, he found "baby still very sick, Lawrence with a severe cold in addition to his cough, and Ray quite worn out." The senior apostles and prophet tried to be accommodating of the young family's needs, but the apostle's sense of duty sometimes led him to accept assignments when Ray desperately needed his support at home. Eighteen months after his call and shortly after his daughter Lou Jean's first birthday, Lou Jean came down with pneumonia. McKay contacted the prophet, who suggested McKay might cancel his planned trip to a stake conference in Rich County. But McKay's traveling companion, Wilford McKendrick of Weber Stake Academy, was not even a general authority, so McKay decided to accompany McKendrick at least as far as Evanston and introduce him to the stake leaders. In Evanston, a boy rather than a stake leader came to the depot in a wagon to fetch the visiting authorities, so McKay continued on to the town of Woodruff. Before he attended the Saturday conference meeting there, McKay phoned friends in Ogden and asked them to check on his family.

6. "Bryan is Given Warm Reception," *Salt Lake Tribune*, Feb. 4, 1907, 2; "Interesting Address," *Salt Lake Tribune*, Feb. 21, 1907, 10; "Charles Henry Owen," Davis County Cooperative Society, dccsociety.org.

7. DOMD, Jan. 27, 1907, Sep. 24, 1967. My description of McKay's weekly routine is based upon my perusal of his diaries for 1906–08.

When word returned that Lou Jean's condition had worsened, he immediately arranged for a buggy ride back to Evanston. Sunday morning at 10:00 he finally arrived home. "I was glad to be by her side, and to be home to comfort if not to help Ray," he wrote. Lou Jean's condition did not improve over the next three days, so McKay canceled his upcoming trip to Wayne County for another conference. Soon after he decided to stay home, Lou Jean rallied, and he "regretted" his haste in calling off the appointment.[8]

As Llewelyn remembered, after McKay's call as an apostle the family "saw little of him, for he left early in the morning and returned late at night." Once as he was leaving home, little Lou Jean blurted out, "Good-bye, call again," as if he were a stranger. Of necessity Ray was the primary disciplinarian, arbiter, and decision-maker in matters related to the children in the home. She reared the children. She often invoked his presence, though, with phrases such as "Your father would want ..." When he was home, McKay "never talked much" in disciplining. He handed out what Lawrence called "the look" and what Bob, his youngest son, called the "finger treatment." The latter involved McKay's tapping Bob on the temple with his finger and warning, "Think about it, boy." Only once did he physically discipline Bob. Bob had been playing basketball with some friends when Ray called him to dinner. "Wait a minute," he replied. Shortly, McKay strode from the house, "marching as fast as he could. McKay "grabbed me by the ear," Bob recalled, "and walked me, in front of all my friends, all the way up to the gravel road and up the back stairs and sat me down at the dinner table." He told Bob, "Don't you ever say, 'Wait a minute' to your mother again." One of the few times McKay lost control of his emotions with his children was when he was playing baseball with his young boys in the backyard. When Llewelyn hit the ball, he cast the bat behind him and inadvertently struck his father in the head. "Don't ever throw a bat!" he reprimanded. "If you can't play baseball better than that ... !" he began, and then left off speaking and retreated to the kitchen. Sometimes on long winter evenings when he was at home, McKay joined Ray and the children in card games like Rook, Pit, and Coquinole. His favorite was a combination of bridge and Five Hundred using Rook cards that the family called "McKay Pirate Rook." Lawrence told his daughter Midene that their father "was just somebody to have a good time with when he was home ... because he was gone so much."[9]

Despite the stresses that McKay's calling placed upon their marriage, Ray and David never let their children hear or see a "disagree[ment] let alone [a] quarrel," according to their son Lawrence. Their self-control was exceptional,

8. DOMD, Feb. 6, 1907, Aug. 13, 1907, Oct. 23–Nov. 3, 1907.

9. McKay, *Home Memories*, 30; McKay, *My Father*, 100–1, 103, 106; Robert McKay, remarks at the David O. McKay Symposium, Brigham Young University, October 1996, box 22, folder 13, Prince Papers; Midene Anderson, excerpts of interview by Greg Prince, Oct. 1, 1996, box 22, folder 13, Prince Papers.

and much of the outward harmony was attributable to Ray. David's frequent absences and the burden of managing a household and raising children, largely on her own, sometimes brought tears to her eyes, despite the resolution she had made as a new mother that "she would never feel bad when David O. had to leave on a church assignment." At times David returned home to find her overwhelmed and in tears. Sometimes they wept together, but she endeavored to be good-natured and supportive by practicing immense self-abnegation and self-control. Perhaps her parents' failed marriage as well as her understanding of her cultural and religious obligations as a wife steeled her determination to avoid conflict at all costs. She strove to cultivate "peace in the home" through an approach that she described to an audience of female college students in 1952 as "being at all times kind, loving, self-sacrificing, ready to help, ready to serve, in fact, loving to do anything the head of the house desires because his desires are also hers." She advised the students to remember that "wisdom is made up of two parts: nine-tenths silence and one-tenth brevity." She continued, "The successful mother must plan, and arise early to carry that plan out. If she does not, the meals are late, the dishes drag, the husband is cross, the woman is flustered.... If she does not plan a year ahead, the gardening, the house-cleaning, and the education of the children are neglected."[10]

As the children grew, McKay occasionally invited one of them to accompany him on trips to stake conferences. Five-year-old Lawrence traveled with him by train to La Grande, Oregon, in the summer of 1907, and in 1909 he joined his father on a memorable trip by train and buggy to conferences in Garfield County. When the buggy was stranded on a remote road by a flash flood, the young boy feared for his life. "Father took me on his lap and held me in his arms all night," Lawrence remembered. In 1910 six-year-old Llewelyn was old enough to accompany his father on a church trip to northern California. In 1912 it was five-year-old Lou Jean's turn to accompany her father to a conference in Provo. Occasionally, David and Ray were able to leave all the children in the care of a relative and travel together, as they did in 1911 when they rode to Arizona on Sunday School business and then on to California for a week.[11]

10. McKay, *My Father*, 12–13, 104. Bringhurst, "Private versus Public," 15, characterizes Ray's approach as "repressed submissiveness" and points out that "David O. had a fundamental advantage in all aspects of their relationship. Physically, he towered over his almost petite five-foot three-inch wife. More importantly, as the male, his status as head of the family was undisputed." Much of this "advantage" was attributable, he accurately points out, to the fact that "Ray seemingly accepted her subordinate status without question." Ray's grandson-in-law Howard Anderson characterized Ray as "infinitely patient" and provided one amusing example. "She asked him to take the mattresses downstairs so she could clean them out. Instead of carrying them down the stairs, he threw them off the balcony in the Huntsville house, down onto the lawn. She said, 'Well, if your husband does that, you'll just have to smile and explain to him that isn't quite what you had in mind.'" Howard B Anderson, interview by Stephen L. Prince, Feb. 7, 1997, box 22, folder 13, Prince Papers.

11. McKay, *My Father*, 81, 83; DOMD, Nov. 10–20, May 26, 1912.

One of the facets of his church work McKay loved most was connecting with his audiences. Early in his ministry he visited a conference in Malad City, Idaho, where many Welsh converts and their descendants had settled. Shortly before the Saturday morning session began, the apostle commented to the stake president, a pure-blooded Welshman, that he had Welsh ancestry too. The stake president appeared skeptical. When McKay arose to speak, he began, "Just before this service began I whispered to President Richards that I have Welsh blood in my veins, but … he implied that I made the claim merely because I am here with you Welsh people. But I wish to say to President Richards and to you that my mother was born in Plasagon House, Cleydyfagwyr Cefn Eved Cwmer, near Merthyr Tydfil, South Wales, and her name was Evans." An elderly Welshwoman on the front row stood and urged him on, "That's it, that's it, you are, you are."[12]

Soon after he began serving in the quorum, McKay was sustained as President Joseph F. Smith's second assistant in the General Sunday School Superintendency. His duties in this capacity increased after he stepped down as Weber academy principal in 1908, although he continued to commute from Ogden. He attended weekly general Sunday School union board meetings; outlined and wrote Sunday School lesson manuals; and regularly attended stake Sunday School conferences where he preached, trained Sunday School officers and teachers, promoted parental involvement, and encouraged organizational improvements. McKay's first solo-authored Sunday School manual, *Ancient Apostles*, was printed in 1918. At times the apostle found his Sunday School work invigorating, as in a conference in Brigham City where he narrated Henry Van Dyke's classic children's tale "The Story of the Other Wise Man." "The tabernacle was crowded … and, as the rays of sunlight came through the window and shone on the smiling faces of the children, it seemed that Heaven was approving the spirit that prompted the great gathering of children," he recorded. At other times he was discouraged, regretting how poorly some leaders performed their callings. After attending a Sunday School conference in Spanish Fork, McKay groused, "The superintendent did not have matters in hand. There was no attention to details. There should be a change in the superintendency."[13]

McKay's work on the general board occasionally brought him into conflict with his former teacher, James E. Talmage, whose Sunday School lectures for several years at the Latter-day Saints University drew large crowds. When the board considered with Talmage whether to continue the university Sunday School in 1907, several years before Talmage became an apostle, Talmage's comments were

12. McKay, *Home Memories*, 24–25.

13. "M'Kendrick Now at Head," *Ogden Daily Standard*, Mar. 12, 1908, 6; "'Ancient Apostles,' A New Book Written by Apostle D. O. M'Kay Printed and Bound in Ogden," *Ogden Daily Standard*, Feb. 1, 1918; DOMD, Feb. 9, 1906; DOMD, June 9, 1912; DOMD Dec. 9, 1906.

"wordy," McKay complained, and "(fight the thought as I would) insincere." McKay concluded that Talmage "must repent or go down spiritually."[14]

Following Joseph F. Smith's death in November 1918, McKay replaced him as general Sunday School superintendent. He selected his dear friends Stephen L Richards and George D. Pyper as his assistants. Recently called as an apostle, Richards had developed a friendship with McKay during their college days at the University of Utah. Pyper had edited the church's Sunday School periodical, the *Juvenile Instructor*, for nearly a decade, and he was a gifted musician, member of the Tabernacle choir (then known as the Mormon Tabernacle Choir), and manager of the Salt Lake Theatre.[15]

The great albatross weighing down general church leaders in the early twentieth century was the continuation of plural marriage, and McKay negotiated that burden with his colleagues as a junior apostle. President Smith issued a second manifesto on the subject in 1904, threatening excommunication for new polygamists, but few were disciplined. As a young apostle, McKay labored on a committee tasked with preparing an official response to charges and criticisms regarding the LDS Church, including the continued practice of plural marriage following the 1890 Woodruff Manifesto, criticisms that circulated widely as a result of the inquest of the Senate's Committee on Privileges and Elections regarding the seating of Senator (and Apostle) Reed Smoot. Through this church committee, church leaders hoped to "represent ourselves rather than to be misrepresented by others," McKay noted. McKay's associates on the committee were Apostle Orson F. Whitney, B. H. Roberts of the Seventy, James E. Talmage, Richard W. Young, LeGrand Young, Nephi Morris, and Franklin S. Richards. President Smith's son Joseph Fielding served as secretary. In McKay's estimation Roberts was "the most able man on the committee" in terms of analytical and expressive capacity, but he manifested less "faith in the gospel and especially in the present leaders" than Elder Whitney. Whitney ranked second in McKay's estimation, being "not so practical as Bro. Roberts" but having "more spirituality." Talmage, whom McKay had admired greatly in his student and missionary days, lagged behind both Roberts and Whitney in McKay's estimation. He admired Talmage's vocabulary and critical acumen but suspected he was insincere in his professions of faith and "a good deal of pretender" whose inflated ego grated on McKay's sensibilities. In truth, both McKay and Talmage struggled at times to keep their vanity in check. In their initial meetings in January, McKay strongly supported church members who continued to live with plural wives they had married prior to the Manifesto. The problem was that under persistent grilling by outsiders, Woodruff had implicitly broadened the

14. DOMD, Dec. 11, 1906.

15. DOMD, Dec. 31, 1918; "D. O. M'Kay is General Superintendent of Sunday Schools," *Ogden Daily Standard*, Nov. 28, 1918, 8.

scope of the Manifesto's prohibitions to include cohabitation with wives. "We have made declarations enough, but unfortunately the facts and circumstances appear to discredit the declarations that have been made," observed Richards. Some on the committee wanted to excuse members from compliance with the Manifesto if they had not personally voted to sustain it when it was presented in general conference, but Roberts pointed out that the document had been approved by the conference and thereby had become binding on the entire church. The best option, Richard Young believed, was to "plead for the indulgence of the people of the world." Somehow, they must uphold President Woodruff's interpretation of the Manifesto applying to cohabitation while still defending the sanctity of "the relations and obligations of the old polygamists" to continue living with and providing for their plural families.[16]

After several days of preliminary discussion, the committee divided into three subcommittees. McKay, Talmage, and Morris were responsible for examining the history and aims of plural marriage, the weightiest of the assignments. They would examine polygamy and the Manifesto within the context of religion and priesthood governance. Whitney, Smith, and Richard Young would draft a statement on the history and character of the Latter-day Saints, and Roberts, Richards, and LeGrand Young would report on the political situation and political connections. In late February the committee of the whole reconvened, read their draft reports aloud, and scrapped much of what they had written. What remained of the committee report was submitted to the First Presidency and distilled into a document presented in the April 1907 general conference. The document acknowledged the civil disobedience of church members who married polygamously after the Supreme Court upheld anti-polygamy statutes in 1878, reasoning that "what our people did in disregard of the law of the decisions of the Supreme Court ... was in the spirit of maintaining religious rights under constitutional guaranties, and not in any spirit of defiance or disloyalty to the government." The final committee report sidestepped the controversial post-Manifesto polygamous marriages of church leaders and attributed plural marriages following the Woodruff Manifesto to the choices of individual members, excusing the church; "in every state and nation there are individuals who violate law in spite of all the vigilance that can be exercised," they rationalized.[17]

The First Presidency issued the committee's report as a declaration to the world during the April conference. The document identified the church as "pure Christianity," testified of the restoration of the priesthood by angels, defended the integrity and morality of the church and its members, and denied that the church had been duplicitous. It censured those who accused the church of

16. DOMD, Apr. 5, 1907; DOMD, Feb. 4, 1907; *Minutes of the Apostles*, 3:374–76.

17. *Minutes of the Apostles*, 3:377, 380; "An Address: The Church of Jesus Christ of Latter-day Saints to the World," Apr. 5, 1907, *Conference Reports*, appendix, 11–12.

"shunning enlightened investigation" and showed that the church valued education and free inquiry. The church safeguarded the sanctity of marriage and family relations, was democratic rather than autocratic or authoritarian, and encouraged but did not compel its members to pay tithing. Members were loyal to the country and its Constitution; their patriotic ardor outweighed and "outlived the memory of all the wrongs inflicted upon our fathers and ourselves." Plural marriage was a religious "principle" introduced by Joseph Smith and practiced by the Latter-day Saints until "every means of constitutional defense had been exhausted." Admittedly, some members had married plurally following Wilford Woodruff's Manifesto, but "the wonder is not that there have been sporadic cases of plural marriage," the authors declared, "but that such cases have been so few" given the fact that "a religious conviction existed among the people, holding this order of marriage to be divinely sanctioned." Finally, there was "nothing treasonable or disloyal in any ordinance, ceremony, or ritual of the Church." Some might argue that Latter-day Saints, who believed the prophet spoke for God, could not "give true allegiance" to the nation, but this was simply untrue.[18]

In the same year that the First Presidency issued their proclamation, the *Millennial Star* office in Liverpool published Talmage's *The Story of "Mormonism,"* in which he enunciated an updated doctrinal understanding for the twentieth-century church, arguing that "plurality of wives was an incident[,] never an essential" feature of the church's doctrine on marriage. Talmage almost certainly promulgated this view in their committee meetings, a view McKay ardently embraced. Years later as prophet McKay stated to his counselors that "the having of more than one wife is not a <u>principle</u> but a <u>practice</u>." The principle was "the eternity of the marriage covenant" and "all the blessings pertaining to that may be obtained by a man with one wife."[19]

Two years after they issued their declaration to the world that McKay helped to draft, the First Presidency in 1909 appointed Francis M. Lyman, John Henry Smith, and Heber J. Grant to investigate ongoing plural marriages and to "summarily" discipline those involved. Other apostles, including McKay, were called upon to assist as part of their duties as the "traveling high council" for the church. For instance, that fall McKay investigated Israel Barlow Jr., who had married Alice Welling, the sister of Bear River Stake president Milton Welling. McKay's investigation provided supporting evidence for Barlow's excommunication the following year.[20]

In 1911, under assignment, McKay interrogated Apostle John W. Taylor, but he was a reluctant, cautious investigator. Taylor claimed that "a superior officer" in the church had advised him to promote polygamy following the Manifesto.

18. "An Address," *Conference Reports,* appendix, 3–16.

19. Talmage, *The Story of "Mormonism,"* 86; McKay, *Confidence amid Change*, 136–37.

20. Alexander, *Mormonism in Transition*, 67; Grant, *Diaries of Heber J. Grant*, 289 (Oct. 6, 20, 1909).

When McKay asked him to identify the officer, Taylor stonewalled, creating the impression that he was lying. Later that month Taylor was excommunicated. But McKay remained sympathetic to him. Years later as church president he would restore Taylor's blessings. Unlike his colleague Joseph Fielding Smith, who, from McKay's perspective, "would condemn all" excommunicated members who died "without having given satisfactory evidence of repentance" to "the Terrestrial and Telestial Kingdoms," McKay believed it was the "right" of the First Presidency and the Quorum of the Twelve to restore the blessings of those individuals.[21]

In 1914, McKay participated in inquests or ecclesiastical trials of at least six polygamists, including Apostle Matthias Cowley. These were heart-wrenching, unpleasant hearings— he called one a "trying ordeal" for both the member and the council, and he often favored clemency. McKay believed that many who had contracted new marriages, along with John W. Woolley, who solemnized many of the marriages, had been misled or "deceived." He voted with six fellow apostles against disfellowshipping Cowley, but the next day Cowley was stripped of his priesthood authority. Years later as counselor in the First Presidency McKay would meet with Cowley and work to restore his blessings.[22]

Shortly after Joseph F. Smith's death in 1918, his successor, Heber J. Grant, instigated a new round of investigations in which McKay loyally assisted. The presiding brethren assiduously ferreted out evidence of an alleged "union" that was actively recruiting new polygamists. Because of his Weber County roots, McKay focused on polygamists there. One was Thomas J. Steed of Ogden, a prominent rancher and investor who was in his sixties. While Steed stonewalled to the council, he later confessed privately to McKay that he had taken two plural wives, and on the strength of that confession he was excommunicated. McKay again favored clemency, this time for Steed's wives, being convinced that they were "sincere in the mistake they have made," but the council overrode his appeal on their behalf.[23]

The church's crackdown on polygamy, in which McKay demonstrated moderation and gentleness, coincided with a broader national effort to police behavior: the Prohibition movement. In the latter crusade, he showed he could be a determined and at times combative crusader. Unlike Apostle Reed Smoot, who prioritized the church's political clout over its moral influence in the fight against alcohol, McKay embraced Prohibition wholeheartedly in his early apostolic career, regardless of the potential political costs for the Republican Party and the church. Progressivism, including efforts by urban middle-class professionals to cleanse society of vice and corruption, was surging nationwide when

21. *Minutes of the Apostles*, 4:57, 60; McKay, *Confidence amid Change*, 591; DOMD, Feb. 16, 1939.

22. DOMD, Jan. 14, 1914; DOMD, June 17, 1914; *Minutes of the Apostles*, 4:79; Grant, *Diaries of Heber J. Grant*, 410 (Mar. 27, 1936); Gibbons, *David O. McKay*, 167–68.

23. "Thomas J. Steed Dies in Ogden," *Davis County Clipper*, Mar. 25, 1921, 1; DOMD, Jan. 12, 15, Feb. 18, 1919.

McKay joined the crusade, linking hands with other Christian reformers in an effort to prohibit the manufacture and sale of alcohol. The Word of Wisdom provided a religious impetus for McKay's fervor, but his missionary service in Scotland, where he had observed up close the ravages of drink, steeled his resolve. The McKays lived in Ogden, a railroad city whose population was exceptionally diverse for Utah. Because of that diversity, the apostle campaigned for prohibition in Ogden and Weber County against considerable odds. In 1908, as a key Prohibition organization, the Anti-Saloon League, perfected its organization in the Beehive State. Fred Kiesel, an Ogden millionaire with heavy interests in the liquor trade, warned Senator Reed Smoot that powerful commercial interests would secede from Utah's Republican Party and reconstitute an anti-Mormon party if the church or the Republican Party campaigned for statewide prohibition. Both Smoot and President Joseph F. Smith mortally feared a rupture in the fragile political truce between Latter-day Saints and non-Mormons. Although Smoot pledged to block prohibition with his Republican network, a bill introduced by George M. Cannon in the state legislature early in 1909 called for statewide, absolute prohibition. Cannon was McKay's associate on the Sunday School General Board, and the young apostle came out squarely in favor of the bill. A committee of two dozen prominent citizens including McKay gathered over 6,000 signatures from Weber County in support of the bill and presented their petition to the county's four legislators. Smoot countered the Prohibitionist campaign, called in his political favors, and secured enough votes to quash the Cannon bill in the Utah Senate. The following week in a council meeting not attended by Smoot, who was in Washington, the apostles "had quite a discussion" on the bill's defeat, spearheaded by Heber J. Grant, the bill's most ardent supporter among the Quorum of the Twelve. Grant feared that Smoot and his political operatives who were "managing the Republican party" had made "some kind of deal ... with the liquor interests." McKay sided firmly with Grant. After Smoot's political organ, the *Herald Republican,* alleged that legislators had rejected the bill because most of their Republican constituents opposed it, McKay led a delegation from Ogden to a mass meeting to counter the newspaper's claims, shame legislators who had rejected the bill, and push for a reconsideration. The following Sunday before an audience of thousands in the Ogden Tabernacle, McKay inveighed against the lawmakers and steeled his audience to hold their representatives accountable when the legislature next met in 1911. Liquor spawned "discord, misery and poverty" in the home, McKay charged. Under prohibition, illicit watering holes would doubtless spring up, he acknowledged, but alcohol would be harder to obtain, and fewer homes and young people would be victimized by it.[24]

24. Alexander, *Mormonism in Transition*, 34; "Prohibition Petitions Presented to Solons," *Salt Lake Tribune*, Feb. 4, 1909, 12; "Cannon Bill is Expected to Be Killed in Senate Today,"

The next year, 1910, McKay redoubled his energies against liquor and gambling interests, helping to organize the Betterment League of Ogden, serving as its president while also chairing the Ogden Dry Committee. When President Joseph F. Smith through his counselor Anthon Lund instructed the apostles to "say nothing of statewide prohibition" that year in order to preserve the fragile alliance between Mormon and non-Mormon Republicans, McKay and two other prohibitionists in the quorum were "chagrined," and he tried to remain true to his convictions while still honoring the prophet. The junior apostle griped to Lund that he "had waged quite a war against the saloon and was [now] nearly winning.'" Lund replied by advising him to "not let up an inch" against the saloon as long as he didn't specifically advocate for a statewide prohibition statute. On the eve of the election, after some Latter-day Saint prohibitionists claimed that they had been "muzzled" by Smoot's Republican machine, McKay advised, "If, as alleged, Utah is in the grip of the liquor interests, then in the name of all that is sacred let us fight until we unloose that grip." Soon after the 1910 election, the new state legislature passed a local-option law providing for referenda on prohibition in every city and town. McKay and his Betterment League closed ranks with Methodist minister Frederick Fisher, who became a close friend, campaigning for prohibition in Weber County. McKay met with the high councils and stake presidencies of each stake in Weber County and secured pledges of support. Speaking for nearly an hour in the general conference in April of that year, McKay implored Saints across Utah to stand "for God's word" by voting for prohibition. On the appointed day, Ogden's electorate rejected prohibition. McKay was convinced that many of the opposition votes were fraudulent and "illegal." Ostensibly burying the hatchet, he stated, "We have only kind feelings for our friends in the opposition. It is a condition we are fighting, not persons." Even so, he worked behind the scenes to unseat Ogden's wet mayor, William Glassman, in the upcoming November election. "The issue today," he believed, "is shall the people rule or Glassman and the saloons?" McKay's activism enraged Glassman, who accused him of turning the election into a religious referendum, but McKay retorted that he had only urged church members to vote their conscience. The apostle was "very disappointed" when Glassman was reelected; the outcome illustrated how limited the Latter-day Saints' political clout was in Ogden.[25]

Intermountain-Republican, Feb. 20, 1909, 1; Peterson and Cannon, *The Awkward State of Utah,* 36–37; Grant, *Diaries of Heber J. Grant,* (Feb. 20, 24, 1909); Smoot, *In the World,* 6; "Attended Mass Meeting in Salt Lake Theatre," *Ogden Daily Standard,* Feb. 25, 1909, 8; "Elder D. O. M'Kay on Prohibition," *Ogden Daily Standard,* Mar. 1, 1909, 4.

25. "Open Meeting of Betterment League," *Ogden Daily Standard,* Jan. 6, 1910, 7; "Leading Citizens See the Gambling," *Ogden Daily Standard,* Aug. 4, 1910, 6; "M'Kay Talks on Prohibition," *Ogden Evening Standard,* May 1, 1911, 5; Lund, *Danish Apostle,* 438; "Betterment League as Viewed by M'Kay," *Salt Lake Tribune,* Nov. 8, 1910, 9; "Prohibition Advocated by M'Kay," *Ogden Evening*

After the 1911 defeat, it took five years for a successful prohibition initiative to materialize in Weber County. In 1916 McKay, still serving as president of the Betterment League of Ogden, urged Latter-day Saints across the county to swamp political mass meetings and elect Prohibition delegates to the state party conventions. The Saints' turnout at these local Republican mass meetings was so heavy that *Goodwin's Weekly* dubbed them "mustang conventions . . . which were really priesthood meetings in the guise of conventions." Badly outnumbered, the local-option moderates who had dominated Utah's Republican mass meetings for years were ousted. Then, with both the Democratic and Republican Parties officially committed in their platforms to statewide prohibition, the way was finally clear for the legislature to enact a "dry-as-a-bone" prohibition statute in 1917.[26]

Three and a half years after McKay's call to the apostleship, while he was in the thick of the Prohibition campaign, he and Ray welcomed their fourth child, Royle, into their family. When Royle was two and a half years old, the energetic toddler began complaining of intense knee pain. Initially Ray suspected rheumatism, an ailment that afflicted her periodically, but the next day when Royle became feverish, his parents suspected his knee was infected. All through that Friday and Saturday morning while McKay was in the Salt Lake Tabernacle fulfilling general conference duties, Royle's fever intensified. By midday on Saturday, the fever was so high that doctors recommended surgery. The exhausted and desperate father wanted to attend to Royle, but he was scheduled to speak that afternoon, and his sense of apostolic duty prevailed. Unbeknownst to most of the congregation, he was expressing his own faith in the face of grave personal stress when he preached, "When a little suffering child burning with fever will look up to his father and in simple faith say, 'Papa, bless me,' I want to tell you that from such homes arise the strength and the glory of any nation. Such are the homes of Latter-day Saints." Racing home following the afternoon session, McKay spent a sleepless night at his son's hospital bedside. At 3:30 a.m. Royle began convulsing, and the attending doctor

Standard, Apr. 10, 1911, 6; "Call for Mass Meeting," *Ogden Daily Standard*, Apr. 8, 1911, 6; "Another Methodist Minister Writes Highly of Mormons," *Logan Republican*, Aug. 3, 1911, 1; DOMD, May 23, 27, June 27, Nov. 3, 1911; "Word of Appreciation," *Ogden Evening Standard*, June 29, 1911, 4; "Directly Charges Church Influence," *Salt Lake Tribune*, Nov. 7, 1911, 2; "Responsibility of Citizenship," *Ogden Evening Standard*, Oct. 23, 1911, 6; "No Undue Church Influence Used," *Ogden Evening Standard*, Oct. 27, 1911, 6.

26. "Statement Issued by David O. M'Kay," *Mt. Pleasant Pyramid*, Aug. 4, 1916, 4; "Straight Talk," *Goodwin's Weekly*, Nov. 11, 1916, 4; Peterson and Cannon, *Awkward State*, 46–48. After Prohibition went into effect, McKay lobbied Ogden authorities to enforce the law. In 1922 he excoriated the Ogden police force for lax enforcement. He was infuriated by a report that people could "purchase a bottle of liquor in a hotel on Twenty-Fifth Street in Ogden as easily as they could before the days of prohibition." "Apostle McKay Flays Police and City Dads in Conference Address," *Ogden Standard Examiner*, Sep. 9, 1922, 1.

rushed him into the operating room. The surgery seemed successful; Royle's fever broke and he rallied, but Sunday evening his condition worsened. A doctor administered medication without effect. Monday evening McKay joined his father and brother in anointing his son Royle's head with consecrated oil and pronouncing a priesthood blessing. The rite calmed Ray's frazzled nerves, and she drifted off to sleep. Early Tuesday morning "his little pulse weakened," McKay recorded, "and we knew that our baby would soon leave us." His last word was "Mama."[27]

Royle's death devastated the McKays and left a raw, aching absence in their home. Ray was inconsolable, and home became a prison for her; everything reminded her of the baby. McKay continued his work as best he could, including his conference travel assignments. The work was therapeutic. "I can stand it, for my life is filled with varied scenes and duties with which Baby was not associated," he told a friend, "but poor Ray is home all the time." When he returned from a stake conference assignment a couple of weeks after the funeral, he "found Ray in inconsolable grief.... She could only weep and sob for comfort.... O this yearning of the heart for our baby boy!" McKay recorded. A month later, Ray sobbed through most of the night. She had faith that she would see her baby in heaven, but the longing for him was still intense. At the time he died, Ray was in the early stages of pregnancy, and the hope of a new infant to love and caress gave her something to cling to, but a few months later she miscarried the six-month-old fetus. "A little baby would have been such a comfort ... since losing our little boy Royle. But we are again deprived of this blessing," the apostle grieved. Eventually three more children would join the family—Emma Rae in 1913, Ed in 1915, and Bob in 1920—but the aching from Royle's death never left entirely.[28]

McKay suffered physical as well as emotional challenges during his tenure as a junior member of the Quorum of the Twelve. In the summer of 1911, he broke his leg in a freak accident: as he was trying to mount his horse the saddle slipped sideways, the mare bolted, and he was thrown violently to the ground. The resultant double fracture in his right leg was agonizing and confined him to bed for nearly two weeks before the leg could be set. Five years later, in 1916, he again sustained severe injuries, this time while driving up Ogden Canyon with his brother Thomas. Due to flooding Thomas had left his car east of a bridge and walked into town the previous evening. As they approached the bridge, McKay had a distinct impression that he should not cross. It was "a warning as distinct as anything that has ever come into my life," he recalled, but "I let my judgement supersede inspiration." Unbeknownst to him, county workers had stretched a cable across the bridge to prevent motorists from passing. The cable,

27. David O. McKay, address of Apr. 6, 1912, *Conference Reports,* 53; DOMD, Apr. 4–7, 1912.

28. DOMD, Apr. 12, 28, 1912; McKay, *My Father*, 85–86.

which was barely visible in the morning fog, struck the radiator of the car, then the windshield, and then McKay's face, fracturing his jaw, knocking out several teeth, and leaving him disoriented. "Tommy drove hastily back to the house and helped Father inside. Father's face was a mass of blood and I watched in shock as he stood over the sink, spitting out pieces of bone and teeth," Lawrence recalled. "What was I doing? Where was I driving?" he kept asking. The injuries kept him from attending the April conference, and over a month passed before he felt well enough to attend any public meeting. He attributed his eventual full recovery and the absence of scarring to two healing blessings and his family's faith and fasting.[29]

By 1920, McKay's apostolic work had settled into a consistent albeit demanding routine of committee and council meetings, stake and ward visits, funerals and weddings, Sunday School work, and curricular writing. His commute from Ogden to Salt Lake, long days of work, and weekend church travels left little time for his children, although he loved them deeply, and Ray faithfully shouldered on. Passionately committed to curbing abuse and vice, he had crusaded indefatigably against alcohol, refusing to prioritize the church's political security over principle. Although he sympathized somewhat with some polygamists who had taken new wives and fathered children following the Manifesto, he had loyally held the line in investigating polygamists and differentiating between plural and celestial marriage. He had shared sacred experiences in council meetings and in private interactions with his fellow apostles. McKay was now a seasoned apostle; only the prophet, his two counselors, and three apostles, Rudger Clawson, Reed Smoot, and George Albert Smith, had served longer in the quorum than he had. He was soon to receive a historically unprecedented assignment, one that would make him, like the ancient apostle Paul, the modern church's most widely traveled apostle to that point.

---

29. "Accident to Apostle M'Kay," *Ogden Evening Standard*, July 15, 1911, 7; DOMD, July 14, 26, 1911; David O. McKay, address of Apr. 9, 1944, *Conference Reports*, 156; McKay, *My Father*, 92–94; "Modern Styles are Condemned," *Millard County Chronicle*, Apr. 13, 1916, 3; "Tabernacle Filled with Friends of Prof. Moench," *Ogden Daily Standard*, May 1, 1916, 10; Woodger, *David O. McKay*, 100–102.

5: World Tour

Shortly after the October 1920 general conference and toward the end of his second year as church president, Heber J. Grant gave McKay an extraordinary assignment: he was to tour the church's missions throughout the Indo-Pacific and possibly beyond. Grant himself had traveled to Japan, and many apostles had visited Hawai'i, but none had visited the South Pacific or the Asian mainland. McKay's world tour became one of the most formative experiences of his entire apostolic career, preparing him to one day preside over the church. No other assignment afforded such a marked concentration of impressive spiritual experiences, and none other did more to expand his worldview, understanding of cultural differences, and insight into the administrative and membership needs of a global church. Grant called Hugh J. Cannon, the fifty-year-old president of the Liberty Stake and McKay's longtime associate on the General Sunday School Board, to accompany McKay as his secretary. In the Salt Lake Temple on December 2, Grant set apart McKay for his mission. Grant blessed the apostle that "the healing power from Almighty God" would attend his administrations, that he would "understand the needs of the various missions" and that a "retentive memory" would allow him to share his insights with church authorities when he returned to Utah. Grant also instructed him to meet with, "encourage and bless" the missionaries he would encounter.[1]

McKay's assignment to travel the world meant months of hardship and worry for Ray. It was not unlike the burden borne by wives of many husbands and fathers serving as Latter-day Saint missionaries. Lawrence was away from home on a mission, but she would be solely responsible for the remaining five children, ranging in age from sixteen-year-old Llewelyn to colicky three-month-old Robert, as well as family finances and the upkeep of their home and yard. On McKay's last day at home, five-year-old Ed was afflicted with tonsillitis, and Ray, who was short on sleep, was often in tears, although she "heroically tried to subdue" her worry and exhaustion.[2]

The two travelers left home on December 4 with letters members had asked them to deliver to their missionary sons and husbands who were serving abroad

1. "M'Kay to Visit Island Mission," *Ogden Standard Examiner*, Oct. 16, 1920, 8; Lund, *Danish Apostle*, 779; DOMD, Dec. 2, 1920; Neilson, *To the Peripheries*, 11.

2. McKay, *My Father*, 111.

and "several pounds of chocolates" crammed into their baggage. On their trip west they stopped briefly to meet with missionaries and church leaders in Portland, Seattle, and Vancouver. On the short passage between Vancouver and Victoria, McKay penned a brief note to Ray. He assured her that she was "the dearest and sweetest of sweethearts.... Never were you dearer to me than you are now." He wrote that he looked forward to their reunion "as a loving family, each one healthy, virtuous, and true." Ten days after her husband's departure, Ray wrote to Lawrence, "Home is very different without you & Daddy. It seems as though our family is very small indeed. I cannot get used to it."[3]

The two travelers embarked from Vancouver on the six-thousand-ton *Empress of Japan*, a ship capable of carrying over seven hundred passengers, on December 7, 1920. McKay felt "downright gloomy" at the thought of not seeing his loved ones again for perhaps a year. A voyage punctuated with bouts of seasickness interspersed with monotonous stretches of "reading, writing, talking, walking and sleeping and counting" did nothing to lift his spirits. "The self-indulgent, so-called elite" on board who spent their time "smoking, drinking, eating and sleeping" annoyed him and he refused to join them in pastimes like playing face cards, which smacked of gambling. After over two weeks at sea, the travelers arrived in Yokohama just before Christmas. They would spend the next two weeks in Japan, traveling nearly two thousand miles and visiting missionaries and members in Kofu, Tokyo, and Osaka.[4]

The Japanese and their country immensely impressed McKay. He marveled at how efficiently the Japanese used their limited arable land. He found the "pine-covered hills and woody glens" as beautiful as any place he had visited. "Japan never disappoints," he emphasized repeatedly in his diary. Of Nikko, a mountain city famed for its waterfalls, lakes, bridges, and temples, he wrote, "I have never seen a more beautifully interesting spot." McKay surmised that religion was largely a form of "fashion" and "convenience" for most Japanese people, although he noted exceptions such as a devout Buddhist next door to the mission home who prayed day and night. From McKay's western perspective, Buddhist and Shinto shrines seemed a mix of "wealth, art, and superstition," and he thought it auspicious for the church that many of the educated class were reportedly "turning away from [the] superstition." McKay admired the Japanese people's capacity for rigorous manual labor; their resilience against the winter cold; their intelligence; and their talent for "keen" imitation, studiousness and frugality. In contrast to many Americans who greeted the New Year with raucous revelry and drinking, the Japanese exercised dignity and restraint: he praised the "total absence of noise and confusion." Instead of wild abandon,

3. McKay, *Pacific Apostle*, 1–7 (Dec. 4–7, 1920); McKay and McKay, *Heart Petals*, 82; McKay, *My Father*, 114.

4. McKay, *Pacific Apostle*, 8 (Dec. 7, 1920), 12 (Dec. 13, 1920), 19 (Dec. 23, 1920).

"houses and yards are all cleaned and decorated, and everybody prepared to pay New Years respects and give good wishes to everybody else." In every respect the Japanese were the equals of "other civilized people."[5]

The apostle was less impressed by the state of the church, its missionary program, and its congregations. Joseph Stimpson, the thirty-five-year-old mission president who had studied at Weber Stake Academy and edited the school paper during McKay's tenure there, was understandably weary and eager to return home after having served a total of nearly twelve years there as missionary and mission president. Although Stimpson possessed the requisite language skills, in McKay's estimation he lacked "leadership and vision." The missionaries were "choice, sweet-spirited young men," but they spent more time studying Japanese in their apartments than proselytizing. The entire Japanese membership tallied only 127, and barely one-third of that number attended church faithfully. Few adhered to the Word of Wisdom, and only four contributed a full tithe. Some functioned in church callings, but many more needed the challenge and opportunity to serve. Through an interpreter he called one of the members, Brother Takahashi, as the Sunday School superintendent. McKay believed more Japanese people might become interested in the church if the missionaries emphasized gospel principles related to community, industry, provident living, and family, including ancestors—in short, "the view of what [the church] will do for Japan."[6]

After two stimulating weeks in Japan, McKay and Cannon arrived in Pusan, Korea, on January 6, en route to China. To their knowledge, no Latter-day Saints lived there, so they passed quickly through the country. Korea was ruled by Japan; impressed by the modern railroad built by the Japanese that conveyed them across the country, McKay believed that the Japanese occupation was "fortunate" for Korea. He was unimpressed by his glimpses from the train windows of the "desolate-looking" countryside gripped in the chill of winter, the "barren, craggy hills," and the grinding poverty. Unless the Koreans were more religiously minded than he suspected they were, the prospects for missionary work seemed minimal.[7]

Crossing the Yalu River into Manchuria, the two travelers passed children sledding and woodcutters pulling heavily laden carts. McKay anticipated that the Japanese, who had acquired control of the railway on which they traveled and a strip of land on either side following the Russo-Japanese War in 1905, would eventually control all of Manchuria "because of their superior

5. McKay, *Pacific Apostle*, 20 (Dec. 23, 1920), 25 (Dec. 27, 1920), 26 (Dec. 28, 1920); 30 (Jan. 1, 1921), 34 (Jan. 3, 1921), 35 (Jan. 4, 1921), 36–40 (Jan. 5, 1921).

6. McKay, *Pacific Apostle*, 31–34 (Jan. 2–3, 1921); "Joseph Henry Stimpson," in *Latter-day Saint Biographical Encyclopedia*, 4:71–72.

7. McKay, *Pacific Apostle*, 41–43 (Jan. 6, 1921).

intelligence and energy." As they traveled south on the train toward Beijing, the two emissaries visited the eastern terminus of the Great Wall at Shanhaiguan, where beggars in rags swarmed them. McKay was more "chilled" by the shocking evidence of their "abject poverty" than by the frigid weather. As they stepped from the train station in Beijing into the packed street, the cacophony of "horns blowing, gongs ringing, and human voices yelling" overwhelmed their senses. Traveling a circuitous route by rickshaw, they eventually arrived at the Grand Hôtel de Pékin with its elegantly appointed rooms.[8]

President Grant had asked McKay to visit China, even though there were no Latter-day Saint congregations there, to set the stage for missionary work. To that end, McKay and Cannon entered the Forbidden City on Sunday morning, walking along a moat until they came to a grove of trees, where they felt strong spiritual impressions. Cannon offered a prayer, and McKay dedicated China for the preaching of the gospel, praying on behalf of the Chinese people for peace, stability, educational opportunities, and relief from famine. He pled that missionaries who would labor there would receive "keen insight into the mental and spiritual state of the Chinese mind" and thereby be able to "make the proper appeal to them." Recalling the experience for a general conference audience the following year, he stated, "God was with us when we stood beneath that tree in old China and turned the key for the preaching of the gospel in the Chinese realm.... No disputant can convince us that our souls were not filled to overflowing with the Spirit of God on that occasion." On Monday McKay and Cannon visited the United States embassy, where they consulted with the American minister to China, Charles R. Crane, about the prospects of stationing missionaries there. Crane said he "approved" of the idea and suggested that the Latter-day Saints could make "a distinct contribution" to China by sharing their knowledge and expertise regarding irrigation.[9]

As the travelers walked along a well-preserved portion of the Great Wall and toured the Winter Palace, they were struck by the contrast between these "stupendous" architectural achievements and the corruption, factionalism, inefficiency, and disorder they perceived in modern China. Quoting an aphorism rooted in scripture, McKay marveled, "How the mighty have fallen." On the train to Shanghai, he appreciated the decorum and courtesy of a Chinese passenger. McKay offered some peanuts to him, and the man reciprocated by ordering tea for McKay. A few days later McKay recorded his overarching impressions of China, which were negative: despite the evidence of a rich, classical past, China seemed "a broken, senile nation ... abounding in poverty," he judged, where "loathsome" beggars mutilated their bodies "to prey more successfully on the

8. McKay, *Pacific Apostle*, 43–47 (Jan. 7–8, 1921).

9. McKay, *Pacific Apostle*, 47–50, (Jan. 9–10, 1921); Neilson, *To the Peripheries*, 29–30; David O. McKay, address of Apr. 7, 1922, *Conference Reports*, 65.

sympathies of the public." The "usual missionary propaganda" would not be effective in preaching Christianity in China, and their "superstitions regarding evil spirits" would need to be overcome.[10]

After stopping briefly in the relatively "modern" city of Shanghai, McKay and Cannon returned to Japan, planning to board a ship bound for Hawai'i. In the handful of days before their departure, McKay hoped to revitalize missionary work in Japan by training the incoming mission president, Lloyd Ivie, who was slated to arrive any day. He was chagrined to learn that Ivie's ship would not arrive until after his departure. His disappointment turned to delight when he learned at the last minute that his own boat's departure had been delayed by two days. "Not in all my experience have I had anything impress me so deeply and convincingly of the immediate intervention of Providence!" he exulted. When the boat from America finally docked, McKay looked for Ivie and was "greatly astonished" and somewhat crestfallen when he learned that he was not aboard. In fact, unbeknownst to McKay, Ivie and his new bride had left Utah only five days earlier. McKay resourcefully recalibrated in the face of this negation of his previous spiritual euphoria. Although he and Cannon had "interpreted our delay only in the light that we were to meet with the new president," he now turned his attention to using his time to devise contingency plans for the mission, just in case Ivie did not arrive before President Stimpson's scheduled departure in three weeks.[11]

Having devised a feasible contingency plan with the mission president, McKay boarded *The Russia* on January 26, bound for Honolulu. Over the next week at sea McKay took the opportunity to learn more about Asia. He closely read *The Sayings of Confucius*, which confirmed for him that "truly great men, and highly civilized peoples lived in China centuries before the Christian era," and read I. William Adams's historical novel set in feudal Japan, *Shibusawa; Or, The Passing of Old Japan*.[12]

When they arrived in Honolulu on Friday, February 4, McKay and Cannon were greeted by Elizabeth Lealoha Kamohalii, a Relief Society leader who had joined the church five years earlier, and Mission President E. Wesley Smith, the Hawai'ian-born son of Joseph F. and Julina Smith. Unlike Japan, where the church had barely established a toehold, the church was well established in Hawai'i, with eleven thousand members. On the north shore of O'ahu, the church operated a recently dedicated temple, a sugarcane and pineapple plantation, and a school with 127 pupils. Church membership was diverse and

10. McKay, *Pacific Apostle*, 50 (Jan. 10–11, 1921), 56–58 (Jan. 16, 1921); "Chinese Floods and Famine Bring Appeal That Rotary Club Help Tree Planting," *Ogden Standard Examiner*, Feb. 20, 1921, 18.

11. McKay, *Pacific Apostle*, 54 (Jan. 15, 1921), 65 (Jan. 24, 1921), 67 (Jan. 25, 1921); "Lloyd Oscar Ivie," Church History Biographical Database, history.churchofjesuschrist.org.

12. McKay, *Pacific Apostle*, 68–71 (Jan. 26–Feb. 1, 1921).

experienced, including prosperous merchants and émigrés from Utah. Over the next 20 days, McKay and Cannon visited four islands (O'ahu, Maui, Hawai'i, and Kaua'i), participated in thirty-four meetings and socials, and listened to every missionary. The visitors were fêted with luaus. They swam in the ocean, rode horseback over the church's plantation, swatted mosquitoes, and hiked the 'Īao Needle, a twelve-hundred-foot-high inactive volcano. McKay marveled at "the dark, lava-colored sides of the precipitous cliff... covered with green grass and heavier foliage." Notwithstanding the abundant mosquitoes, McKay reveled in the natural beauty of the islands. On the Big Island of Hawai'i, McKay and Cannon visited Kīlauea. Standing near the crater's rim in the middle of the night, McKay thought the churning lava sounded like "a blacksmith's bellows raised to the nth power." The view from the brink of the crater was unforgettable: "rivers of molten lava flowing in a sea of fire and brimstone, bubbling and spurting from 10,000 cauldrons!" A young missionary, Virginia Budd, later recalled that McKay joined three elders on a lava ledge just inside the crater. The four had been there just a short time when McKay said he felt they needed to "get out of here." Shortly after they made their way back to the rim, "the whole balcony crumbled and fell with a roar into the seething lava below." Budd later judged, "We had witnessed inspiration if not revelation."[13]

McKay was struck by the refinement, industry, and education of many Hawai'ian church members. Anthropologist Louis Sullivan of the Bishop Museum in Honolulu seemed to encourage his theory that Polynesians were related to American Indians and therefore descended from Book of Mormon peoples. From Sullivan, McKay also learned that Japanese immigrants and their descendants comprised over 40 percent of the islands' population, and more were arriving every year. Based upon his observations and interviews, he identified the church's needs in the islands: Japanese-speaking missionaries, a high school where members could obtain better education, and more mature and experienced missionaries, including couples, to provide support for each branch.[14]

On Maui, McKay and Cannon, accompanied by President Smith and two elders, Samuel Hurst and David Keola Kailimai, visited a small church at Pulehu, a village where Cannon's father, George Q. Cannon, had labored. The group gathered under a pepper tree, and McKay offered a prayer of gratitude for the missionary labors of Joseph F. Smith and George Q. Cannon. At the close of the prayer, Elder Kailimai stated in Hawai'ian that he had seen "a hand and arm extended to [Hurst] in the attitude of shaking hands." When McKay heard

13. McKay, *Pacific Apostle*, 74–75 (Feb. 4, 1921), 100–2 (Feb. 23, 1921), 90 (Feb. 12, 1921), 78, 96 (Feb. 20, 1921), (Feb. 7, 1921), 84 (Feb. 9, 1921), 88–89 (Feb. 10, 1921); "[Auto]biography of Edith Virginia Farnes part 2," Entry for Edith Virginia Budd [Jacobsen Farnes], KWCJ-PGT, Family Search, familysearch.org.

14. McKay, *Pacific Apostle*, 97–98 (Feb. 21, 1921), 100–2 (Feb. 23, 1921).

the English translation of the report, he stated that he did not know the precise spiritual meaning of Kailimai's vision but explained that "the veil between us and the other world was very thin." Cannon then stated suggestively, "There was no veil at all," only hinting that he had seen more. That evening in a church meeting in Wailuku, McKay referred to the earlier manifestations and, turning to Cannon, testified, "My Brother, you have been closer to your father today than you have ever been before."[15]

Following their tour of Hawai'i, the two travelers planned to steam directly to Tahiti, but when they learned that no departures from Honolulu were imminent, they decided to return to California instead and book passage on the first steamer bound from San Francisco for Tahiti. When Ray heard the news, she mused, "Wouldn't it be great if he could drop in and say Halloo! Before starting out again? But of course he could not, using Church money.... Oh, it makes me feel so lonesome to think of his being 'so near and yet so far.'" The burden of David's absence was even greater than she had anticipated due to some unforeseen financial problems. A substantial bill had come due, and the McKays' bank had failed. She had only managed to pay the debt through the generosity of a member of her stake presidency, who had dropped by and asked if she needed anything.[16]

On March 1, the two world travelers floated into San Francisco Bay. McKay felt gloomy at the sight of the American mainland, knowing he was only a day's journey by train from Utah, but he felt duty bound to proceed as soon as possible to Tahiti. Unbeknownst to him, President Grant had invited Ray and Hugh's wife, Sarah, to accompany him and President Anthony Ivins to California for a surprise reunion. Unfortunately, McKay and Cannon disembarked before Grant's party arrived at the dock, and the two travelers went directly to the British consulate to obtain a New Zealand travel visa. Because their passports indicated they were missionaries, the consular staff informed the men that they must first obtain a missionary permit, which could only be issued in New York or Washington, DC. McKay and Cannon were leaving the consulate downcast when some missionaries Grant had dispatched found them and shared the news that their wives were in town. No news could have given him "more true joy," McKay wrote, than knowing he would soon be holding Ray and their six-month-old baby, Robert, in his arms. After spending the rest of the day with their wives, McKay and Cannon met the following day with Grant and Ivins, recounting their experiences, sharing their findings, and discussing how to proceed. McKay and Cannon had already scheduled conferences with

15. McKay, *Pacific Apostle*, 82–83 (Feb. 8, 1921); Nielson, *To the Peripheries*, 44; Anderson, "Prayer under a Pepper Tree," 57–59.

16. McKay, *My Father*, 123; Emma Ray Ashton, "Emma Riggs McKay," *Relief Society Magazine*, June 1967, 488–89.

the Saints across the South Pacific over the coming months, but the only way they could visit New Zealand would be to wait for a missionary permit and visa. An emergency telegram from Salt Lake informing the prophet that his counselor Anthon Lund had just passed away made up their minds for them. For over a week Lund had been confined to his bed, resting and recuperating from complications caused by an ulcer, but no one had expected him to die. Now they decided to all return to Salt Lake for the funeral, write to Washington for the requisite missionary permit, and then leave for Tahiti on a ship scheduled to depart in about a month.[17]

If McKay hoped to spend much time at home following his return, he was sorely disappointed. He estimated he spent 90 percent of his waking hours away from home in meetings. "Since coming home, he has had to go to Salt Lake every day," Ray lamented. Even when he was home, the house was generally full of visitors. McKay regretted being unable to spend more time alone with Ray and the children, but he felt his presence had still been therapeutic, as he and Ray were able to resolve their "perplexing financial difficulties." Complications from David's recent typhoid inoculation deprived him and Ray of a blissful final evening. Instead, McKay suffered a miserable night beset with fever, chills, and aching joints. The next day after he left, Ray wrote, "It broke my heart to see him go away again."[18]

McKay arrived on Sunday in San Francisco feeling considerably better, only to learn that their boat's departure for Tahiti had been delayed by a day. In a rash decision that nearly proved fatal to their world tour itinerary, he opted to make a whirlwind trip south to Santa Monica to confer in person with Grant, who was resting there prior to the upcoming general conference. The trip down to Los Angeles was uneventful, and the visit with Grant was productive, but when McKay attempted to buy a return ticket to San Francisco following his visit, he learned he could only travel as far as Bakersfield; no seats were available on the train from Bakersfield to San Francisco. Having no other option, he bought a ticket to Bakersfield, hoping he would not be thrown off. Before the train left, Mission President Joseph McMurrin explained to the conductor the importance for the entire church of McKay's world tour and persuaded him to allow McKay to remain aboard beyond Bakersfield. The train arrived late in San Francisco, with only an hour to spare before the ship's scheduled departure. The British consulate had refused to release McKay's visa to Cannon, so McKay raced against time to the consulate, snatched his visa in a frenzy, sped to the docks, and boarded the *Marama* just

---

17. McKay, *My Father*, 123–24; DOMD, Mar. 1–2, 1921; Nielson, *To the Peripheries*, 56; Lund, *Danish Apostle*, 791.

18. DOMD, Mar. 26, 1921; McKay, *My Father*, 124.

in time. The feat was a godsend in the face of McKay's impetuous decision to visit southern California.[19]

En route to Tahiti, McKay continued his tradition of educational reading about countries on his itinerary by reading *Tahiti Days* by Scottish travel writer Hector MacQuarrie and *History of New Zealand* by Alfred Saunders. He also enjoyed conversing with his fellow passengers, who struck him as likable, unpretentious folk. They held talent shows and a costume ball but maintained appropriate decorum on Sundays. One Mr. Beard, however, struck him as "the most painful example of a man afflicted with exaggerated Ego that I have ever seen—a pretender of the first degree."[20]

The *Marama* made good time between California and Polynesia. After passing Tikehau and Mataiva, atolls with coconut palms sprouting from coral rock a couple hundred miles northeast of Tahiti, they arrived on April 9 in Papeete, "a quiet and unruffled tropical town" of six or seven thousand residents on Tahiti's north shore. McKay was incredulous when he learned that Mission President Leonidas Kennard had made no preparation for his arrival or for meetings with the members in the islands. This was because Kennard had been absent from headquarters and out of communication for about three months visiting scattered branches. These extended absences were unavoidable, the missionaries explained, because trading schooners traveling between Tahiti and the other islands did not operate on a consistent timetable; the only means of relaying messages between Tahiti and the outer islands was by boat. There were nearly sixteen hundred church members scattered across French Polynesia, but only a few dozen lived in Papeete. The largest branches were on Tubuai, an island 370 miles to the south, and in the Tuamotu Archipelago, several hundred miles to the east. Naturally, the mission president spent much of his time on those islands. The four elders at mission headquarters, two of whom were themselves waiting for a boat to take them to new assignments, inquired for McKay about the possibility of traveling to the Tuamotus to meet with members there. A boat would soon depart for the islands, but if McKay took it, it would be a month or more before he could return to Tahiti. Alternately, the church could charter a schooner, but that might cost as much as $1,500, an unwarranted expense, McKay believed. At length the two travelers decided to separate temporarily. Cannon would remain for three weeks in Tahiti to conduct their planned business with the mission president, if he managed to return, and then depart for New Zealand. There he would rejoin McKay, who would continue westward

19. DOMD, Mar. 28–29, 1921; Nielson, *To the Peripheries*, 57. McKay apparently made the trip to seek Grant's advice, but he could have accomplished the same task by telegram. He wanted to fulfill the prophet's directions to visit all of the missions abroad, but he feared that it might be infeasible to travel thousands of miles around the African continent just to visit South Africa. Grant advised McKay to do as he saw fit.

20. DOMD, Mar. 29, Apr. 2, 1921; Nielson, *To the Peripheries,* 58.

on the ship that brought them to Tahiti so as not to disrupt their arrangements for conferences elsewhere.[21]

Eager to experience at least a bit of Tahiti during his brief visit, McKay toured the legendary Sunday market at daybreak and observed barefooted men and women bargaining over chickens, ducks, tropical fruits, and brightly colored fish for the traditional Sunday meal. Later that day the visitors attended Sunday school with eight Tahitian adults and two children. Thirty attended the afternoon sacrament meeting. The missionaries apologized for the small congregation, reminding McKay that most church members lived in the Tuamotu islands, but the apostle sensed that much more could and should be done to proselytize on the main island of Tahiti, with its far greater population. His diagnosis: "missionary work in Papeete seems to be in an expiring condition.... Remedies must be sought and applied as soon as possible." Following the meeting, as Cannon was removing his trunk from the ship, McKay heard, "apparently in an accidental way," that the ship Cannon planned to take to New Zealand in three weeks "would not sail as previously scheduled." The timely discovery enabled the duo to change plans and continue on together, leaving a message for Kennard to meet with them in a few months in New Zealand. Looking back on the timing, McKay credited divine intervention: "We knew [God's] guiding hand and acknowledged His overruling providence, when replacing our judgement by His inspiration He moved us to do something which our own judgment had told us not to do."[22]

On the way to New Zealand the travelers stopped at Rarotonga in the Cook Islands, where their ship anchored long enough for them to take an "interesting and instructive" excursion around the island. Mission President George Taylor met the travelers in Wellington on April 21. With a recorded membership of nearly 6,000, most of them Māori, the church had a larger base in New Zealand than anywhere else in the South Pacific. After retrieving their luggage, McKay and Cannon stopped at the office of Māui Pōmare, a member of Parliament, minister for the Māori people, and friend of the Latter-day Saints. In a speech before Parliament, the minister had praised the Saints for their sobriety and industriousness. McKay was thrilled when Pōmare remarked that he "wish[ed] all the New Zealand Maoris were Mormons; if they were, they would be good citizens." Pōmare praised the educational work being accomplished at the Māori Agricultural College, a vocational school for boys operated by the church. Mission leaders were thinking about establishing an agricultural colony to improve members' financial security, and Pōmare pledged to help them navigate the

21. McKay, *Pacific Apostle*, 103–5 (Apr. 9, 1921), 106–7 (Apr. 10, 1921); Nielson, *To the Peripheries*, 59–61; R. Lanier Britsch, *Unto the Islands*, 51.

22. McKay, *Pacific Apostle*, 105–7 (Apr. 10, 1921); Nielson, *To the Peripheries*, 61; David O. McKay, address of Apr. 7, 1922, *Conference Reports*, 66.

legal requirements. Next the leaders met with James Hislop, the undersecretary for internal affairs, hoping to increase the quota of American missionaries, but he was unable to help.[23]

President Taylor had scheduled a "Hui Tau," or mission conference and cultural celebration, in Huntly, a small community three hundred miles from Wellington. As the visitors approached the meeting ground, they saw large circus tents that had been pitched for the occasion. A chorus of women greeted them by chanting "Haere mai, Haere mai" ("welcome"), and then a group of men performed a traditional haka war dance. After local dignitaries formally greeted the visitors, the crowd of members stepped forward to shake hands and rub noses with them. Over the next two days, McKay presided and spoke through his Māori interpreter, Stuart Meha, a faithful and widely traveled church member, in multiple sessions of the conference, and feasted at lavish communal dinners. McKay noted only that "as a number of the hundreds in attendance understand English very well, we speak continuously until the address is finished, then Bro. Meha repeats. The efficiency and fluency with which he does this is simply marvelous." From Meha's perspective, though, a different dynamic was at work, one that confirmed his testimony of the church and his faith that McKay spoke with divine power. "What I saw convinced me that the people knew and understood clearly what was being said by an apostle of the Lord" before they heard the translation, Meha recorded. He saw "heads bowed and tears running down the faces" of elderly people who "did not know English, but here, on this occasion, they knew—for a servant of God had blessed them that they might have the ... interpretation of tongues."[24]

Through much of the conference, McKay was fighting a cold, a toothache, and an upset stomach. By Sunday afternoon his voice was hoarse, and just as the meeting started, he excused himself and vomited. "After the vomiting spell, I rested a moment or two, prayed for strength to do my duty, and returned just as the last of a long list of local names were being read and voted upon," he wrote. Five minutes into McKay's sermon, a member of the Reorganized Church of Jesus Christ of Latter Day Saints interrupted him, calling out that "Joseph Smith didn't receive the revelation on polygamy." McKay's own father-in-law had become a Reorganite, so the interchurch competition hit close to home. A melee might have broken out had not McKay motioned for silence and quipped, "What is that saying that when the Sons of God met together, the devil came also?" The congregation's laughter defused the tense situation, and the rush of adrenaline that washed over the apostle seemed to improve his raspy voice. As McKay continued to speak, a strapping Māori, James Rongotoa

23. McKay, *Pacific Apostle*, 109–10 (Apr. 13, 1921), 113–17 (Apr. 21, 1921); Britsch, *Unto the Islands*, 291–93; James N. Lambert, address of Oct. 10, 1920, *Conference Reports*, 160.

24. McKay, *Pacific Apostle*, 119–23 (Apr. 22–23, 1921); Selwyn Kātene, *Turning the Hearts*, 145.

Elkington, hefted the detractor, carried him from the tent, and dropped him over a fence at the edge of the meeting ground. McKay later thanked Elkington for his resourcefulness and likened the Reorganite missionaries to "a boil on the Church body— the more one irritates it the sorer it gets." Following the Hui Tau, he traveled north to Auckland to inspect the mission headquarters and chapel and engaged a dentist to pull the decaying tooth that had caused his head to throb for weeks.[25]

McKay's next scheduled meetings with members were in Tonga, but the travelers' course led them through Fiji. McKay and Cannon shared a sleeping compartment on the boat with two Catholic priests, whom they initially mistook for Protestant ministers. Expecting unpleasantries, McKay mischievously broke the news of his religion to the roommates, announcing, "This must be a specially favored room to be reserved for two ministers and two Mormons." The two priests seemed not to know how to respond, and no one said anything for the next half hour as Cannon and McKay struggled to maintain straight faces and repress the inclination to snicker at their fellow passengers' supposed discomfort. Lamentably, they missed an opportunity to counter prejudices and learned little of each other over the next five days. During the voyage, McKay wrote some articles narrating his trip for church magazines. When the boat stopped for a day and a half in Suva, he and Cannon visited a botanical garden and sampled kava, a traditional drink made from the root of *Piper methysticum*. The depressant tasted "woody" and bitter to him. While the town was "picturesque," McKay distrusted the dark-skinned Melanesians—a prejudice he would transcend decades later when he championed missionary work and chapel construction in Fiji and authorized the ordination of Melanesian converts to the priesthood. That was all in the future, though. In 1921 he wrote, "They are repulsive to me as the Polynesians are attractive!" Although he enjoyed their harmonious singing, he was "sure their grandfathers were cannibals." He "left with the distinct impression that there are other people better prepared for the preaching of the Gospel than the Fijians are."[26]

From Suva the travelers proceeded to Tonga. As the ship approached the low-lying coral island of Tongatapu, the endlessly varied, exquisite deep-blue, emerald, and purple hues of the ocean enthralled McKay. "There may be more beautiful ocean settings, but thus far, I have not seen them," he judged. Because the ship had come from Fiji, where a measles epidemic was raging, no one was permitted to land without quarantining for two weeks. The Tongan government was sensitive to the hazards posed by ships carrying infectious diseases;

25. McKay, *Pacific Apostle*, 117–21 (Apr. 22, 1921), 121–24 (Apr. 23–24, 1921), 127 (Apr. 29, 1921); McKay, *My Father*, 129; entry for James Rongotoa Elkington, LTHW-8LS, Family Search, familysearch.org.

26. McKay, *Pacific Apostle*, 128–32 (May 1–7, 1921); Britsch, *Unto the Islands*, 502, 505–6.

a vessel from New Zealand carrying passengers infected with the Spanish flu had brought that deadly illness to Tonga in 1918, killing 8 percent of Tonga's population. In a rare outburst of doubt, McKay mused, "Surely it seems that luck and Providence have forgotten us this time!" McKay had planned to spend only a day on the island, and a lengthy quarantine seemed a high price to pay for visiting a small branch. Wanting to keep busy, McKay decided to continue to Samoa instead and possibly return later. Mission President Mark Vernon Coombs, an enthusiastic, impetuous thirty-year-old, sent two letters to the ship, trying to persuade McKay to submit to the quarantine and visit the Tongans first. He pointed out that even if McKay went first to Samoa, he would still have to isolate himself in quarantine when he returned. Unimpressed by the young president's unsolicited advice, McKay rejected it. He did assent to Coombs's request to accompany him to Samoa.[27]

The boat stopped for several hours at Utu Vava'u, the second-largest island in Tonga. The ocean had eroded sections of the island, creating numerous bays and inlets and a deep natural harbor. On the wharf stood a crowd of islanders who watched the ship approach. McKay marveled when he saw a man nonchalantly disrobe, jump into the water, swim to a nearby boat, row it to shore, and then matter-of-factly take up his cloth pareu and wrap it around his waist. Among the crowd on shore were two elders laboring on the island, Stirling May and Reuben Wiberg. When Coombs called out to them that an apostle was aboard, they ran and assembled the Latter-day Saint youth who had formed a brass band under May's direction. While standing on the dock, the band played several numbers for the passengers. McKay was impressed by May's achievement, especially since the elder was largely self-taught, and praised his "energy and pluck," including his desire to extend his four-year mission to six in order to translate the Book of Mormon into Tongan. President Coombs had managed to sell McKay on Tonga. McKay had known almost nothing of this "small mission" with its approximately eight hundred members, but from what Coombs had told him, he now concluded it was "one of the most promising missions of the Church."[28]

An enchanting aura enveloped the travelers as they approached the verdant, mountainous backdrop of Apia on German Samoa. Unable to go ashore until morning, the passengers spent one more night on the boat, where they basked in a breathtaking sunset. "The reflection of the afterglow of sunset upon the peaceful surface of the sea this evening was most splendid," McKay rhapsodized. "The sky was tinged with pink, and the clouds lingering around the horizon were fringed with various hues of crimson and purple, while the heavier cloud farther to the west was sombre purple and black." The artist's palette of colors reflected

27. McKay, *Pacific Apostle*, 133–35 (May 8–9, 1921).

28. McKay, *Pacific Apostle*, 136–39 (May 10, 1921).

in the "clear blue of the [calm] ocean" had a soothing effect. As the shadows lengthened and the colors faded, a pale crescent moon cast its reflection on the sea. After he fell asleep, McKay dreamed "a beautiful vision ... suggested no doubt by the scene" at sunset and dusk, he later wrote. Rather than recording the details of his dream at the time, he scribbled cryptic references to it in the margins of his typed diary the next day. His notes read, "City—multitude led by Savior" and "these are they who have renounced the world—who have truly been born again." The sacred experience, a vision of the Heavenly City and a witness of the Redeemer of whom he testified as an apostle, was one of the most deeply personal manifestations of divine approbation that McKay ever shared. Several weeks later in a meeting in New Zealand the apostle divulged the experience publicly, perhaps for the first time.[29]

The next morning twenty-two men rowed McKay ashore in a longboat festooned with tropical flowers and greenery. A large crowd greeted McKay and Cannon on the wharf, including a brass band from the church school in Sauniatu playing "God Save the King" and "The Star-Spangled Banner," the national anthems of German Samoa, which was ruled by New Zealand following World War I, and American Samoa. After receiving formal greetings from twenty-five Samoan chiefs, McKay and Cannon shook hands with hundreds of people. Seated in an automobile, they paraded much like colonial administrators down the main thoroughfare lined by curious citizens who had heard that an apostle had arrived. Eventually they reached the mission home, a "dilapidated" structure in the village of Pesega. Nothing they had experienced in Polynesia to this point, even the Hui Tau in New Zealand, rivaled the grand reception in Samoa. An estimated fifteen hundred well-wishers, including King

29. McKay, *Pacific Apostle*, 141 (May 11, 1921). A fuller account appeared in a selection of McKay's experiences collected by Clare Middlemiss. Middlemiss reported that the account was written on May 10, and indeed his description of the sunset in Apia harbor appears in his diary. But the following morning, May 11, he made only the brief notations above. Middlemiss removed the assertion that the account was "taken from President McKay's World Tour Diary" before her book was revised and reissued. "I then fell asleep," the account published by Middlemiss reads, "and beheld in vision something infinitely sublime. In the distance I beheld a beautiful white city. Though it was far away, yet I seemed to realize that trees with luscious fruit, shrubbery with gorgeously tinted leaves and flowers in perfect bloom abounded everywhere. The clear sky above seemed to reflect these beautiful shades of color. I think saw a great concourse of people approaching the city. Each one wore a white, flowing robe and a white headdress. Instantly my attention seemed centered upon their leader, and though I could see only the profile of his features and his body, I recognized him at once as my Savior! The tint and radiance of his countenance were glorious to behold. There was a peace about him which seemed sublime—it was divine! The city, I understood, was his. It was the City Eternal; and the people following him were to abide there in peace and eternal happiness. But who were they? As if the Savior read my thoughts, he answered by pointing to a semicircle that then appeared above them, and on which were written in gold the words: *These Are They Who Have Overcome the World—Who Have Truly Been Born Again!*"

See Middlemiss, *Cherished Experiences* (1955), 101–2, and Middlemiss, *Cherished Experiences* (1976), 59–60.

Malietoa Tanumafili and numerous high chiefs, provided a royal welcome. In a special chief's house erected for the occasion, McKay was offered the first bowl of kava as a sign of respect. The guests along with several hundred islanders then feasted on pork, beef, chicken, fish, taro, fa'ausi, and coconut under a huge bowery. Next, delegations from each village presented gifts. "We were literally buried in Samoan presents, many of them rare and costly," he wrote. The festivities continued into the evening, with songs and dances performed by pupils from church schools.[30]

Over the next three days McKay presided and spoke in conference sessions attended by hundreds of members. Taking 1 John 4:4–8 as his text, he enjoined love and inveighed against malice. McKay listened as well as taught, demonstrating an interest in local leaders' perspectives. In a meeting with Samoan chiefs, including Pola, David Creighton, Tapusoa, Kippen Su'a, and Sa'egahe, he asked how the church might better serve them; they recommended additional and improved schools including a high school, seasoned missionaries familiar with Samoan culture, larger meetinghouses, and a plot of land near the pier where members from outlying islands could camp while selling their crafts and farm products. McKay sympathized with the chiefs' desire for seasoned workers but defended the young missionaries; "though frequently inexperienced," they had "the love of the work at heart," he said.[31]

From Western Samoa the church leaders traveled eastward by chartered boat to Tutuila, the main island of American Samoa. Wedged into a forty-two-square-foot platform atop the boat's engine, the passengers suffered intense discomfort and nausea as waves pitched the small craft. When the breathtaking coast of Tutuila with its lush mountain peaks came into view, few had the energy to appreciate it. After regaining their composure ashore, they covered eleven miles by truck, horse, and foot through driving rain before arriving waterlogged at Mapusaga, a village of ninety-seven inhabitants where a missionary house, school, and sizable plantation were located. Mission leaders had dedicated the plantation as a gathering place for members nearly two decades earlier. The school band stood in the driving rain, serenading the visitors as they arrived. The following day, the Sabbath, was filled with meetings, including an afternoon conference attended by 230 people from around the island. On Monday, McKay visited the school, listened to reports from the missionaries, and studied a petition from twenty-five high chiefs on the island pleading for trained male and female teachers for the school. "Scarcely one" of the missionaries had any pedagogical training, and although they were working hard to teach school, their inexperience handicapped them. Sensitive to the feelings

30. McKay, *Pacific Apostle*, 141–59 (May 11, 1921).

31. McKay, *Pacific Apostle*, 151–52 (May 12, 1921); Conference program notes included in DOMD, May 12, 1921.

of animals, McKay was troubled by the mistreatment of the plantation's work horses. The inhumane treatment of animals rankled him deeply throughout his life; he chastised the mission president and missionaries, telling them that he "didn't believe in preaching the gospel of love from the pulpit, and then persecuting and punishing God's creatures in life."[32]

Back in Western Samoa by the following weekend, McKay and Cannon visited Sauniatu, the site of a church plantation, major school, and gathering place on the island of Upolu. Residents lined the road leading into town, waving palm branches, the men on one side and the women attired in white dresses on the other. Their demonstration of reverent respect brought tears to McKay's eyes. On Sunday, McKay presided over and spoke in multiple conference sessions, including an afternoon meeting where taro, a starchy tuber, served as sacrament bread. That evening McKay and the missionaries dined with eighty-four-year-old Sai Masina, the village headman, and his extended family in their traditional home, an open-sided bowery with a thatched roof and pebble floor. McKay was impressed by the cleanliness of the Masinas' dwelling, the well-disciplined and talented children who sang for them, the excellence of the food, and the spirit that prevailed. He preferred this meal, which felt more authentic, "in a Samoan hut, prepared and served by Samoans, and eaten in Samoan fashion" to the much grander banquets that had been held in his honor. The following evening McKay held "a very profitable and impressive meeting" with the missionaries and their leaders. McKay commented, "If the elders could but retain the spirit with which they were blessed on this occasion, they could never cast the least reflection upon the Church of Christ." One of the missionaries, Lewis Parkin, fondly remembered that meeting and the holiness he felt in McKay's presence: "of all the influences and places I have ever been in, I never felt as we did in this meeting. Tears were shed by everyone present. When it was my turn to speak I sobbed so I could hardly speak, and I wasn't the only one either . . . all the elders and even Apostle David O. McKay. The meeting lasted for six hours, and it was the shortest six hours I ever spent."[33]

Sauniatu was not without its problems. McKay was disappointed with the church plantation when he inspected it. The boggy, low-lying tract was poorly suited to cattle ranching and coconut farming, and the residents were discouraged by the results. The cattle were scrawny and unhealthy, and many of the coconut palms were struggling and unfruitful. Twice in the previous year the headmen had recommended that the plantation be closed and a better one established elsewhere. Some of the members who worked on the farm resented

32. McKay, *Pacific Apostle*, 160–68 (May 20–25, 1921); Nielson, *To the Peripheries*, 91–92.

33. McKay, *Pacific Apostle*, 171–75 (May 28–30, 1921); Beatty, "The Devil in Our Pews," 81–83; Nielson, *To the Peripheries*, 97–98; Lewis Betts Parkin, diary, quoted in "Lewis Betts Parkin's Mission to Tonga," entry for Lewis Betts Parkin, KWCH-X53, Family Search, familysearch.org.

their Anglo missionary supervisors, who sometimes treated them imperiously. Yet the backdrop of volcanic peaks blanketed with thick, green vegetation rising abruptly from the village was enchanting, and the members treated McKay with such touching reverence and awe that his prevailing impressions were positive. Shortly before McKay departed on Tuesday morning, parents crowded around him begging him to bless their children; others reverently knelt and kissed his hands. Through tears, Brother Masina declared that a lifetime of prayers had been answered. "I have seen an apostle of the Lord," he rejoiced, "and now I am ready to go." McKay and Cannon mounted their horses and were escorted to the edge of town by the school band and the residents. Were it not for the rain that began, the crowd might have followed them for some time. About a quarter mile down the road, McKay turned to mission president John Adams and said he felt they should "return and leave our blessing." "I think that's inspiration," seconded Adams. For the rest of his life, McKay cherished memories of the next hour. "As we approached the sobbing crowd, I could not help but thrill with the picturesqueness of the scene!" he recalled. "The green avenue—lined with stately trees whose intertwining branches formed a vista ending only at the village, the white dresses of the women and the red turban of the band boys' uniforms stood out in beautiful contrast to the various shades of green surrounding them." McKay imparted an apostolic blessing, pronouncing the place "one of [God's] first temples," and asked for heavenly protection from evil, kind and wise leadership, health, material prosperity, and economic success for the plantation. Rarely had he felt nearer to heaven.[34]

On his last evening in Samoa, McKay sized up matters in the islands he had visited, drawing upon his keen powers of observation. By asking the Samoan high chiefs' advice, personally greeting and visiting with members in their homes and chapels, and receiving their expressions of faith and gratitude, he had tried to understand the church from the Samoans' perspective, working through translators. He had also met with the missionaries and listened to them. That evening he incisively appraised the strengths and weaknesses of the mission organization and staff and advised the missionaries and leaders accordingly. The missionaries "with perhaps one possible exception" were diligent and effective, and the baptismal rate was high, but their living quarters were unkempt. Acting upon recommendations he had received from Samoan members and chiefs, McKay announced he would recommend that couples be called to staff the church schools and to manage the plantations; the young missionaries lacked the experience and training to do so. Brass bands being conducted by the missionaries were excellent public relations tools and developed discipline and

34. Britsch, *Unto the Islands*, 394; Nielson, *To the Peripheries*, 98; McKay, *Pacific Apostle*, 175–78 (May 31, 1921).

talent. He pledged to purchase musical instruments with church funds so that the players would no longer have to borrow them.[35]

Having completed his tour of Samoa, McKay returned to Tonga. While traveling with McKay, President Coombs had convinced him to return and undergo quarantine. Cannon would proceed to New Zealand on the original schedule and conduct business there. McKay and Coombs, along with four new missionaries who had been waiting in Samoa for a boat to take them to Tonga, would quarantine along with the other passengers on Makaha'a, a five-acre speck of sand and coconut palms offshore from Nuku'alofa. McKay whiled away the hours writing articles for church magazines, combing the beaches and tidepools for seashells, singing hymns with the elders, and reading Shakespeare's *As You Like It* to them. One of the elders, Lewis Parkin, a twenty-three-year-old World War I veteran, professed disinterest in Shakespeare, but McKay the literature teacher insisted that "interest can be awakened by producing mental pictures of personality and action." Parkin was captivated by the apostle's vivid dramatic reading. Later that day he wrote, "Today Brother McKay started to read Shakespeare's play called 'As You Like It'. The first time I ever liked Shakespeare was today for he explained it as he went and the expression is wonderful." The stresses of the quarantine tried McKay's patience, as did the immaturity of the thirty-year-old mission president. After President Coombs amused the missionaries with tales of some of his youthful indiscretions, McKay gave him a "mild rebuke," and Coombs "seemed to chafe under it." The apostle let him stew.[36]

After enduring eleven days and nights of quarantine, the party entered Nuku'alofa and traveled to the mission headquarters for dinner. McKay preferred the relaxed nature of this welcome to the formal reception he had received in Samoa. A group of missionaries sang "Song of Greeting," which one of them had written. It reflected an admixture of sincerity and settler-colonial paternalism: "We greet you here with hearts sincere, Apostle of the Lord / It may look queer and strange appear the hue our Saints here show / But underneath the copper sheath, their true white hearts do glow." Conference meetings and other events proceeded over the next five days. After every meeting, members queued up to shake the apostle's hand. Some requested blessings. Others wanted to practice speaking English. Every night, Saints who had traveled to the conference visited, danced, and sang into the wee hours of the morning with "a vigor that seems incapable of exhaustion," preventing him from sleeping. "I can rejoice with them, but I find that energy goes out of me in such streams that I must get a little respite in my sleep in order to recuperate the supply," he confessed.[37]

35. McKay, *Pacific Apostle*, 181–86 (June 6, 1921).

36. McKay, *Pacific Apostle*, 187–98 (June 9–20, 1921); "Lewis Betts Parkin's Mission," familysearch.org..

37. McKay, *Pacific Apostle*, 199–216 (June 22–July 1, 1921). The lyrics to the "Song of Greeting" appear in DOMD, June 23, 1921.

While he was in Tonga, McKay attempted to improve the church's reputation and legal standing by visiting government leaders. McKay learned that keen opposition from politically influential Christian ministers had threatened the church's legal status. As a corrective, McKay requested an audience with Viriami Tungi, the premier of Tonga and husband of Queen Sālote Tupou III. Tungi was a Wesleyan Methodist, educated in Wesleyan schools, and although he professed neutrality in his interview with McKay and Coombs, he actually believed the government should deny visas to Latter-day Saint missionaries because of polygamy. The premier told the Latter-day Saints that the leaders of other churches resented the Mormon missionaries for stealing their congregants. Although the government had rejected the mission president's request to lease land for a new school, Tungi claimed disingenuously that the government had no objections to the church's educational initiatives.[38]

After spending nine days at Nuku'alofa, McKay departed on a star-crossed two-hundred-mile voyage to Ha'apai and Vava'u. On their first night at sea, waves crested the boat, washing a lifeboat overboard and nearly carrying some of the deck passengers with it. The inebriated captain tied the helm and staggered below deck, where McKay had a berth. "My seasickness was replaced by actual horror when I detected him hugging a full quarter bottle of whiskey—*full* excepting what he had drunk of it! Then flashed through my mind a combination of evils that would be difficult to duplicate for danger—a *mad sea, midnight* and pitch darkness, seventy people aboard a small vessel, sixty-eight of whom were exposed on the open deck, dangerous reef ahead—and the commander intoxicated!... I became alarmed!" he told Ray in a letter. "Soon without his knowing what had become of it, I had the whiskey under my pillow." Everyone survived the voyage. After arriving in Ha'apai twelve hours late with the boat's rudder damaged, church leaders held a ninety-minute meeting with 116 Saints. The next day after the rudder had been repaired, the group departed for Vava'u but was blown off course and arrived too late to hold their Sunday morning and afternoon meetings. Instead, that evening McKay spoke at a general church meeting. On Monday morning he traveled five miles overland to meet with the Haalaufuli Branch in their small chapel. That evening he dined at the home of a faithful member, Leva'itai, and her husband Iki Tupou Fulivai, the harbormaster and a member of the Tongan nobility. Iki had been one of the missionaries' first converts, but he had stopped attending. Leva'itai urged McKay to administer to Iki, who was seriously ill. Iki's experience with McKay was pivotal. He recovered and became a stalwart member and missionary.[39]

38. McKay, *Pacific Apostle*, 207 (June 28, 1921); Britsch, *To the Islands*, 439.

39. McKay, *Pacific Apostle*, 214–21 (June 30–July 4, 1921); McKay, *My Father*, 141–42; Sikahema, "Church Culture." Coombs's account of the storm-tossed voyage is printed in Nielson, *To the Peripheries*, 103–4.

From Vava'u, McKay traveled back to Samoa and then on to Fiji. In Suva, McKay wrote and mailed letters. Walking through town two hours before his ship's departure, McKay bought a newspaper at the editorial office. As he perused the paper, he saw the headline "Mormon Missionaries—Many in Nuku'alofa—Not Wanted by the Tongans." Incensed by what he believed to be inaccurate reporting, McKay returned to the newspaper office, complained to the editor, and responded to the editor's invitation to refute the charges by hammering out a hastily composed response, which the editor promised to publish the next day.[40]

After his visit to Tonga, McKay returned to Auckland by way of Samoa and Fiji and rejoined Cannon on July 18. They would spend the next two weeks touring portions of the North Island of New Zealand that they had not previously visited, with their talented Māori interpreter Stuart Meha. On Thursday evening and Friday, they met with members in the Bay of Islands district, near the upper tip of the north island. It was winter, and after his tour of the tropical South Pacific, McKay was uncomfortably cold. Back in Auckland, McKay and Cannon addressed a crowd of six hundred in a rented auditorium in the city hall. McKay felt prejudices were allayed through the talks he and Cannon delivered and the music provided by a choir of missionaries and members, notwithstanding a disturbance by a Reorganite missionary following the meeting who "made all present feel the spirit of hell." Contrasting McKay's dignified sermon with the antagonism of the interloper, one visitor commented to McKay following the meeting, "I wish you success. I like your style." From Auckland the church leaders made their way south. In Porirua, a short distance from Wellington, they tried to stir members of a dysfunctional branch from their lethargy. McKay doubted that his "long, wearisome dissertation on the folly and sinfulness of backsliding" had done much good. By contrast, the seasoned, faithful leaders of some other branches they visited impressed him. In the Dannevirke Branch, Cannon and McKay enjoyed the hospitality of Eriata [Elliot] Nopera, a wealthy landowner whose elegant home and well-trained family dazzled them. Nopera had joined the Church in 1886 when he was twenty years old and lived on a three-hundred-acre estate on the outskirts of town. A few years hence he would become the first Māori district president.[41]

The following day they dined at the beautiful home of Wiremu Takana, whom they called William Duncan, and his wife, Takare Aperata Takana. The couple had traveled to Utah in 1913 to be sealed in the temple. Takare, a mainstay in the Relief Society, spoke little English, so McKay's interaction with her was limited, but he praised her husband as "a remarkable man, one of the

40. DOMD, July 13, 1921.

41. McKay, *Pacific Apostle*, 227–35 (July 18–27, 1921); Nielson, *To the Peripheries*, 108; "Story of Meha, Stuart," *Dictionary of New Zealand Biography*, teara.gov.nz.

biggest and strongest in the Church, not excepting anyone." Brother Takana regaled the visitors with Māori legends, and before McKay and Cannon left, the Takanas presented them with expensive woolen steamer rugs. Next, they visited Māori Agricultural College, a vocational high school for boys that the church had established in Hastings, near the southeastern coast of the north island, in 1913. Some rambunctious students hoisted the visitors onto their shoulders and paraded around the hall singing "For He's a Jolly Good Fellow." At the college McKay requested a private bedroom. "People will undoubtedly think me selfish ... but I cannot rest sleeping with another man," he wrote. He would rather wrap himself in a rug and sleep well on the floor than spend a sleepless night in a shared bed. "If I do not get my rest I cannot keep up," he admitted. The former educator visited classes taught by the missionaries, toured the campus, and inspected the adjacent training farm where harvests had been unimpressive. He judged the training in animal husbandry and woodworking to be "fairly good" but found the English instruction abysmal. After inspecting the infertile, unproductive farm, McKay met with the school board and urged them to find a more suitable tract for an agricultural college and to convert the existing college into a girls' school.[42]

Having completed their work in New Zealand, the church leaders entrained for Auckland, where they boarded a vessel bound for Australia. En route to Sydney, McKay sagely evaluated the status of the church in New Zealand. As had been the case in Japan, he felt that local members should be given greater responsibility and deference in managing the church. He had been impressed by the capability of Stuart Meha, William and Takare Takana, and Eriata Nopera. "Some of our Elders appear like 'upstarts' presiding over experienced men," he wrote. This heightened appreciation for the abilities of local members was the most consequential product of McKay's visit to New Zealand for the church there.[43]

After a five-day passage on rough seas, Cannon and McKay disembarked in Sydney on Sunday, August 7, 1921. Missionaries had established a branch there in 1852, but nearly seven decades later, because of emigration to Utah, the entire continent had only 1,025 members—fewer than in the geographically smaller Tahitian, Samoan, New Zealand, or Hawai'ian missions. McKay and Cannon planned to spend their time in southeastern Australia, where nearly all the members resided. That afternoon McKay attended the Sydney Branch's fast and testimony meeting in a rented hall where he spoke on "the peace that comes from true conversion." Many members relished meeting an apostle, but McKay failed to measure up to one young member's expectations. "Well,

42. McKay, *Pacific Apostle*, 235–38 (July 28–30, 1921); Nielson, *To the Peripheries*, 110; Kātene, *Turning the Hearts*, 146.

43. McKay, *Pacific Apostle*, 239–40 (Aug. 2, 1921).

Brother McKay, you're just a man after all," remarked the disenchanted young man. "Well, I hope so," McKay bantered. "What did you think I am?" On Tuesday and Wednesday McKay accompanied Cannon and Robert Bischoff, a missionary, to the famous Jenolan Caves. McKay was enchanted with the "labyrinthian" limestone caves, where electric lighting accentuated the exquisite stalagmites and stalactites, although the tour guides seemed disappointingly disengaged or ignorant.[44]

Next the two visitors from Utah traveled to Melbourne, a city of 700,000 where the Church had a substantial branch. A combined meetinghouse and missionary living quarters was under construction, but for the time being the branch was meeting in a rented hall. The Relief Society hosted a welcome tea that evening with food, singing, recitations, and a piano solo. The next day McKay interviewed the six elders working in the city, whom he judged to be above average in strength, judgment, and intelligence. That evening the apostle addressed a congregation of 130 members and investigators including William Spence, a labor union leader and former member of parliament who had befriended the missionaries and exerted "a good influence among officials on [the church's] behalf."[45]

During a brief visit to Tasmania, McKay interviewed the four missionaries laboring there, dined with members, and spoke to an audience of one hundred in the town hall. The audience was "attentive," but the non-members there seemed so skeptical that McKay wryly concluded that the church there was "generally about as popular as the measles."[46]

The visitors' next stop was Adelaide, a city of a quarter million where they discovered the mission president had bungled their lodging arrangements. After wandering the streets for several hours searching for a place to stay, McKay wrote that he had seen "more drinking in saloons that afternoon than I have ever seen before in my entire life." The temperance worker in him was disgusted by "stupid-looking men swilling the whisky down like pigs." The next day, McKay met with eight missionaries, some of whom had traveled 1,600 miles across the continent from Perth for the occasion. Their reports were bleak: only one convert had been baptized in the previous year in all of South Australia. The "remarkable" devotion of some members thrilled him, though; one of them, John Allen, was blind. Allen's brother-in-law, a prominent Anglican minister, opposed his decision to be baptized. But the blind man testified "he would not exchange his knowledge of the Gospel with his blindness for the position, salary, and eyesight of the highest bishop in the Church of England."[47]

44. McKay, *Pacific Apostle*, 243–47 (Aug. 7–10, 1921); Britsch, *Unto the Islands*, 207.
45. McKay, *Pacific Apostle*, 248–50, (Aug. 13–14, 1921).
46. McKay, *Pacific Apostle*, 251 (Aug. 17, 1921).
47. McKay, *Pacific Apostle*, 254–56 (Aug. 20–21, 1921).

His tour completed, McKay spent several days at the mission home in Sydney with mission and Relief Society presidents Don and Elizabeth Rushton. On the weekend he joined a party of thirty-eight on an excursion to Warumbul in Australia's first national park, where they spent the day picnicking, playing baseball, singing, and admiring the native animals and plants, especially the deep-red flowers of the coral trees. The next day McKay blessed two babies in church, interpreted Joseph Smith's prophecy on war as a prelude to the recently completed world war, and spoke in a missionary fireside on his "reasons for being a Mormon." A non-member in the audience told him afterward that as he spoke she had seen "a white robe put over [his] shoulders" that later changed to purple and gold. "I did not attach much importance to it," the apostle recorded. On Monday, in what he deemed "a very impressive and important gathering" with the Rushtons and nine missionaries, McKay advised the missionaries to spend less time visiting members and more time interacting with outsiders, to avoid "too frequent use" of the pretentious title "elder" and to be dignified in demeanor so that their lives would be "eloquent sermons." The former English teacher offered pointers on proper grammar and advised the missionaries to ensure that candidates for baptism were fully prepared. As he had done elsewhere, he emphasized that local men should be given meaningful priesthood responsibilities and callings.[48]

McKay found the red tape of securing visas for his upcoming travel to Java, India, and Egypt vexing. Restrictions on travel imposed during the First World War were still in place, and it appeared that he and Cannon would not be able to secure the requisite documents before the scheduled departure of their ship. As he often did, McKay left the details to Cannon, assuring him that the way would be providentially opened. "Even though a stone wall appears to cross your path, go as far as you can, and you will usually find an opening through which you can pass," he declared. This proved generally true, but Cannon was the one who was consistently left to devise the means of resolving the daunting logistical challenges. In this case, McKay decided to visit the Brisbane Branch while Cannon was left to collect the visas and tickets, board the ship, and meet him when the ship docked in Brisbane. McKay met with the Saints and some of their friends on Sunday in the only chapel owned by the church in Australia. That evening, Gertie Orth, a twenty-two-year-old convert who had told her boyfriend she could not marry him until he joined the church, handed the apostle a note, thanking him for his sermon on pure religion and virtue, and pledging to "live that pure, undefiled religion" of which he had spoken. McKay's message had hit its mark. The following day he advised the missionaries to combat anti-Mormon prejudice by distributing a series of three tracts and by focusing on teaching the

48. McKay, *Pacific Apostle*, 258–60 (Aug. 25–29, 1921).

friends of members. On Tuesday afternoon, September 6, Cannon showed up on the ship with the necessary tickets and visas, and McKay walked aboard.[49]

McKay would now visit vast areas of the globe between Australia and Syria, where the church had no official presence. His primary task of touring the church's missions that had never before been visited by an apostle was "practically complete," and had it not been for the prospect of seeing the Holy Land and his missionary son, Lawrence, in Europe, McKay "should be tempted," he confessed, "to take a boat to San Francisco" and reunite with his family. He was "surfeited with sightseeing and associating with strangers and [wanted] to be home," he wrote his wife. McKay had the names of a handful of expatriate Latter-day Saints scattered across the Indian Ocean whom he was to try and contact as he appraised the prospects for missionary work there. Although it was not part of his official assignment, he would also become better informed about non-Christian religions and gain a greater appreciation of the good in non-Western cultures, although he would see much that he did not understand and disparage some of the practices he encountered.[50]

In Java, McKay and Cannon visited the sole Latter-day Saint of record on the island, Frank Becraft, a former Weber Stake Academy student whom McKay had taught. Becraft supervised the sale, installation, and operation of filters in sugar factories on the island. Becraft drove the two men around the island, playing tour guide. From their observations and conversation with Becraft, they concluded that "the low moral standard" of the inhabitants would make it difficult for missionaries to preach successfully there. Another two days' voyage brought them to Singapore, a city whose polyglot populace rekindled the tourists' fascination with the exotic, non-Western cultures that they had experienced in Polynesia. In Burma, they visited the golden Shwedagon Pagoda, a sacred Buddhist site. The pagoda's umbrella crown, or spire, rising high above the stupa, was adorned with diamonds and rubies. "Images of Buddha greet the visitor or the devout worshipers at every turn. In some niches, he is sitting, in some reclining, and in others standing," McKay wrote.[51]

McKay and Cannon spent over two weeks on the Indian subcontinent, home to nearly one-fourth of the world's population. Landing in Calcutta, they traveled over 800 miles to Agra and then north about 150 miles to Delhi before heading southwest to Bombay on the coast, 900 miles from Delhi. The duo were appalled by the caste system they observed but thrilled by architectural masterpieces including the Taj Mahal and Delhi's grand seventeenth-century mosque,

49. McKay, *Pacific Apostle*, 261–66 (Sep. 1–6, 1921); Nielson, *To the Peripheries*, 117. Orth's boyfriend joined the church in 1928, and she married him. "Glimpse into the Life of Gertrude Orth Shirra," entry for Gertrude Orth, KWC4-15H, Family Search, familysearch.org.

50. McKay, *Pacific Apostle*, 266 (Sep. 6, 1921); McKay and McKay, *Heart Petals*, 97.

51. McKay, *Pacific Apostle*, 266 (Sep. 6, 1921); McKay and McKay, *Heart Petals*, 97; Nielson, *To the Peripheries*, 121–22, 130; McKay, *Home Memories*, 88, 90.

the Jama Masjid. On the train in central India between Agra and Delhi, McKay was favorably impressed by the hospitality of a "Persian" merchant and equally embarrassed by the egotism of a European passenger, manifesting a healthy awareness of Western cultural deficiencies. McKay, Cannon, and the European unwittingly sat in a compartment that the merchant and his sons had reserved. Rather than ousting them, the merchant apologized for inconveniencing them and invited them to remain. When the European ordered lemonades only for the white westerners, McKay hastily interposed, doubling the order and offering to pay. "We Europeans assume a haughty, dignified air towards the Orientals, but, by goodness, the Orientals are far ahead of us in courtesy and good manners!" he reflected. McKay had the names of several members of the church in India, each of whom he hoped to meet. For this reason, they traveled north from Agra to Delhi. By letters awaiting them there, they learned that only one of the members, John Currie, was still a believer, and he lived in a remote region well beyond the railroad terminus. Transportation difficulties made it impractical to visit him. After praying about the matter, they decided to go directly to Bombay, where a ship was scheduled to depart the following week. McKay found Bombay to be a relatively westernized, "thriving" entrepôt, but he was overwhelmed by the "abject poverty and squalor," which seemingly exceeded any place they had visited since Peking. Seven days after arriving in Bombay, as they stood aboard the *Egypt* watching the shoreline recede, they mused on the religious devotion and morality of many Hindus they had met. McKay marveled that the country seemed more upright than many Christian nations. Years later, as church president, he would explore the possibility of opening India to missionary work.[52]

Aboard the *Egypt,* McKay and Cannon crossed the Arabian Sea and entered the Red Sea. McKay visited with a fellow passenger, Major General Theodore Fraser, a Scotsman with extensive military experience in the Near East. When McKay told Fraser he planned to visit Latter-day Saint Armenian refugees in Syria, the general tried to discourage him. The Armenians, he said, were "despicable," lazy cheats "with whom no other peoples can live" and warned McKay that conditions in Syria were volatile. If he insisted on going, he should "be prepared to leave your head behind." McKay good-naturedly replied that his head was "not worth much but I don't want a Turk to have it!" Passing through the Suez Canal, they landed at Port Said before daylight on October 25 and arrived in Cairo by afternoon. For the next four days, the two Utahns played tourist, visiting the Grand Pyramid of Cheops, made of gigantic blocks of stone—"monuments," McKay wrote, "to the tyranny as well as the greatness of the ancient Pharaohs." They toured the treasure trove of ancient artifacts in the Egyptian Museum, visited the Sultan Hasan Mosque and traveled by camel to

52. Nielson, *To the Peripheries*, 126–31; McKay, *Home Memories*, 93–96.

the ancient city of Memphis. He playfully wrote his son Llewelyn, "I accept as absolute facts every plague of Egypt named in the Bible, and add to them the *plague of fleas*, which Moses forgot to mention."

McKay caught his first glimpse of Jerusalem—"the most historic place in the world" and the high point for him as an apostle of Christ on his world tour—shortly after noon on October 30, 1921. McKay measured his tour guide's comments and his own observations at the sites they visited against his careful study of the New Testament gospels. When they passed the "Apostles' Fountain," where the guide claimed Jesus announced he would raise Lazarus from the dead, McKay noted that the Gospel of John identified a different location for the announcement. When they visited the Garden of Gethsemane, an elaborate Franciscan basilica was under construction surrounding a rocky slab. He found the "modern" trappings excessive and distracting but accepted without question the traditional "rock—thank heaven they can't change that—on which the three disciples sat and watched." He was disgusted by the hostile rivalry between the Roman, Greek, and Armenian branches of Christianity; each owned a corner of the alleged site of Christ's birth and jealously guarded their turf. "The spirit of contention, of bigotry, and of jealousy has banished the spirit of Christ from the place of his nativity!" he lamented.[53]

McKay's visit to Jerusalem coincided with the fourth anniversary of the controversial Balfour Declaration, Britain's pledge to support a Jewish homeland in Palestine. McKay approved entirely of the declaration. Within nine months of McKay's visit, the League of Nations would advance Lord Balfour's agenda by approving a British mandate in Palestine. McKay's guide was bitterly opposed to the declaration and swore under his breath that "the Jews shall never rule over Palestine." Steeped in Zionism from his reading of the Bible, McKay retorted, "I want to tell you something to remember: No matter how much the Mohammedans and Greek Christians oppose the Jews' coming back to Palestine, the Jews are coming and will possess this land!" Anti-Semitic riots broke out in Jerusalem later that day, and a bomb was thrown into a crowd, killing one and wounding others. Three Jews were clubbed to death. McKay, a large man, tried unsuccessfully to yell and use his cane to shield a handful of Jewish men, women, and children from an angry mob armed with sticks and stones. British police arrived just in time to rout the mob. In his mind's eye McKay envisioned the return of more Jews to Palestine, which he anticipated would further inflame Palestinian "hatred" and precipitate a bloodbath. Influenced perhaps by apocalyptic Biblical prophecies, McKay wrote, "I seemed to see not many years hence, those doorways and stone steps [of Jerusalem] covered with blood in the great struggle that is impending." The following afternoon Cannon and McKay

53. DOMD, Oct. 30–31, 1921.

climbed the Mount of Olives, knelt beneath a secluded fig tree, and "rebuked" the "spirit of opposition" toward the Jews' return, "that it should not prevail." They prayed, moreover, for inspiration and protection in their upcoming tour of the battle-scarred Armenian Mission.[54]

Although Cannon and McKay had planned to hire a driver to take them directly from Israel to Syria, they felt "strongly impressed" to take the train to Haifa instead, hoping somehow to rendezvous with Joseph Wilford Booth, the new mission president, who was on his way to Aleppo to begin a relief mission, even though they had been unable to contact him. As they exited the train station in Haifa, someone tapped McKay on the shoulder, and McKay turned to see Booth standing there. The men marveled at their perfectly timed reunion and concluded that it was not coincidental; instead, "[their] coming together thus was the direct result of divine interposition!" Booth knew the terrain well, having spent the better part of a decade between 1898 and 1909 in the Ottoman Empire as a missionary and then mission president. Booth hired a car and driver to take them to Aleppo in Syria. There they visited the American consul, a friend of Booth's, who counseled them not to go to Aintab, a city in Turkey, where thousands of impoverished Armenian refugees, including a few dozen Latter-day Saints, lived in fear that the massacres of Armenians in 1915–16 would resume after the French occupation forces retreated. Despite the consul's warning, they proceeded the next day to Aintab, passing a burned-out car on the roadside. A hastily called church service drew thirty members and forty of their friends, some of whom requested baptism. Following the meeting, McKay blessed their children and listened to the refugees' horrific tales; only one-fifth of the twenty-five-thousand Armenians who had lived in the area a decade earlier remained, he was told. One devout woman who regarded him as God's servant grasped his hands and gazed directly into his eyes. "We have been in hell for seven years," she declared, but now, seeing an apostle, "we are in heaven." Following this reception, McKay and his companions felt certain they were "where the Lord desired us to be." The French had announced earlier that day that they would pull out of Aintab in a few weeks, leaving the Armenians defenseless. Because of their timely visit, McKay was able to authorize Booth to relocate every member to Syria within ten days.[55]

Traveling through Israel on their return to Port Said, McKay and Cannon visited Nazareth, Jesus's hometown. The closely nestled white homes amid the green olive and fig trees and the city shops enchanted McKay. The old town well was "gushing forth the same pure water that filled Mary's jug every morning," he imagined. At the well he met a comely woman. "I pictured her as the Madonna,"

54. DOMD, Nov. 2–3, 1921.
55. DOMD, Nov. 3–8, 1921.

McKay wrote, and the sight of small children at play on the street reminded him of the lyrics, "He played as little children played the pleasant games of youth."[56]

Back in Port Said on November 16, McKay and Cannon reclaimed their stored souvenirs and luggage and booked passage on a ship bound for Italy. A whirlwind trip up the Italian peninsula left little time for sightseeing aside from an "intensely interesting" excursion to Pompeii and two days for guided tours of the Coliseum, the Parthenon, Circus Maximus, the Basilica of St. Paul, the Sistine Chapel, and the burial vaults of early Christians in the catacombs of Rome.[57]

The sites in Italy were impressive, essential elements of any cultured world tour, but McKay was more excited for his imminent planned reunion with his missionary son, Lawrence, in Switzerland. As they exited the train station in Lausanne, McKay spied Lawrence, whom he described as "a straight, dignified young man," about a block away. As they embraced, McKay recorded, he felt "pure joy." For the next ten days, father and son toured the mission, combining meetings with the Saints in Lausanne, Basel, Frankfurt, and Liège with tours of famous sites, including the Cologne cathedral, "a cold, elegant edifice"; Waterloo, where the guide's historical knowledge was disappointingly shallow; the Louvre, where McKay wished he could spend a week; and the Eiffel Tower. Predisposed to dislike it by his anti-Catholic bias, McKay found Notre Dame Cathedral to be "a cold dismal place in which the representatives of the Apostate Church sit begging for contributions and charge visitors a franc to see their 'treasures.'"[58]

Britain was merely a steppingstone between the continent and the boat that would take Cannon and McKay home; they spent only two full days there. McKay did visit Glasgow, where he had preached the gospel nearly a quarter-century earlier. Many of the Saints he'd known had emigrated or died, but he met with several friends, including Elizabeth Noble, who had been the housekeeper at the mission headquarters when he was there. She cried for joy and wryly quipped that time had gotten the best of McKay: "Ah, but ye're nae my bonny laddie, you've changed."[59]

Having completed their mission, the weary travelers crossed the Atlantic in eight days and arrived in Utah on Christmas Eve.[60] Just over a year had elapsed since their departure the previous December. The round-the-world tour had given McKay a global perspective on Mormonism. Aside from their visits to Hawai'i and Heber J. Grant's mission to Japan, none of McKay's fellow apostles had traveled beyond North America and Europe, and they all perceived the church and missionary work through a Euro-American lens. McKay's

56. DOMD, Nov. 15, 1921.
57. DOMD, Nov. 16, 22, 24, 1921.
58. DOMD, Nov. 26, Dec. 1–2, 6, 1921.
59. DOMD, Dec. 8, 1921; McKay, *My Father*, 155.
60. McKay, *My Father*, 155.

travels and the faith-promoting miracles and providential interventions he experienced had reinforced his religious convictions and deepened his spirituality while also broadening his understanding of the diversity of human experience, religious beliefs, and cultures. His travels had reinforced some western biases, but they had shaken others. In some interactions he had observed, non-Western peoples had demonstrated greater nobility of character than their European and American counterparts. Time would show that his world tour, as well as his subsequent travels, helped to make McKay less dogmatic and more tolerant of cultural differences than some of his less-traveled colleagues. McKay's tour had also enabled many church members in the South Pacific and Japan to meet their first apostle. In greeting, hosting, or visiting with him and listening to him preach, many of the faithful sensed a connection to something much larger than themselves. For some, McKay was a tangible link to the administrative structure of the church. Others, like Jione Mau of Tonga, who sensed his spiritual mantle, felt closer to God in his presence. After a meeting, Mau slipped a small paper into McKay's palm. On it he had written, "Not until I have ceased breathing will I forget your teachings. I thank the Lord that I have lived to see you, to hear your voice and to touch your hand."[61]

61. Jione Mau to David O. McKay, June 30, 1921, box 6, folder 20, McKay Papers, hereafter cited as McKay Papers.

6: A Year at Home and Two More Abroad

Following his world tour, McKay joyfully reunited with his family. The extended family members who showed up at the train station to welcome him thoughtfully said their goodbyes at the station because they sensed "the main family should be alone for awhile," Ray wrote appreciatively. "This last week has been simply wonderful!... I have never in all my life seen or heard anyone so interesting as Papa. For eight days now we have been traveling in strange countries, seeing naughty and good people, seeing their queer habits and costumes," Lou Jean wrote to her brother. In the new year, though, family and friends clamored for McKay's time, inviting him to dinners and speaking engagements to hear of his travels. "Papa has been dined and entertained continuously by his relations and friends," Ray wrote three weeks after her husband's return. "He has given some wonderful talks & the halls are so crowded that the aisles cannot be used."[1]

In the new year McKay also resumed his former routine of visiting stake conferences and Sunday School conventions on weekends and attending committee and council meetings on Tuesdays and Thursdays. He spoke at funerals; performed weddings; and attended corporate, university, and hospital board meetings. His summer was hectic. In June he was awarded an honorary master's degree from Brigham Young University in recognition of his work as a teacher, principal, and church commissioner of education and his "contribution to the church teacher-training work." He began participating in a weighty assignment to standardize, simplify, and modernize the temple endowment ceremony, working alongside Joseph Fielding Smith, Stephen L Richards, John A. Widtsoe, and George F. Richards. In the course of this assignment, which would last for several years, he pondered the temple's essential messages and symbols. The committee committed to writing previously unwritten but crucial portions of the ceremony, including the wording of covenants, and revised instructions regarding rituals and ceremonies, eliminating inessential or outmoded trappings. Writing to Lawrence mid-summer in 1922, McKay indicated, "Church duties are keeping me busy as usual. There is so much to do, so many appointments to

1. McKay, *My Father*, 156–57; DOMD, Jan. 10, 16, 18, 25, Feb. 1, 3, 8, 12, 19, 1922.

fill that one wishes one might turn night into day and not get weary. But after all, such a wish is foolish; for rest and relaxation are just as essential to success as work." To that end, the family spent a week in late summer at Yellowstone. Less than a day's drive away, the park with its hot springs, wildlife, and fishing opportunities was one of McKay's favorite vacation destinations.[2]

Less than nine months after completing his world tour and soon after he returned from Yellowstone, McKay received a call to preside over the church's European Mission, headquartered in Liverpool. President Grant knew the timing was inopportune, coming as it did on the heels of the world tour, but the current president, Orson F. Whitney, needed to return home for urgent medical care, and McKay seemed best qualified among the apostles to replace him due to his vigor, relative youth, former service in the British Mission, and acumen derived from his world tour. McKay would share this calling with Ray, who would accompany him and preside over the mission's Relief Societies. This would be the weightiest church administrative assignment of her life. David casually broke the breathtaking news to Ray as she was working in the kitchen, enhancing its shock value. His letter to Lawrence exuded enthusiasm: *"Your Mama, the kiddies, and I shall leave for Liverpool about Oct. 15th!* ... What do you think?" In the quarterly conference of the Quorum of the Twelve on September 26, John A. Widtsoe prophesied that McKay would "return and declare in this room that his mission was a joy to him."[3]

Over 2,000 friends packed Berthana Hall in Ogden on the evening of November 2, 1922, to bid adieu to the McKays. Ray played the part of loyal wife. "You have to live with a man to know him," she said. "I have lived with my husband for twenty years and I know how he loves and works for you." That work often came at her expense, but she did not demur publicly. Instead, minimizing her own calling to preside over the Relief Society in Britain, she playfully bantered that she had to "tag along behind" her husband in order "to keep up an acquaintance" with him. Already he had devised an agenda for the next three years. He informed the well-wishers that he intended to focus on three timely goals as mission president: visit and encourage missionaries and members in Europe, enhance the reputation of Utah and its people, and carry the message of Christianity and peace to lands ravaged by the Great War that had ended only four years earlier.[4]

---

2. McKay, *My Father*, 159; DOMD entries for Jan.–Oct. 1922. See for instance Jan. 8, 15, 17, 19, 29, Feb. 8, 10, 12, 14, 15, 24, 27, Mar. 17, 1922. On his honorary degree see "Talmage-M'Kay Receive Honorary Degrees," *Provo Daily Herald*, June 2, 1922, 1. For the Richards Committee's work on the endowment ceremony see DOMD, July 22–23, 25, 27, 1922; Buerger, "Development of Mormon Ceremony," 54; Alexander, *Mormonism in Transition*, 302.

3. McKay, *My Father*, 159, 216; Woodger, *David O. McKay*, 139–40; "Churchman is Named for European Mission," *Salt Lake Telegram*, Sep. 15, 1922, 21; DOMD, Sep. 26, 1922.

4. "Apostle and Mrs. D. O. M'Kay Guests at Farewell Party," *Ogden Standard Examiner*, Nov. 3, 1922, 16.

On November 8, the McKays embarked on their new adventure. En route to New York, they attended church in Chicago and visited Niagara Falls. From New York the family traveled to Montréal and then to Liverpool, arriving on November 25. Given his service in Britain as a young missionary it seemed "almost a homecoming," McKay wrote, especially since his family was with him. The mission headquarters, Durham House, consisted of offices and a chapel on the main floor, an apartment for the family on the second, and the printing and editorial offices of the *Millennial Star* on the third. In his first editorial for the *Star*, McKay introduced what would become a key emphasis of the mission: "every member" had the "pleasure, duty and obligation" to share the gospel through word and deed. Later that month he announced an ambitious goal for the new year: each member should strive to bring someone into the church. "Our aim is to have ever member a missionary, not in the sense of leaving their homes or work, but in the sense of opening the way for elders to get in the presence of men and women who honestly desire to know the truth," he wrote the following March.[5]

The goal would be difficult, given the church's abysmal standing. McKay was shocked that the church's reputation, which had been subpar when he was a missionary in the 1890s, had seemingly worsened since then despite the excommunication of new polygamists. After Liverpool College refused to admit their children because of their faith, the McKays searched for over a month to find a "suitable" school that would enroll them. A nun who turned away sixteen-year-old Lou Jean from a Catholic school explained, "Although we accept people of other denominations, this is such an exceptional case, isn't it? People just shudder when a Mormon is mentioned and we must consider our people." Popular culture reinforced anti-Mormon prejudice. A film recently made and released in Britain, *Trapped by the Mormons*, portrayed the hypnotic powers of missionaries who duped young women and spirited them away to Utah to become polygamous wives in harems. Ministers warned their parishioners against Mormons, and the press circulated allegations of Mormon lechery and perfidy. When a group of missionaries landed in Liverpool, a reporter asked them incredulously, "If you aren't here to entice young girls to go to Utah, why are you here?" "People really do believe us unchaste and lawless," McKay wrote in amazement. Many Britons associated Mormonism exclusively with polygamy, disregarding the lofty Christian moral principles taught by missionaries and the charitable activities of Relief Societies.[6]

5. DOMD, Nov. 3, 13–14, 25, 1922; McKay, *My Father*, 160, 163; David O. McKay, "A Word of Greeting," *Millennial Star*, Dec. 7, 1922, 777; "Minutes of the London Conference," *Millennial Star*, Dec. 28, 1922, 829; David O. McKay to Rudger Clawson, Feb. 5, 1923, quoted in Gibbons, *David O. McKay*, 126.

6. DOMD, Nov. 26, 30, Dec. 5, 1922, Jan. 5, 7, 11, 1923; McKay, *My Father*, 160; "Minutes of the London Conference," *Millennial Star*, Dec. 28, 1922, 829; D'Arc, "The Mormon as Vampire," 172–75.

McKay took up his pen to respond to the charges in an editorial printed on December 28, 1922, in the *Millennial Star*. Its circulation was largely limited to Latter-day Saints, but it was the only organ he controlled, and he wielded his pen ably. He pointed out that every American missionary was admitted to England with the permission of both the American and British governments. They served without remuneration and sought to "strengthen" congregations and to counteract prejudice through "upright living, noble desires, and unselfish service." They preached the original gospel of Jesus Christ as restored through the prophet Joseph Smith. When McKay learned the next month that a group of ministers in Cardiff had organized a vigilance committee, allegedly to shield women from missionaries, McKay denounced them in the *Millennial Star:* "They cannot sincerely and conscientiously believe the absurdity that elders, whose lives are above reproach, are in the mission field to lure girls to Utah." Anyone who condoned such talk, he wrote, was either "inexcusabl[y] ignorant of the facts" or a "hypocrite." McKay encouraged members and missionaries to maintain the moral high ground by exercising self-control and eschewing violence. He praised a robust missionary in Newcastle who, when struck with a cane while tracting, "controlled himself and received several blows without retaliating" even though he could have "readily" overcome his assailant. For his part, McKay made an appointment to meet with William Aitken, commonly known as Lord Beaverbrook, the Canadian-born owner and publisher of a prominent newspaper, the *Daily Express*, and asked for fair-minded, accurate reporting. Thereafter "the worst of the excesses stopped," recalled Llewelyn, who had finished his mission and was working with his father in the mission office.[7]

McKay occasionally parried prejudice with biting satire. When he learned that a town council in Wales had forbidden a church member from holding services in his home because "nearly thirty girls" had disappeared from a large nearby village two years previously, McKay asked the town council facetiously if they had "gone far enough." He continued, "If you have the right to prevent his singing hymns and of speaking, in the presence of his family and of friends, of the grace and goodness of God, you also have the right to order him to cease his prayers; because 'He is a Mormon.'" Ridiculing the council's kneejerk reaction to the alleged disappearance of thirty girls, McKay wrote, "You know that whenever any girl leaves any town in Great Britain, the 'Mormons' are responsible, just as the early Christians were responsible for the overflowing of the Tiber River." He ridiculed their logic as "unbecoming a body of intelligent men" and

7. David O. McKay, "Why They Are Here," *Millennial Star*, Dec. 28, 1922, 824–25; David O. McKay, "Where Knowledge Is Absolute," *Millennial Star*, Jan. 11, 1923, 25–26; David O. McKay, "Christ's Teachings Regarding Right Thinking," *Millennial Star*, Jan. 18, 1923, 41; McKay, *My Father*, 164.

concluded, "it is difficult for me to conceive that the people from whom my mother comes can be so bigoted."[8]

McKay also sought to shore up the church's reputation by cultivating relations with government officials and complying with legal requirements. Shortly after arriving in England, he met with Fred Kerr, Canada's emigration agent in Liverpool and a personal friend of Apostle George Albert Smith. McKay also conferred with Horace L. Washington, a consul from the United States. When President Serge Ballif of the Swiss-German Mission, who operated under McKay's supervision as did all mission presidents on the continent, cabled him about increased legal restrictions on the movement of American missionaries in Germany, McKay instructed that all missionaries should obey the law scrupulously, even if that meant leaving the country to conform to official edicts. In an attempt to improve relations with governments in Scandinavia that continued to discriminate against the church and deny visas to missionaries because of polygamy, McKay traveled there with Apostles John A. Widtsoe and Reed Smoot on a diplomatic mission. As a US senator, Smoot navigated most of the diplomatic negotiations, but McKay had the opportunity to become acquainted with America's ministers in each nation, whom they relied upon to facilitate appointments with government officials: Robert Bliss in Sweden, Laurits Swenson in Norway, and John Prince in Denmark, whom McKay characterized as "a prince by name and a prince by nature."[9]

While he defended the church's noble aims, McKay struggled to remedy the members' and missionaries' shortcomings as he toured the branches. The leadership of nearly every congregation lacked experience in "church organization, church discipline, and the proper conduct of presiding authorities." The "great majority" of missionaries were "choice, able young men" who were "ready to do anything they are asked to do and to go where they are asked to go." But some missionaries evinced "a spirit of inactivity" or fanned "turmoil and contention." McKay wished for "more frequent and closer contact" with the young, unsophisticated missionaries to keep them from danger, especially since a few indiscreet actions could further inflame public prejudice. Some missionaries were addicted to tobacco. One young man recently arrived from Arizona was accused of "sinful relations," and although he maintained his innocence on that count, his admittedly "indiscreet actions" made the accusation believable and necessitated an emergency transfer. Another missionary fell in love with seventeen-year-old Muriel Banham, a member of the Bradford Branch. He abandoned his post in Liverpool, traveled to her hometown, and proposed to her. "He is infatuated, has lost the spirit of his mission," McKay despaired.

8. David O. McKay, "Back to the Medes and Persians," *Millennial Star*, Apr. 10, 1924, 233–34.

9. DOMD, Nov. 30, 1922, Jan. 15, Mar. 28, July 20, 23, 26, 1923. See also Thomas, "Apostolic Diplomacy," 130–65.

The elder desired an honorable release; he believed in God and testified that he had been providentially healed by a priesthood blessing during the influenza epidemic so that he could serve a mission. But he felt he could not continue to serve without his sweetheart at his side. McKay gave him the choice of being dishonorably released or promising not to visit her again. The young missionary pledged to stay clear of his girlfriend, but a week later he was back in Bradford. McKay summarily released him in order to "protect" the church from "the results of his indiscretion," and a month later the couple married. Other elders were guilty of grosser offenses, including two who were excommunicated for taking up with prostitutes. By contrast, some missionaries served masterfully. Elder David Goddard of Ogden, who served as McKay's "excellent" mission secretary, was "at [the] typewriter constantly" and ably presided over one of the Scottish conferences. McKay was especially impressed with a young elder from Idaho, Ezra Benson, whose planning and management of the Newcastle District Conference was "the nearest to ideal of any conference" in Britain.[10]

In his first full year as mission president, McKay visited and spoke at the semiannual gatherings of all fourteen conferences, or districts, in Britain. Often Ray accompanied him, meeting with Relief Society leaders and speaking too. McKay also visited and spoke in ten district conferences on the continent—Liège, Rotterdam, Copenhagen, Kristiania, Stockholm, Hamburg, Frankfurt, Berlin, Zürich, and Lausanne. At a missionary meeting following each conference, he asked each missionary to share their spiritual impressions, their challenges, and their suggestions. At one conference in Berlin attended by over 207 missionaries, he heard from each missionary and provided instruction in a marathon nine-hour meeting. Many in attendance marked their diaries with red letters because of the "especial spiritual feast" where they gained "a clearer understanding of what it means to be a missionary of the Church of Christ in the world." McKay wrote editorials at least twice monthly for the *Millennial Star*, reviewed and responded to correspondence, prepared a pamphlet entitled *Slanders Refuted*, and prepared mission reports, transfers, and releases. An extrovert, he despised days spent writing alone in the office. "Eight or ten hours constant writing and dictating wear on one's nerves," he complained. When he was traveling on the Continent, he interspersed church meetings and interviews with sightseeing and shopping to rejuvenate himself. These trips were especially pleasant when Ray accompanied him, as she did in February 1923 on his first three-week tour of the Continent. After an "excellent" conference in Zürich, the McKays took the train to Dresden, where they toured an art gallery.

10. DOMD, Jan. 21, Feb. 17, July 16, 1923, Dec. 8, 1922, Jan. 4, May 10, Feb. 17, 1923, Dec. 4, 1922, Apr. 13, 22, 23, July 19, Sep. 15, 1923, June 8, 1924, Oct. 14, 1923; "Minutes of the Nottingham Conference," *Millennial Star*, Nov. 23, 1922, 748; entry for Willis McCracken Smith, KWD3-HZG, Family Search, familysearch.org.

The next day in Berlin, they ambled along the Siegesallee, a grand avenue of monuments running through the Tiergarten. Although he did not always enjoy shopping, he wrote that a day spent shopping with Ray in Paris on their way home was simply "grand." Toward the end of their trip, David dreamed one night that he and Ray were visited by her deceased mother. "Her beauty, strength of character, and reserved dignity impressed me deeply," he recorded. He cherished the experience as a "significant" visionary manifestation.[11]

McKay relished the opportunity to show family and friends the places where he had visited and worked as a young missionary in Scotland. Accompanied by Ray and Kathleen Wright, a senior missionary couple from Ogden, the McKays visited Stirling Castle, where their inebriated tour guide simultaneously disappointed and amused them. McKay led them past the house where he and his companion had boarded and took them to see Wallace monument and the Trossachs. In Edinburgh, he stopped in on Sister Whyte, whose home he had stayed in whenever he visited the city as a young missionary. In Glasgow he renewed his acquaintance with Janet Leggat, the widowed, lonesome matriarch of a large Latter-day Saint family, most of whose children had emigrated to Utah.[12]

One year into McKay's mission, Mary Booth, a sister of Apostle James E. Talmage, arrived in Liverpool. She was on her way to Aleppo to join her husband, mission president Joseph Booth, whom McKay had met the previous year in Haifa. David and Ray seized the opportunity to escort her the rest of the way. The trip would be pleasurable, but it would also allow McKay to succor the displaced and impoverished Armenian members whom he had met on his world tour in 1921. Lou Jean would skip school for six weeks to care for the younger children while her parents were away. The travelers left Liverpool on January 7, 1924, crossed France, and boarded a ship in Marseilles bound for Alexandria in Egypt. McKay relished disabusing a "bright, clever traveling companion" aboard the ship of her anti-Mormon prejudice. Missionaries were "infesting" Edinburgh "for the purpose of inducing young girls to go to Utah," she told him; her sister had even been approached by one of the young imposters and offered a pamphlet. "She was very much embarrassed when I told her who I am and what the facts are," McKay wrote. After visiting Alexandria, they met President Booth in Beirut and toured the ruins of Baalbek, with its

11. DOMD, Apr. 12, 1923, Feb. 11, 15, 19, 28, Oct. 12, 1923. G. Martin Hopfenbeck, "After Fond Adieus," *Millennial Star*, Dec. 11, 1924, 793. McKay's participation in each conference and his activities in the office are chronicled in his diary for 1923. It appeared to McKay that there was "plenty of food and plenty of money in Germany," despite the nation's recent defeat in the Great War. He believed that what Germany needed most was an honest government to manage the resources. DOMD, Nov. 21, 1923.

12. DOMD, May 24, 26, 29, 1923; entry for Janet Chalmers [Leggat], KWZS-ZMZ, Family Search, familysearch.org.

Roman temple to Jupiter built on the foundation of an earlier Sumerian shrine. The following weekend, the leaders convened a branch conference in Aleppo and remained there for several days, with Booth interpreting for David and Ray. McKay's interactions with refugees of war and religious persecution sensitized him to the magnitude of international humanitarian crises that a worldwide church faced. McKay hoped to colonize the Armenian Latter-day Saint refugees and provide them with a suitable economic base. He and Booth met with a landowner to investigate the possibility for renting land along the Euphrates for a colony, but they found the prospects unsuitable.[13]

Leaving the Booths in Aleppo, David and Ray returned by train to Beirut and hired a driver to take them to Nazareth and Jerusalem. David was especially impressed with the colonies of Jewish immigrants in the region, "giving promise of the return of the Jews," which he believed to be divinely ordained. In Jerusalem and Judea, they joined another American couple, the Webbers, in visiting the standard tourist sites. The group marveled as they viewed what was purportedly the "original arch that formed part of the judgment Hall in which Pilate said, 'Behold the man!'" and "walked on the original stones on which the Roman soldiers played games and from which Jesus began his way to Golgotha." Continuing to Cairo, the Webbers and McKays visited sites there. McKay was impressed by the beauty and immense fertility of the Nile Valley, the primitive farming techniques he observed, and the "quaint towns with mud bricks and flat-roofed houses" insulated with corn stalks. They traveled by boat from Alexandria to Brindisi on the Italian coast and then crossed Italy by train, stopping in Naples to see Pompeii, where they saw evidence in paintings and sculptures of the former inhabitants' "voluptuous lives." In Rome the McKays "enjoyed every minute" of their visit to the Forum and the Basilica of St. Paul Outside the Walls but bristled at the "heathenish forms of worship" they observed "amidst untold wealth and magnificence" at St. Peter's Basilica, which they attributed to Constantine's corruption of Christianity. They marveled at Michelangelo's fresco on the ceiling of the Sistine Chapel depicting an embodied God ("a person") creating Adam because it harmonized with Latter-day Saint theology. In the Gallery of the Academy at Florence, they followed the historical progression of Christian art from its rude early stages to Michelangelo's master sculpture of David. In Milan, McKay, as a modern apostle, carefully studied da Vinci's interpretation of the face of each of the original apostles. A train conveyed the McKays from Italy to Paris, where they celebrated Valentine's Day. They arrived back in Liverpool on February 16, 1924, having enjoyed an unforgettable adventure together that finally qualified Ray as a bona fide world traveler.[14]

13. DOMD, Jan. 2, 7–10, 13–16, 19–23, 1924.

14. DOMD, Jan. 26, 28, Feb. 1, 4–6, 9–12, 14, 16, 1924.

Barely a week after arriving home, McKay set out again, this time without Ray, for three weeks of travel and conferences with missionaries and members in Belgium, Germany, and Switzerland. Late in the trip he came down with a severe cold that dampened his spirits. After recovering at home, he resumed his travels: between April and October, he spoke and presided at thirteen two-day conferences in Britain and spent another six weeks conducting church business, including mission and district conferences, on the Continent. Each mission there had its own full-time president, but McKay as head of the European Mission counseled and taught the missionaries and members and represented the church in negotiations regarding missionary quotas and visas with government authorities. Additionally, he accompanied Ray, who represented the church in her role as president of the British Relief Societies, to a five-day convention of the International Council of Women dedicated to "prevention of the causes of war." Founded in 1888 by American suffragists, the international body was working closely with the League of Nations to promote international peace. Ray reported in the *Millennial Star* that key sentiments voiced in the conference included arms reduction and achieving social justice through constructive dialogue and mutual understanding. In an editorial inspired by his attendance at the conference, McKay wrote that the proposed solutions were impractical unless "governments as individuals will practice the simple though sublime teaching of the Redeemer." For centuries the world had only known a "pseudo-Christianity," but now the "Gospel of the Redeemer" was "being preached to the nations of the world" by the missionaries, he editorialized.[15]

Although McKay expected when he was called as mission president that he would serve the standard three-year term, President Grant released him to return home after two because of his extended absence from home on his world tour. "The American mail contained a letter from the First Pres. announcing my release to take effect about two months hence.... My trip around the world visiting foreign missions counted in my three years' mission, so the letter states," he recorded matter-of-factly early in September 1925. McKay had "hoped to stay longer," Lawrence surmised, but the apostle did not complain publicly. McKay made the best of the remaining weeks of his mission, continuing with his previously scheduled conferences in Manchester, Belfast, Nottingham, and Blackburn. En route home from Blackburn, he realized his tire was flat. Lacking a spare, he slowly drove the remaining twenty-six miles on the tire rim. On his last trip to the Continent, McKay dedicated a meeting hall in Amsterdam and presided at a special conference in Hamburg—"one of the best ever held in the Church"—where he asked each missionary to draft and present a one-minute gospel message.[16]

15. DOMD, Apr. 7, May 5–7, 1924; David O. McKay, "Conference on the Prevention of Causes of War," *Millennial Star*, May 22, 1924, 331.

16. DOMD, Sep. 4, 28, Oct. 12, 1924; McKay, *My Father*, 170.

Nearing the end of that last trip, he took two days from his schedule to fulfill a private obligation known only to himself and a nonmember Englishwoman, Gertrude Kemp, whom he had met in New Zealand on his world tour. The incident illustrates McKay's endearing courtesy and personal sense of honor. In 1915 Kemp had married Hoani Wineera, a Māori Latter-day Saint soldier whom she met in London while he was convalescing from a wound received at Gallipoli. Following their son's birth in 1917, Gertrude pledged to her husband that if he died in combat, she would take their son to New Zealand to be reared as a Māori. In 1918, Hoani was wounded a second time and evacuated to a military clearing station in France, where he died. He was interred in a British military cemetery at Trois Arbres. True to her pledge, Gertrude relocated with her son to New Zealand, a land she had never before visited. Eventually she married Hoani's older brother Hohepa, who cared for her and her son. After meeting McKay in New Zealand on his world tour, Gertrude asked him to find her husband's grave and dedicate it if his work ever took him to France. Four years later McKay was determined to honor her request. It was a small, private matter but one that he treated as seriously as a public commission. On a Sunday, he made his way from Paris to Trois Arbres and tried unsuccessfully to locate the cemetery. The next day with the help of a local woman, he visited the cemetery, located the grave, and dedicated it. A few weeks later he penned a tender report to Gertrude, including a detailed description of the cemetery and a photograph of the grave. He reported, "I offered the dedicatory prayer in which we remembered with heartfelt solicitations the little woman who kept her promise to her soldier husband and return[ed] to his people with her only son." He wished Gertrude peace and happiness. Several years after experiencing the apostle's kindness, she joined the church.[17]

James E. Talmage, McKay's replacement, arrived in Liverpool early in November. McKay oriented the new president, and together they attended a conference in London where McKay introduced Talmage to the presidents of the fifteen districts, or conferences, in Britain. McKay also introduced Talmage to the American consul-general, Horace Washington, and showed Talmage church properties and other potential building sites. On December 6 he and his family boarded the ship that would carry them across the Atlantic. Their two-year mission had concluded, and McKay now solidly understood the church's condition and needs across Europe.[18]

17. DOMD, Oct. 19–20, 1924; Gertrude Wineera to Elder McKay, [December 1921?], box 7, folder 8, McKay Papers; David O. McKay to Mrs. Hohepa Wineera, Nov. 13, 1924, box 1, folder 12, McKay Papers; "391 Lance Corporal Hoani Te Okoro WiNeera," Porirua War Stories, poriruawarstories.com; entry for Gertrude Victoria Kemp [Wineera], LKG6-MK4, Family Search, familysearch.org.

18. DOMD, Nov. 4–11, 1924; Hopfenbeck, "After Fond Adieus," 792.

In his tenure as mission president, McKay largely fulfilled two of the major goals he set for himself at the outset and made some progress on the third. He largely realized his first goal of visiting and encouraging members and missionaries. He did so by traveling almost weekly to be with them. As one missionary, Martin Hopfenbeck, editorialized in the *Millennial Star*, McKay engaged in almost "continual travel" to be with the members and missionaries. He had a remarkable ability to "remember faces and names" and "it was his pride to know each Elder in the field." His encouragement and instruction extended to organizational matters, where Sunday Schools and Mutual Improvement Associations were "following as nearly as possible the outlines prescribed by the general boards." The McKays encouraged members to adapt, though, where general procedures and lesson outlines were "inapplicable." He had tried to standardize religious practices, discouraging rituals such as dedicating the water prior to a baptism or stating, "If you will now give attention, we will ask the blessing" on the sacrament, and he had instructed priesthood holders to recite the sacrament prayers from memory rather than reading them. Baptisms increased modestly, and the presidents of the conferences credited much of the increase to the missionary efforts of members. The mission reported 615 baptisms in 1923–24—far from the idealistic goal of one baptism for each of the 5,000 adult members of record but up from 447 in 1920–21. Indeed, the number of baptisms in Britain in 1924 was greater than in any year over the previous decade.[19]

Through his sermons and editorials printed in the *Millennial Star*, McKay advanced his second goal of promulgating Christianity and peace in war-torn Europe. His direct audience was largely limited to church members and those who were studying with the missionaries, but he used the media available to him. He made modest progress toward his third goal of enhancing the reputation of Utah and the Latter-day Saints. He had worked diligently to do so by meeting with government leaders and communicating with newspaper publishers and editors. Whenever the subject of polygamy arose in casual conversation, he refuted allegations that the church continued the practice. As he reported to the First Presidency, by the end of his mission, street meetings were held

19. "Apostle and Mrs. D. O. M'Kay Guests at Farewell Party," *Ogden Standard Examiner*, Nov. 3, 1922, 16; Hopfenbeck, "After Fond Adieus," *Millennial Star*, Dec. 11, 1924, 793–95; Morrell, *Highlights*, 76; David O. McKay, "The Ordinance of Baptism," *Millennial Star*, May 24, 1923, 329; David O. McKay, "Administering the Sacrament," *Millennial Star*, July 10, 1924, 440; David O. McKay, "Good-bye Nineteen Twenty-Three," *Millennial Star*, Dec. 27, 1923, 824; "Statistical Report of the British Mission for the Year Ending December 31st, 1920," *Millennial Star*, Mar. 3, 1921, 135; "Statistical Report of the British Mission for the Year Ending December 31st, 1921," *Millennial Star*, Mar. 16, 1922, 167; "Statistical Report of the British Mission for the Year Ending November 30, 1923," *Millennial Star*, Mar. 13, 1924, 167; "Statistical Report of the British Mission for the Year Ending December 31st, 1924," *Millennial Star*, Mar. 19, 1925, 183. *Millennial Star* did not print a mission statistical report for 1922 in March 1923.

regularly "without molestation" in most places, and worship services and proselytizing in rented halls had proceeded without a single interruption for two years. "Leading newspapers now [refused] to print scandalous articles about the Mormons" and attendance at conferences had increased considerably.[20]

20. Morrell, *Highlights*, 76.

7: Seasoned Apostle

The McKays arrived at the train station in Ogden on the winter solstice and were met there by their extended family. "Weather cold, but warm welcome at station, warm and heartfelt," McKay noted. They spent a quiet Christmas morning at home and later dined with extended family at the home of McKay's sister Jeanette. Over the holidays he visited Huntsville, toured a new gymnasium at Weber Stake Academy, and celebrated with friends at numerous dinner parties.[1]

The apostle soon returned to his office in Salt Lake. In a meeting with the First Presidency and in the quarterly conference of the Quorum of the Twelve, he reported on the status of missionary work in Europe and recommended changes to the missionary program. The church was wasting money by renting halls for services, he observed. It would be better to purchase lots and construct chapels. This recommendation, a legacy of his service as mission president, would be fully implemented decades later and become a hallmark of his administration as church president. He recommended that the Swiss-German Mission be divided (a new Austrian and German mission was created later that year), that a general authority visit each foreign mission at least annually, and that the church discontinue its standing practice of expecting the apostle called to preside over the European Mission to also serve as president of the British Mission. The work was simply too great. A separate individual should be appointed to head the British Mission, as was the case in each mission on the Continent. (This was done in 1928.) The Church was barely established in France, he said, but small branches were slowly growing in Switzerland, and congregations of respectable size worshipped in Amsterdam. The church had a foothold in Syria and was growing "rapidly" in Belgium. But it was in Germany that "the work [was] growing by leaps and bounds." Conferences there were well-attended, and choirs of 75 to100 furnished music for the services. In Berlin, 1,286 Saints and friends had recently attended a district conference.[2]

Although the decade following McKay's tenure as mission president is unevenly documented, with large gaps in his diaries, it is clear that he settled in

1. DOMD, Dec. 21, 25, 1924, Jan. 1–3, 1925.

2. DOMD, Jan. 12, 1925; Morrell, *Highlights*, 76. McKay's report on the church's growth in individual nations, as recorded in the April general conference, reiterated information he shared with general church leaders. David O. McKay, address of Apr. 4, 1925, *Conference Reports*, 13–14.

to a routine. He generally visited stake conferences or stake Sunday School conventions three weekends each month. He met weekly with the Quorum of Twelve Apostles, followed by a joint council meeting with the First Presidency and the Quorum of the Twelve. Occasionally the First Council of Seventy joined in the Thursday meetings. On one such occasion, Seventy B. H. Roberts, "tried to convert" the Quorum of the Twelve to the idea that "Seventies have more authority than High Priests." For some time, Roberts had lobbied the prophet on this point, marshaling scripture and quotations from Joseph Smith and Brigham Young to argue that "what the Apostles can do the Seventy can do," including ordaining stake presidents, setting apart bishoprics and stake presidencies, and performing marriages. He cherished Brigham Young's statement recorded in the manuscript history of the church that "the Seventy were ordained Apostles and when they went forth into the ministry they went with power to build up the kingdom in all the world, and consequently they have power to ordain High Priests and also to ordain a High Council." Although Roberts presented apt documentary evidence, the First Presidency and the apostles were unmoved. McKay reported tartly, "He failed." On Tuesdays, McKay met with committees including the Church Board of Education, the Sunday School Superintendents, and the Sunday School General Board. He played a key role in establishing a missionary home in Salt Lake where newly called missionaries would receive instruction prior to their departure for the field. He taught outgoing missionaries "what it means to be a missionary" and devoted several hours each week to setting them apart.[3]

McKay also accepted sensitive and consequential ad hoc committee assignments. In 1929 he served on a committee with George Albert Smith, Joseph Fielding Smith, Stephen L Richards, and Melvin J. Ballard to review B. H. Roberts's book manuscript *The Truth, the Way, the Life: An Elementary Treatise on Theology*. Roberts traced the plan of salvation in detail in this manuscript, which he intended for curricular use in the church. He regarded it as his magnum opus, a "harvest of all that I have thought, and felt and written through the nearly fifty years of my ministry ... on the theme of the title." McKay and his colleagues on the committee met twice weekly over multiple months to discuss and evaluate the manuscript in light of scripture, the teachings of the temple, and official messages of the First Presidency. While they approved of most of the manuscript, they felt that Roberts's treatment of topics including pre-Adamite beings on the earth and God's progression in knowledge countered scripture or were conjectural. Wary of doctrinal speculation, they opined conservatively that "the general authorities ... should not present as doctrine that which is not sustained in the standards of the Church." Joseph Fielding

3. DOMD, Mar. 9, 1932, Jan. 13, Mar. 5, 12, 1925, Jan. 8, Mar. 31, 1926; Roberts, *Autobiography of B. H. Roberts*, 250–53.

Smith, the most impassioned critic on the committee, furnished many of the scriptural references and arguments that figured in the committee report. Roberts had posited that in the physical creation, Adam was "the first flesh" on the earth, placed there before the plants and animals. The committee objected to his reasoning because it countered the account of the creation found in the scriptures and in the temple. They dismissed Roberts's speculation that God continues to learn new principles as fields of knowledge develop. "While we believe in eternal progression and that God is progressing, it is not in quest of hidden truth or laws yet undiscovered to Deity," they wrote. Roberts's notion of a pre-Adamite race, wiped out by a cataclysmic disaster prior to the appearance of Adam and Eve, was "not sustained in the scriptures" and would provoke "endless controversy." Committee members tried to persuade Roberts to edit the manuscript to address their concerns. Roberts made a few small changes but refused to undertake fundamental ones. By July, McKay was beginning to look elsewhere for a Sunday School manual for the following year, fearful that Roberts would not eliminate "the personal opinions which do not conform to the revelations of the Lord." The theological duel between Roberts and Smith continued to play out intermittently before McKay and the rest of the apostles over two more years. Due to the impasse, the manuscript remained unpublished.[4]

Following the sudden death of the presiding patriarch, Hyrum G. Smith, in 1932, the First Presidency asked McKay, along with George F. Richards and James E. Talmage, to serve on a committee to identify the patriarch's "rightful successor." Hyrum's oldest son, Eldred, was only twenty-five years old at the time, and although he was faithful and had served an honorable mission, he lacked gravitas. McKay therefore opposed his appointment and, along with Richards, supported Grant in his inclination to appoint his son-in-law Willard Smith, who was then forty-seven years old. Many in the quorum opposed Grant's proposal, though, and consequently Grant chose to leave the position vacant.[5]

McKay shared with his fellow apostles the responsibility of visiting missions in North America. Generally, he spent between two and four weeks each year on these visits. In 1925 he toured the Eastern States Mission, holding almost daily meetings. The next year he spent a week visiting congregations in eastern Nevada and investigating the feasibility of establishing a small, far-flung stake headquartered in Ely. Later that year he toured the Southern States Mission and presided in meetings of missionaries and members in Virginia, North

4. Allen, "Story of *The Truth*," in Roberts, *The Truth, The Way*, clxxi-clxxxviii; "Doctrinal points questioned by the Committee which read the Manuscript of Elder B. H. Roberts, entitled—The Truth, the Way, The Life," quoted in Roberts, *The Truth, The Way*, 297, 418; Rudger Clawson to George Albert Smith et al., Oct. 3, 1928, *Minutes of the Apostles*, 4:285; George Albert Smith to Rudger Clawson et al., Oct. 10, 1929, *Minutes of the Apostles*, 4:287–90.

5. Grant, *Diaries of Heber J. Grant*, 365–66 (Mar. 26, 29, 31, Apr. 1, 1932); DOMD, Mar. 31, 1932; Bates and Smith, *Lost Legacy*, 173–80.

Carolina, Kentucky, Georgia, and Florida. The two-day conference in Atlanta was typical, consisting of "six meetings—six addresses [by McKay], besides special dinners, socials, etc." In 1927, he visited branches, districts, and missionaries in the Central States Mission. On some of these tours, McKay managed to break away for sightseeing. In the Southern States Mission he visited Stone Mountain, a massive slab of exposed granite where the United Daughters of the Confederacy had commissioned a giant panoramic sculpture to honor Confederate war heroes. Reflecting the prevailing quest of white Americans of his generation to achieve a reconciliation of former Unionists and Confederates, a goal that swept Black Americans and their civil rights to the margins of Civil War history, McKay was impressed by both the scale and intent of the proposed monument to honor those "who fought so sincerely and so heroically for what they thought was right," but he wished for an equally heroic monument on the other side of the cliff, a monument to Northern soldiers and their ideal of the Union's "imperishability." In 1929, McKay visited the Canadian Mission for several weeks, an exhausting ordeal. A week and a half into his tour he wrote Ray, "I am wearying of meetings! meetings, meetings, from one to five every day but one, for ten successive days, and the end not yet in sight." He vowed to "not accept another such schedule" because of the strain. Four days later, after his twenty-fifth meeting, he hinted at the pressure in a letter to Ray: "Traveling thousands of miles and attempting to keep speaking powers on 'high speed' on an average of twice a day for two weeks requires an expenditure of more nerve energy than some people think." He found it challenging to be ready constantly to inspire and motivate members and missionaries. Nevertheless, McKay did his best to serve the Saints and enhance the church's reputation. On one occasion, the apostle accompanied Mission President Charles Hart to a hospital in Ottawa to administer to a missionary. The assistant superintendent there treated them "contemptuously," and McKay stood up for his rights as was his custom when faced with religious bigotry. He protested the treatment and exposed the underlying religious prejudice in letters addressed to both the assistant superintendent and the mayor. When McKay read his draft letters to Hart, the mission president "seemed a bit frightened and mildly suggested some gentler terms instead of 'insult', 'ignorance', 'bigotry' etc."[6]

For nearly twenty years following his call as an apostle, McKay had commuted between Ogden and Salt Lake. Prior to their mission, he and Ray had considered moving to Salt Lake but decided to remain to accommodate Llewelyn, who desired to graduate from Weber Stake Academy. Now, memories of the wearisome commute between church headquarters and Ogden, the fact that

6. DOMD, Aug. 9–15, 1925, Nov. 21–26, 1926; McKay and McKay, *Heart Petals*, 109, 116; McKay, *My Father*, 173–75, 180, 182; "Apostle M'Kay Writes of Tour," *Ogden Standard Examiner*, Dec. 17, 1926, 3.

their oldest children who attended Weber Stake Academy were now grown, Lawrence's residence in Salt Lake, and the fact that Ray's dearest relatives on her side of the family were also there made relocating all the more attractive. The three children at home were still in elementary school. It would be easier to uproot now than when they were teenagers. Ray's cousin Belle helped them locate a commodious apartment north of Temple Square, and the family moved in nearly a year after they returned from Europe. David and Ray celebrated their move by walking down the street to attend the performance of Handel's *Messiah* in the tabernacle on New Year's Day, 1926. They viewed the apartment as a way station until they could save enough for a home. For the time being, finances were tight because they had not yet sold the house in Ogden. In 1934, a financially desperate time for most Americans, they examined several properties on the east side of Salt Lake but could not find one they liked in their price range. Finally, after selling their house in Ogden in 1939, they closed on a substantial box-style house at a prominent address down the street from grand mansions and the Salt Lake Temple itself, 1037 East South Temple Street.[7]

What the McKays lacked in money in the 1920s and 1930s they made up for in prestige and personality. Within a six-month period between December 1927 and June 1928, the McKays' three oldest children, Lou Jean, Llewelyn, and Lawrence, married. Although romantic attachments governed their marriage choices, each child dated peers from prominent families, and from his niece Flora McKay Crawford's perspective, McKay influenced the three older children's selection of spouses. Lou Jean married Russell Blood, the son of Minnie and Henry H. Blood, a prominent businessman, politician, and stake president who would be elected governor of Utah in 1932. Lawrence married Mildred Dean Calderwood, the daughter of Emily and William Calderwood, a wealthy Salt Lake obstetrician, president of the Utah State Medical Association, and medical director of the Beneficial Life Insurance Company. Llewelyn married Alice Kimball Smith, the daughter of Heber and Lileth Smith, the caretakers of Joseph Smith's birthplace in Vermont, and a granddaughter of President Joseph F. Smith. Shortly before Lou Jean's wedding, McKay wrote her a note while traveling on church business. He later informed Ray that "tears began to blur my eyes so I had to bring it to an abrupt close." He explained, "The first break in our lovely, charming family group gives me a feeling in my heart akin to a pang."[8]

McKay enjoyed taking the younger children who were still at home on outings, generally to Huntsville. He spent parts of New Year's Day and Washington's

7. McKay, *My Father*, 175; DOMD, Jan. 1, 1926, undated notes from pocket diary 1934, May 24, 1939; Bringhurst, "Private versus Public," 23.

8. Entries for Heber Chase Smith, Sr., KWCW-657, William Robert Calderwood, KWJ8-VNT, and Henry Hooper Blood, KWCW-K53, Family Search, familysearch.org; McKay and McKay, *Heart Petals*, 110.

Birthday in 1932 sledding in Huntsville with Ed and Bobby. After the snow melted, their outings to the McKay homestead often doubled as work parties. Emma Rae and Bobby joined him in planting potatoes on Memorial Day.[9]

McKay's coworkers in church administration shared his allegiance to the church, but their strong personalities sometimes clashed, breeding resentments in a hierarchical organization where those at the top expected loyalty from their subordinates. By virtue of his assignments and associations, McKay was pulled in to these disputes and had to take sides in unpleasant controversies. Often, he attempted to play the role of peacemaker. In 1931–33, it fell to McKay, as advisor to the Primary Association, to work with Presiding Bishop Sylvester Cannon to resolve an acrimonious dispute over management of the Primary Children's Hospital. The dispute pitted Primary board member Emily Smith Stewart, a daughter of Apostle George Albert Smith, against Primary General President May Anderson. In a meeting where Stewart and her fellow board member Vilate Raile aired their grievances, Anderson pulled rank, and the rest of the board loyally rallied to President Anderson's defense. Stewart complained she had been "crucified" in the meeting. A couple of weeks later, in a "very unpleasant" interview with Anderson, her counselors, and Stewart, McKay and Cannon broached the possibility of releasing Stewart if she refused to "set herself right." A follow-up meeting was scheduled for the next day to try and effect a reconciliation, but in the hours before the meeting Stewart complained to her father. "Sorely grieved at the injustice," George Albert Smith phoned McKay and informed him that he had "prohibited" his daughter from attending the meeting McKay had called. McKay believed Smith's stand was "most certainly inimical to his daughter's interests." Two months later, the First Presidency announced their decision to uphold McKay and Cannon's recommendation by releasing Stewart and Raile. The aggrieved women continued to press for apologies and reinstatement, though. At year's end, George Albert Smith sought out McKay, hoping to convince the apostle that his daughter's release had been ill-conceived. "I fear he [McKay] doesn't realize the attitude he assumes may be wrong," Smith wrote. On February 2, 1933, as a last resort, the devoted father petitioned the First Presidency to intervene and "correct" the mistake that had been made by "vindicat[ing]" Emily and Vilate Raile. President Grant refused to budge. Privately he confided to McKay that "if the father and husband and relatives would tell these girls to behave themselves and quit talking it would be a great blessing. I fear serious consequences if they do not." McKay and Cannon did agree to meet once more with Raile, Stewart, their husbands, and President Anderson. In the meeting Anderson agreed to excise from the minutes statements that were critical of the two women, but she would go no further. As

9. DOMD, Jan. 1, Feb. 22, May 13, 25, 1932.

McKay pointed out, reappointing the two women to the board would be no more than a face-saving "farce." After two more months, under pressure from Grant, Smith agreed to drop the matter. "I know how hard it is for parents to judge their own," Grant wrote sympathetically.[10]

At the same time that McKay was trying to mediate the dispute between Anderson and Stewart, he was drawn by assignment into another contest of wills between his best friend and fellow apostle Stephen L Richards and President Grant, a man whom he revered above all others and felt duty bound to sustain. The conflict stemmed from Richards's thoughtful sermon in the April 1932 general conference entitled "Bringing Humanity to the Gospel." In his talk, the apostle inveighed against "dictatorial dogmatism, rigidity of procedure and intolerance." He celebrated change and tolerance. "I would not hang on to a practice or conception after it has outlived its usefulness in a new and ever-changing and better-informed world," he said, pointing out that the church was "a live, vital institution." For example, "some important changes in the ordinances, form, and methods have been made in recent years." This phrase, with its oblique reference to recent changes in sacred rituals, seemed ill-advised to some church leaders. More objectionable to Grant, though, were some of Richards's statements about the Word of Wisdom, an emotionally fraught topic in view of the heated nationwide debate over Prohibition. Although he said nothing directly about alcohol, Richards expressed sympathy for members who struggled with addictions to tobacco, tea, coffee, "and other harmful beverages." He acknowledged the "tremendous temptations" young members faced to indulge in these substances with "the appeal of brilliant, seductive advertising, the universality of the practice, the ridicule you must endure to stand out almost alone." Richards called upon parents and church leaders to be understanding; he feared that well-meaning zealots had "estranged many from the Church or at least contributed to their estrangement by attributing to violation of our stands of health, harmful as it may be, a moral turpitude and sinful magnitude out of proportion of the real seriousness of the offense." Although he stressed that he had "no intention to lower standards" and that he would not "abandon the campaign against cigarette smoking, tea and coffee drinking," he stated that he would "modify the campaign and the counsel and surround the campaign and the counsel with safeguards which I think have been lacking." He would explain the hazards of smoking but not disparage the smoker.[11]

10. DOMD, Jan. 8, 11–13, Mar. 3, Apr. 18, May 31, 1932; George Albert Smith, diary, Dec. 30–31, 1932; Feb. 2, 3, Mar. 21, 23, Apr. 1, 1933 in *Minutes of the Apostles*, 3:319–24; Pusey, *Builders of the Kingdom*, 288–89; Grant, *Diaries of Heber J. Grant*, 377–79, (Feb. 2, 3, Mar. 21, 23, Apr. 1, 1933); Woodger, *Against the Odds*, 162.

11. Stephen L Richards, "Bringing Humanity to the Gospel," *Sunstone,* May–June 1979, 43–46. The published version differs slightly from the version that was delivered. Some differences are discussed in Joseph Geisner, "Very Careless," *Sunstone Magazine Podcast*, sunstone.org.

Some general church leaders and mission and stake presidents feared Richards's remarks in conference might give license to disobedience, and Grant felt Richards had spoken out of turn by stating that he would "modify" the church's campaign. Following the session, the First Presidency and Quorum of the Twelve met to discuss whether the talk could be "published in full at this time." Ultimately, they determined the answer was no. Grant tasked a doctrinal hard liner, Joseph Fielding Smith, and Richards's best friend, McKay, with working with Richards to edit the talk for publication. It was a thankless task. The full quorum considered the talk again on April 28 but came to no resolution. The following week in a heated interchange, Richards announced to his brethren that he would resign his apostolic office before he would bowdlerize the text. Grant pulled McKay aside and remarked that Richards had "made a mistake when he delivered that address, but today he made a fool of himself." Caught between his loyalty to his friend, whose actions had been impugned, and his covenantal obligation to uphold Grant, McKay kept his own counsel. The prophet provided Richards with some time to reflect and privately opined that Richards would eventually recant. Three weeks later a penitent Richards confessed to Grant that "he had made a mistake by preaching." The confession made Grant "very happy." Fearing that publication of an edited version of the speech, with an explanatory note, would draw undue attention to the excised portions, Grant determined to "let the matter drop and if it doesn't appear in the Conference Pamphlet it will soon be forgotten that the speech was made." A compromise was effected; Richards would not have to edit his remarks, but the church would not publish the talk.[12]

In the decade following his return from the European Mission, McKay acquitted himself ably in his responsibilities, including these delicate mediating and peacemaking assignments, earning President Grant's confidence and respect. Even in his relations with fellow apostles in matters pertaining to the patriarch to the church, the leadership of the Primary, and the content of conference talks, he loyally upheld Grant's perspective and direction. His judgment in matters pertaining to doctrine, including the conjectural interpretations of B. H. Roberts, was safely conservative. He would soon receive a new calling that would reorient his church service.

12. DOMD, Apr. 26, 28, May 5, 1932; Geisner, "Very Careless," *Sunstone Magazine Podcast*, sunstone.org; Grant, *Diaries of Heber J. Grant*, 306–7; *Minutes of the Apostles*, 4:318.

8: A New Calling: Counselor to Heber J. Grant

By 1934, after serving for twenty-eight years as an apostle, McKay's arduous routine had become familiar and therefore manageable. That changed in the fall. On a gorgeous Thursday afternoon, the McKays motored up Big Cottonwood Canyon as the guests of Heber J. and Hulda Grant to enjoy the vibrant fall foliage. Whenever the McKays spent time in the mountains, it was in Huntsville, so this was David and Ray's first visit to the majestic canyon, and they were enthralled. As they returned from the outing, little did they suspect that their connections to the prophet would change markedly within a week. Grant's first counselor, Anthony Ivins, had celebrated his eighty-second birthday just a few days earlier. Although Ivins's strength had flagged lately, he seemed essentially healthy and was planning to take a short fishing trip later in the month. Late on Friday, though, Ivins suffered a serious heart attack and passed away early Sunday morning.[1]

Ivins's death left a vacancy in the First Presidency just two weeks before general conference. After the funeral on September 27, Grant conferred with his remaining counselor, J. Reuben Clark, to discuss a possible replacement. Clark deferred to the prophet, saying that "anyone whom you want will suit me." Grant replied that his "mind had rested upon Brother McKay," and Clark concurred: "I am very glad; he is the man that I had thought of and would like. I started with the head of the quorum, and when I got to Brother McKay, I did not have a desire to go further." Grant phoned McKay and asked to meet with him. When McKay arrived at the prophet's home, the two exchanged pleasantries, and then without warning Grant called the apostle to serve as his second counselor. McKay recorded that he was "entirely overcome," but after regaining his composure, he accepted the call. Following a lengthy visit, the two men embraced, and Grant bestowed an affectionate kiss. The prophet recorded, "I felt sure he would do all in his power to aid in fulfilling the duties of the Presidency of the Church." McKay likely shared the news with Ray, but she made no mention of it to their children. On Conference Sunday, October 6, McKay

1. DOMD, Sep. 20, 1934; "Venerable L.D.S. Leader Succumbs to Heart Attack," *Roosevelt Standard,* Sep. 27, 1934, 1.

was sustained in his new calling. Later that day Ray wrote to Lawrence of the "wonderful honor that has come to your father." People coming up to congratulate him had stated, "it has been the universal prayer since Pres. Ivins died that David O. should be chosen the new counselor." Later that month McKay wrote to his children, "Recently there came to me the highest honor and greatest responsibility of my life.... Hundreds of letters and telegrams ... have brought congratulatory messages.... I have noted that in many of these messages your loving mother is included.... I want at least her loved ones to know that she rightfully shares in *all* achievements and honors." Without her toleration of his many absences, her steady hand in managing the household and the children, her service with him in the European Mission, and her faith in him and in the church, he could not have performed his duties so capably. In a patriarchal organization where male priesthood leaders are honored and sustained by virtue of their callings while their wives receive no sustaining vote and far less public recognition, McKay wanted his children not to underestimate their mother's essential and taxing role or the fact that his work was a mutual endeavor.[2]

The new calling placed even more demands upon McKay's time, limiting his interactions with his unmarried children. At the time of McKay's call to the First Presidency, Emma Rae was nearly twenty-one and was teaching speech and drama at Granite High School; Ed was turning nineteen and was studying medical science at the University of Utah; and Bob was fifteen and attending West High School. Ed and Bobby still accompanied McKay on work outings to the farm in Huntsville, and the three children enjoyed summer family vacations and fishing trips in Yellowstone and at Fish Lake, but there was little time for their other traditional outings. Emma Rae was delighted that her parents both managed to attend some of the high school plays she directed.[3]

The calling to the First Presidency shifted and expanded McKay's responsibilities. Gone were the routine assignments to preside and speak at stake conferences and Sunday School conventions, as were the weekly meetings with auxiliary boards. As second counselor in the First Presidency, McKay met regularly with the First Presidency and the Presiding Bishopric. As the preeminent governing body in the church, the First Presidency exercised broad administrative latitude, identified priorities, focused resources, and steered the church. As Francis M. Gibbons, secretary to a later First Presidency, explained in his biography of McKay, "While the Twelve confer regularly with the First Presidency in their weekly temple meetings, they usually are not privy to the wide range of Church responsibilities discharged by the latter, matters pertaining to finances,

2. Grant, *Diaries of Heber J. Grant*, 399 (Sep. 27, 1934); DOMD, Sep. 27, Oct. 11, 1934; McKay, *My Father*, 191–92, 195–96.

3. DOMD, July 11, Oct. 19, 1935, Aug. 13, 1937, Aug. 19–25, 1938, June 2, 1939; McKay, *My Father*, 198, 200.

physical facilities, personnel, temple work, public relations, and the myriad of activities carried on under the umbrella of the Corporation of the President."[4]

When McKay entered the presidency, Grant, nearly seventy-eight years old, needed the vigor and support of younger counselors. His first counselor, J. Reuben Clark, only two years older than McKay, was energetic, but under a unique arrangement supported by Grant, Clark worked in New York City as general counsel and later as president of the Foreign Bondholders Protective Council, a government entity tasked with recovering bond payments owed to American citizens by Europeans. This responsibility, in tandem with Clark's legal work for an oil company, kept him away from Salt Lake City on non-church business for over a third of the time during McKay's first decade in the First Presidency. While he was out of town, Clark corresponded frequently with McKay and Grant about Church business, but in his absence, much of the daily work devolved upon McKay, especially until 1940.[5]

Prior to McKay's call, Grant personally answered official correspondence addressed to him; shortly thereafter Grant began relying upon his counselors to answer most of the incoming letters. On an especially busy day in 1936, McKay replied to sixty-eight letters to the First Presidency. Returning to the office after an absence over the Christmas holidays later that year, he signed 150 letters in one day; some of those letters announced what he described as "important decisions."[6]

Working with the Presiding Bishopric, the First Presidency addressed all types of pecuniary matters related to the church, from financing chapels to investing funds in stock and bond markets. Grant and Clark possessed greater financial acumen and business expertise than McKay, but he was also required to participate in the regular board meetings of church-owned businesses, including Utah State National Bank, Zions Securities, the Hotel Utah, the Temple Square Hotel, the Heber J. Grant Co., Utah Home Fire Insurance Company, ZCMI, Zion's Savings Bank and Trust Company, and Beneficial Life Insurance Company. Over time he became familiar with the businesses' fiscal operations.[7]

Along with the other members of the First Presidency, McKay superintended the construction and administration of temples, the sites of the church's crowning rites. Seven temples operated when McKay entered the First Presidency, and the prophet was eager to build more. McKay and his colleagues investigated possible temple sites in Boise and Idaho Falls, Idaho, solicited and considered architectural plans for a temple in Los Angeles, California, and

4. Gibbons, *David O. McKay*, 170. The frequency of First Presidency meetings changed over time. Meetings were less frequent until 1938, when Grant announced that presidency meetings would be held on Monday, Wednesday, and Friday mornings. Grant, *Diaries of Heber J. Grant*, 424 (Dec. 9, 1938).

5. Quinn, *Elder Statesman*, 62–63, 65, 76, 110.

6. Quinn, *Elder Statesman*, 78; DOMD, June 1, 1936, Jan. 8, 1937.

7. DOMD, Apr. 14–15, 1936.

weighed (and ultimately rejected) an invitation from the Church of Christ (Temple Lot) for a jointly operated temple on the site designated by Joseph Smith for a temple in Independence, Missouri. The presidency brainstormed ways to enhance temple worship for younger adults, such as temple sessions with specialized instructions regarding temple symbolism, clothing, covenants, and rituals. Fearful that the temple failed to engage young members, McKay, the professional teacher, lamented that "so many young people have been disappointed after they have gone through the House of the Lord." They felt overwhelmed by the "mechanics" of the ceremony and "failed to comprehend the significance of the message." With better instruction and preparation, he hoped, young initiates would transcend the mechanics and focus instead on the importance of "cleanliness" of body and mind. The "clean linen" used in temple ritual "gives to man a sense of dignity, of purity, all through life" including "the eradication of every ill feeling" and "the elimination of every vulgar thought," he taught waves of new missionaries preparing to enter the temple. In the temple, volunteer workers with no professional training in acting represented Adam, Eve, and others as they portrayed the creation of the world and the story of the Garden of Eden, where "man entered into mortality ... and everything which man desired was placed before him." In observing the reenacted drama with amateur actors, he warned a group of new missionaries, "you may sit in your seat and criticize the man or the woman, if you wish; you may look at his dress and count the buttons; you may look at her dress and criticize. If you do, I am sorry for you. Or you may sit there and see through the symbolism" to deeper messages such as the battle between selfishness and self-denial. "Selfishness, the law of nature, would say, 'I want the best; that is mine.' But God said: 'Take the firstlings of the flock and offer a sacrifice unto me.' That is the story. The best shall be given to God; the next you may have. God is the Center." Spiritually attuned individuals would leave the experience "filled with a desire and determination to walk uprightly before God," McKay hoped.[8]

The First Presidency administered a large bureaucracy. They selected leaders for the church's auxiliaries and worked with the Quorum of the Twelve to select and call general authorities. McKay sustained Grant's personnel decisions, but as his confidence grew he counseled freely in the deliberations leading up to those decisions. When the prophet proposed the former president of the Southern States Mission, LeGrand Richards, as presiding bishop, McKay recommended someone whom he felt would "make a better executive," but he assured Grant that whatever he decided was "of course ... all right." McKay questioned the prophet's proposed call of May Green Hinckley as the new Primary general president because she was "not well enough educated." Later he

8. DOMD, Apr. 27, May 8, 1936, July 12, 1940; Anderson, "Mormon Modern"; Anderson, *LDS Temple Worship*, 264–69.

backpedaled; he had been thinking of "the wrong Hinckley," he said, and was "a hundred per cent for Sister Hinckley." In some cases the Quorum of the Twelve lobbied against the First Presidency's united administrative recommendations. In 1941, the presidency decided to call five additional apostles who would not be members of the Quorum of the Twelve but would shoulder some of the responsibilities that physically frail apostles could no longer fulfill. The five included McKay's brother Thomas. But when half of the members of the quorum objected, the five were designated instead as assistants to the Quorum of the Twelve in the April general conference even though Grant continued to feel it would be better to ordain them as apostles.[9]

Presidents McKay, Grant, and Clark oversaw the church's auxiliaries too, although members of the quorum served as immediate advisors. At one point Clark and McKay feared that the auxiliaries were "getting out of hand" and needed firmer direction. They fretted especially about the Sunday School, whose superintendent, George Pyper, had passed away recently, and the Young Men's Mutual Improvement Association, led by George Q. Morris, whose assistant, Joseph J. Cannon, was unable to provide the support Morris required. The counselors worried too that the church's reliance upon "expert" full-time employees threatened to "break down influence of Church leadership." McKay ruefully observed, "It does look as though we are getting into Commissions and Committees, just as the Government is doing." For decades while serving as church president, Joseph F. Smith had also served as general superintendent of the Sunday School. McKay suggested that he as a First Presidency member could pick up the reins of the auxiliary "without undue work" if he had a free hand to call new assistants and a new board. His position as superintendent would make him head of the church union board, which also would allow him to assist other auxiliary leaders more directly. After considering the breathtaking proposal, the prophet chose instead to call another talented educator and administrator, Milton Bennion, the dean of education at the University of Utah, as general Sunday School superintendent.[10]

In his fourth year in the First Presidency, McKay wound up in the hospital. While seated on the stand during the April general conference, he experienced stabbing pains in his side. Ray saw his grimaces and slipped out of the Tabernacle to call a doctor. The examination revealed a serious kidney infection. The infection worsened, and McKay endured five days in the hospital. By mid-May he still had not "fully regained [his] strength," he lamented. Finally, ten days

9. DOMD, Jan. 3, 1936; Grant, *Diaries of Heber J. Grant,* 421, 436 (Apr. 6, 1938, Dec. 14, 1939); *Minutes of the Apostles,* 4:372. The five were Marion G. Romney, Thomas E. McKay, Nicholas Smith, Alma Sonne, and Clifford Young.

10. DOMD, June 24, 1942, Jan. 27, 1943; Quinn, *Elder Statesman,* 123; "Dean Bennion Heads LDS Sunday School," *Salt Lake Telegram,* Mar. 2, 1943, 1.

of rest in California seemed to restore his vigor. Clark responded to the emergency by beginning to scale back his activities in New York.[11]

A year and a half later, near the end of 1939, McKay suffered a more protracted health setback due to a double hernia. McKay underwent surgery, and coming out of anesthesia he blurted, "I don't think it's worth it!" The truth of that drug-induced exclamation became painfully clear in the coming days. While convalescing in the hospital, he had difficulty breathing, caused by a clot blocking a pulmonary artery. He remained in the hospital until January 14, six weeks after his surgery, and he continued to experience severe lung pain, flu-like symptoms, and extended absences from the office for five full months. During that time President Grant suffered a debilitating stroke. With McKay still unable to fill his responsibilities, Clark reduced his legal activities even more and finally shouldered more than his share of the administrative burdens at church headquarters. Clark's biographer, D. Michael Quinn, has written that "from 1940 to 1945, Reuben was often the only member of the First Presidency at the office for weeks or months at a time." This is somewhat of an exaggeration, but McKay was absent from the office on church business for over a month late in 1940, and again in 1941 and in 1943. He also suffered a frightening attack of Ménière's Disease, complete with vertigo, violent nausea, and near unconsciousness in August 1941. But Clark also traveled on church business to Canada and the Pacific Northwest during those years. Nevertheless, Clark overshadowed McKay as an administrative leader in the 1940s.[12]

During these years of increasing health challenges, McKay's three youngest children married. In 1939, when McKay was nearly sixty-six, Emma Rae married Conway Ashton, the son of Rosabel and Elias Ashton. A prominent and wealthy Salt Lake attorney, Elias had passed away in an accident in 1919. Following his mission to Germany, Ed went to medical school, served as a doctor in the US Navy, and in 1942 married Lottie Lund, who had minimal background in the church and had only a few months earlier been sealed in the temple to her parents, Mary and Francis Lund. After Bob completed his mission to Argentina and service in the US Army, he married Frances Ellen Anderson, the daughter of Nettie and Edward O. Anderson, head architect for the church. Bob recalled that his father "let me have my free agency ... when it came to choosing a companion." McKay took great pride in each of his children's accomplishments. On his forty-third wedding anniversary, he rejoiced that all six children who had lived to adulthood had graduated with a bachelor's degree from the University of Utah. Education mattered to him.[13]

11. DOMD, Apr. 3, 4, 11, 16–21, May 13, 19, 30, 1938; Quinn, *Elder Statesman*, 86–87.

12. McKay, *My Father*, 207; DOMD, Dec. 1, 31, 1939, Jan. 14, Apr. 7, Nov.–Dec. 1940, Aug., Nov. 1941; Quinn, *Elder Statesman*, 92.

13. McKay, *My Father*, 208–9; entries for Conway Alan Ashton, KWC6-GVD, and Francis

In his role as a member of Heber J. Grant's First Presidency, McKay devoted a great deal of time to advising leaders of congregations, stakes, and missions on a variety of challenging issues involving members. One Southern stake president appealed for advice after church members asked their bishop to bar two Black members from attending a bi-ward Relief Society activity. Although segregation was routine in many Southern cities at the time, Grant and his counselors warned that the women should not be excluded from the activity. Instead, they suggested a bitter compromise, acquiescing to the prejudice of the white complainants: the bishop should "discretely approach" the Black members and ask them to "sit at one side or in the rear or somewhere where they would not wound the sensibilities of the complaining sisters." One bishop contacted McKay for help in mediating a dispute between two families in his ward over ownership of a strip of land. McKay recommended that the families engage a surveyor to resolve the matter. If those in the wrong rejected the survey, the rightful owners would then be justified in going to court, he advised. Another bishop asked how to counsel a recently returned veteran who had become "embittered" and wanted to renounce his church membership. McKay tried to interpret the veteran's disillusionment in a broader context: "a little learning is a dangerous thing, and these young men think because they have a little knowledge, they know everything." Local leaders also sought McKay's counsel on difficult worthiness matters. A stake president requested advice before ordaining a seventy-year-old man, a "good husband, and honorable citizen," to the Melchizedek priesthood; the man qualified fully aside from his smoking habit. McKay advised the stake president to tell the brother "that they would like him to set the example to the Elders, some of whom are now using tobacco." He was "not to exact a definite promise [as a precondition to ordination], but [to] appeal to him to conform more fully to the teachings of the Priesthood." Local leaders who were themselves downhearted also sought relief. One "very depressed" stake president whose two daughters were suffering from tuberculosis wondered if it was time, after six years of faithful service, for him to be released. McKay promised that the authorities would pray for the two daughters in the temple and consider the man's request. A few months later he received an honorable release.[14]

As a counselor in the First Presidency, McKay made three to four out-of-state trips per year on church business. Now that their children were grown, Ray regularly traveled and spoke alongside him. On these trips he spoke at

---

Lorenzo Lund, KWCD-PL2, Family Search, familysearch.org; "Edward O. Anderson Gets Church Post," *Ogden Standard Examiner*, Nov. 20, 1943, 1; DOMD, Jan. 2, 1944; Robert McKay, remarks delivered at David O. McKay Symposium, Brigham Young University, Oct. 1996, box 22, folder 23, Prince Papers.

14. *Minutes of the Apostles*, 4:389; DOMD, Aug. 18, 1939, Aug. 21, 1940, Feb. 8, 1944, Dec. 7, 1949; entry for Carl Daniel Greenhalgh, KWZM-M1P, Family Search, familysearch.org.

conferences or dedicated chapels in Chicago, Indianapolis, New York, Portland, San Francisco, Sacramento, and Washington, DC, among other cities. In 1938, under assignment from President Grant, he and Ray visited the Sacred Grove and Hill Cumorah, Joseph Smith's birthplace, Nauvoo, and Carthage. In Palmyra, New York, they witnessed a pageant, attended by thousands, entitled *America's Witness for Christ*, written by H. Wayne Driggs. McKay delighted in the "elegant" costumes and "impressive" performance. The evening concluded with a dramatic depiction of Jesus that reminded him of the scripture, "Come unto me ... and I will give you rest" (Matthew 11:28). Addressing the cast of missionaries, McKay enumerated concrete "reasons for accepting Joseph Smith's testimony," including the tangibility of the golden plates, the testimonies of the three and eight witnesses, and the quality of the Book of Mormon itself. In 1941, he visited Hawai'i on church business and dedicated a new stake tabernacle on O'ahu with a beautifully landscaped courtyard and an imposing 141-foot tower. At the dedication, only a few months before bombs would fall on Pearl Harbor, he delivered President Grant's warning to the Hawai'ian members of coming "days of trouble" and the "trials which follow" and pled, "May the Lord bless and preserve you." A favorite conference assignment for McKay was visiting the Teton Stake in southeastern Idaho. In both 1935 and 1942 he presided at that stake's conferences, followed by a day or two of fishing. In 1942, he and Ray accompanied his brother Thomas and Bishop Joseph L. Wirthlin to the stake. After arising early on Monday, they drove to a site along the Gros Ventre River where they breakfasted on fish, fried potatoes, bread, butter, and jam. The men spent the day fishing while the women visited Jenny Lake in the Tetons. That evening, they enjoyed a chicken dinner in the mountains.[15]

Second Counselor McKay spoke and represented the church and prophet at religious gatherings, civic events, and funerals. His evident love of people, affability, gift for storytelling, use of poetry, optimism, and ability to discern God's hand in everyday life particularly endeared him to the Saints, and he was much in demand as a speaker and officiator at weddings. In a single week in 1935, he performed fourteen temple weddings. McKay was a popular speaker at Sunday evening firesides, where he often spoke about courtship, marriage, and family life, articulating ideals of courtesy, honesty, chastity, and companionship. "God has instituted marriage and the family as the proper conditions of expressing in our lives the divine attribute of love," he counseled. He advised parents that "no other success can compensate for failure in the home," directing his advice especially at men: "When the club becomes more attractive to any man than his home, it is time for him to confess in bitter shame that he has failed to measure up to the supreme opportunity of his life and flunked in the final test of true

15. DOMD, Oct. 26–29, 1935, July 24, 1938, Aug. 17, 1941, Aug. 8, 1942.

manhood." He admonished, "Make home your hobby; for, if anyone makes a loving home with all his heart, he can never miss Heaven."[16]

McKay's profound spirituality enlivened his addresses. In one emotionally taxing speaking assignment on Christmas Sunday in 1938, President McKay ministered to the family and friends of twenty-four high school students who lost their lives in a train-bus collision in Salt Lake County, their bodies so torn and mangled that it was initially impossible to identify some of them. He praised the deceased students' relatives for their courage, quoted scriptural promises of peace and resurrection, and asked them to entrust their departed family members to God's care. "Let not your heart be troubled.... In my father's house are many mansions.... I go to prepare a place for you, that where I am, there ye may be also," the apostle read. At a reunion for missionaries of the Eastern States Mission who had served under President Frank Evans, who had recently died, McKay sensed that Evans's spirit was present. He cited scriptural examples of the thinness of the veil between life and the world of spirits to illustrate the possibility of Evans's presence, including the account of Christ's raising of Lazarus; the appearance of Jesus to Paul; and the ministration of Peter, James, and John to Joseph Smith. He then shared a lesser-known, modern example of contact with the spirit world: following his untimely death, twenty-year-old Arthur Wells, the son of a prominent Latter-day Saint couple, appeared to his mother, Almena[17]

Despite his gifts and popularity in public speaking, occasionally President McKay ate humble pie as a speaker, as at a fireside held in conjunction with the Chicago Stake conference in 1938. After thirteen musical numbers and addresses by members of the Sunday School and Primary General Boards, the time was spent. "I was the last speaker, and my remarks consisted of one sentence only," he recorded. Following a stake meeting in Vernal, Utah, where he spoke on "eternal verities in a changing world," he felt disappointed by his performance. "It was a very unimpressive talk and occupied too much time," he lamented. He felt better the next day about a talk he gave prior to dedicating a church building in which he honored those who had sacrificed to build the chapel, including a boy who contributed $225 he earned by washing cars, shining shoes, and selling newspapers.[18]

Until shortly before McKay's call to the First Presidency, rank-and-file members could walk into the Church Administration Building and obtain an audience with the prophet himself, as McKay had done in his youth with Wilford Woodruff. According to James Moyle, a prominent Utah politician,

---

16. DOMD, June 17–22, 1935, July 23, 1944, May, 2, 1937, Jan. 7, 1945; "Challenge Given to Church Youth," *Deseret News*, June 9, 1941, 1, 5.

17. "24 Killed in Bus Crash," *Salt Lake Telegram*, Dec. 1, 1938, 1; "Resurrection Explained to Bus Wreck Survivors," *Deseret News*, Dec. 26, 1938, 3; DOMD, Dec. 3, 1950.

18. DOMD, Feb. 25, 1938, July 23–24, 1949.

"when President Clark came upon the scene" in 1933, "the public was fenced out." Members could still walk into the administration building and gain an audience with a church authority, but access to members of the First Presidency was increasingly screened. McKay's secretary, Clare Middlemiss, abetted this screening. In the spring of 1935, just a few months after McKay's call to the presidency, Middlemiss, a twenty-four-year-old returned missionary working as a secretary in the Church Missionary and Financial Office, was appointed as McKay's secretary. Nervous about working under the thumb of such an eminent man, she considered turning down the transfer, but her supervisor, Arthur Winter, lectured her, "Sister, when the First Presidency speaks, you go." Quickly adapting to her new work environment, Middlemiss took charge of McKay's appointment book. Visitors lacking special credentials who desired to see the apostle in his office had to seek access through Middlemiss, unless they or their friends and family knew how to contact him directly.[19]

Despite the restricted access, many rank-and-file members still managed to meet with the counselor. To a greater degree than Clark or even President Grant, he appeared approachable and affable. As a reporter for the *Deseret News* observed, McKay was "known for his intimate acquaintanceship with hundreds of church members." In office consultations McKay dispensed advice related to major life decisions, an individually tailored ministry that required a blend of judgment, moral rectitude, respect for others' agency, and compassion. One visitor sought leave to propose marriage to someone who had returned prematurely from her mission for health reasons. McKay advised him to proceed. A couple sought advice on marital difficulties. At the end of their appointment, they committed to "try it again," each concentrating on overcoming their deficiencies and trying to cooperate for the sake of their son. McKay counseled the wife to stop gossiping about her husband and persuaded the husband to seek psychiatric help. A young woman sought President McKay's inspiration on whether she should serve a mission. He advised her to study French in college for a year and then return for more direction if she desired. Shortly after the United States entered World War II, a young man inquired if he should enlist in the US Marines or serve a mission. McKay replied that it was "a matter that he and his father must decide." Another member wondered if she should break her engagement after her fiancé confessed to a moral indiscretion. McKay told her that "if he has confessed and promises to do it no more, then if your own heart tells you to go ahead it is your right to do so." A recently widowed father of two toddlers called seeking advice about a married friend who wanted to divorce her husband, marry him, and raise his children. "You must not do it," McKay instructed, and the man discontinued the relationship. A recently widowed mother of two small children requested an audience with McKay to discuss her

19. Quinn, *Elder Statesman*, 78; Prince and Wright, *David O. McKay*, 406.

future. She hoped to leave her children in her relatives' care while she served a mission for the church. McKay advised her to "stay home" instead.[20]

McKay as counselor marshaled the priesthood and his revelatory capacity to minister to ailing members, including Rose Marie Liddle, a middle-aged schoolteacher who had raised her siblings after her parents died and now feared she was going blind. In the weeks after McKay blessed her, Liddle's vision markedly improved. Vivian Taylor, a fifty-six-year-old whose husband, Lester, had kidney problems, approached the counselor at a Saturday event at BYU and begged him to administer to Lester in their home. McKay explained that he had no time to visit but promised that the apostles would pray for Lester in their next council meeting. That evening while driving back to Salt Lake, he could not forget her look of disappointment, so the next day he made the one-hundred-mile round trip to Provo to bless Lester Taylor. A few months later doctors removed one of his kidneys; he remained active in business and lived for another thirteen years.[21]

In addition to his official responsibilities in the presidency, McKay proactively reached out to some in need. These private acts reflect a gentle desire to right wrongs and assist others. In 1942, he crossed paths with a troubled teenager. Police apprehended the fifteen-year-old high school freshman for taking McKay's car on a joy ride. A mechanic had inadvertently left the keys in the ignition outside the Church Administration Building. McKay, the former high school teacher, took an interest in the lad that redoubled when he learned of the boy's troubled home life. He interceded with the juvenile court system on behalf of the boy and met with him over several months in his office. When the court determined that the young man's mother was unable to care for him, McKay phoned the judge and the governor to secure a solid foster placement. McKay's efforts likely enhanced the boy's prospects. Although the boy eventually discontinued his meetings with McKay, his prospects improved. He graduated from high school and earned a bachelor's degree in California. Another person who benefited from McKay's voluntary outreach was Amy Brown Lyman. In 1943, church leaders excommunicated her husband, Apostle Richard R. Lyman, for adultery. Sister Lyman was serving as general president of the Relief Society at the time, the most prominent female leadership position in the Church. Humiliated by her husband's conduct and the public revelation of her private life, she stayed away from her office for over a week. When she did return, McKay "escorted her ... so that her return after the excommunication ...

20. "Pres. Smith Commends Workers Who Aid Project on Labor Day," *Deseret News*, Sep. 6, 1950, 40; DOMD, Jan. 8, 1941, Aug. 29, 1947, June 7, 1938, Dec. 11, 1941, Apr. 16, May 31, Sep. 13, 1945.

21. DOMD, May 22, Dec. 29, 1944, Mar. 12, 13, 1949; Vivian Taylor, "Lester R. Taylor History," KWC8-PWC, Family Search, familysearch.org.

would not be so difficult." Several weeks later, she called to thank him for "having assisted her in her distress" and "referred particularly to [McKay's] having taken her to her office, and having insisted on her performing her duties in order to get her mind off her troubles."[22]

While serving in the First Presidency, McKay's private ministry also extended to those beyond the church. In 1942 Tomiharu "Tom" Hiratzka, a Japanese American who had been forced to leave medical school in California, requested an appointment with McKay. He could legally leave the Japanese internment camp, Topaz Internment Camp, in Delta, Utah, to continue his education if he could obtain the necessary funds and a post away from the West Coast. Hiratzka was not a Latter-day Saint, but Mabel Mills, a placement officer with the War Relocation Authority, had advised him McKay was influential and might be willing to help him. McKay phoned his friend Laurence Ellison, president of the Utah Bankers Association and the Layton Sugar Company, and asked him to intercede to secure funding and a medical internship in Ogden for Hiratzka so that he could complete his training. It was "because of our intercession," McKay later noted, that Hiratzka "was able to finish his medical studies." Hiratzka went on to a distinguished career at Wayne State University and Wesley Hospital in Wichita, Kansas.[23]

During his tenure under President Grant in the First Presidency, McKay also ministered to acquaintances who became polygamists. Despite the church's efforts to stamp out polygamy, Mormon fundamentalism gathered steam about the time that McKay entered the presidency in the 1930s, as witnessed by the establishment of a new refuge for polygamists along the Utah-Arizona border at Short Creek, the formation of a vast network of cooperatives affiliated with the Kingston group based in Davis County, and a flowering of fundamentalist promotional literature. From his time as European mission president in the 1920s, McKay knew firsthand that rumors, let alone evidence, of persistent polygamy stymied the church's growth and poisoned its reputation.

McKay took a gentle, persuasive approach to the problem with his former academy student Charles Owen, who in 1928 married a second wife, Earline Hull. Owen's first wife died in 1931, returning him to the monogamous camp, but he reentered polygamy when he married Delsa Edgel against her parents' wishes in 1934. McKay tried to reclaim Owen, who credited the apostle with having persuaded him to return to school and earn a diploma after he dropped out as a teenager in 1905. Shortly after he entered polygamy for the first time, Owen asked McKay to read an article he had written on "the

22. DOMD, Nov. 9, 10, 17, Dec. 4, 1944, Jan. 4, 12, 16, 25, Feb. 9, 20, Mar. 2, 29, May 9, 1945; *University of California Register,* 87; DOMD, Nov. 20, 1943, Jan. 18, 1944.

23. DOMD, May 25, 1942, Jan. 17, 1948; for Tomiharu "Tom" Hiratzka, see "Obituaries—November–December 1998," *Stanford Magazine,* Nov.–Dec. 1998, stanfordmag.org.

fullness of the Gospel, including plural marriage." As Owen recalled, McKay complimented him on his research but warned him that it would be wrong to live the principle. In their conversation, Owen did not admit to having married polygamously, nor did McKay press him to do so, but Owen did ask McKay a hypothetical question: if in fact he had two wives, would McKay advise him to turn the second out of his home? Owen recalled McKay's reply: "No, every bit of manhood in my nature would rebel against that, but there should be no more children" born to the union. McKay did not pursue the matter further. A few years later in 1934, McKay heard rumors that Owen had taken another wife, but he did not seriously investigate until 1937, following the death of Owen's second wife Earline. By that time Owen's lifestyle was again monogamous. McKay spent much of one Sunday in 1938 working on the Owen case, likely in preparation for church disciplinary action, but he still hoped that his former student might be restored to church fellowship. Early in 1941, he met with the Owens repeatedly over a week's time and then phoned their bishop to apprise him of their progress. A month later Edgel and Owen legally married in Davis County. Eventually they were sealed for time and eternity in the temple.[24]

McKay could be more intrusive and dogged in his investigation of the polygamous marriages of others whom he did not know well, working with local church leaders and law enforcement officials. In 1934 he began investigating Price Johnson, a rancher in Short Creek, on the Utah-Arizona border, who reportedly proposed marriage to an eighteen-year-old as his fourth wife that year. The following year Arizona authorities, with encouragement from church leaders, arrested Johnson, his wife Helen, and four other residents of Short Creek. Additionally, the Zion Park Stake high council excommunicated twenty-one residents of Short Creek, including Johnson. McKay, who was monitoring the crackdown, reported on it to the Quorum of the Twelve and the First Presidency in a council meeting. Subsequently Johnson was convicted of unlawful cohabitation and sentenced to eighteen to twenty-four months in prison. McKay also monitored the activities of other polygamists, including Arnold Boss and Joseph Musser. In 1939, McKay reprimanded two bishops for not taking action against Clyde Neilson and Alonzo F. Cole after they published a tract seeking to legitimize and advocate plural marriage. In his attempts to ferret out polygamists as a member of the First Presidency, McKay interviewed relatives and associates of suspected polygamists. With help from her parents, McKay documented the marriage of eighteen-year-old Mary Athlene Mills to the prominent polygamist and naturopath Rulon C. Allred. McKay

24. DOMD, undated entry in 1934, Sep. 7, 1937, Nov. 20, 1938, Jan. 11, 16, 1941; "Charles Henry Owen," Davis County Cooperative Society, dccsociety.org; entry for Charles Henry Owen, KWCD-LNS, familysearch.org.

prepared a file documenting Allred's activities and relayed the information to Mills's bishop. In 1940, McKay tried unsuccessfully to persuade Virginia Budd Jacobsen, a returned missionary and former student body president at the University of Utah, to implicate her father, George Henry Budd, who was rumored (accurately) to be a closet polygamist and a recruiter for the fundamentalists. In 1942–43 he repeatedly interviewed Addie Athay, the wife of James Leroy Athay, and their daughter, Pauline, regarding James's alleged ties to fundamentalist leader and pamphleteer Joseph Musser.[25]

In addition to these dogged investigations of individuals, in 1937 McKay helped to expand hard-nosed institutional efforts to expose and discredit polygamists. President Clark engineered the probe, but McKay served as his loyal lieutenant. Less impassioned about polygamy than Clark, McKay nevertheless pursued fundamentalists, whom he believed to be a threat to the church, as part of the probe. Fred Curtis, bishop of the Hawthorne Ward in Salt Lake City, where several polygamists resided, was asked to superintend a handful of "special missionaries" called by Clark and McKay, including Reuel Alder, a former polygamist; Kaspar Fetzer; George Lund; Eugene Neff; and Cornelius Zappey, "to try and save young people's souls from the clutches of the [fundamentalist] cult." In 1943, McKay's supervision of the committee's activities mushroomed. Between January and September, the apostle received updates on the fundamentalist probe in at least seventeen meetings and conversations. McKay relayed tips from city and county law enforcement officials to the special missionaries and shared much of the data gathered by the church team with Utah's attorney general, Grover Giles, in preparation for criminal prosecutions. The special missionaries monitored the homes of suspects, including the large residence of Heber Kimball Cleveland in Salt Lake, where six adult women resided. They stood on the sidewalks and streets outside homes including Cleveland's where special "fast meetings" were held, discouraging people from entering and sometimes recording the license plate numbers of attendees. The First Presidency and Presiding Bishopric relayed the information to attendees' bishops and stake presidents. Some local church leaders used the data to convene disciplinary membership councils, but others refused to act. "Shouldn't all bishops and stake presidents be informed about this issue and face it?" the frustrated investigators asked McKay in one meeting. When public sympathy for the polygamists surged as news leaked of the church's surveillance, Fetzer and Zappey met with McKay to strategize about whether it might "be better

25. DOMD, undated entry in 1934, undated entry in front of 1935 diary regarding July 14 meeting, Feb. 8, 1935, Sep. 19, 1935, Mar. 8, 1939, Nov. 17, 19, 20, 1938, Apr. 19, 1940, June 10, 1940, July 7, 29, 1942, Dec. 8, 1943; Bradley, *Kidnapped from that Land*, 48–57; Driggs, "After the Manifesto," 378–80; Nielson and Cole, *Four Rejected Revelations*. See also DOMD, May 9, 1940, Apr. 8, July 21, Aug. 9, 1943, Jan. 24, 1948.

to discontinue the work of Brother Curtis or others, to report car numbers or attendance at these meetings ... since they [the fundamentalists] are looking for persecution and now claim the Church leaders are so doing." A few months later McKay, aware of imminent legal action by the government, directed the special missionaries to "not be too active" in the near future but to wait instead for "agents of the law" to act. Within two months, in a dragnet operation, law enforcement officials arrested forty-six, several of whom had been monitored by the special missionaries, on charges including conspiracy to advocate polygamy, cohabitation, kidnapping, and circulation of obscene materials. "We commend and uphold the federal government in its efforts ... to bring before the bar of justice those who have violated the law," the First Presidency stated.[26]

In addition to administering and safeguarding the church, staffing its organizations, managing its finances, and rendering service through counseling and assistance, the First Presidency members coped with the unique challenges of their era. The calamities that engulfed the world during President Grant's prophetic tenure elicited vigorous temporal and spiritual vision and leadership from McKay, Clark, and Grant. The urgency of these immense external challenges focused the creative energies of the presidency and broadened the salience and reach of their initiatives and perspectives. People were looking for answers, and audiences who otherwise might have been inattentive were willing to listen.

The immense economic depression that unfolded following the stock market crash in 1929 cast a long shadow over the church's operations, deeply affecting the lives of most members, igniting doubt and fear, posing fiscal challenges

26. DOMD, Jan. 24, Feb. 18, Apr. 8, June 28, July 21, 1943, Jan. 12, Mar. 7, 1944; "Justice Denies Cultist's Plea," *Ogden Standard Examiner*, Oct. 2, 1944, 2; "Polygamy Probe Nabs 46," and "Officials of LDS Church Commend Action Against Polygamists," *Salt Lake Telegram*, Mar. 7, 1944, 1; Watson, "The Fred E. Curtis Papers," Audio, *Sunstone* Salt Lake City 2001 Symposium, session 263, sunstone.org. For an account of the arrests of March 7 and the subsequent trials see Bradley, *Kidnapped from that Land*, 64, 68–90. McKay's pursuit of polygamists slowed after the 1944 raids, although he continued to meet periodically with Curtis and investigated the temple recommend status of Joseph McKnight, the defense attorney who represented the arrested polygamists in court. With McKay's encouragement, the special missionaries passed information to the Federal Bureau of Investigation (FBI) regarding additional polygamy cases they uncovered. DOMD, Aug. 15, 16, Sep. 1, 9, 1944, Nov. 2, 1949. Ironically, McKay's friend who assisted him in vice investigations, Emmanuel Henry "Harry" Clarke, was married to Bertha Clara Langton, who had been sealed, per fundamentalist authorities, to polygamist John Albert Burt prior to her 1921 temple marriage to Clarke. The couple came to McKay in 1948 concerned about the validity of their temple sealing because of Bertha's previous relationship. McKay advised them that in 1906 President Joseph F. Smith had "recalled any authority" to seal people outside the temple. He assured her that her first sealing had been done "without authority" and was invalid before God. DOMD, Sep. 20, 1948; entry for Bertha Clara Langton [Clarke], KWZ7-KZK, Family Search, familysearch.org. McKay warned congregation leaders in 1955 that "excommunicants are moving into wards where they are not known, and are being or have been used in teaching classes." He advised leaders to be vigilant to ensure that "the spirit of an apostate [is not] poisoning the minds of our youth." David O. McKay, address of Oct. 1, 1955, *Conference Reports*, 90.

for the church, and incentivizing innovation. Although his own position was economically secure, in his travels prior to his call to the presidency, McKay witnessed the plight of faithful members in rural regions who were upended by record drought and rock-bottom commodity prices. During McKay's 1934 visit to Metropolis, a hard-pressed Nevada farming community, local leaders informed him that every farm in the ward was mortgaged for more than the land was worth. That same year he visited congregations in Jerome and Wendell, Idaho, where farmers had "not more than 10%" of the normal water supply. In some urban wards and stakes, members were equally desperate. In the Southgate Ward of South Salt Lake, over 60 percent of the heads of households were unemployed. As a new member of the First Presidency, McKay visited the bishop's storehouse in Pioneer Stake just before Christmas in 1934 to investigate progressive policies that were being implemented under Stake President Harold B. Lee. Few local leaders were as proactive as Lee. To meet the challenge, President Clark had been campaigning for a centralized church response to the Depression for over a year. When McKay entered the First Presidency, Clark gained a sympathetic ally who, unlike Grant's former counselor Anthony Ivins, agreed that the church should mobilize its economic resources independent of the government to provide for its members. Latter-day Saint students provided additional impetus for church action, petitioning the First Presidency late in 1934 for greater engagement with "social and economic problems," including "definite help" with medical insurance. The First Presidency took up the challenge and began to explore cooperative insurance options for tithe payers and priesthood quorums.[27]

Several concerns galvanized the presidency's quest for a church welfare program. Deficit spending as a means of financing government welfare programs was financially reckless, they feared. Large government bureaucracies were inefficient, they warned; by relying upon volunteer labor the church could supply welfare more cheaply than the government. Moreover, they believed welfare was a Christian, neighbor-to-neighbor obligation rather than the responsibility of the national government. Their distrust of the government's approach increased when they heard that government employees had discriminated against a few needy church members. For instance, some women whose husbands were serving missions had been denied welfare on the grounds that their husbands were already "employed" by the church. The presidency feared that government welfare programs were sapping members' work ethic and independence; some who could support themselves reportedly chose welfare over work, and some government agencies doled out money with no expectation of work in return. In the spring of 1935 Clark pushed the prophet to announce a new

27. DOMD, undated notations from trip to Idaho in front of 1934 diary, July 7, Oct. 2, Dec. 18, 1934, Apr. 1, 1935; Mangum and Blumell, *The Mormons' War*, 96, 102.

church-wide program that he had outlined, but Grant demurred. Although Grant and McKay assured Clark that "we are united with you in the thought that the Church has . . . the responsibility to demonstrate to the world what it can do in taking care of its poor and unemployed without resorting to government aid," Grant sensed, in the face of opposition from some church leaders, that the time was not yet right.[28]

After the April 1935 conference, while Clark was away on business, Grant and McKay invited Harold B. Lee to the Church Administration Building, shared with him Clark's outlines, and asked him to devise plans based upon those outlines for a program that would permit the church to care for its own. Lee "expressed his perfect faith that the plan should be carried out and our people taken care of by going back to the old system of taking tithes in kind and building warehouses to take care of surplus crops in one section and moving them to another." Lee submitted a preliminary report and organizational plan the following month, and McKay deemed it "feasible," but Grant still feared the membership would "not sustain it." With Clark out of town and Grant indecisive, McKay informed Lee that he "felt incapable of taking the initiative" although he believed the church should do something. By fall, Grant's confidence had increased. To build support for the program, the presidency decided to gather data on the number of Latter-day Saints currently on relief. "We must not be forced to shape our course by false or inaccurate data," they observed. By January 1936, the survey was complete. It revealed that nearly one-fifth (17.9 percent) of church members in the western United States were on welfare and that nine-tenths of those on welfare received aid from the government. The survey also showed that ward and stake leaders believed 13–19 percent of their members on welfare could support themselves without the aid if they fully used available resources, including their own farmland. In February, McKay asked Lee, along with Campbell Brown Jr., the director of welfare programs for Utah Copper Company, to review and summarize the survey materials and to revise their recommendations in light of the new data. Over the next three weeks, the duo worked feverishly to comply with McKay's directive to "revise, simplify, and extend" Lee's original recommendations. When they presented their revised plans to McKay on March 15, Lee recalled, McKay enthusiastically "slapped the table with his hand and exclaimed: 'Brethren, now we have a program to present to the Church.'"[29]

In a meeting with ward, stake, and mission leaders following the final general session of the April 1936 conference, the prophet invited McKay, who had superintended Lee and Brown's work and knew it intimately, to present the

28. Cannon, "'What a Power We Will Be in This Land,'" 66–68, 70.

29. Cannon, "'What a Power We Will Be,'" 68–69; Harold B. Lee, diary, quoted in Goates, *Harold B. Lee*, 141–44.

results of the survey and to introduce the new program. He indicated that funds for the program would come from tithes and fast offerings; to that end local leaders were asked to encourage each member to donate 10 percent of their income to the church and to pay at least $1.00 in fast offerings in the coming year. By the fall, each bishop should collect enough necessities through donations and food storage to feed and clothe every needy member over the winter. A church relief committee would work with the Presiding Bishopric to reallocate fast offering funds and furnish employment on church and other properties. Each able person who received commodities from the program would be expected to labor for what they received. Although the First Presidency hoped to eventually provide for all needy members, for the time being only those who were on the dole, receiving direct assistance from the government without performing any labor in return, and any needy members who were unable to obtain government assistance would be cared for by the church. The estimated cost for the year would be $842,000. The church must "lead out and set an example to the world in the alleviating of suffering among our people … for the world is looking for leadership in this regard," McKay urged.[30]

Soon after the conference, McKay began meeting regularly with the General Church Committee, composed of Lee, Apostle Melvin J. Ballard, retired sugar company executive Mark Austin, and President Grant's son-in-law Bert Judd. In June, an article in the church magazine the *Improvement Era* announced that the "ultimate objective" of the program was "eventually to take care of all of its people exclusive of government relief." The program was no longer being billed publicly as merely a supplement to Franklin D. Roosevelt's New Deal. Presiding Bishop Sylvester Cannon, a New Deal supporter, believed this competitive, separatist objective was unnecessary and financially impossible. Late in 1937, Clark complained to Grant and McKay that Cannon had "willfully failed to support" the plan. The following April, Grant released Cannon from his position. Two months later, Grant told a reporter that the church had to that point been unable to remove all members from relief employment because they had failed to cooperate. "Because it has proved impossible to persuade many of the members to resist the temptation to lean on the government, we now have to be content with urging those who go to work on WPA jobs to try to give an honest day's work for their money," Grant was quoted as saying. Criticizing government relief and some recipients, he continued, "I have watched men at work on these government jobs. I have counted slowly to four between their shovelfuls. In some cases, I have counted to as high as forty between shovelfuls—and they were mighty skimpy shovelfuls at that."[31]

30. Cannon, "'What a Power We Will Be,'" 69–70; "An Important Message," *Deseret News*, Apr. 7, 1936, 1.

31. DOMD, May 8, 1936, Mar. 17, 19, 1937; Henry A. Smith, "Church-wide Security Program

Although the Church Security Program, later renamed the Welfare Program, was Clark's brainchild and would not have materialized without his persistent lobbying and Grant's culminating endorsement, McKay was responsible for the program's quotidian development and implementation, an integral contribution that is sometimes overlooked. As Clark's biographer, D. Michael Quinn, noted, prior to 1940, McKay had "primary responsibility for governing the Welfare Program" as well as forging ahead in the face of gainsaying by many members. In this sense the program was as much McKay's as it was Clark's. In 1936 it was McKay who coached and worked with Lee to finalize the blueprint of the program. Often, he was the only representative of the First Presidency in the general committee's meetings where decisions were made regarding purchase and development of productive facilities such as farms. In the summer of 1937, while both Grant and Clark were away on a three-month visit to congregations in Europe, McKay convened a meeting for all general authorities and auxiliary officers to advance the program.[32]

Initially the conservative press heralded the security program as a visionary alternative to the New Deal, a view that thrilled the First Presidency and suggested that the church might set the standard for the nation. "What a power we will be in this land and in the earth," Clark exulted. The early results of the security program were significant, although not as sweeping as the presidency had hoped. In 1937 and 1938 the church spent over $1.7 million on welfare work. By the end of 1938 the Church had amassed clothing valued at $9,400; over $114,000 worth of food; and fuel worth over $3,700 for distribution. In 1939 the Church employed nearly 7,200 members on work projects and assisted an average of 12,955 members, 1.6 percent of the Church's membership, each month. Many Latter-day Saints remained dependent upon government assistance, though. In December 1939, close to 41,500 Utahns received government welfare checks. Not until later in the century would the Welfare Program facilitate cooperation, service, and mutual assistance on a truly massive scale.[33]

Opponents of the Church Security Program charged the First Presidency with being impervious to the plight of needy Americans in their criticisms of government welfare programs. The charge was defensible, although McKay, Grant, and Clark sincerely believed they were acting in the best interests of

---

Organized," *Improvement Era,* June 1936, 337; J. Reuben Clark to First Presidency, Oct. 19, 1937, box 358, J. Reuben Clark Papers; Howard Wood, "Lure of WPA Foils Mormon Self-Aid Aims," *Chicago Tribune,* June 6, 1938, 1.

32. Quinn, *Elder Statesman*, 458; Gibbons, *David O. McKay*, 171

33. Arrington and Hinton, "Origin of the Welfare Plan," 68; Joseph F. Darowski, "The WPA Versus the Utah Church," in Cannon and Embry, *Utah in the Twentieth Century*, 172; Cannon, "'What a Power We Will Be,'" 71–72; speech by J. Reuben Clark, minutes of special priesthood meeting in the Salt Lake Tabernacle, Oct. 7, 1935, "Beginnings of Church Welfare Plan," Volume II, box 196, J. Reuben Clark Papers.

needy church members and the nation. Their warning that the nation was mortgaging its future through deficit spending was trenchant, and their vision of welfare as a neighborly obligation called forth the best in the human spirit. Their hope that the church could care for its own in the short term hinged upon exceptional generosity and creativity in communities plagued with high unemployment and poverty. Unfortunately, the resources members mobilized and donated were insufficient to care for all church members on government welfare. Under those circumstances, the First Presidency's continued criticism of laborers, including members, employed on government welfare projects and their persistent distrust of an expanding federal welfare bureaucracy was likely facilitated by their insulation from personal economic deprivation. All came from economically modest backgrounds, but by the 1930s, serving on the boards of church-owned businesses, they perceived labor problems from the perspective of management. They were also financially comfortable. Grant possessed a large amount of assets and a fine home in Salt Lake's upscale Avenues neighborhood. Clark was very wealthy; he earned an annual salary of $15,000, the equivalent of over $324,000 in today's money, for his work with the Foreign Bondholders Protective Council. By doing legal work for the Mexican Eagle Oil Company beginning in 1935, he raked in an additional $108,000, or over $2.3 million today. The least secure financially of the presidency members, McKay still received a yearly stipend of $6,000, a modest though certainly adequate amount for an executive of a large organization, equivalent to roughly $128,000 today. Financial gifts from Clark, who wanted to share some of his income with McKay as he shouldered Clark's ecclesiastical responsibilities during his prolonged absences, totaled over $14,000 in 1936 alone.[34]

From their economically secure position, McKay and his associates readily opposed not only New Deal welfare efforts but also other facets of Franklin D. Roosevelt's modestly redistributionist, big-government, pro-union programs during the second half of the 1930s. On the eve of the 1936 election, the entire First Presidency signed and published an editorial, drafted by Clark at Grant's insistence, opposing Roosevelt's bid for reelection and questioning his fidelity to the Constitution. In 1937, they agreed, as Grant wrote, to exert their influence behind the scenes "to overturn the President's attempt to pack the Supreme Court." In 1938 they extended a calling to BYU President Franklin S. Harris to run on an anti–New Deal platform against Utah's pro–New Deal senator Elbert Thomas. Although some individual Latter-day Saints heeded the First Presidency's counsel in these matters, the majority of Utahns voted to return Roosevelt and Thomas to office.[35]

34. Quinn, *The Mormon Hierarchy*, 13, 56–62, 174–75; Quinn, *Elder Statesman*, 142.

35. Grant, *Diaries of Heber J. Grant*, 416, 445, 470 (Apr. 7, 1937, Sep. 4, 1940, Dec. 7, 1942); Cannon, "'What a Power We Will Be,'" 72–74. The 1930s were the heyday of organized labor, an

Just as the Depression had done, the Second World War necessitated vigorous leadership on McKay's part as a member of the First Presidency. While working in his office on a Sunday morning in December, McKay learned that Pearl Harbor had been bombed. A week later he addressed an audience of two thousand students and townspeople packed into the church's Logan Institute of Religion, "one of the most attentive audiences" he had "ever addressed." He echoed American public opinion and placed the blame squarely on the Axis powers. The Japanese attack was an act of "deceit and treachery" while the Nazis had "willfully broken" their promises by invading other nations. "Political chicanery has replaced international trust and good will," he observed. What was to be done? McKay did not criticize the United States for entering the war, but he warned that war itself would not produce lasting peace. The world needed a "modern Moses who can lead us out of this wilderness" by promulgating a "unified ideal" grounded in Christian charity. While he did not claim to be that modern Moses, he opined, "A social order is needed in which God's will shall be done, in which love and good will and service to fellow man are working ideals." In short, "the world needs God." McKay did not explain how that ideal was to be achieved in a world of competing religious systems where atheism was gaining ground, but given the premium he placed upon moral agency, he almost certainly believed it could only be achieved by voluntary conversion.[36]

Five months following the attack on Pearl Harbor, in a message likely drafted by Clark for the April 1942 general conference, the First Presidency proclaimed that "the Church is and must be against war." McKay supported this view in a conference address, showing by thoughtful exegesis that "war is incompatible with Christ's teachings." This did not mean that members should be conscientious objectors, though. The presidency distinguished between the institutional church's opposition to war and the "highest civic duty" of its members who were "citizens or subjects of sovereignties over which the Church has no control" to serve in the military of their nations when called upon according to "constitutional law." McKay taught, "We serve our country as bearers of arms, rather than to stand aloof to enjoy a freedom for which others have fought and died." McKay went beyond the First Presidency statement, reflecting his

important constituency of Roosevelt's New Deal coalition that enjoyed unprecedented federal cooperation and protection, including the right to compel workers to join unions under closed shop arrangements. McKay shared the prejudices of the business class and especially opposed the closed shop. In 1937 he commiserated with Dan Seegmiller, a department store employee who lost his job after refusing to join the union. "No man who does not wish to join a Union should be compelled to do so," McKay intoned. But his suspicion of unions ran deeper than concerns about agency. He declared that he "would not advise a man to join a union unless it is absolutely necessary." DOMD, Mar. 9, 1937, Mar. 10, 1938.

36. DOMD, Dec. 7, 1941; "Leader in LDS Sees Ideals as War Antidotes," *Salt Lake Tribune*, Dec. 15, 1941, 10; "Pres. McKay Prescribes Ideals for World at War," *Deseret News*, Dec. 15, 1941, 16.

independent thinking as he justified Allied military action despite the presidency's observation that "both sides cannot be wholly right; perhaps neither is without wrong." There were conditions, he reasoned and taught, under which "a Christian nation may, without violation of principles, take up arms against an opposing force." One was in the face of "an attempt to dominate and to deprive another of his free agency." Another was in response to "lawless encroachments from without" such as the Japanese "treachery"; no function of government was greater than the protection of its citizens. He raised the possibility of a third circumstance under which war might be justifiable for a Christian nation, although he did not probe into the matter. It was "defense of a weak nation that is being unjustly crushed by a strong, ruthless one." He concluded by praising American soldiers for "fighting for an eternal principle fundamental to the peace and progress of mankind."[37]

In a second official statement six months later that was largely written by Clark and read by him at general conference, the presidency called upon the warring nations to "abandon the fiendishly inspired slaughter" and broker a negotiated settlement that would be "honorable and just for all." They warned that "wicked and designing men" intended to use the war as the means of "the worldwide establishment and perpetuation of some form of communism on the one side, or of some form of Nazism or fascism on the other." These outcomes must be prevented. Moreover, if war continued until one side was defeated on the battlefield, the statement warned, it would merely sow the seeds for subsequent conflicts. "Enduring peace ... will never be imposed by armed force."[38]

On the following day in his conference address, McKay adopted a more militant stance than the one taken in the official statement Clark had read. He denounced the "wickedness" of the Axis powers and insisted that "the conflict must continue." "The upsetting of the world has forced us into war, and we should be recreant not to go forward." The apostle assured young men called up to the military that their cause was noble. "We all realize with you that ... peace cannot come until the mad gangsters having in their hands science-produced explosives, mechanized equipment, and giant tanks, are defeated and branded as murderers, and their false aims repudiated, let us hope for ever."[39]

The dissonance of the two messages struck many listeners. Noting that the "85-year-old President Grant has long been ill," one reporter interpreted the two speeches as evidence of "disagreement in the First Presidency itself" between the two counselors. Some asked whether the First Presidency statement truly

37. "Message of the First Presidency," address of Apr. 6, 1942, *Conference Reports*, 94; David O. McKay, address of Apr. 6, 1942, *Conference Reports,* 70–74.

38. Quinn, *Elder Statesman*, 475; "Message of the First Presidency," address of Oct. 2, 1942, *Conference Reports*, 15–16.

39. David O. McKay, address of Oct. 3, 1942, *Conference Reports,* 68.

represented the views of the entire presidency or only of Clark. Biographers have also noted the dissonance. D. Michael Quinn wrote of the "diametrical opposition" as evidence of "disagreement." Francis M. Gibbons wrote of "a basic divergence of opinion" between the two men.[40]

The difference between portions of the two statements was undeniable, one calling for an end to hostilities and the other calling for military defeat. But common threads ran through the two counselors' thinking, making the First Presidency statement a document that reflected both men's views. Like Clark, McKay taught that war could not sow the seeds of lasting peace. The war, he predicted early in 1943, would be won by the side with the "greatest armies, the most airplanes, the most death-dealing bombs," but "peace will be maintained only by men and nations turning their hearts towards God and his righteousness." The two counselors shared the statement's strongly articulated contempt for and wariness of fascists and communists. Given that fact, the call for a negotiated settlement was hardly a recommendation to diplomats to blithely trust Josef Stalin or Adolf Hitler at the negotiating table. In his conference address, McKay embraced the same Christian idealism that infused the First Presidency statement. "Some of you listening in will call it trite," he admitted. The saving ideal was "Christ's plan of love and service" embodied in the golden rule of "brotherly consideration." "Even in so-called Christian lands men have spurned the teachings as being impractical. The result is that the earth has literally been drenched in blood," he warned. Echoing the First Presidency statement, he advised that "His [Christ's] doctrine of arbitration as a means of settling difficulties and quarrels if applied by warring nations would in itself do away with war."[41]

Following the war, McKay reiterated a warning he had consistently issued throughout the war; enduring peace could be achieved only by applying Christian ideals. "Peace on earth is not achieved," he warned in a 1945 Christmas message. In the coming days the world could choose "peace through the triumph of [Christian] principles or the possibility of destruction through the misuse of atomic energy." Chastising the Allied victors for their refusal to mention God in the Charter of the United Nations on the grounds that the document must be acceptable to all, McKay protested, "As long as God is only 'a noble and beautiful thought,' and not a Reality in the minds and hearts of men, their efforts will come to naught who strive to avert war and to establish peace."[42]

As second counselor to Heber J. Grant, McKay rendered yeoman service. During Clark's extended absences in the 1930s, Grant relied primarily upon his second counselor. Between 1935 and 1939 Grant was also away from the

40. "Mormon Mixup," *Time Magazine*, Oct. 19, 1942, 41; Quinn, *Elder Statesman*, 142–43; Gibbons, *David O. McKay*, 201.

41. DOMD, Jan. 24, 1943; David O. McKay, address of Oct. 3, 1942, *Conference Reports*, 67–70.

42. David O. McKay, "Principles of Peace in the Post-War Period," *Deseret News*, Dec. 29, 1945, 22.

office for two to three months each year. McKay assumed more than his share of the First Presidency's daily responsibilities, including significant amounts of the correspondence and many of the consultations and meetings, as well as overseeing the development and implementation of the Church Security Program. Following McKay's pulmonary embolism and protracted recovery from surgery in 1940, Clark stepped forward and assumed that primary role as counselor. In his role as a member of Heber J. Grant's First Presidency, McKay provided temporal and spiritual leadership, advising the prophet, serving on the boards of church-owned corporations, helping to superintend temple construction and worship, advising stake and mission leaders, and supporting the church's campaign against new polygamy. He also interacted with and served individual members, officiating in weddings, speaking at firesides and conferences, and advising members on personal matters. All these duties were expected, normal functions of a First Presidency member. But major external events, the Great Depression and the Second World War, also demanded responses, and the First Presidency, including McKay, met the demands with vigorous, resourceful spiritual and temporal leadership. Perceiving both crises through lenses shaped by their religious commitments and their economic situations, they laid the foundation for an ambitious church welfare program and justified America's military objectives while criticizing both the United Nations charter and the New Deal. They led boldly in temporal and political as well as ecclesiastical matters.

9: Counselor to George Albert Smith and Supervisor of Missionary Work

In May 1945, only a few days after the Second World War ended in Europe, President Grant died. George Albert Smith succeeded him as church president, reappointing Clark and McKay as his counselors. Although he was fourteen years younger than Grant, Smith battled chronic anxiety and low stamina and needed the support of strong counselors. Unlike Grant in his later years, President Smith managed his own correspondence, but aside from this procedural shift, little changed initially in McKay's administrative responsibilities. By 1948, though, as Smith's health declined rapidly, meetings of the entire First Presidency became briefer and less frequent. In 1949, while Smith was resting in California for two and a half months prior to general conference, he transacted business entirely by phone or letter. McKay and Clark increased their administrative load, as they had during President Grant's waning years. Smith was "extremely close" to Clark and often summoned his first counselor to discuss matters privately. In these informal meetings, the two formed tentative conclusions that they later discussed with McKay. At times they made decisions without informing McKay. In June 1950, a reporter asked McKay about "the Church's decision to accept no applications for new chapels until 1951." McKay, who normally had a great deal to do with building projects, was flummoxed. He told the reporter that he would "have to take up [the matter] with Bishop Richards and President Clark, that I have had nothing to do with the matter." As second counselor McKay dutifully deferred to Presidents Smith and Clark. In 1950 he authorized a reporter for the *Salt Lake Tribune* to publish a story on the soon-to-be-built Los Angeles Temple. The *Deseret News* complained, showing that the minutes of a previous First Presidency meeting promised that the *News* should carry the story first. McKay was forced to retract his promise, indicating that he was "outvoted" in the matter.[1]

In his first two years as Smith's counselor, McKay devoted a large amount of time to planning Utah's centennial celebration. It may not have been "one of the most challenging assignments [he] had ever faced," as biographer Francis

1. Woodger, *Against the Odds,* 197–99; Quinn, *Elder Statesman*, 110, 125, 127, 144; DOMD, Apr. 12, 1948, Mar. 30, 1949, Apr. 9, June 8, Dec. 11, 1950; Pusey, *Builders of the Kingdom*, 316.

Gibbons avers, but it was a consequential responsibility. Nearly a decade before the one-hundred-year anniversary of the pioneers' arrival in Utah, McKay began chairing the committee responsible for planning the centennial at the request of Governor Henry Blood, the father of Lou Jean's husband, Russell. Blood's successor, Herbert Maw, renewed McKay's appointment in 1940, an olive branch of sorts after having released McKay as a trustee of the Agricultural College of Utah, a release that deeply disappointed McKay. Much of the daily preparation for the centennial devolved upon Gus Backman of the Salt Lake Chamber of Commerce, who was eventually named director of the celebration, but McKay as chair was ultimately responsible. In mid-January 1947 after years of planning, he kicked off the centennial in the capitol rotunda with a musical gala in which the centennial queen was crowned. A host of carefully planned events ensued, including an international ski competition, the dedication of a massive historical monument near the mouth of Emigration Canyon, banquets, and a reception honoring the 236 surviving pioneers. As the festivities multiplied, so did McKay's commitments and correspondence. He began "dictat[ing] in the early morning almost every day, in the evenings, and on Sunday in order to clear [his] desk of the letters that [were] being received." Missteps or unforeseen complications could embarrass Utah and the church, so McKay was gratified when the centennial parade in July passed off without embarrassment. It was "the longest, the most colorful, the most expensive and best attended of any in the history of the state." After hearing for the first time the score for *Promised Valley*, a musical theater production commissioned for the centennial, McKay "felt as though [he was] walking on air." He deemed the composer, Crawford Gates, "a genius." After two performances were rained out, he authorized a new final performance on a Sunday evening. When some general authorities opined that the planned performance would violate the Sabbath, McKay replied that he had "given this matter full consideration" and was "willing to face my Maker on this decision." Unlike *Promised Valley*, McKay was embarrassed by the centennial movie, *Ramrod*, directed by André de Toth. It was "a very poor picture" he judged.[2]

As a churchman, McKay seized the opportunity provided by his post as centennial chair to promote the gospel. In an interview with a reporter from *Time*, the apostle shared religious pamphlets and instructional materials, a short history of the church, and copies of the Book of Mormon and the Articles of Faith. In response to a reporter's question, he stated that divine revelation impelled Wilford Woodruff's 1890 Manifesto curtailing plural marriage. By contrast, he said, the church welfare program, which he had helped to bring forth, "was not

2. Gibbons, *David O. McKay*, 242; DOMD, June 22, 1938, Apr. 22, 1946, Jan. 16, Feb. 27, Mar. 28, May 1, 4, July 23, 24, 1947; Gunther, *Inside U.S.A.*, 207; Lythgoe, *Let 'Em Holler*, 23, 31; McKay, *My Father*, 215.

a revelation" but "just a program of the Church." He identified the two most important functions of the church as missionary work and education (encompassing, he expansively indicated, art, literature, music, recreation, and temple work).[3]

Rather than defining his role as centennial chair narrowly, McKay creatively used it as a bully pulpit to fight government corruption, arguing that a city founded by Latter-day Saint pioneers should conform to its founders' ideals. Much as he had done while working with the Betterment League of Ogden during the Prohibition campaign of the 1910s, McKay assiduously promoted ethical government, continuing his crusade well beyond the centennial's close. McKay's campaign demonstrated his continued appetite for coercive moral reform. It also showed how difficult it was for a churchman in the Beehive State to wield civic power without implicating the church.

McKay's moral crusade in Salt Lake followed on the heels of a political controversy into which he was drawn in 1944 involving Kent Bramwell, the youthful mayor of Ogden. The Bramwell scandal convinced McKay that bribes and payoffs pervaded local government. McKay's involvement clarified his motives, illustrating the premium he and other church leaders placed upon moral rectitude and their determined resistance to compromising alliances that might undercut their moral influence. Bramwell, a counselor in a bishopric in Ogden, had been elected as a reform candidate with local church support. Subsequently he accepted a $600 loan and received a $500 bribe from the gambling operators he had pledged to fight. Once Bramwell was caught in this carefully laid trap, a newspaperman threatened to publicize his misdeeds. Local stake presidents, who wanted to "keep this from becoming a scandal," asked McKay as a former Ogdenite to exert his influence. They feared Bramwell's actions, if they came to light, could "reflect negatively upon the Church," whose local leaders had supported his candidacy and been "proud" of his election. "You have been unwise in dealing with [gambling operators]," McKay advised Bramwell. "You cannot handle pitch without becoming defiled. When you shake hands with these fellows or deal with them in any way, they tar you." The stake president released Bramwell forthwith from the bishopric, and McKay extracted a pledge from the hostile newspaper owner that if "Bramwell will resign, join the Army, and get out of town nothing [in terms of publicity] will be done about it." The next morning, Bramwell resigned and immediately enlisted, and news of the scandal was suppressed for the time being.[4]

With fresh evidence that bribes greased the wheels in his hometown, McKay

3. DOMD, July 2, 14, 1947.

4. Transcript of interview between President David O. McKay and Kent R. Bramwell, Mar. 11, 1944, in DOMD, Mar. 11, 1944. See also DOMD, Mar. 12–13, 1944. See detailed accounts in Parkinson, *S. Dilworth Young*, 199–207, and Holley, *25th Street Confidential*, 82. In litigation following the war Bramwell was acquitted of charges that he sought and accepted a bribe. "Jury Acquits Bramwell of Bribery Count," *Ogden Standard Examiner*, June 9, 1946, 1.

visited the following year with a colorful friend, Albert M. J. Prichard, sexton at the Salt Lake City cemetery and a former sheriff's deputy and detective. Prichard told McKay about illegal gambling operations with ties to Salt Lake's government and implicated two city commissioners, Public Safety Commissioner L. C. "Rennie" Romney and Parks and Recreation Commissioner Fred Tedesco. By January 1946, Prichard had fingered sixteen gambling establishments in the city for McKay. Armed with Prichard's data, McKay launched his centennial moral crusade from the tabernacle in the April 1946 general conference, wading into politics and alleging that Salt Lake City was a haven for "gambling, the slot machine, and race horse betting" and decrying "immorality on the public streets." A few days later, Police Chief Leonard Crowther denied McKay's charges and accused him of slander. McKay pledged to substantiate his charges if Crowther would visit his office. Instead Crowther dispatched Detective Odes B. Record, an active Latter-day Saint, to meet with McKay and apologize on his behalf. According to Record, Crowther instructed him, "Tell him [McKay] for me that I am sorry that I wrote what I did in the article about his sermon, and that I shall be glad to cooperate with him in cleaning up the city." In the course of his conversation with McKay, Record corroborated his charges of lawbreaking. When McKay stated that he was "sure that some of the officers have been acting in conjunction with the 'bunco' men who have been operating in this city," Record replied, "There is no doubt about it."[5]

Former city attorney Fisher Harris, who had cracked down on prostitution and gambling in the city during a previous administration, began working closely with McKay. Harris and McKay questioned Commissioner Romney about his rumored boast that he had ousted the former police chief and appointed an officer who was soft on crime as head of the department's vice unit in return for "a cut" on illegal betting operations. Romney denied the accusations. A few months later, Harris and McKay met with the mayor and city commissioners in the Church Administration Building to discuss corruption charges against Tedesco, who was out of town. McKay and Harris accused Tedesco of using city equipment and laborers to construct bleachers for the Salt Lake Seagulls, a professional football team in which Tedesco held stock. City officials confirmed the charges, but after Tedesco reimbursed the city for $885, they excused him with only a reprimand. Upset that Tedesco had not been ousted, McKay fumed that the city had been defrauded. A private corporation had received services at a far lower cost than could have been obtained from private contractors, and the city had been denied the services that its employees might have provided if their time had not been tied up in developing a private football park. He continued, "The trouble lies not with our laws, but with the

5. DOMD, Apr. 27, Sep. 20, 1945, Jan. 21, Apr. 17, 1946; David O. McKay, address of Apr. 7, 1946, *Conference Reports*, 135–41; "Conference Talk Angers Police Chief," *Deseret News*, Apr. 10, 1946, 11.

officers elected and appointed to enforce the laws. In keeping with the cleanup campaign now functioning all over the state in anticipation of the Utah centennial celebration, the city commissioners have been urged to make a moral and a physical cleanup of this city. Three months have passed, and little or nothing has been accomplished."[6]

Through the rest of 1946, McKay continued to amass evidence of Romney's ties to illegal gambling. He enlisted the investigative services of a Salt Lake attorney, D. Ray Owen Jr., former secretary to the Utah Senate. In mid-January 1947, McKay asked Owen to obtain "affidavits … against Mr. Romney" and promised him $500 for his work. The money, which McKay refused to touch lest the church be accused of meddling in politics, was contributed by private citizens through Ed Ashton, a Salt Lake realtor, bishop, and former president of the Salt Lake Chamber of Commerce. Through his investigation, Owen concluded that Ralph Harmon, owner of the Mint Café at 61 East 200 South, "controlled … all gambling and bookmaking and probably prostitution" in the city. For a share of the profits Harmon and his cronies allegedly received protection from Chief Crowther, who in turn was shielded by Commissioner Romney. When McKay confronted Romney with some of his evidence, Romney retorted that it was "a downright lie" and swore he would "meet those who thus accused me face to face." Despite Romney's denial, McKay remained convinced that "if we could get Romney and Tedesco out, the way would be clear for a good administration." After he unsuccessfully urged Romney to bow out from politics and avoid a public shaming. McKay tried to recruit an upstanding, viable candidate to run against him. His first choice, a wealthy and highly respected businessman and banker, John L. Firmage, declined on account of poor health. Eventually Elmer Thomas, a retired army colonel and Latter-day Saint, agreed to run against Romney in a round-robin race in which four candidates vied for two seats. McKay told Thomas that as a churchman he could not openly campaign for him, but he helped recruit a campaign manager and raised hundreds of dollars from private donors for campaign literature. Rather than extolling his own strengths, Thomas foolishly devoted his campaign to besmirching Romney: Thomas finished last in the four-way race, and Romney was reelected.[7]

Following the disappointing election, McKay pushed for a grand jury investigation of corruption and encouraged Clifford Ashton, Ed Ashton's half

6. DOMD, Apr. 22, 24, 29, July 21–Aug. 6, 1949; "City Equipment 'Misuse' Is Aired at Meet," *Salt Lake Telegram*, July 26, 1946, 13; "McKay Issues Blast at City Officials," *Salt Lake Telegram*, Aug. 6, 1946, 11.

7. DOMD, Aug. 6, 7, 16, 22, Sep. 3–6, 12, 17, 18, 25, 30, Oct. 1, 24, Nov. 7, 8, 23, Dec. 20, 1946, Jan. 21, Feb. 8, Apr. 27, July 3, 18, Aug. 14, 26, 27, Sep. 6, 20, Oct. 10, 15, 25–31, 1947, Jan. 12, 1948. For appreciative views of Harmon's sponsorship of sports in Salt Lake County see Hack Miller, "'Top Friend' of Sports Dies," *Deseret News*, Sep. 19, 1968, 6C, and John Mooney, "Hardly Seems Like New Season Without Ralph at Counter," *Salt Lake Tribune*, Sep. 6, 1968, 1C.

brother, to serve as special prosecutor. McKay gave Ashton "an outline of alleged facts that we have on hand that seem to link one or two city officials with the underworld of this city." As the investigation proceeded, Owen appeared before the grand jury and disclosed, with McKay's cautious approval, that McKay, as chair of the centennial commission, had asked him to "investigate existing conditions with respect to 'bunco' men ... in order that we could have a clean city" and that when they uncovered the extent of the corruption they "could not turn our backs on such lawlessness." When the jurors asked to meet with McKay to hear all that he knew, he initially agreed to testify but later reneged, fearing that his appearance before the jury might be used as evidence of church political interference. He said he would meet only privately with the judge and with Ashton to share his perspective. Without McKay's testimony, the jurors returned five indictments but failed to indict Romney or Tedesco, showing that they had been unimpressed by allegations of ties between the commissioners and the underworld. Instead, they disparaged many of the reports of putative corruption they had received in phone calls and letters as "groundless rumors and fabrications" and "a grave injustice ... to honest and conscientious public officials." The jurors did censure the police department for not enforcing gambling and liquor-licensing statutes, and they criticized county officials for failing to enforce laws regarding bookmaking, pinball machines, and punch boards. Behind these operations was "a large and well-organized system of gambling," they concluded.[8]

McKay's campaign as centennial chair to clean up Salt Lake City had largely failed. His position as a member of the First Presidency had amplified his voice, but it undercut his ability to openly electioneer and testify. Although McKay's crusade to unseat Romney and Tedesco and discredit Crowther withered, it did push Crowther to appoint a new chief of the vice squad, Golden Haight, a Latter-day Saint bishop. Haight complained that Crowther gave him officers who "wouldn't be much support," but in time he led his men in several successful raids, resulting in the confiscation of slot machines and some arrests for gambling. To McKay's relief, Tedesco left city government in mid-1949 to take a position at a soft-drink bottling company, and Romney stepped down as commissioner of public safety to take Tedesco's job as commissioner of parks and recreation.[9]

George Albert Smith's presidency and McKay's anti-vice crusade coincided with several health challenges for McKay. In the fall of 1946, he underwent surgery for another blockage in his pulmonary artery. The recovery period kept

8. DOMD, Mar. 22, 24, Apr. 3, 28, 30, June 3, Nov. 23, 1948.

9. "Record Named Crowther's Deputy," *Salt Lake Telegram*, Mar. 12, 1949, 1; "Board Appoints Lingenfelter to Fill Vacant Tedesco Post," *Salt Lake Telegram*, June 2, 1949, 1; "Salt Lake Has New City Commissioner," *Salt Lake Telegram*, June 22, 1949, 14; entry for Golden Haight, KWC8-SGL, Family Search, familysearch.org.

him from his office duties for nearly two months. In mid-December, he finally felt strong enough to return to "active duty." Eighteen months later he felt dizzy and checked in to the hospital. His cardiologist detected an "unequalization between the pulse and heartbeat" and warned that he was working too hard. McKay summarized the diagnosis: "due to strenuous, unwise efforts I overtaxed my heart. I was going for 14 to 16 (sometimes 18) hours a day." McKay's stamina lagged for the next five months, a sobering portent of weakness to come. He was learning, he wrote, "that a man past three score and ten cannot run so fast as he could when he was in his forties." Although McKay dutifully pruned his appointment calendar, his ailments multiplied. While training a horse in August 1948, he tripped and fell, dislocating his shoulder. The onset of severe side and gastric pains a month later added to his discomfort. Conditions improved somewhat, but in July 1949 after a full day's work he again left the office "complete fatigued." He admitted he should follow his doctor's advice and work only half days, but he maintained that "the continual stream of letters, interviews, speaking appointments, in addition to my other duties associated with this office" made that "impossible."[10]

McKay's most crucial assignment in the First Presidency, supervising the church's missionary efforts, continued under President Smith despite health challenges. From the perspective of his assistant Franklin Murdock, McKay was the ideal presidency member for this assignment: he was "naturally a missionary," "enthused about every phase of missionary work," "deeply endowed with the welfare of the individual," and professionally "well prepared" to instruct missionaries. Christ's injunction to his ancient apostles to "preach the gospel to every creature" placed proselytizing efforts at the core of the church's mission, and McKay boldly but good-naturedly embraced the task. When Lewis Browne and Sinclair Lewis, two popular authors and lecturers, spent a day in Salt Lake as part of a nationwide speaking tour, McKay took them on a tour of Temple Square. When they asked if he would arrange a special tour of the temple for them, he reportedly quipped, "Certainly. All you have to do is adhere to the faith, give up alcohol and tobacco, and donate to the Church one-tenth of your income."[11]

McKay conducted preliminary investigations and interviews with prospective mission presidents, called many of them, and advised them on concerns and problems throughout their tenure. Every six months he interviewed mission presidents who were visiting Utah for general conference about a host of issues, including chapel construction, finances, member worthiness, personnel needs, mission statistics, and problem missionaries. McKay gave mission

10. DOMD, Oct. 17–21, Dec. 16, 1946, June 15, July 6, Aug, 25, Sep. 27, Oct, 13, Nov. 20, 1948, July 20, 1949.

11. Franklin J. Murdock, interviews by Gordon Irving, Mar. 28–30, 1973, 50, 66; Gunther, *Inside U.S.A.*, 194.

presidents a free hand in many matters. In 1950, President David Stoddard of the California Mission asked if the church had a policy on missionaries preaching without purse or scrip, a practice that some members in California opposed. They complained that missionaries requested food and lodging and then spent their allowance from home on souvenirs and luxuries. McKay informed Stoddard that the matter was "entirely in the hands of the mission president" and encouraged him to "handle his mission the way he thought best under the guidance of the spirit."[12]

As chair of the church missionary committee, which included two additional apostles and two seventies, with Murdock as secretary, McKay extended thousands of mission calls in his sixteen-and-a-half years as counselor to both Heber J. Grant and George Albert Smith. In 1950 alone, he issued over 3,000 calls. In a typical Tuesday meeting, the committee reviewed application packets. McKay or Murdock would read aloud the bishop's recommendation, noting the applicant's home ward and stake, health, schooling, language and musical ability, church leadership experience, worthiness, height, weight, and ethnicity. Prospective missionaries could express an interest in serving in a specific mission or country, and the committee considered that preference. The committee also considered mission presidents' requests for missionaries with specific talents and abilities. For instance, Japanese Mission President Edward Clissold desired elders who were athletically inclined or avid scouters in order to help him establish church sports and scouting programs there. After spending "a minute or a minute and a half" reviewing the application, McKay would look at a chart showing personnel needs in the missions and propose, "Well, we'll send that young man to the Eastern States Mission. If you brethren have any feelings about this, you speak up." But they nearly always concurred. Murdock recalled that one father asked him to tell McKay that "if the Lord would inspire you to assign his son to the Southern States Mission, he would certainly appreciate it." McKay "leaned back and laughed" and said, "Well, bless his heart. We'll let him go to the Southern States Mission." Some missionaries or their parents took the liberty of appealing a call that had been issued. If McKay deemed the suggestion meritorious, he sometimes acquiesced; but in other cases, he advised the petitioners to serve where they had been called.[13]

McKay monitored the safety of missionaries in times of political and military turbulence. In 1950, police arrested and imprisoned Elders Stanley Abbott and Aldon Johnson in Czechoslovakia. McKay phoned the missionaries' parents and released a statement to the press. He asked Utah Senator Elbert Thomas to appeal to the US State Department to negotiate the elders' release

12. DOMD, Apr. 8, Nov. 23, 1948, Nov. 2, 1950.

13. DOMD, June 7, 1940, Feb. 3, 1949, Oct. 21, 22, 1947, Mar. 4, 1948, Mar. 21, 1949, Feb. 21, 1950; "Statistical Report," Apr. 6, 1951, *Conference Reports*, 9.

from jail and departure from the country, subsequently working with other church authorities to remove all missionaries from the country. That same year he and Murdock devised preliminary plans to evacuate missionaries from East and West Germany. In 1951, after the US State Department advised Americans in Hong Kong to evacuate, McKay instructed the mission president to comply with the recommendation.[14]

Although Murdock devoted much of his time in the office as a full-time church employee to missionary needs, a surprisingly large number of missionary problems required McKay's attention. Parents who worried about their sons' or daughters' health or testimony contacted McKay, as did mission presidents seeking advice regarding missionaries who wanted to abandon their posts. After McKay learned that a young elder in Norway had asked his mission president to send him home because of religious doubts, McKay telegraphed the young man, whose parents he knew, advising him to "pause," consider how his actions might break his parents' hearts, and then write to McKay with his final decision. When a mentally unstable missionary tried to drown himself, necessitating his return home, McKay phoned the parents to compassionately explain the situation. The parents of another missionary who had been sent home for treatment in a mental hospital requested that their son be allowed to return after his condition stabilized. McKay explained that the strains of missionary work had unduly taxed the elder and instead extended an honorable release. The apostle contacted parents of missionaries who deserted their assignments and disappeared and then solicited help from law enforcement officials to try to keep them safe.[15]

Murdock recalled that in most groups entering the mission home there were "one or two" who particularly struggled to adjust. In the case of one young man whom he saw moping "off in a corner," he inquired if the missionary had financial problems, if someone in his family was ill, if he was missing a girlfriend, if the food disagreed with him, or if he had trouble sleeping. None of these common issues was the problem. Finally the missionary confessed that he "had a saddle horse" at home. "I just can't go on this mission till I see that horse once more," he pled. Murdock took the matter to McKay, and it struck a sympathetic chord. "Bless his heart," Murdock recalled McKay saying. "You just let him go down overnight and see that horse again. A boy that thinks that much of a horse, he'll be a good missionary."[16]

Complications involving missionary romances also landed on McKay's desk. Although the church seldom called married couples on missions after World

14. DOMD, Feb. 8, July 5, 7, 26, 1940, Jan. 11, 13, 1951.

15. DOMD, Sep. 27, 1943, Mar. 2, July 10, 19, 1945, Aug. 26, 1947, Feb. 22, July 11, 1949, Dec. 11, 1950.

16. Franklin J. Murdock, interview by Gordon Irving, Mar. 28–30, 1973, 89.

War II, McKay called some husbands and wives to serve together if they were unable to have children. However, he advised couples who planned to delay their families so they could serve to "stay home and build up a family." In an era when the church still called married men on missions, some applied to serve, noting on their applications that their wives had pledged to support them financially. Others who eloped before their missions neglected to indicate on their applications that they were married. If a clandestine marriage came to light in the Salt Lake Mission Home and the spouse met the age requirement for missionary service, McKay sometimes permitted her to serve separately from her husband in the same mission. Temple marriage was the church standard, so those in the mission home who had married secretly were only allowed to proceed if their spouse could travel to Salt Lake for a temple sealing. Occasionally a missionary in the field with a wife at home fell in love with someone else. In one unusual case, McKay decided that "nothing would be gained by bringing this Elder home" if he and his wife both said they no longer loved each other but that to avoid a dishonorable release he must "adhere to mission rules and stop courting" while on his mission. If his wife fell in love with someone else at home and sued for divorce, though, that would be "a different matter." When single missionaries fell in love with someone in the mission field, McKay advised them to cease communicating with their love interest for the balance of their mission, return home, and then wait at least six months before resuming the relationship.[17]

Before President Grant's death, McKay's oversight of the church's missions, including physical facilities, had taken him and Ray to Mexico in 1943, a nation that Clark knew much better, having served there as United States ambassador prior to his call to the First Presidency. McKay had wanted to visit Mexico for a quarter century, and he marveled at its "expansive forests and sublime mountain ranges." He enjoyed "a spectacle of a lifetime" when he rode on horseback to Parícutin, a cinder cone volcano, where he gazed at eruptions of "fire and smoke that seem[ed] to touch the stars." McKay felt overwhelmed by the contrast between "magnificent cathedrals and artistically carved palaces" he saw and the "extreme poverty and wretchedness" of the common people. Although he spoke no Spanish, on this visit he was able to begin making amends for a course taken the previous decade by the First Presidency in response to a mass defection, a course he had once strongly advocated.[18]

Over 1,200 members had defected from the church in the mid-1930s as part of the Third Convention, a nationalist movement within the church that demanded that the First Presidency call church leaders who were Mexicans, including a Mexican mission president. Although their ultimatum and defection violated church protocol, the protesters highlighted definite inequities

17. DOMD, Feb. 10, Oct. 16, 1947, June 20, 1949, Apr. 24, Aug. 30, 1950.

18. DOMD, Oct. 17, 1943.

that McKay had witnessed in the South Pacific on his world tour in the 1920s, where he observed white missionaries presiding over mature, capable converts. Reliance upon leaders from the western United States to staff and manage the church's international missions and districts would continue to retard the development of local talent in the years to come in many lands where the church struggled for a foothold. In a 1936 letter to mission president Harold W. Pratt, Grant and McKay had dismissed the members' concerns. "The privilege of their receiving the Gospel should merit their appreciation and support of those who have been sent down, appointed, and set apart to preside over that Mission," they instructed. "The Lord will dictate when reappointment or reorganization should be made." Early in 1937, McKay on behalf of the First Presidency instructed Pratt to initiate excommunication proceedings against the leading protesters and arranged for former mission president Antoine R. Ivins and Apostle George F. Richards to inform the protesters of the decision. McKay likely hoped the leaders would appeal to the First Presidency, repent, and be readmitted quickly, but no one appealed.[19]

By the 1940s, McKay had mellowed. When he called a new mission president, Arwell Pierce, to serve in 1942, he urged Pierce to make amends with the defectors, saying, "You are the Abraham Lincoln who must save this union." Touring the mission with Pierce in 1943, McKay met with members, missionaries, and leaders and inspected church buildings and building sites. He reached out to Othón Espinosa, a prominent Third Conventionist, visiting his home and blessing his granddaughter. He was moved by the faith exhibited by many members. Juan Pineda, a poorly clad man he met in the branch in Zentalpan, left a lasting impression. Through an interpreter, Pineda told the apostle that he had received death threats when he joined the church. Over time, his neighbors' hearts had softened as they saw the salutary impact of gospel principles in his life. The apostle observed the substandard meeting places of the Saints, including a small adobe building on the outskirts of Piedras Negras and a rude structure near a manure yard in Cabrera. After visiting a congregation of nearly one hundred in Cabrera, McKay noted, "They deserve a little chapel." In location after location, missionaries reported that what was most needed to advance their work was "a respectable chapel in each branch." McKay dedicated a new building in Zentalpan and inspected several building lots. Upon his return, McKay pushed the First Presidency to reconsider the excommunication of participants in the mass defection.[20]

In 1946, the First Presidency, acting upon Pierce's and McKay's recommendations, reduced the Third Convention leaders' penalty from excommunication

---

19. Heber J. Grant and David O. McKay to Harold W. Pratt, n.d., quoted in Tullis, "Shepherd," 131, 156; DOMD, Feb. 20, 1937.

20. Tullis, "Shepherd," 139, 145, 157; DOMD, Oct. 13–Nov. 12, 1943.

to disfellowshipment. Later that year in a master stroke of reconciliation, President George Albert Smith visited Mexico, graciously greeted the members, and extended an olive branch by inviting a prominent Third Conventionist, Abel Páez, to address the congregation. Two years later the McKays returned to Mexico for a second tour. In company with mission leaders Arwell and Mary Pierce and Moroni Abegg, Ray and David visited a small lean-to without a roof that the Third Convention had occupied. McKay determined that the structure should be roofed and used for a recreation hall and that a chapel should be erected alongside it. In Ozumba he inspected another former Third Convention property, a "fairly convenient meeting house with one room." McKay believed the building should be expanded and a piano provided. In Cuautla he dedicated a chapel and cultural hall that seemed to be "the most imposing building" in the city. Over nine hundred attended the dedication, notwithstanding the opposition of Catholic zealots who circulated anti-Mormon literature in the days leading up to the event. The Catholics' actions reinforced McKay's prejudice against Catholicism. In San Marcos, Hidalgo, at one of the oldest and strongest branches in Mexico, McKay spoke to a congregation of over three hundred. After the meeting, he recommended that the church purchase a building lot near the place where two Latter-day Saints, Rafael Monroy and Vicente Morales, had been executed for their faith during the Mexican Revolution. The modern building would be a fitting memorial to the martyrs. Heading north toward the border, McKay presided at conferences in Monterrey and Piedras Negras.[21]

McKay's visits to Mexico sensitized him to the need for greater accommodation of Spanish-speaking members. Two years after his first visit, McKay attended the first "Lamanite conference" held under the auspices of the Spanish American Mission in the American Southwest. A group of two hundred members from both sides of the border gathered at the Mexican Branch chapel in Mesa for meetings, followed, he recorded, by "the first temple session in this dispensation of the Gospel conducted in any but the English language." McKay assured the attendees that they were a chosen people and that the Book of Mormon had been written specifically to them as descendants of Lehi. He would attend and speak repeatedly at Lamanite conferences in the coming years.[22]

In addition to his efforts to reunite the church in Mexico, President McKay seized the opportunity as supervisor of missionary work to establish new missions abroad following World War II. The church's international expansion, which would become a hallmark of McKay's prophetic ministry, actually gathered steam during his years as President Smith's counselor. "There never has been a time in the history of the Church when people generally seem to be so favorably inclined to listen to the message of the restored Gospel," he reflected.

21. Tullis, "Shepherd," 145–47; DOMD, Feb. 13, 14, 18, 22, 24, Mar. 4, 1948.
22. DOMD, Nov. 2, 4, 5, 1945, Oct. 17, 1948.

Sobered by the devastation of world war, "intelligent men and women [were] beginning to recognize how applicable are the principles of the Church to the alleviation of ill-will among men." For decades missionary work had largely been confined to North America, northern and western Europe, and the Pacific Islands. Only 1,200 members lived in South America, and only two missions existed there, one in Argentina and the other in Brazil. Although McKay's support and vision were key in sending missionaries to new places in South America, the impetus came from a member who used his contacts to secure an appointment with the prophet. In August 1946 former Argentine Mission president Frederick S. Williams obtained an appointment with George Albert Smith through the graces of a former Argentine missionary who happened to be Smith's nephew. Smith in turn invited McKay as supervisor of the church's missionary efforts into the meeting. Williams, who had worked for several years in Venezuela and Uruguay, proposed sending missionaries to additional places in South America. McKay told the prophet that he was glad Williams had come and recommended that they "should do something about" his proposal. Williams came away from the meeting with an assignment; he was to place his recommendations in writing "concerning the opening of new missions in South America." By October he had drafted a twenty-page document including a recommendation regarding the sequence for taking the gospel to the nations: Uruguay should be first, followed by Peru, Chile, Paraguay, Ecuador, Colombia, and Bolivia. Early in 1947 the McKays' son Bob hosted a social gathering for fellow returned missionaries from Argentina at his parents' home. McKay asked the former missionaries if they thought it was feasible to send missionaries to Uruguay. Their enthusiastic response "convinced" McKay that the time was right, he wrote. A few months later, under assignment, McKay phoned Williams and asked, "Do you remember recommending opening a mission in Uruguay? How would you like to go down and open it?" The mission opened under Williams's direction later that year, and the following year missionary work commenced in neighboring Paraguay. At about the same time, missionary work also expanded in Central America, with the first elders arriving in both Guatemala and El Salvador in 1947.[23]

In 1948, the Japanese Mission was officially reopened, and early in 1949, McKay recommended that "definite steps be taken toward the organization of a mission in China." Communist forces had recently defeated the Nationalist army in Manchuria, and within a few months the Nationalists would be routed from the entire mainland, a defeat that the presidency did not anticipate. They believed that the best place to headquarter the mission would be

23. DOMD, Jan. 8, 1943, Jan. 11, May 7, July 22, 1947; Williams and Williams, *From Acorn to Oak*, 201–4, 219; Turley and Christensen, *An Apostolic Journey*, xxiv-xxvii; Cannon and Cowan, *Unto Every Nation*, 270–73.

Hong Kong but were uncertain what type of passports the missionaries would need. A few weeks later, under the prophet's direction, McKay called Hilton A. Robertson, former president of the Japanese Mission, as the new president. Robertson recalled that McKay met him by appointment and asked him "who would be the most likely person in the Church to send to China" to supervise missionaries there. Hilton named four men before McKay informed him that he was the unanimous, inspired choice of the First Presidency and the Quorum of Twelve Apostles. They felt that Robertson knew more about Asian peoples and cultures "than any other man in the Church." McKay called Henry Aki, a Chinese-speaking member in Hawai'i whom he knew, as Robertson's counselor. Missionaries arrived in Hong Kong in 1950 and served for the better part of a year, baptizing eighteen people before being recalled to Hawai'i due to the Korean War.[24]

As part of his stewardship over missionary work, McKay represented the church in negotiations with government officials regarding missionaries. When the military intelligence command and the division of economic warfare within the US Department of Justice wanted to enlist American missionaries to conduct observations and gather information in South America during World War II, the request came to McKay, who conveyed the First Presidency's determination that the request was "premature." In 1949, the FBI requested the names of missionaries returning from Europe so that they could interview them about conditions abroad. McKay promised that the presidency would "consider the matter very carefully" but pointed out that the church had pledged to foreign governments that missionaries would "not participate in any way" in political affairs.[25]

McKay worked diligently to accommodate draft laws and policies while maintaining the church's missionary force and mission leadership. In March 1942, fifteen months after Pearl Harbor, he instructed mission presidents to refuse all requests from missionaries to extend their term of service, lest the church violate its "tacit understanding" with the government regarding missions and military service. That same month the church instructed ward and stake leaders to process mission calls only for older men who held the office of seventy or high priest. "We shall not knowingly call anyone for the purpose of having him evade military service, nor for the purpose of interfering with or hampering that service in any way," the First Presidency announced. Under the new policy, in 1942 only 643 missionaries passed through the mission home in Salt Lake, and at the end of 1943, only 852 full-time missionaries were serving throughout the church. When draft boards during World War II raised concerns about the calling of specific missionaries, mission office staff,

24. DOMD, Jan. 27, Feb, 3, 28, 1949; Muriel Jenkins Heal, "We Will Go: The Robertson Response," *Ensign,* Apr. 1982.

25. DOMD, Jan. 8, Feb. 16, 1943, May 18, 1949.

and members of bishoprics, McKay conferred with Arnold Rich, director of Selective Service in Utah, to resolve the concerns. In 1943, a recently returned missionary claimed exemption from the draft on the grounds that his mission president had asked him to return and serve as branch president; McKay ruled that the man was "subject to call from the government" regardless of his contemplated church calling.[26]

In 1948, three years following the end of World War II, Congress passed the postwar Selective Service Act requiring all men between the ages of 18 and 26 to register and be classified by their local draft board. Congress exempted those studying for the ministry and ordained ministers from military service but still required them to register. Most ordained ministers were over the age of 26, but the church's 3,000-plus missionaries fell almost entirely in the draft-age range. McKay helped to negotiate an arrangement with the government whereby those with mission calls who had been notified by a draft board of their "acceptability of service" should "cease all preparation for coming into the Missionary Home" and instead prepare for military service. Those who had already been ordained and were serving missions would be exempt from the draft until after they returned.[27]

The outbreak of the Korean War in June 1950 set the stage for misunderstandings, frustrations, and resentments between military authorities in Utah and McKay and his associates in the Missionary Department. When the war began, about 591,000 soldiers were serving in the American army. Over the next three months, Congress and the executive branch authorized a force with just under 1.1 million men. In November, the secretary of defense boosted the authorized size to 1.26 million, excluding members of the National Guard. In order to maintain its missionary force without impeding the military, the First Presidency reduced the minimum age of missionary service for men from twenty to nineteen in September. They did so after Frank Murdock, the secretary to the Missionary Department, consulted with Oscar Gray, the assistant director for Selective Service in the state. Murdock came away from the meeting understanding that the military preferred older, "experienced men" over nineteen-year-olds. McKay and Murdock expected that young men would serve missions and then return at age twenty-one, more mature and capable, for military service. By lowering the minimum age for missionary service, McKay and Murdock primed the pump for a flood of applications from nineteen-year-olds, increasing the number of missionaries entering the field by a whopping 27

26. DOMD, Mar. 18, 1942, Jan. 13, May 18, 1944, Jan. 9, 1943; "Message of the First Presidency," Apr. 6, 1942, *Conference Reports,* 91–92; "Annual Report," Apr. 6, 1943, *Conference Reports,* 104; "Annual Report," Apr. 6, 1944, *Conference Reports,* 19.

27. Selective Service Act of 1948, Pub. L. No. 80-759, 62 Stat. 604, or 50 USC Appendix §§ 451–473 (2025); DOMD, Nov. 10, 1948, Jan. 18, 1951.

percent. The increase infuriated Gray, who denied he had ever expressed a preference for older recruits, and his boss, Brigadier General J. Wallace West. Both were Latter-day Saints, Gray more involved in church matters than West, but neither offered McKay much sympathy. The increase in applications made it appear that the church was shielding its members from the military. Suspecting the worst, some draft boards tried to prevent anyone with a physically fit (1-A) classification from serving a mission. A few even summoned young men from their jurisdictions who were already serving missions. McKay represented the First Presidency in delicate negotiations with Gray, West, and other officials, trying to maintain the church's right to call missionaries while minimizing the risk of negative publicity and charges of disloyalty.[28]

In mid-January McKay admitted to government officials that the age change for missionary service had been "a mistake," albeit an innocent one. Gray recommended that the church call only young men who were classed as IV-F, or physically impaired. Eager to avert a return to the emergency restrictions that had decimated the missionary force during World War II, McKay suggested instead that young men contact their draft board and obtain clearance from the board before submitting a missionary application. Both Gray and McKay came away from the meeting erroneously believing that they had prevailed. Two days later, based upon his understanding of what had been decided, Gray directed draft boards to "only consider registrants to fulfill missions" who were ineligible for military service. The letter infuriated McKay, who accused Gray of changing course midstream. In a hastily convened follow-up meeting, Gray agreed to amend his directive and permit local boards to clear men for "various reasons," a category sufficiently broad to encompass missionary service. The revised directive, dated Friday, January 19, was not shared with McKay or distributed to draft boards for several more days. In the interim, a group of young men with mission calls was scheduled to enter the mission home on Monday, January 22. Under the January 15 directive draft boards could not defer physically fit young men, but knowing that Gray had agreed to issue revised orders, McKay took liberties and admitted the young men to the mission home. From Gray's perspective, McKay violated the spirit of his pledge that young men would need to be cleared by their draft board before applying for a mission. McKay defended his actions, saying he had not intended his pledge to "cover boys who have already been called and assigned to their missions," especially because boards under Gray's former directive had been barred from clearing

28. Mark A. Olinger, *U.S. Army Mobilization During the Korean War and Its Aftermath*, Land Warfare papers no. 70W (Institute of Land Warfare, 2008), 2, 7; Minutes of a meeting of David O. McKay, General West, and Colonel Gray in DOMD, Jan. 16, 1951; "Funeral Service for Oscar Walton Gray," *Salt Lake Tribune*, May 21, 1985, 29; "Gen. J. Wallace West Dies Monday In Salt Lake," *Pleasant Grove Review*, Nov. 9, 1978, 6.

physically fit young men. The young men had already outfitted themselves for missions and obtained passports. "In justice to the boys, we had to let them come in to the Home," he insisted, "and we will stand on that and take it right back to Washington if necessary." Members of some draft boards were incensed by McKay's unilateral action, and General West assured them that the Selective Service had "not concurred in any actions of the Latter-day Saints church in admitting registrants into the mission home without first obtaining written release from their local boards." The boards should process the young men and summon them for classification "in the same manner as all other registrants." If they failed to show up, they could be arrested. Hot under the collar, McKay insisted that West vouch for the church's integrity. "It is not fair to say that we have not kept faith because we have." Those in the mission home were "not draft evaders." They had entered the mission home "in good faith" and were "entitled to go on their missions."[29]

Despite his bluster, McKay knew that the church had been backed into a corner. The nation was at war against communism, and an Associated Press reporter had "got a story from somewhere that there is a disagreement between the Church and the State Selective Service." The public relations risk of continuing to insist upon exemptions from the draft in order to maintain a large missionary force was too great. Privately he admitted to his fellow apostle and friend Stephen L Richards that the church would have to require those he had admitted to the mission home to obtain permission from their draft boards before continuing their missions. Almost certainly this would mean that at least one hundred young men in the mission home would have to enter the military instead. For his part, General West issued a circular apologizing indirectly and assuring that he had not intended to "cast any reflection upon the integrity of the Church or its authorities." On January 30, the First Presidency instructed bishops and stake presidents not to recommend any person for missionary service who had been classified by a draft board as physically fit for service. Nor were they to recommend anyone of draft age who had not yet been classified by a board. Young men were no longer to petition their draft boards for exemptions, and those with mission calls who were found by their boards to be fit for military service would have their calls rescinded. It pained McKay to draft a letter rescinding the calls, and he consoled the recipients as best as he knew how. "We share your disappointment," he wrote. "You may be assured, however, that the Lord, who knows the real intent of every heart, will accept your desires to serve Him, and bless you accordingly.... When He gives a commandment to any of his children to perform a specific work in His name, and those who are thus called accept that work and then are prevented by untoward influences to complete their assignment, the Lord will 'require that work no more at the

29. DOMD, Jan. 13, 15, 19, 22–27, 1951.

hands of those sons of men, and will accept of their offerings.'" Under the new policy imposed by the military, the number of missionaries dropped by over 48 percent between late 1950 and the end of 1953. Even after the war ended, reduced restrictions on missionary service continued. Beginning in the summer of 1953, bishops could recommend one young man from their congregation each year for missionary service. Two years later the quota was increased to two. Eventually the quotas on mission calls were eliminated entirely, and late in 1959, the Church announced the goal of having 12,000 full-time missionaries in the field.[30]

McKay left his mark on the church during his six years as counselor to George Albert Smith primarily through his supervision of the church's missionary effort. Despite the frustrations of navigating Selective Service requirements that greatly reduced the church's missionary force, McKay, with President Smith's hearty approval, facilitated the opening of more nations in Asia and Latin America to missionary work. While touring the Mexican Mission, McKay gained an appreciation for the faith and heritage of the Saints there, approved the construction of new church buildings, and recognized the desirability of temple sessions and special conferences in Spanish. In the state and community, McKay directed Utah's successful centennial celebration. With considerably less success he attempted to combat political corruption and vice in the Salt Lake Valley.

30. DOMD, Jan. 26, 1951; First Presidency to presidents of stakes and bishops of wards, Jan. 30, 1961, in DOMD, Jan. 30, 1951; First Presidency to missionaries rescinding their calls, Feb. 6, 1951, in DOMD, Feb. 6, 1951; "Statistical Report," Apr. 6, 1951, *Conference Reports*, 9; "Statistical and Financial Report," Apr. 5, 1954, *Conference Reports*, 65; "New Change in Draft Policy for Missionaries," *San Juan Record*, July 23, 1953, 1; "More Missionaries Permitted," *Manti Messenger*, Sep. 2, 1955, 1; Poll, *Divine Miracle*, 200–1. McKay's frustrations with the draft continued to bring out his combative instincts. Gordon B. Hinckley recalled a time when McKay met with Stephen L Richards and a stake president from Idaho to discuss the predicament of a missionary who had been ordered to report for duty after serving a mission for seventeen months. "President McKay put his fist down on Brother Richards' desk and said, 'We'll fight this! We'll fight it all the way to the Supreme Court if it takes everything the Church has!' ... Richards, who was more deliberate, said, 'Well, President McKay, we can fight it, but what if we lose it? If we lose it, we lose our whole missionary program. This young man has had seventeen months in the field, and my feeling is he'd better come and take the Army now and we'd better not disturb our missionary program." McKay wound up agreeing with Richards. Gordon B. Hinckley, excerpts from interview with William Robert Wright, Dec. 10, 1996, box 23, folder 1, Prince Papers.

10: The First Year as Prophet

In August 1950, George F. Richards, the senior member of the Quorum of the Twelve, passed away, and McKay became next in line to succeed an increasingly frail President Smith. After months of weakness, Smith rallied for the October general conference and appeared "vigor[o]us and well," McKay reported. The respite soon ended. After January 9, 1951, the prophet did not return to his office. He spent nearly three weeks in the hospital in February, and from that point until his death on April 4 he was often disoriented. On April 2, for the first time Smith failed to recognize McKay when he visited. The realization that the prophet was so near death "came as quite a shock to my nervous system," McKay reported. Two days later, Smith's family summoned him to the president's home to pronounce a priesthood blessing, and McKay "broke down with emotion." Smith died a few hours later, only two days before the opening session of the April general conference. As senior apostle, McKay was suddenly in charge, nearly forty-five years after his apostolic ordination.[1]

The following day, Thursday, McKay met with the apostles in the temple. The fourteen men took their seats in order of seniority, with McKay taking the first seat. As McKay began to speak "concerning the status of the Church and the need for reorganization of the Presidency," Spencer W. Kimball experienced "a sudden flow of warmth." To Kimball's view, the senior apostle took on a hue of "majesty and power.... For me, the mantle fell upon him that moment. There was no doubt in my mind," Kimball recorded. Later that day McKay spoke "with great difficulty and deep emotion" at the Primary Association's conference and returned home "completely exhausted." On Friday April 6, he opened the general conference. The Saturday morning and afternoon sessions were canceled for President Smith's funeral, where McKay presided and conducted. Following the Sunday afternoon general session, the apostles met in the temple. Joseph Fielding Smith moved that McKay be sustained as church president, a motion the apostles unanimously sustained. Then McKay presented the names of his counselors. Church members and leaders anticipated that Clark, who had served as first counselor to both Presidents Grant and Smith, would

1. DOMD, Oct. 1, 1950, Apr. 2, 4, 1951; Quinn, *Elder Statesman*, 129–30; Gibbons, *George Albert Smith*, 366–68.

be retained in that position. Despite his seniority in the quorum, McKay had served for decades as second counselor. Although he had never publicly questioned the ranking, he had long felt that counselor assignments should reflect seniority. Now he moved to rectify the situation; he designated his closest friend in the quorum, Stephen L Richards, as first counselor and named Clark, who had served less time as apostle than Richards, as second counselor. The announcement "stunned" several apostles, who walked back to the Church Administration Building "numb … our hearts breaking for [Clark]," Spencer Kimball recorded. It was difficult not to interpret this reversal as an embarrassing demotion and implicit rebuke. Although McKay did not see it that way, it seemed to some an insensitive elevation of principle over people. The next day in the final session of the conference, designated as a solemn assembly, Clark stoically read the names of the new First Presidency for sustaining; it was a painful ritual of humble loyalty to McKay as church president that "wasn't easy," he later confessed. McKay attempted to smooth matters over in the solemn assembly, explaining that the "guiding principle" in his ranking of counselors was seniority in the quorum and insisting that Clark's new appointment was not a "demotion." He pledged to his brethren, "I shall do my best so to live as to merit the companionship of the Holy Spirit." The following Thursday in a sacred rite in the Salt Lake Temple, McKay was formally ordained to his new position by President Joseph Fielding Smith. Ten months after calling his two counselors, McKay underscored his admiration for both of them in a council meeting. "I sense more clearly than ever, and wish to express here in your presence, my appreciation and gratitude for the support of those two noble men," he testified. Nevertheless, by disposition he was much closer to Richards than Clark, much as President Smith had been drawn more to Clark than McKay. According to Ernest Wilkinson, whose manipulative tendency and affinity for power politics likely colored his record, McKay confided in 1960 that his relationship with Clark over the years had sometimes been challenging. Wilkinson quoted him as saying that their shared commitments and ideals had enabled them to "get along," but "if I ever had any inspiration, it was when I selected Stephen L Richards as my first counselor, against all precedent."[2]

As his son Lawrence observed, the 1950s were "years of prime activity" for McKay, especially through 1958. Lawrence's statement must be interpreted in context; nearly 78 years old when he was sustained, McKay was far less vigorous than he had once been. Still, his health was relatively good in the early years of

2. DOMD, Apr. 5, 7–9, 12, 1951, Feb. 21, 1952; Spencer W. Kimball, journal, Apr. 5, 8, 1951; Quinn, *Elder Statesman*, 145, 147, 149; J. Reuben Clark, "Sustaining of Church Authorities," *Conference Reports*, Apr. 9, 1951, 136–47; David O. McKay, remarks made on Apr. 9, 1951, *Conference Reports*, 150–51; Jack Reed, "David O. McKay Completes One Year as President of the LDS Church," *Salt Lake Tribune*, Mar. 30, 1952, 56.

his presidency, and he used his strength to travel widely, meet with the Saints, oversee "a massive international building project," and teach masterfully.[3]

McKay hit the ground running. The morning following his sustaining, he convened a meeting of the First Presidency and announced that henceforth they would meet every weekday that they were in town, a rigorous schedule that his predecessors had been unable to maintain in their old age. Daily presidency meetings continued for the next eighteen months until McKay eliminated the Monday meetings. Local church leaders, members, representatives of the press, and the managers of church-owned businesses clamored to meet with the new president. In one interview McKay told a reporter that the church had already organized a branch in China (Hong Kong), intended to expand its reach into new countries, such as India, and would stand as a bulwark against communism in Cold War America. He hoped, he later indicated, to establish not only chapels but "schools for the little children who have no opportunity now even to go to school" in China. A backlog of items caused by President Smith's extended absence from the office needed McKay's attention. The first weeks of his presidency were thus "the most strenuous and trying" of his life to that point. As the stress mounted, he and Ray entrained for Southern California in late April to rest. Shortly after returning home, McKay awoke in intense pain and rushed to the hospital where he was diagnosed with an enlarged prostate. He called President Richards that evening for a blessing. The following day he underwent surgery, followed by a second blessing administered by President Clark and Llewelyn. Three weeks later as his recovery flagged, his doctors imposed an additional week's rest, chastening him for "not following their orders closely enough" about staying away from work.[4]

In early June, McKay was able to resume his full schedule, including attending the board meetings of church-owned corporations, among which were ZCMI, Zions Bank, Beneficial Life Insurance Company, the Hotel Utah, and the Utah Home Fire Insurance Company. Within a two-week period in early June, he spoke to the graduates of BYU, the University of Utah, and Temple University, receiving honorary degrees from each institution. He also performed temple weddings, including the marriage between Fletcher Hicks, a visually impaired BYU student from Columbus, Georgia, and Lilly Glauser, a musically gifted student from Montpelier, Idaho. Despite his busy schedule, he observed, he was "thankful" he could officiate at the wedding and reminded of "how blessed we are to possess our eyesight."[5]

Everywhere McKay went, members rushed to greet him. After he dedicated

---

3. McKay, *My Father*, 240.

4. DOMD, Apr. 10, 19, 22, 25, 27, May 3, 4, 24, 1951, Sep. 29, 1952; David O. McKay, "Dedication speech for the Hyde Park Chapel," in Lampropoulos, *A Vision Splendid*, 59.

5. DOMD, June 3–4, 8–9, 12, 27, 29, 1951.

a new stake center in Castle Dale, Utah, in July, McKay stood for two hours shaking hands and autographing dedicatory programs. The experience left him drained. Three days afterward, he again greeted a large crowd after speaking at the Nephi Centennial Pageant. In August, McKay spent three exhausting days in upstate New York visiting and evaluating church historic sites, attending the Hill Cumorah Pageant, and speaking to the cast, composed of missionaries, in the Sacred Grove. "I've never seen such delighted people as these were to meet the new president," Ray wrote. "People who had never seen a church president before, newcomers and converts to the Church were thrilled. There were hundreds of Kodaks and people everywhere wanting to shake hands." One who thrilled to meet the new prophet at the pageant was Kim Ho Jik, a graduate student who had joined the church while studying at Cornell. After meeting the prophet, Brother Kim "cradled his right hand in his left" and repeatedly mused, "'I have shaken the hand of the Prophet of God.'" McKay reported that the enthusiastic pageant audience of twenty thousand, seated on chairs and benches or watching from their automobiles, "impressed me almost as deeply as the pageant itself, which was presented on a professional scale." Still the trip was enervating; it kept him "busy every minute" and was "one of the most strenuous assignments [he had] had in some time."[6]

Before leaving New York, the exhausted church president experienced chest pains and feared a heart attack might be imminent. The pains portended future heart problems, but back in Salt Lake his cardiologist, Louis Viko, assured him his heart was basically sound and attributed the chest pains to frazzled nerves and fatigue. Viko prescribed several days of rest at home, but even at home people came to meet with him, and the press of business kept him awake at night. After returning to the office after his enforced break, he found that on many days, after three to four hours of work, his strength was spent, and he had to return home. Four weeks after experiencing his first chest pains he told Middlemiss that his nervous system was still not "entirely recovered." To speed his recovery he and Ray drove to California for a week's reprieve prior to the groundbreaking of the Los Angeles Temple. The modest presidential cottage on the sun-washed coast of Emerald Bay in Laguna Beach had enthralled him ever since he visited Grant there in 1921. He called it "the most restful place in the world." But on this brief trip, the handful of days he had allotted were insufficient to allow him to recover fully.[7]

Although he needed more rest, the temple groundbreaking provided its own tonic. It was a momentous occasion, foreseen by Heber J. Grant but delayed for

6. DOMD, July 8, Aug. 10, 12, 1951; McKay, *My Father*, 217; Jack Reed, "David O. McKay Completes One Year as President of the LDS Church," *Salt Lake Tribune*, Mar. 30, 1952, 56; reminiscence of Don C. and Geneal Wood, quoted in Denny Roy, "Kim Ho Jik: Korean Pioneer," *Ensign*, Jul. 1988.

7. DOMD, Aug. 17, Sep. 11, 1951; Jun. 22, 1959.

many years due to the Depression and the Second World War. "I now declare the first shovel of dirt raised over the site of the Los Angeles Temple which is to be reared to the glory of God and to the salvation of his people," the prophet proclaimed. Four days after the groundbreaking, McKay arrived back in Salt Lake, feeling "pretty well" but conscious that his nervous system was "still impaired." Over the coming months, he would return to southern California, mixing business with rest in November, January, February, and April.[8]

In October, McKay presided and conducted at his second general conference as prophet, calling Marion G. Romney, whom he had first met as a missionary in Australia on his world tour, as a new apostle and naming four assistants to the Quorum of the Twelve: ElRay Christiansen, John Longden, George Q. Morris, and Stayner Richards. Following the general conference priesthood session, McKay shook hands with hundreds of attendees, including a group of deacons from Kingman, Arizona, whose bishop, Ralph Harmon, had driven them to Salt Lake. McKay complimented Harmon on his "close companionship" with the boys, something he hoped all bishops would cultivate. The day after the conference, he traveled to Provo to install Ernest Wilkinson as BYU's new president. Just a few days later, he left for Washington, DC, to attend a conference with President Harry S. Truman and other "leading citizens" to discuss national problems and policies. His time in Washington, including a ten-minute personal visit with Truman, was "wholly worthwhile," he felt.[9]

In meetings with his counselors during his first year as church president, McKay confronted a variety of administrative issues ranging from management and personnel concerns at the *Deseret News*, to staffing the church's missions and auxiliaries, to requests for financial contributions from the church. The presidency considered the monetary needs of those who had joined the church abroad and immigrated to Utah under the sponsorship of members and the question whether the church would enroll its employees in the Social Security program. Some advisors, including Henry D. Moyle, believed the church should steer clear of contributions to Social Security; he had no faith in the government's ability to operate a long-term pension plan and predicted that its "bonds would probably become worthless." Notwithstanding his previous criticism of New Deal programs, McKay countered that he "did have faith in the government," and pointed out that too much was at stake for Social Security to fail; if the government defaulted on its welfare obligations "everything would fail." Increasingly critical of what he perceived to be shortcomings of the church welfare program, he said he preferred the government's impartial approach to welfare to the church's approach in which "assistance is dependent upon the

8. DOMD, Aug. 12, Sep. 27, 1951; Joseph Fielding Smith, "The Los Angeles Temple," *Improvement Era,* Nov. 1951, 784.

9. DOMD, Oct. 6, 11, 19, 22, 23, 1951.

judgment of the bishop or coordinator." He preferred to have "each person ... treated alike and no favoritism shown."[10]

McKay's counselors expressed themselves freely, and McKay listened. As they searched for a president of the new Central American Mission, McKay proposed David Haymore, a native of the Mexican colonies who spoke Spanish fluently and had previously presided over the Spanish American Mission. Richards objected, feeling that Haymore was insufficiently "progressive" and dynamic. McKay asked his counselors for additional recommendations and ultimately selected Gordon Romney. The prophet also listened to the female leaders of auxiliaries. Bertha Reeder, Young Women general president, questioned why men conducted the annual June conference sessions for women's auxiliaries. McKay and his associates considered the matter and decided that it was not only permissible but "proper" for Reeder and the other female presidents to conduct their conference sessions.[11]

During his first year as prophet, McKay sensed God's guiding hand in his life, and his confidence increased in the spiritual impressions that came. On a trip to Los Angeles in November, McKay "felt impressed to come home earlier" than he and Ray had planned. They arrived shortly before a severe snowstorm, and McKay acknowledged and expressed gratitude for the prompting. A couple of months later he was again in Southern California for a seminary conference. When the event was postponed for a week due to torrential rain, McKay felt prompted to return immediately to Utah rather than remain in California and rest for a few days. Soon after he arrived in Salt Lake, a business emergency arose at the Layton Sugar Company, where he served as president. McKay reflected, "The wisdom of following my impressions has been demonstrated."[12]

McKay spoke on behalf of the church at many organizational functions during his maiden year. In the eleventh month alone he spoke at the fiftieth anniversary of the Salt Lake Chamber of Commerce, officiated and spoke at the groundbreaking for Weber State College's new campus, dedicated a new Primary children's hospital on the foothills north of church headquarters, and was the featured speaker at Founders' Day for the Agricultural College of Utah. He used his addresses to admonish and inspire as well as celebrate and entertain. At the hospital dedication he reminded his audience that "the great purpose of man's mortal existence is to master selfish, animal instincts and propensities, and to develop qualities and attributes of the spirit." He won over his young audience at the state agricultural college with a bit of doggerel: "My grandad, viewing earth's worn cogs / Said things were going to the dogs. / His grandad in his house of logs / Said things are going to the dogs. / His grandad in the

10. DOMD, Dec. 27, 1951, Jan. 2, Apr. 4, 1952.
11. DOMD, Nov. 26, 1951, Mar. 31, 1952.
12. DOMD, Nov. 9, 1951, Jan. 22, 1952.

Finnish bogs / Said things are going to the dogs. / His grandad in his old skin togs / Said things are going to the dogs. / There's one thing I have to state / The dogs have had a good long wait." After admitting the tendency of older people like himself to bemoan the younger generation's lapses, he pinpointed genuine concerns about the nation's moral fabric. Highlighting a topic that had recently captured newspaper headlines, increasing juvenile crime, he argued that the nations' schools must "teach citizenship and noble character." The greatest good that the state agricultural college could achieve, he emphasized, would be to "inspire students to the truth that character is higher than intellect."[13]

By the end of his first year as church president, McKay had traveled over 50,000 miles, spoken to numerous church and civic groups, dedicated six chapels, visited five states and the District of Columbia, and accepted three honorary degrees. He had broken ground for a massive temple in Los Angeles, installed a new president at BYU, attended a conference of prominent leaders across the nation and visited with the President of the United States, and evaluated church historic sites in upstate New York. All this action had come at a cost to his aging body. He had been hospitalized twice and spent the better part of two months convalescing.[14]

Beyond his first year, one facet of his calling continued to defy mastery: the stresses of the job. The busier he became, the more tired he felt and the poorer he slept. In his second year he canceled Monday morning meetings with his counselors and decided that the First Presidency would no longer meet with the General Welfare Committee in their weekly meetings. Welfare, which had been a key priority during the Depression, was "being given too much prominence"; the presidency's attendance at the committee meetings privileged welfare over other church programs and needlessly involved the presidency in preliminary discussions. Moving to limit the program, he announced that purchases of new welfare farms by local church units would be "curtail[ed]."[15]

Two years into his presidency, McKay's son Edward, a doctor, implored him to take Mondays off and spend less time each day in the office. A year later, Ed and Dr. Viko stressed that he needed to rest and relax on Mondays. But McKay's idea of resting was not what his doctors had in mind. He was a workaholic. "In keeping with the doctors' instructions, I did not go to the office today. Spent the day on the farm in Huntsville, attending to the many chores I have neglected for so long," his secretary recorded in McKay's diary.[16]

13. DOMD, Mar. 2, 7, 1952; "Corporate Leaders Arrive for S.L. Chamber Jubilee," *Deseret News*, Feb. 20, 1952, 17; "Weber Day Closes Books," *Weber College Signpost*, Mar. 19, 1952, 1.

14. Jack Reed, "David O. McKay Completes One Year as President of the LDS Church," *Salt Lake Tribune*, Mar. 30, 1952, 56.

15. DOMD, Oct. 15, Nov. 5, 1952.

16. DOMD, June 15, 1953, Apr. 13, 19, 1954.

11: The People's Prophet

Latter-day Saint regard for and veneration of David O. McKay was intense and unprecedented, at least since the days of Brigham Young. Youth groups studied his life in church meetings, especially after Deseret Book published Llewelyn's *Home Memories of President David O. McKay* in 1956. To many of his followers, McKay looked the part of a prophet more than his predecessors. McKay's associate in church administration, assistant Church Historian Preston Nibley, described him as a "tall, handsome man with a shock of white hair, immaculately dressed" in a double-breasted suit. Unlike artistic depictions of bearded Old Testament figures or his late-nineteenth- and twentieth-century predecessors, McKay sported no beard to frame his winsome smile. He appeared quintessentially wholesome and modern, reflecting the clean-shaven visages of modern American presidents and executives. "He didn't look like Moses, but he looked like a Supreme Court Justice.... He was truly a lovely looking man," recalled Renee Pyott Carlson. "He broke down so much prejudice. He looked the part of a prophet," recalled one of his traveling companions. His was "an affable new image of Mormonism," *Time* magazine reported, "to a world that had previously seen the Mormon leaders as dour, dark-suited figures." Never as influential nationally as Billy Graham or Pope Paul VI, he was nevertheless a leader who commanded respect not only within but also beyond the Latter-day Saint fold. "He was a loveable person by the Jew and the Gentile and the disaffected Mormon," recalled the composer Crawford Gates.[1]

People clearly loved McKay as their prophet. While McKay's biographers have acknowledged that fact, they have focused more upon his relationships with family and prominent men and women than with rank-and-file Latter-day Saints. As McKay was filling his tank with gasoline at a North Salt Lake service station in 1951, just a few months after he was sustained as church president, a man approached him cautiously and apologetically to offer some advice. "Please do not drive this car yourself," he implored. "You are too precious; the

1. DOMD, Jan. 18, 1947, July 19, 1956; Nibley, "David O. McKay,"; Renee Pyott Carlson, excerpts from interview by Greg Prince, Jun. 2, 1994, box 22, folder 13, Prince Papers; "Prophet, Seer and Innovator," *Time Magazine,* Feb. 2, 1970, 49–50; "Nixon Heads List of 'Admired Men,'" *New York Times*, Jan. 4, 1970, 3; Crawford Gates, excerpts from interview by Greg Prince, Aug. 17, 2001, box 22, folder 13, Prince Papers.

Church needs you; you must be careful." McKay was "deeply touched" by the man's sincere concern. For as long as McKay's schedule would permit, the faithful pressed in upon him to shake his hand as he entered or left the tabernacle during general conference. "Some took his hand in both of theirs and stared into his eyes, unable to speak," Middlemiss recorded. Many asked him to pose with them for photographs or tried to establish a personal connection with him by dropping the name of a friend or relative he might know. After conference, one woman brought a homemade pie into the tabernacle and presented it to him as an expression of her love.[2]

At a filling station in Nephi in 1955 he was thronged by a "choice group" of high school students until he was "completely closed in." They brought out a chair from the school to make him comfortable and invited him to sit as he autographed their papers and books for over an hour. At a Cedar City service station in 1957, three young boys ran over to shake his hand. "Nothing pleases me more than to have these children come around—to shake their hands, and to partake of their sincere spirit is always a joy to me," he told his secretary. Although Dr. Viko advised him that year to conserve his strength and protect his weakening heart by "reduc[ing] to a minimum the strenuous handshaking after meetings," he kept it up because the Saints expected it and because he relished being among them.[3]

Celebrity status, money, power, and personal connections with McKay's associates facilitated some individuals' access to him. Friendship with a highly respected, influential religious leader could confer political, economic, or other benefits that some politicians and business leaders such as President Lyndon Johnson sought, but at least some prominent individuals were spiritually inspired or even transformed by their association with McKay. Fred Schluter, a wealthy New Jersey industrialist who owned Thermoid Rubber, was scouting out possible locations for a western automotive rubber plant when he met McKay in 1946. Upon their meeting, Schluter recalled, "I was suddenly conscious that here was one of the 'biggest' men I had ever met... a great and kindly spirit." Schluter was not particularly religious, and his private life and marriage were in shambles. McKay sparked "some of the spiritual side of me that had been too long dormant," Schluter wrote. Five years later, Schluter introduced McKay to his new wife, Dorothy Miskell. She quickly became interested in the church and requested baptism in 1953. Seven months after Dorothy's baptism, McKay baptized Fred, and he subsequently officiated their temple sealing. Fred wrote a biographical tribute to McKay, and he and Dorothy donated funds for a David O. McKay scholarship at BYU.[4]

2. DOMD, Oct. 27, 1951, Oct. 5, 1952.
3. DOMD, Oct. 19, Nov. 11, 1955, July 19, 1956, May 8, 31, 1957.
4. Schluter, *Convert's Tribute*; DOMD, June 12, 1951, Apr. 11, 14, Nov. 2, 1953, Apr. 7, 1958,

Like Schluter, James Brewster Conkling, who worked as president of two major record companies and chaired the National Academy of Recording Arts and Sciences, was not a Latter-day Saint when he met McKay. Conkling's wife, Donna Driggs, of the renowned King Sisters, was a lifelong member. McKay visited with the Conklings following the nationally televised Grammy Awards gala in which the Tabernacle Choir sang and received a Grammy. "Just for him to have the opportunity to be in your company for a few precious moments was more than I could ever dream would happen," Donna wrote following their meeting. Soon afterward, Jim told his wife that he had decided to join the church; two years later he was baptized, and later he worked for the church as managing director of the church's short-lived International Educational Broadcasting Corporation and then as an executive of the church's media holding company, Bonneville International.[5]

In spite of his general desire to accommodate others and visit with them, on vacations McKay pulled back from the limelight, insisting upon personal and family time. In 1956 he traveled with Robert and Edward to Wyoming, primarily to claim and retrieve some saddles stolen from their Huntsville property that had been recovered but also to spend a day fishing in Yellowstone. When the bishop of the Jackson Ward learned that McKay had checked in to a motel in town, he phoned to invite him to speak to a group of members that evening. McKay politely declined, explaining that he had been driving all day, was exhausted, and had an appointment at 5:00 the next morning. A few minutes later leaders from the ward's youth organization descended on the motel, hoping McKay would speak to them. Again he demurred. The following evening, when the McKays checked into a room at West Thumb after a successful day of fishing, a group of teenage workers from the lodge surrounded him. Would he be willing to address about one hundred workers at the lodge later that evening? McKay told the disappointed teens that he could not speak to them because he was "very tired" and planned to leave the park at 5:00 the next morning.[6]

At times, McKay gave in to the pressures of the office, time constraints, and physical exhaustion and refused to give blessings. He once showed Dick Isaacson a long list with the names of those who had written to him requesting blessings in a six-month period. "No man in his 40's could have done what these people had asked President McKay to do," Isaacson judged. "He tried to do the ones that he felt were most important." During his 1953 visit to Scotland,

July 10, Oct. 3, Nov. 16, 1968. Schluter sought to move beyond a checkered past. His first wife filed for divorce in 1948 on grounds of desertion. Schluter v. Schluter, 17 NJ Super. 496, 86 A.2d 300 (1951). In 1956 federal officials investigated his company and prosecuted him for tax evasion. He was pardoned by President John F. Kennedy. Cumbler, *Social History*, 141.

5. DOMD, Nov. 27, 1959, Donna Conkling quoted in Dec. 5, 1959; Prince and Wright, *David O. McKay,* 130; "Broadcasting Executive James Conkling Dies," *Deseret News*, Apr. 16, 1998.

6. DOMD, July 10–12, 1956.

when members of the Edinburgh Branch asked him to bless their children, he declined, stating that "that was not what he was there for." When one elder, Frederick Buchanan, asked the prophet to administer to another missionary who was suffering with ear problems, McKay advised Buchanan to give the blessing himself. "You have the same healing power as anyone else," he instructed. After McKay's visit, "some members went inactive," resenting McKay's seeming disregard for them. "I think they were expecting some special attention from him, though it was small-minded of them," Buchanan reflected.[7]

Convinced of McKay's exceptional faith and spiritual clout, devout Latter-day Saints petitioned him for healing blessings. He especially tried to accommodate victims of paralyzing or terminal illnesses. On his first trip to Germany as prophet, McKay met two children whose mother had been paralyzed by a stroke. She sent her children to the conference to meet McKay, convinced that if they shook his hand and relayed the handshake to her, she would "be blessed." After shaking their hands, McKay gave them a white handkerchief to carry to their mother "with his blessing." McKay learned later that the mother's condition had improved; she was able to leave her bed on her own and perform simple kitchen duties like washing the dishes while seated in a chair. Tales of this miraculous healing spread. In 1952, the prophet surprised nuns serving at Holy Cross Hospital when he entered the lobby and asked for directions to the room of Julene Butler, a three-year-old polio victim. Although the ravages of the disease persisted, she lived to adulthood, earned a PhD, and became BYU's head librarian. In 1954 Lucille Worthen, a forty-five-year-old mother of three who had been afflicted with polio fourteen years earlier, wrote to McKay. For some time, she had felt that if she received a healing blessing from the prophet and exercised sufficient faith, she could be "completely healed." Touched by her desire and conviction, McKay made an appointment for a blessing. As the blessing concluded, Worthen felt a tingling sensation in her legs and stood briefly before her legs gave out. A few days later a letter arrived from McKay. It indicated that as he blessed her the thought had entered his mind that "daily massaging of her limbs and gradually standing on them would show her willingness to cooperate with divine aid that she needs." McKay hoped that if she did so "the Lord would eventually grant unto her the desires of her heart." McKay's compassion and his readiness to combine his faith with hers almost certainly inspired her. Although Worthen never fully recovered, she knew that the man she sustained as God's prophet cared deeply about her.[8]

7. Richard Isaacson, excerpts from interview by Greg Prince, Mar. 20, 1995, box 22, folder 13, Prince Papers; Frederick Buchanan, excerpts from interview by Greg Prince, May 21, 1996, box 22, folder 13, Prince Papers.

8. DOMD, Dec. 19, 1952, Dec. 16, 1951, Nov. 14, 1954; Helen Julene Butler, interview by Becky B. Lloyd, Mar. 27, 2010, Everett L. Cooley Oral History Project; entry for Lucille Beardall Worthen, KW8J-X9D, Family Search, familysearch.org.

Following a church service in St. George where he spoke in 1955, McKay motored to a small home in nearby Leeds to meet with Ross Eager, a twenty-one-year-old polio victim who had undergone years of medical treatments in California. Eager's determination and persistence since his diagnosis, as reported in the press, had made him a minor celebrity, and a caravan followed McKay's car to witness the blessing. As Eager later recalled, McKay advised him, "Satan meant to hit you so hard that he wanted to wipe you clear off this earth, and he is frustrated now because his plan did not work." McKay recorded, "He is a brilliant young man, and I felt that he would recover, and so blessed him to that end." Eager rebounded sufficiently to marry, attend school, father two children, and become an insurance agent in Cedar City before his health began to fail again four years later. He died in 1962.[9]

Another polio victim, Sara Minson, who had been paralyzed from age eight but had learned to walk with braces, visited the prophet in 1960. She had worked as the chief accountant for two state agencies in Boise for over thirty years, but due to hip degeneration she now used a wheelchair. She and her sister traveled to Salt Lake to visit with McKay, who provided "assuring words of encouragement," she wrote. Although she was not physically healed, "the love and spirituality" radiating from McKay's face lifted her. "Here was a man who was willing to consider my personal problem despite his anxiety over his wife's health and the terrific responsibility which is his," she gratefully reflected.[10]

Early in 1956, LaMont Maurice Larson, a nineteen-year-old cancer patient, attended the dedication of a new seminary and chapel at Intermountain Indian School, which was operated by the federal government, near his home. He hoped to receive a blessing from the prophet, who was officiating in the dedication. McKay's packed schedule left no time for a blessing, but after he returned home, he could not forget the disappointment on LaMont's face. On the following Saturday McKay drove sixty miles to Larson's home to pronounce the requested blessing. Larson and his nurse were astonished. "I was very glad that I had taken the time to come to his home," McKay reflected. Two months later the young man passed away.[11]

The prophet advised faith and courage in the face of terminal illnesses. When

9. DOMD, Apr. 17, 1955; Eager, *Man of Faith*, 92, in entry for Ross Eager, KW8Z-3D8, Family Search, familysearch.org.

10. Sara Minson to Secretary [Clare Middlemiss] in DOMD, May 17, 1960; Minson, *Autobiography*, 13, entry for Sara Minson, KWZR-JH6, Family Search, familysearch.org. As a preventative measure McKay encouraged healthy people to obtain a polio vaccine. After the vaccine was released in 1955, complications from a vaccine virus led to hundreds of new cases and ten deaths. Some local church leaders advised their congregations to shun the vaccine and rely exclusively upon God. McKay disagreed with their approach "because the Lord expects us to do everything we can to make use of all the improvements and inventions and discoveries that come through his inspiration." DOMD, Jan. 25, 1957.

11. DOMD, Jan. 26, 1956.

a cancer victim died despite a healing priesthood blessing from the prophet, his family and friends wondered how this was possible. McKay advised that "the Lord does not always answer our prayers affirmatively; sometimes the answer comes negatively." He pointed out that "if we always had an affirmative answer, there would be no death at all." He reminded Cecil Briggs, a returned missionary afflicted with cancer, that "the sufferings of this world are part of our mortal existence, that this life is so brief compared to the eternities to come." He encouraged Briggs to have faith in God's timing and assured him of God's love.[12]

McKay also cared for the mentally ill. He took exceptional interest in an eighteen-year-old high school dropout from Sacramento named David who made his way to Salt Lake City in 1958. General church leaders in Salt Lake City helped the young man secure work at Welfare Square, but he soon quit the job, and the church paid his bus fare back to California. Less than a year later, David was back in Utah, visiting McKay "almost nightly" at his home over the course of several months. McKay helped him find several jobs, but he was unable to hold any of them for long. He wrote to the young man's father, urging him to intervene, and David subsequently reported he had received some money from home, but later that same day, he said the funds were insufficient to buy a bus ticket. McKay did not know what to believe. He referred David to Police Chief Cleon Skousen for help. "I have had much pity and sympathy with this boy, but it has reached a point where there is not anything I can do for him," McKay lamented. A few days later, during McKay's birthday party, the young man came by the house; McKay sent Llewelyn to the door to say he could not meet with him that evening. "I am really worried about the boy, and do not wish to see him get into any more trouble. He really needs care and should be with his folks," McKay reflected. In 1961 the young man stole a car and drove it to Missouri, where he was arrested. McKay asked the mission president there to visit David, work with his court-appointed attorney, send someone from the church to visit him, and try to obtain proper psychiatric care for him. "He is not mentally responsible," McKay advised.[13]

McKay's personal ministry extended beyond those who were physically and mentally ailing. "He made every single one of us feel special when we so easily could have been just one of hundreds," recalled Irene Bates, a Relief Society leader in England. "He made you realize that everybody was important in the sight of God. That was it. You were an individual. You were a daughter or a son of God." One day when British Saints were standing in "endless lines" waiting to shake his hand, McKay glimpsed "an elderly lady quite far back, bent and tired." Excusing himself from the front of the line, he made his way to the woman, held out his hand and exchanged pleasantries with her to spare her the

12. DOMD, Oct. 17, 1951, Feb. 6, 1958.
13. DOMD, July 23, Sep. 6, 1959, Oct. 2, 1961.

strain of standing on her feet any longer. "How could we help loving such sensitivity and consideration?" Bates reflected. On another occasion, a father asked the prophet to meet with his daughter. She was engaged to marry a Catholic stationed at Hill Air Force Base, but as the wedding approached, she worried about her decision to marry outside the faith. The woman walked away from her interview with McKay feeling renewed and hopeful. It was "one of the supremely great experiences of her life," the father reported. Two days later she and her fiancé married. Their marriage endured until his death nearly fifty-six years later, and his memorial services were held at both her Latter-day Saint ward and his Catholic chapel.[14]

McKay's close associates and fellow church leaders, including future prophets, sought counsel in deeply personal matters and trusted his counsel would comport with God's will. "I am at a crossroads and badly need direction. Can you give me some counsel?" wrote Spencer Kimball in 1957. "I know that as the Lord's prophet you are entitled to and do receive His revelations and … that He will inspire you to direct me … I have total confidence in your judgment and inspiration." Kimball had throat cancer, and after taking a biopsy, his doctor would likely recommend removal of the vocal cords. Through a hole in his neck, Kimball might learn to make intelligible sounds, but it would be "impossible" for him to preach. Kimball's voice was integral to his work, and because of that, "to lose permanently [his] voice" seemed "worse than death." If McKay advised him to meet with the cancer specialist in New York and proceed with a biopsy and possible laryngectomy at the risk of losing his voice, he would do so. If he advised otherwise, he would continue working as long as his voice and strength lasted. McKay advised Kimball to go to New York, and if necessary, undergo a complete laryngectomy. In the end, the surgeon entirely removed one of his vocal cords and half of the other. Kimball regained the ability to speak with a raspy voice and lived for twenty-eight more years, serving for twelve of them as president of the church. In 1965 a middle-aged couple, Russell and Dantzel Nelson, visited the prophet, seeking inspired counsel regarding an offer that Russell, a renowned heart surgeon, had received to chair the division of cardiovascular and thoracic surgery at the University of Chicago. He was serving at the time as president of the Bonneville Stake, and the family lived in a beautifully appointed home in one of Salt Lake's finest neighborhoods. The Nelsons were concerned about the implications of their decision for their children and obtained the appointment through the graces of their stake high councilor, Joseph Anderson, who worked as secretary to the First Presidency. The ninety-two-year-old prophet "laid back in his chair, closed his

14. McKay, *My Father,* 260; Bill and Irene Bates, excerpts from interview by Greg Prince, Oct. 5, 1999, box 22, folder 13, Prince Papers; DOMD, Dec. 27, 1958, Jan. 6, 1959; obituary for John George Bonk, *Ogden Standard-Examiner,* Nov. 19, 2014, standard.net.

eyes, and communed with the Lord in supplicating an answer that would be a guide for us." The appointment lasted for seventy-five minutes, and McKay remained "nonresponsive" with his eyes closed for so long that the Nelsons "began to wonder if he was still alive." Then, Nelson recalled, McKay opened his eyes, gazed directly into theirs, and advised them to turn down the offer. Nelson recalled the substance of his remarks: "I wouldn't be in a hurry to change neighborhoods. It doesn't feel good to me.... People will come from all over the world to you because you are here. I don't think you should go to Chicago." A few months later Nelson was appointed head of a thoracic residency program involving four hospitals in the Salt Lake Valley, two of which, Latter-day Saints Hospital and the Primary Children's Hospital, were operated by the church.[15]

The prophet reached out to acquaintances who had become alienated from the church. After speaking at the Agricultural College of Utah in Logan, McKay drove to the nearby home of Henry Peterson. Five years his senior, Peterson had grown up near McKay in Huntsville, had studied at the University of Chicago and Harvard, and had served under McKay decades earlier on the General Sunday School Board. In 1911 Peterson had resigned under duress from BYU in a highly publicized controversy over academic freedom, and thereafter his involvement with the church had lagged. Ignoring McKay's plea, he had resigned from the general board in protest of his dismissal. McKay's impromptu visit softened Peterson, who expressed remorse for resigning from the board years earlier. Peterson seemed "humble and contrite" and "bore his testimony regarding the divinity of the Church." McKay deemed the visit "one of the most satisfying ... in many a day." Four years later at the suggestion of a relative, McKay invited Peterson to obtain a recommend and attend the Los Angeles Temple dedication. During his interview in the church offices, Peterson acknowledged that for years he had resented the church for his dismissal from BYU; now, he said, he felt "no resentment whatsoever." Recommend in hand, Peterson left the office "very happy indeed," and McKay felt gratified and hopeful.[16]

The prophet also manifested goodwill toward lapsed Mormons like University of Utah philosophy professor Sterling McMurrin, perhaps hoping that he might reclaim them. According to McMurrin, McKay offered in 1954 to testify in his behalf if his stake leaders subpoenaed him to appear before an ecclesiastical council. While serving on the Utah Centennial Commission, McKay worked closely with Gus Backman, a cultural Mormon who admired the church but had rarely attended services since his early teens. In 1947, while still serving

15. DOMD, July 18, 1957, Dec. 13, 14, 1965; Spencer W. Kimball, journal, Jun. 28, 1957; Kimball and Kimball, *Spencer W. Kimball*, 263–65, 301–12; Condie, *Russell M. Nelson*, 148–50.

16. DOMD, Mar. 7, 1952, Mar. 5, 1956; Richard Sherlock, "Campus in Crisis: BYU, 1911," *Sunstone*, Jan.–Feb. 1979, 15.

on the centennial commission, McKay contacted Backman's bishop, pointed out that Backman was an ordained deacon, and asked the bishop to "take an interest in Brother Backman." Four years later, just a few days before McKay became church president, Backman contacted his friend, hurt by a church leader's reported characterization of him as "anti-church." He assured McKay that he would do "anything" McKay asked for the church. McKay pledged that anyone who questioned his friend's loyalty to the church would "receive a reprimand from me." During his presidency, McKay met regularly with both Backman and John Fitzpatrick, editor of the *Salt Lake Tribune*, in Fitzpatrick's office for friendly banter and also to discuss civic matters.[17]

McKay's home on South Temple Street was well-known and accessible. No guards patrolled the grounds, and he could sometimes be seen reading the paper on his front porch or working in the yard. At all hours, visitors stopped by unannounced to seek counsel or blessings, request favors, or simply wish him well. "Very rarely do we have an evening free at home—members of the Church are continually calling there," he reported in 1958. Some of the callers brought gifts. Viola West, a teenager, baked a birthday cake and delivered it to his home in 1956. Calvin Arneson, a Californian, rang the bell in 1959, dropping by a case of strawberries simply to express "appreciation." McKay had performed Arenson's wedding sixteen years previously, so the man felt a personal connection to him. Some callers were inconsiderate. In the middle of one summer night, a caller knocked repeatedly at the back door, calling out in a raspy voice, "President McKay, President McKay." The McKays ignored the calls, and eventually the intruder left.[18]

An especially disquieting visit occurred one June evening when a distraught couple knocked on the door. The father claimed he had been trying to teach his three-year-old son to float in the Great Salt Lake, assuming that the salt water would keep him afloat, but the son drowned. McKay feared the father was guilty of negligent homicide. The parents pled with McKay to go to the county hospital, pray over the body, and restore the child's life. He acquiesced, but when they arrived at the hospital, they learned that the body had already been taken to the morgue. The parents again pled for a blessing, and McKay advised them, "The boy is gone; we cannot bring him back," although he consented to say a prayer with them. He then assisted the parents in making arrangements for an undertaker. McKay was troubled the next morning when the father again showed up on his doorstep, telling him he had received spiritual assurance during the night that "all is and will be well in every way." The encounter with the troubled

17. Prince and Wright, *David O. McKay*, 55–56, 333–34; DOMD, Mar. 31, 1947, Mar. 28, 1951.

18. DOMD, Aug. 25, 1958, Sep. 9, 1956, May 10, 1959, Aug. 25, 1957, Mar. 25, 1958.

parents was "one of the most disturbing tragedies with which I have ever been associated," he reflected.[19]

Some members, primarily women, stopped at the McKay home seeking marital counseling and intervention. A temple-endowed member from Nephi, over eighty miles south of Salt Lake, whose husband was not a practicing member, was distressed by her husband's request that she no longer wear temple undergarments. McKay advised her to tell her husband that "she will take them off if he so demands, but that he will have to bear the consequence" of her action. Whatever the effect of the counsel, the husband eventually began attending church. Eight years later, a few months before his death, he and his wife were sealed for eternity in the temple. Another woman who had been married for a decade knocked on the door at 9:30 one winter evening. McKay invited her in, and for the next half hour she tearfully recounted her marital difficulties and lamented that her husband no longer loved her. McKay phoned the husband and asked him to come over. After he arrived, the couple commenced arguing and continued until well after midnight, when McKay ushered them to the door, urging them to forget bygones and start anew in order to give their daughter a happy home.[20]

Although they lacked appointments for formal visits, many admirers of the prophet devised "coincidental" rendezvous with him. Nina Shern, a young woman living in Salt Lake's Avenues district, passed the prophet's car daily while walking to work. One day she deliberately timed her walk to coincide with the prophet's routine arrival at the office. She walked up as he exited the car, greeted him with a handshake, and then froze, embarrassed that she had not rehearsed what to say next. She mumbled a few words and then took her leave. It was not quite the interchange she had imagined, but she never forgot it. In a BYU devotional early in 1960, assistant Church Historian Preston Nibley spoke on the character of President McKay. He told the students that the prophet was an early riser; perhaps they could greet him as he arrived at his office early some morning. A few days later, a student who had attended the devotional stood in the parking lot at 6:15 a.m. waiting for the prophet. When McKay arrived, he invited the student into his office to visit briefly.[21]

After the McKays moved to an apartment in the Hotel Utah in 1960, groups of students often converged on the hotel seeking impromptu meetings. Some waited in the elegant lobby to greet the prophet as he walked to and from work each day. Sometimes so many students were waiting that he spent

---

19. DOMD, June 20, 1959; "Lake Waters Claim Life of S. L. Child," *Salt Lake Tribune*, June 21, 1959, B1.

20. DOMD, Apr. 28, Aug. 1, 1956, Feb. 16, 1958.

21. Nina Liechty, interview by Brian Cannon, August 2022; Nibley, "David O. McKay"; DOMD, Feb. 9, 1960.

an hour or more crossing the lobby. Others came to his apartment. His journal records that on a Sunday in 1960, "people [came] calling at the apartment in the Hotel all day." Some persistent callers, including missionaries in training at the nearby mission home, went down the hallway in the hotel ringing doorbells until they found the right one. In 1962, two BYU students, Susan Ward and Sondra Pinegar, knocked on the doors of "grumpy hotel guests" for hours until a maid helped them find the prophet's apartment. Years later, Susan recalled her memorable visit: the prophet "looked surprised but didn't say anything. Neither did I; I couldn't. I felt like I had a key to the celestial kingdom but did not belong—I was not worthy to be in his presence. I started to cry. He took me by the hand and said, 'Won't you come in?' I waved to my friend down the hall and entered the prophet's home. Our discussion remains personal, but the resulting impact changed my inner direction dramatically."[22]

For every person who visited the prophet's home or office, many more wrote to him. McKay received "thousands of letters" that his secretaries screened and managed. "Crank letters" went into a separate file and were kept for a few months and then discarded. Middlemiss reviewed "every important letter" with him, she insisted, even though "every letter cannot receive personal acknowledgement." In most cases, she categorized the letters and out of necessity wrote the responses "in accordance with [his general] instructions." Elaine Reiser, a part-time secretary in the office, explained, "We answered" the letters "and "then we would go through them and just tell him basically what it was as he signed them. So he knew what we answered." Similar inquiries received similar responses, taken from previous letters that had been sent. "I had books of those [previous] letters, and I would take a paragraph from this and paragraph from that ... but once in a while [McKay] would pull me in to take a dictation," recalled Clare's assistant Lola Gygi Timmins. When he had time to examine them, letters from members offered McKay a look into their lives and challenges and provided a glimpse of the church's operation at the local level. In 1959, Mary Quist Mays, a thirty-seven-year-old mother of six young children and an avid genealogist, wrote to the prophet about a matter that fixed his attention. She noted that *Teachings of the Prophet Joseph Smith* recorded Joseph Smith's instruction that "the greatest responsibility in this world that God has laid upon us is to seek after our dead." Yet she found little support for that proposition from her local priesthood leaders, who prioritized other matters. Moreover, she rarely heard genealogy discussed in general conference. As a busy mother, she did not have time to devote to unimportant matters. Should she omit genealogy from her schedule? "I turn to you ... because with all my heart I believe you are a true Prophet of God," she wrote. McKay replied to her stake

22. DOMD, Oct. 30, 1960, Dec. 6, 1961, Jan. 11, 1962; Susan [Ward] Easton Black, reminiscences of Susan Easton Black, Witnesses of the Book of Mormon, witnessesofthebookofmormon.org.

president and copied her on the response, affirming that Joseph Smith's statement was true. The prophet agreed with Mays that "too few people take interest in this very important work," but "the failure of the people to do their duty affects in no way the truthfulness of the statement made by the Prophet Joseph Smith." He insisted that "the fact is that the Church is putting forth more effort at the present time for the salvation of the dead than at any other time in history." Recently he had met with twelve stake presidents who stated that the Salt Lake and Logan Temples were inadequate to accommodate the members who desired to attend. "Anyone who can even just get a glimpse of this one phase of salvation for the dead can readily understand how this 'greatest responsibility' will require not only our present activity, but … will extend even through the Millennium." A few weeks later, McKay made temple and genealogical work the primary focus of the general conference priesthood session.[23]

McKay responded to some letters with a call to repentance. Dee Leavitt, a twenty-seven-year-old college-educated World War II veteran who described himself as an "inactive" church member, wrote to the prophet in frustration following the October 1953 general conference. A habitual smoker, he complained that church leaders' and members' intolerance of smoking, including McKay's recent denunciation of it as the "'root of all evil,'" was "driving" him and "hundreds" of other members like him "away from the Church." Why the denunciation, he inquired, when smoking "harms … only the user"? McKay advised Leavitt he was "foolish" for "permitting the honest condemnation of an enslaving habit (unequivocally condemned by the Lord Himself)" to keep him away from "doing something he knows to be right" by attending church. He bore Leavitt no ill will; "one can condemn an evil without condemning the man," he maintained. Quoting from the anti-drug crusader Charles B. Towns, he questioned the notion that smoking harmed only the smoker. Cigarette smokers set a poor example for those around them, injured others, and polluted the atmosphere. Eleven years later, Leavitt again wrote to McKay, this time thanking him for his gentle but firm rebuke. In the intervening years Leavitt had suffered "greatly" and been humbled, but he now was an active church member, married in the temple, whose testimony was "bursting into bloom."[24]

Letters also elicited instruction from McKay. In 1965 a student serving

23. DOMD, Nov. 29, 1965; Elaine Reiser Alder, excerpts from interview by Greg Prince, Jun. 3, 1995, box 22, folder 13, Prince Papers; Lola Gygi Timmins, excerpts from interviews by Greg Prince, Oct. 28, 1998 and Mar. 18, 2000, box 22, folder 13, Prince Papers; Mrs. Onas Mays to David O. McKay, Mar. 13, 1959, copy in DOMD, Mar. 13, 1959; David O. McKay to Mrs. Onas Mays, Mar. 24, 1959, copy in DOMD, Mar. 24, 1959; David O. McKay to Cecil Bryant Kenner, Mar. 24, 1959, copy in DOMD, Mar. 24, 1959; addresses delivered in general priesthood meeting, Apr. 4, 1959, *Conference Reports*, 37–50.

24. Dee L. Leavitt to David O. McKay, Oct. 14, 1953, McKay to Leavitt, Nov. 9, 1953, Leavitt to McKay, Nov. 21, 1964, copies in DOMD, Dec. 2, 1964.

on the Program Bureau at BYU wrote concerning a university ban on "stomp dancing," a fad that was easily mastered and involved rapid, athletically strenuous movement and stomping of the feet on the dance floor. Stomp dancing had been criticized at BYU for being undignified, but the student was unconvinced; she also wondered why BYU did not permit "electronic bands" to play for dances. "I am one of the *very* many kids here at the Y who really enjoy doing these dances and I have a lot of fun wearing myself out. I don't think the dances we do are dirty. I know they *can* be made very dirty but I have never seen any that way around here," she wrote. She and her friend had started attending stomp dances off campus after BYU stopped hosting them. She wanted clarification and pledged to "surely follow your counsel no matter what the answer." Filtered through Middlemiss, McKay replied by commending her on her willingness to follow counsel. In his opinion, a prerequisite for good dancing was "good dance posture," and stomp dancing violated that prerequisite. McKay agreed with the student that she and her friends might "not have any evil intentions" in stomp dancing, but dancing should "suggest nothing but style and good grace" to onlookers. Stomp dancing "to many of us," he said, "appears to be vulgar dancing." Electronic bands could play "moderate and modest music" but they were generally "not approved," he said, because of their "very loud beat which is inconsistent with the standards we desire to have observed."[25]

In a large church, the branch, ward, stake, and mission leaders were primarily responsible for weighing the sinful conduct of members according to standards of justice and mercy. But the prophet reviewed applications for cancelation of temple sealings, many of which resulted from infidelity, neglect, or cruelty. The task weighed heavily upon him. By virtue of his position, he also became the ultimate arbiter in difficult cases that local authorities could not resolve or that were appealed. In these cases, McKay tended toward clemency for sincerely repentant lay members. A woman who chose at age seventeen to have an abortion after learning that the father of her child was already married later fell in love with someone else, married, and served faithfully in her ward congregation. Eventually her husband joined her in attending and serving in the church. When the couple requested permission to be sealed to each other and to their children in the temple, the request landed on the McKay's desk because of her checkered past. McKay judged that the woman as a teen "had been more sinned against than sinning" and concluded, "she has confessed. They have done all they can. Now let us give them a helping hand." When two elders undergoing orientation and training in the church's mission home in Salt Lake City confessed to sexual relations with their girlfriends prior to their missions, the apostles debated whether the men should be released or allowed to continue

25. Jamie Chandler to David O. McKay, Nov. 27, 1965, McKay to Chandler, Nov. 29, 1965, copies in DOMD, Nov. 29, 1965.

serving. The general policy to that point (1961) had been that any who confessed sexual transgressions in their interviews with leaders in the mission home were "returned to their homes." McKay modified the policy and allowed both men to remain, stating "that we must never lose sight of the principle of repentance." Especially if the sexual offenses had been isolated occurrences, McKay stressed that leaders should prioritize "the possibility of saving a soul." The president reminded his associates, "There is power in repentance" and "we are not justified in sending a boy home who makes a confession, and who has kept himself clean since his transgression ... if he has truly repented." Otherwise, he warned, "The Lord will not be pleased with us. When we say we shall not send any [such] boy on a mission, we are taking judgment into our hands, and that decision really belongs to the Lord."[26]

McKay was far less indulgent of sin in church officers, including those who were serving as missionaries at the time of transgression. "There is no justification for young missionaries set apart to serve in the missionary cause to succumb to temptations of this kind," he ruled, pointing out that excommunication was the requisite penalty. When a charismatic, beloved bishop in southern California confessed to immorality, it became necessary to release him from his calling and excommunicate him. His stake president contacted the prophet, looking for a way to release the bishop without causing an uproar. Would it be permissible to invite the bishop to address his ward one last time, as was typical when bishops were released? McKay was firm: the bishop must not speak in church, and the stake president should simply announce from the pulpit that he had resigned. "He has labored very devotedly in the Church," the stake president pressed. "That does not matter, the man must be dealt with," McKay insisted. Former church officials who had been released and excommunicated could be rebaptized only after they demonstrated prolonged and sincere repentance. When asked in 1951 why he and his associates had not done more to reclaim the excommunicated former apostle Richard R. Lyman, McKay pointed out that Lyman "had not showed much repentance nor desire to come back into the Church, so we had just let it stand."[27]

---

26. DOMD, Dec. 23, 1957, Jan. 20, 1961, Nov, 8, 1960.

27. DOMD, Mar. 19, 1964, July 12, 1957, July 16, 1951, May 15, 1952. Lyman and McKay corresponded regularly, and eventually Lyman manifested acceptable contrition. After visiting with Lyman on assignment from McKay, Spencer W. Kimball and LeGrand Richards reported that Lyman "had come a long way." They recommended rebaptism. In the council meeting where Lyman's appeal for rebaptism was discussed, Joseph Fielding Smith reportedly raised concerns about Lyman's putative ambition to have his apostolic calling restored. McKay dismissed the concern, stating that it was "quite a stretch" from baptism to apostleship. McKay, his counselors, and the Twelve authorized his rebaptism in September 1954. The following month, McKay phoned Lyman, speaking first with his wife and then with him and sharing the news. Lyman later wrote to McKay, "With tears in our voices and in our eyes we both tried to say: 'A thousand thanks President McKay and God bless you!' Your good will and kindly feelings toward me, reported by our mutual friends, have been a source

McKay reflected the dominant social attitudes of his era in his stance toward homosexuality. In 1965, Presidents Hugh B. Brown and N. Eldon Tanner noted the seemingly increasing prevalence of gay students at church schools and gay missionaries. Brown believed that "some of them may be helped to overcome their perversion, while others have reached a point where they are a menace to others." McKay's diary records that he advised that "they should be excommunicated without any doubt" if they were "confirmed homosexuals"; he believed they had "no right to membership in the Church."[28]

When apostles expressed strongly felt convictions on controversial topics, McKay acknowledged both their entitlement to inspiration that came with their apostolic calling and their capacity for fallibility. In 1954 Joseph Fielding Smith promulgated his anti-evolution views in *Man, His Origin and Destiny* and encouraged the book's adoption in seminaries and institutes of religion. In response to queries from some seminary and institute faculty about the degree to which the book should be regarded as official doctrine, McKay acknowledged that the authorship of the book by the president of the Quorum of the Twelve "makes it more or less authoritative," but he gravitated decisively toward the latter. "It is no more to be taken as the word of the Church than any other unauthorized book," he instructed. He refused, however, to publicly criticize or privately reprimand Smith for disseminating his views, tolerating Smith's strongly held views. This same respect for personal inspiration extended to rank-and-file church members, so long as their inspiration did not counter official church doctrine. When an eighty-six-year-old member, Alvin Allen, visited his office to discuss Allen's plans to print a book regarding why golden plates were buried in the Hill Cumorah and how they came to be located there, along with the contents of a vision Allen believed he had received, McKay told him that he was free as an American citizen to publish anything he cared to, but cautioned him against implying in any way that McKay was familiar with the book's message or endorsed it.[29]

In addition to his relatively broad tolerance of others' views, McKay's relatability, extending to his passion for fine fashion and sleek automobiles, endeared him to the people. In his son Llewelyn's mind, his father had two flaws, "One he drives too fast. And two, his vanity." Both characteristics made him appear fully human. Tales of his lead foot and love of speeding were legion, and teenaged church members especially loved them. On his frequent trips to Huntsville, he often drove well above the speed limit. Ted London, a highway

of great encouragement." Richard R. Lyman to David O. McKay, Nov. 3, 1954, DOMD; Lola Gygi Timmins, excerpts from interview by Greg Prince, Aug. 4, 2000, box 22, folder 11, Prince Papers; Spencer W. Kimball, journal, Sep. 21–23, 1954.

28. DOMD, Mar. 30, 1965.

29. DOMD, Sep. 13, 1954, Jan. 30, 1958.

patrolman from Morgan County, pulled McKay over on one of those drives. According to Ted's grandnephew Brett London, when Ted approached the car McKay asked, "Have you forgotten who I am?" Ted replied, "Of course not. You are David O. McKay—Prophet, Seer, and Revelator." He issued the ticket and went on his way. According to family folklore, a few weeks later McKay called London into church headquarters. In recounting the story, London said, "What do you mean he didn't hold a grudge? He sat me down in his office and called me to serve as Bishop." London held the calling for the next fifteen years. According to another tale, when McKay as an old man was pulled over, he thanked the officer for the ticket and quipped. "Some have said I am slowing down [but] this is proof that I'm not." Concerned about his safety, at one point his children had a governor installed on his Buick that limited the car's speed. According to his grandson Dick, when McKay returned from Huntsville, "he came storming into the house. 'What's wrong with that car?… He made such a ruckus that they had to take it down and take the governor off." They never did tell him what they had done.[30]

As a leader, McKay struggled to balance institutional imperatives with the interests and feelings of individual members. He once observed that in church administration "we are dealing with human hearts." Cognizant of the tenderness of feelings and the "sacred" nature of individual rights, McKay cautioned that "we cannot run the Church as we would a business." He could be sharp, though, and "had the ability to discipline," Paul Dunn stated. "I never had him angry at me, I'm grateful to say," recalled Gordon B. Hinckley. "But he could get angry. He could get upset." In one temple meeting of the general authorities, Bernard Brockbank was scheduled to provide a briefing. He was unprepared and requested an extra week to complete his report. McKay reprimanded him sharply, asking questions such as "Did you and I have an agreement that you were going to teach this morning?" and concluded, "Brethren, you have to take these things seriously." At the end of the meeting, he asked Brockbank to walk with him back to the office. As they exited, Paul Dunn sensed McKay was "giving this General Authority an increased amount of love." Although he was willing to make tough decisions and did discipline church leaders and employees, including firing some, he waffled on many decisions as he calibrated and recalibrated his use of power. To efficiency-minded associates, McKay could be frustratingly double-minded, but before old age began to cloud his judgment, his indecision arose from his sense of personal honor and morality and the value he placed upon personal relationships.[31]

---

30. Dew, *Go Forward with Faith*, 182–83; London, "Highway Patrol Uncle," *London Edition*. londonedition.home.blog; Bringhurst, "Private versus Public," 25, 29; Richard and Vivian McKay, excerpts from interview by Greg Prince, May 21, 1996, Prince Papers.

31. DOMD, May 17, 1962; Gordon B. Hinckley, excerpts from interview by William Robert

McKay's handling of a staffing challenge in the Tabernacle Choir illustrated both his ability to have hard conversations to safeguard institutional interests and his willingness to rescind decisions and provide second chances to individuals. In 1957 J. Spencer Cornwall, a distinguished musician who had directed the Tabernacle Choir for over two decades, placed McKay in a bind when he resigned immediately after the First Presidency raised the prospect of his eventual retirement and indicated that they intended to begin recruiting an appropriate successor. His ego bruised, Cornwall declared that if they intended to replace him eventually, he would safeguard his honor and resign immediately. The Presidency had already determined, based upon feedback from choir members, that Cornwall's assistant, Richard P. Condie, was temperamentally unsuited to the position, although he was the best candidate currently available for the job. In the long run, a better candidate appeared to be Newell Weight, an assistant professor from BYU, but he was scheduled to be out of state for two more years until he completed his doctorate. Counting on Condie's need for employment in the near term, McKay offered him three options: he could continue working as assistant director, be appointed acting director, or be named director, with a two-year fixed term. When Condie asked if the two-year position could be converted into a permanent one if he performed well, McKay leveled with him, stating, "No, I should be frank with you," and Condie took the two-year appointment. The following Sunday, McKay announced Cornwall's resignation and Condie's new appointment to a stunned choir, many of whom disliked Condie. Ten days later, McKay had a follow-up conversation with Condie. The prophet prefaced the conversation with a question. "I heard one of your worst enemies making a comment. Do you want to hear it?" When Condie asked McKay to proceed, he told Condie that choir members complained about his short fuse: "That you have a Scot temper perhaps." When Condie pledged to try to school his feelings, McKay quoted a line from the poet Alexander Pope: "Your defects to know / make use of every friend / and every foe." Condie's performance improved dramatically over the ensuing two years, although he never fully conquered his temper. In those two years the choir began a fruitful collaborative relationship with Eugene Ormandy and the Philadelphia Orchestra, improved the quality of its tone, released three albums, and released a single, Peter Wilhousky's stirring arrangement of "The Battle Hymn of the Republic," which eventually would rise to number thirteen on the charts. Admitting that Condie had "really done a wonderful job" and that even many in the choir who had originally opposed his appointment were "now reporting that they have received more definite instruction and training than they have ever had before," McKay flexibly rescinded his original plan and promoted Condie permanently.

Wright, Dec. 10, 1996, box 23, folder 1, Prince Papers; Paul H. Dunn, excerpts from interviews by Greg Prince, Feb. 18, 1995, Jan. 15, 1996, box 22, folder 13, Prince Papers.

"When are your two years up?" he asked Condie on September 1, 1959. Condie replied that he had two weeks left. McKay smiled wryly and responded, "Well, you go right on," to which Condie replied, "As one Scotsman to another, I love that." Condie directed the choir until he retired at age seventy-six in 1974.[32]

McKay's reversal of his original decision to limit Condie's term as choir director to two years likely promoted the church's interests, given Condie's achievements in the preceding two years. McKay also reversed course repeatedly as he weighed the proposed relocation of Ricks College from Rexburg to Idaho Falls. In this instance, he ultimately prioritized his morally based sense of honor and duty to individual residents of Rexburg over the unanimous, data-driven recommendations of his key associates and advisors, along with the majority of church leaders in eastern Idaho. Better than any other event in his presidency, this incident demonstrated McKay's conviction that faith, trust, and human hearts were of greater worth than institutional growth or efficiency and that "we cannot run the Church as we would a business."[33]

In 1954 rumors of a contemplated move of the college, based upon informal investigations being conducted by Church Commissioner of Education Ernest Wilkinson, spread like wildfire in eastern Idaho. Grover Hemming, the president of the Eighty-Fourth Quorum of Seventy in Rexburg, sent a telegram to McKay inquiring about the rumors. McKay replied, "Rest assured there will be no change in Ricks College." The prophet reiterated that message a few months later in a letter to the Rexburg Chamber of Commerce and Rotary Club: "The college is not going to be moved from Rexburg." Likely unaware of these assurances, Wilkinson continued to gather data on church membership and college enrollment in eastern Idaho, building a case that a college in Idaho Falls would be more centrally located and serve a larger student population. In the spring of 1957, the First Presidency and Wilkinson met with Ricks College President John Clarke and the presidents of fifteen stakes in Eastern Idaho to consider Wilkinson's proposal to relocate the college. Most of the stake presidents favored the move, to the consternation of those from Rexburg. Later that month the Church Board of Education, including McKay, voted unanimously in favor of Wilkinson's proposal to move the college. The next day the presidents of the two stakes in Rexburg, Delbert Taylor and Orval Mortensen, and their counselors sent a letter to the First Presidency, reminding McKay he had given his "assurance" back in 1954 that the college would not be moved. Letters poured into the church offices in Salt Lake from Rexburg encouraging the church to maintain the college there. One strongly worded missive from Rexburg physician Blaine Passey aroused McKay's ire but made a deep impression. Over the

32. McKay, *Confidence amid Change,* 186, 289; DOMD, Sep. 13, 25, 1957; Hicks, *Mormon Tabernacle Choir*, 113–16.

33. DOMD, May 17, 1962.

previous three months, Passey averred, the church had "lost more respect … than the work of a dozen missionaries in the field could hope to recoup," adding, "We are disgusted and ashamed of the Church in this action."[34]

The day after he read Passey's letter, McKay informed Stephen L Richards that he had decided it would "not be worth the cost to move Ricks College." Richards pushed back, and McKay agreed with him that they were not legally obligated to keep the college in Rexburg. But, he stated, "the fact remains that [they] decided as a Presidency that it would not be moved" and so informed the community in "that letter … two or three years ago." Later that morning McKay informed members of the executive committee of the board of education, "The Church is built upon Faith and Trust. Once confidence is lost, the foundation of society begins to crumble.… Our integrity will be measured by our conduct." To their great relief, he informed four leaders from Rexburg of his decision that afternoon.[35]

McKay would reverse course once more over a year later, after Wilkinson informed him that the Idaho Board of Education might establish a junior college in Idaho Falls, essentially cutting off the supply of students from eastern Idaho to Ricks, unless the church preempted the proposal by relocating Ricks College. In light of this new information McKay and his counselors agreed with Wilkinson that the college must be moved. McKay traveled to Rexburg to explain his reversal to the local leaders, whom he had assured the previous year that the college would remain in Rexburg. If Ricks did not move, "we would have a two-year college at Idaho Falls, a state college, and a two-year college at Ricks at Rexburg, with a dwindling attendance, and a successful attendance at the State College in Idaho Falls," he pointed out. J. Reuben Clark praised McKay afterward for maintaining his composure during the tense two-hour meeting, but McKay was troubled by the accusation that he "had broken his word." "Breaking your word, that is an awful thing," he observed. After stewing about the matter for several more months, McKay again reversed course. McKay's "peace-loving soul" caused him to shrink from decisions that would arouse "violent objection," Wilkinson believed. On June 30, 1959, McKay acknowledged in a council meeting that he felt "cloudy" whenever he considered moving the school to Idaho Falls. The following November McKay announced that he "had never been satisfied with the decision … to move Ricks College to Idaho Falls" and declared that the "decision should be reversed and Ricks College left at Rexburg." Integrity, personal honor, and trust had trumped all other considerations.[36]

---

34. Hemming, "Ricks College," 60–61, 69–70; DOMD, Jul. 6, 1957.
35. DOMD, Jul. 11, 1957.
36. Hemming, "Ricks College," 81–82, 88, 103, 105; DOMD, Oct. 31, Nov. 15, Dec. 28, 1958, Nov. 23, 1960.

For a generation of Latter-day Saints, David O. McKay set the standard for what it meant to be a prophet. With his tall frame, wavy white hair, clean-shaven face, piercing eyes, and dapper dress, he looked like a twentieth-century, modern prophet. "In this white suit, clear down to the white shoes, he'd walk through that door, and it really took your breath away, as many times as you saw him," remembered Elaine Reiser Alder. Tall and good looking, he was "witty, literate, and urbane, the most directly attractive Mormon prophet since Joseph Smith," opined admirer Eugene England. Even more important than his appearance and urbanity, McKay loved people in a grandfatherly way, and his compassion, wisdom, and spirituality drew and held people. "I cried as though he were my own father when he died," recalled Cleon Skousen. "My association with him would be relatively casual … and I felt like everybody else did, that you were just a very close friend or confidant. That's the feeling you got." Ray once told her granddaughter, "I think if Dade had his way he would spend his entire time marrying people and preaching funerals, because he just feels that's a real way to be with them and help them." Howard Anderson reflected, "Whenever he talked to you, you … [felt] that you had his total attention and focus, and that he was truly interested in you and in who you were. That is an incredible quality for an individual to have." People sought his counsel, petitioned him for healing blessings, and looked for opportunities to shake his hand, bring him gifts, or knock on his door. He generally prioritized people over policies and programs and was willing at times to compromise institutional benefits to maintain his integrity or demonstrate compassion. He was a man well attuned to his times and widely adored by his people.[37]

37. Elaine Reiser Alder, excerpts from interview by Greg Prince, Jun. 3, 1995, box, 22, folder 13, Prince Papers; Eugene England, "The Place of David O. McKay in Mormon Culture," *Sunstone*, Feb. 2000, 21; W. Cleon Skousen, excerpts from interview by Greg Prince, Feb. 21, 1995, box 22, folder 13, Prince Papers; Midene Anderson, excerpts from interview by Greg Prince, Oct. 1, 1996, box 22, folder 13, Prince Papers; Howard B. Anderson, excerpts from interview by Greg Prince, Dec. 8, 1996, box 22, folder 13, Prince Papers.

12: Unto Every Nation

When McKay was ninety-five years old, a reporter asked him to pinpoint "the most outstanding accomplishment" of his ministry. He responded, "The making of the Church a world-wide organization." He had done so, he said, through "visits to every foreign mission; meeting leaders of nations, ambassadors and other government officials; personally greeting all members of the church and investigators; holding meetings in every mission and stimulating the work of local members and missionaries." McKay's self-assessment was apt. At the end of his life, the church's membership stood at over 2.8 million, an increase of more than 150 percent from when he became prophet. Most of the growth took place in nations where the church had long been established. But during his administration the church also gained a foothold with organized congregations and official proselytizing initiatives in over a dozen more nations, largely in Central and South America. The expansion and explosive growth occurred during an era dubbed by *Time* and *Life* editor Henry Luce the "American Century." The Church of Jesus Christ of Latter-day Saints was a homegrown American religion; American leadership and vision were at their zenith economically, culturally, militarily, and politically around the free world in the 1950s; and Latter-day Saint values of family and faith in God were broadly shared.[1]

McKay greenlighted a Central American Mission in 1952 after he determined that the church's priesthood and temple ban as applied to people with African ancestry would "inhibit" missionary work in only two Latin American nations. Soon missionaries began proselytizing in Honduras, Nicaragua, Chile, Peru, Ecuador, and Panama. In Asia, the church established or reestablished footholds in Hong Kong, Taiwan, South Korea, the Philippines, Singapore, and Thailand. In Europe, missionaries were sent to Italy, and the church obtained government recognition in Spain. In the Pacific, Fiji and Saipan were opened to missionary work. In some of these cases, McKay's support was decisive. As an assistant to the Quorum of the Twelve, Gordon B. Hinckley met with President Clark when McKay was out of town to inquire if the time had come to send missionaries to the Philippines. Clark "hesitated, and finally

1. Alden Whitman, "Missionary President," *New York Times*, Jan. 19, 1970, 1, 26; "Statistical Report – 1950," *Conference Reports*, Apr. 6, 1951, 9; "Statistical Report for 1969," delivered Apr. 6. 1970, *Conference Reports*, 115.

didn't feel well about it," so he dropped the matter. A few months later, Hinckley broached the subject with McKay in the temple. "He put his head back and said nothing for some time. Then he said, 'Follow your inspiration,'" Hinckley recalled. On his next visit, Hinckley rededicated the land for missionary work. Although the international ambitions of McKay and others in Salt Lake City helped to drive this expansion, Latter-day Saints and others not of the faith living in those countries sometimes jump-started it, at times moving faster than McKay deemed wise. For instance, in 1952, "Billie" Fotheringham, a Latter-day Saint employed by the Eastman Kodak Company, was transferred to Santiago. He wrote to the Argentine Mission president, Lee Valentine, asking him to send missionaries to Chile. In 1956 Valentine forwarded the request to Salt Lake. Fotheringham had already spoken with Chilean officials who assured him that missionaries would be welcome, but McKay proceeded cautiously. He sent Henry D. Moyle to visit the country and confirm Fotheringham's report. After Moyle's visit two elders were transferred to Chile.[2]

Concerned about the safety of missionaries and the overwhelmingly American church's relationship with foreign governments, McKay at times blocked zealous mission leaders. When President Vernon Sharp of the Andes Mission proposed sending missionaries to Ecuador in 1960, the prophet objected, judging that "the relationship between America and South America will have to be more definitely established, and favorably established, before we do anything." Five years passed before the first missionaries arrived.[3]

Although the church's ambition to take the restored gospel to the world advanced during McKay's tenure, vast areas of the world remained closed to missionary work when he died: missions did not operate in the Communist bloc, the Islamic world, most of Africa, or generally on the Indian subcontinent. Government policies were a key obstacle, but church leaders' concerns about race, centralized control, and assimilation also delayed the church's movement into India and Africa.

McKay shared the racial prejudices of many white Americans of his generation, but they were tempered by his belief that Christians should treat all people with dignity. On his mission, he attended a concert given by the Fisk Jubilee Singers, an African American performing group from Fisk University, and warmly shook hands with the performers. These talented "beautiful singers" earned a "warm spot in [his] heart," he wrote, even though his general inclination was to "not care much for the Negro." As president of a church that

2. DOMD, Nov. 15, 1952, Feb. 14, 1956; Cannon and Cowan, *Unto Every Nation*, 106–9, 272–77, 322–91; Gordon B. Hinckley, excerpts from interview by William Robert Wright, Dec. 10, 1996, box 22, folder 23, Prince Papers; Steven J. Iverson, "Chile," *Ensign*, Feb. 1977; "Chile, Stories of Faith: Slow Start, Explosive Growth," Global Histories, churchofjesuschrist.org.

3. DOMD, Oct. 4, 1960; Cannon and Cowan, *Unto Every Nation*, 272.

baptized people with African ancestry, he opposed segregated congregations but not segregated schools. He privately opined that the Supreme Court's order to southern school districts to desegregate speedily was undesirable. "We should like to leave the solution for the Southern states people to handle," he told a church leader in South Carolina. "If the Government judiciary had kept out of this the Southern States would have handled it properly." He feared rapid educational integration would handicap white children "inasmuch as the negro child is two or three grades below the white child of the same age." He opposed social integration as well. When he learned that the federal government planned to house hundreds of Black Americans at Tooele Ordinance Depot west of the Salt Lake Valley, he declared, "We do not welcome negroes into our social affairs because if we did it would lead to inter-marriage, and we do not favor inter-marriage."[4]

McKay's concerns about intermarriage were greatest in the case of people with African ancestry because of the priesthood and temple ban, but he also opposed intermarriage with races and nationalities that faced no temple restrictions, including Mexican, Japanese, Chinese, and Hawai'ian people. He took this stance, he explained, "for the ... good [of] family harmony and peace." These were common, albeit contested, views of his era.[5]

McKay also opposed compulsory integration of hotels and restaurants because he felt it would be "unfair to the majority of the citizens of this country" who might prefer segregation and would violate entrepreneurs' rights to manage their businesses as they saw fit. In 1963 he approved a last-minute First Presidency statement in support of "full civil rights," drafted by Sterling McMurrin at Hugh B. Brown's behest, to stave off protests by the National Association for the Advancement of Colored People (NAACP) at general conference, but he neither instigated nor championed the statement. In a meeting of the First Presidency soon after the statement was issued, McKay reportedly downplayed it, saying that it was made "in fulfillment of a promise" and "in response to a request" from

4. McKay, *What E'er Thou Art*, 82, (Mar. 30, 1898); Buchanan, "Missionary Roots," 195; DOMD, Apr. 2, 1956, June 13, Sep. 26, 1961.

5. DOMD, Dec. 15, 1961. Soon after he completed his mission in Hawai'i and returned to Utah, a missionary who had fallen in love with a Japanese-American woman there agreed to meet with McKay at his parents' request. In this case the relationship was complicated by the fact that both sets of parents disapproved of the relationship. The returned missionary told McKay he deeply loved the woman and had promised to marry her, but McKay advised him "not to follow through with his intentions." A few weeks later in a second interview McKay raised the stakes, fearing the impact upon members and missionaries in the islands. If he returned to Hawai'i to court the girl, his honorable release from his mission would be revoked, and he would be required to reimburse the church the cost of his return passage to Utah after his mission. McKay told him that "he would be making a serious mistake to marry this girl—that it would bring disappointment to both of them if he insisted upon consummating this marriage." They ended their relationship. DOMD, Dec. 4, 1948; the missionary married Joy Beck [Van Wagoner]; see entry for Joy Beck Van Wagoner, KW-ZG-6Y6, Family Search, familysearch.org.

the NAACP and that "no more would be said about it." In 1964 Middlemiss reported his remark that "the Civil Rights Bill is now passed and it is the law of the land. Some of it is wrong—the Negro will now have to prove himself."[6]

Long after McKay's death, a handful of individuals recalled private conversations or chance encounters in which McKay intimated that he strongly desired a change in the church's priesthood and temple ban and sought to overturn it. McKay's tendency to listen and respond sympathetically in conversations with both liberals and conservatives makes it difficult to ascertain the depth of his convictions on the subject. On one occasion he did state it was a "tragedy" that Black youth who grew up in largely white congregations had to witness their peers receiving the Aaronic priesthood while they were held back. "I think the Lord is not pleased with it," McKay opined. He felt he needed more than an impression of divine displeasure, though, to initiate a change. "Only the Lord can change it," he added. In 1965 he stated that he stood "with all former Presidents of the Church that [those] having Negro blood cannot have the priesthood." He was more open to the possibility of future change than staunch defenders of the ban, including Harold B. Lee and Joseph Fielding Smith, and less confident in his ability to overturn the ban than Hugh B. Brown and Marion D. Hanks. The best evidence available from a close church associate for the assertion that McKay pleaded fervently for a reversal of the ban comes from Greg Prince's notes jotted down retrospectively of a "rambling monologue" in which Hanks recalled that while McKay was awaiting surgery in the hospital, he confided to Hanks that he had "prayed, and prayed, and prayed to know if they should be given the priesthood, but there has been no answer." There is no compelling evidence that McKay pleaded as frequently or as confidently and optimistically as Spencer W. Kimball would do as church president in the following decade.[7]

From the outset of his administration, McKay had his eyes on India. A few weeks after his ordination, McKay told a reporter, "We have in mind entering India and establishing an Indian Mission." Ten years later after conversing with the Iranian ambassador, McKay mused, "I think there is an opening for us in Iran [where Latter-day Saint academics from Utah had been working as part of the Point Four Program and its successor, the US Agency for International Development], as well as in India, to preach the gospel." Two months later, he observed, "India should be opened for missionary work, as should also Iran and Pakistan." The following year when Elder Richard L. Evans received an invitation to visit India on behalf of Rotary International, McKay encouraged him

6. DOMD, Dec. 15, 1961, June 19, Oct. 8, 1963, Jul. 1964; Prince and Wright, *David O. McKay*, 69–70.

7. DOMD, Oct. 9, 1962, Jun. 4, 1965. Prince and Wright, *David O. McKay*, 103–5, posit that McKay engaged in "intense prayer on numerous occasions" regarding the lifting of the ban. In support of their view they cite interviews recorded long after McKay's death with secretary Lola Gygi Timmons and architect Richard Jackson as well as Hanks.

to make the trip, seeing it as a possible "opportunity for us to make an entrance into India as a Church." Evans subsequently spent a month in India, where he met with Paul Thiruthuvadoss, a forty-four-year-old who first learned about the church in 1954 and who convened his own Sunday schools in which he taught from church curricular materials. He and his wife operated a school in a small village near Coimbatore and claimed to have several hundred followers. The church would need to "move in modestly, quietly, and discreetly," working largely through Indian citizens like Thiruthuvadoss because of the "cool to very reserved" attitude of government officials toward foreign churches, Evans reported. Two years later, Gordon B. Hinckley, the apostle assigned to supervise missionary work in Asia, visited Thiruthuvadoss's congregations with Jay Quealy, president of the Southern Far East Mission. Hinckley was "greatly troubled" by what he witnessed and reported that he did "not know what we should do." "These are earnest people, but they have been schooled in the Pentecostal ways, which are not our ways," Hinckley observed. How would the church assimilate these followers into a correlated, recognizably Latter-day Saint faith? Despite Hinckley's concerns, Thiruthuvadoss and his family desired baptism, and it seemed wrong to deny them this saving ordinance. Shortly after Hinckley's visit, President Quealy returned with two missionaries to baptize Thiruthuvadoss and his family. The missionaries remained for six months on tourist visas. While there, they baptized six other Indians. Twenty-four more were baptized in 1968, but thereafter the members had only sporadic contact with representatives from the mission for many years.[8]

Similar grassroots interests spawned opportunities for the church in West Africa. In the late 1950s, Honesty John Ekong began writing to headquarters expressing interest in the church and requesting visitors and materials. LaMar Williams, an employee of the church Missionary Department, began sending materials to Ekong, who shared them with others. In 1960 the First Presidency asked Glen Fisher, who was completing his term as South African mission president, to stop in Nigeria on the way home and investigate conditions. He reported that several congregations claimed affiliation with the church and were using church literature in their meetings. They petitioned Salt Lake for money to replace their ramshackle meeting places with more substantial structures. Meanwhile, hundreds of other West Africans wrote to Salt Lake requesting an affiliation with the church. In light of Christ's injunction to teach the gospel to all people, McKay felt obligated to "permit these people to be baptized and confirmed members of the Church if they are converted and worthy"

8. DOMD, Apr. 25, 1951, June 5, Aug. 24, 1960, Mar. 8, 22, 1962; Thiruthuvadoss, "First Indian Convert's Testimony," 96–99; John Aki, "My Missionary Experiences in India, 1965," *Liahona*, July 2014, A3–5; Rutherford, "The Internationalization of Mormonism," 37–60. On the Point Four Program see Garlitz, *A Mission for Development*, and Embry, "Church Follows the Flag," 141–79.

even though they could not receive the priesthood or temple blessings unless the Lord "let us know."[9]

McKay initially planned to dispatch South African mission president Layton Alldredge to Nigeria to visit Ekong in 1961. Alldredge could do so on his way back to South Africa after he attended a seminar for mission presidents in Utah. But McKay's counselor in the First Presidency, Hugh B. Brown, had a better idea. His nephew, N. Eldon Tanner, an assistant to the Quorum of the Twelve serving as West European mission president, knew Sir Alfred Savage, a former British colonial official who had been Nigeria's finance minister. Tanner could solicit advice from Savage before the church committed itself in Nigeria. Having studied up on the conditions, Tanner could then visit on behalf of the church. Savage told Tanner that pleas to western churches for affiliation were often ploys for obtaining personal benefits such as status and funds. He warned Tanner "that they read an article in some magazine about some church, and then immediately contact the organization relative to joining it." Savage's warning provided context for the letters from Africa. McKay advised Tanner in July to "perhaps" correspond with the Nigerian letter writers but not to travel there yet. Pleas for an emissary from Salt Lake continued to arrive in Utah, though, and after Brown confronted McKay with new letters from Adewole Ogunmokun in Nigeria, the presidency decided to send Williams from the Missionary Department in the fall of 1961 as an "entirely unofficial" visitor. Ogunmokun had reinforced McKay's previous line of reasoning when he wrote, "I appeal ... to the President David O. McKay and the Presidency to help me and my people.... You must not refuse our plea for baptism and the laying on of hands by those in authority for the Gift of the Holy Ghost." To try to gauge their sincerity, Williams was to inform them that the church had no paid ministry and that converts of black African descent could not be ordained to the priesthood.[10]

Williams returned from his trip enthused about the possibility of preaching and baptizing in West Africa; thousands of Nigerians desired baptism despite the priesthood restriction, he reported. McKay reflected that the modern church faced "as great" a challenge as the one Peter had confronted regarding preaching to the Gentiles. That step had been taken only after Peter received a revelation: "it took the Lord to do it." There were so many things he did not know. "If only we could give them the Aaronic Priesthood. I suppose there is no way to differentiate. The Lord will have to do it," McKay reflected. Brown, who believed the policy could be adjusted without waiting for a revelation, added that he "hoped that the time would come when we could give them the Aaronic Priesthood." But McKay qualified his hope, pointing out that "only the Lord can change it."[11]

9. Allen, "Would-Be Saints," 212–15; DOMD, June 22, 30, 1961. Stevenson, *Cause of Righteousness,* places the church's involvement in Africa within a broader intercontinental perspective.

10. DOMD, July 19, Aug. 16, 1961; Allen, "Would-Be Saints," 218.

11. DOMD, Jan. 9, Feb. 28, Mar. 1, Oct. 11, 1962.

How would branches be established without conferring the priesthood on the converts or making other adjustments that would incite demands from Black members in the United States for similar accommodations? Could auxiliaries like the Sunday School function in African branches with black superintendents under the direction of mission presidents? How many missionaries and how much money would be needed to take care of African congregations? Would the church unintentionally precipitate a large-scale migration from Africa to the United States? "The question of intermarriage bothers me more than anything," McKay remarked. Despite the unknowns, McKay ultimately determined to send Williams back to Nigeria along with two missionary couples. Williams would act as temporary mission president under Tanner's direction. The missionaries would baptize converts, organize them into branches, and select and set apart auxiliary leaders. Then the two couples would visit the branches periodically to administer the sacrament. Church leaders decided that polygamous converts legally married under Nigerian law would be permitted to "keep their wives."[12]

When their Nigerian visas did not arrive on time, Williams and the missionary couples were forced to postpone their departure. As a Canadian citizen, Tanner received his visa easily, so he traveled to Nigeria without Williams and the missionaries in December 1962. There he visited with government officials, applied for permission to establish a mission, and dedicated the land for missionary work. Nigerian officials informed Tanner that the church would receive permission to organize within two months, but complications soon slowed the process. First the government required a deposit, ostensibly to guarantee the missionaries' return to America. Then some Nigerians studying in the United States wrote to the Nigerian press, publicizing and condemning the church's racial policies, and the NAACP stepped up its criticisms of the church. As Nigeria imposed additional stipulations, McKay ruled that the church would not be bullied or blackmailed. Those who had petitioned the church for missionaries would need to lobby their own government. Moreover, the church would "make no concession" regarding its doctrine or policy. A few days later, a request for a $25,000 loan arrived from the leader of one Nigerian congregation. As Sir Alfred Savage had warned, some leaders, desperate for funds, hoped to milk the church for money.[13]

Notwithstanding these setbacks, when Williams finally obtained a tourist visa through the intercession of Utah Senator Wallace Bennett, McKay authorized Williams to travel to Nigeria, meet with government officials, and again request permission to establish the church. During his nine-day trip early in 1964 Williams was unable to assuage the government's concerns. Back in Utah

12. DOMD, Jan. 6, Mar. 1, Oct. 9, 1962.
13. DOMD, Nov. 21, 1962, Jan. 10, June 5, 13, 1963; Allen, "Would-Be Saints," 230.

Williams applied for a permanent visa and was denied. Still, McKay remained convinced, he told his counselors in 1965, "that [the church] should go into Nigeria and give them what we can give them in accordance with the revelations of the Lord," if the government would permit it. "We are prepared to do anything we can to make it possible for the people in Nigeria to enjoy the blessings of the Gospel," McKay stated, but he did "not feel that we should urge the government to grant us visas." Tanner had advised Williams in June to "do nothing further" regarding a visa for fear of alienating Nigerian authorities, but two months later Williams received a new visa, along with the assurance that the government would convert it to a residential permit if he traveled to Nigeria. The First Presidency authorized Williams to travel and "register the Church there and then apply for a residential visa." The church would not proselytize for the time being, but Williams as acting mission president could screen applicants for baptism, baptize those who were worthy, and then establish auxiliary organizations under the direction of local members. Only missionaries would be authorized to officiate at the sacrament table. Shortly before Williams left, McKay warned him to baptize no one until he obtained a residential visa.[14]

Williams traveled to Nigeria shortly after the October 1965 general conference and made headway on receiving a permanent visa. He estimated that "somewhere between 7,000 and 20,000 people" desired to affiliate with the church. The church took pains to conceal news of his trip from the NAACP in Utah. Three weeks after his departure, Williams's wife, Nyal, contacted Gordon B. Hinckley at the Missionary Department. She warned him to take extra precautions to be sure that Monroe Fleming, a Black member who worked as a waiter at the Hotel Utah, did not learn of Williams's trip because of his possible connections to the NAACP. Hinckley shared her concern with the First Presidency and the Quorum of the Twelve in a momentous council meeting on November 4. Harold B. Lee reacted with alarm, characterizing Williams as impetuous and unreliable, a sentiment Tanner shared. His mission to Nigeria unwisely exposed the church to risks of adverse publicity and potential obligations. It was rumored that Williams had speculated that Nigerian converts might be ordained to the Aaronic Priesthood to enable the church to function, an idea Brown had actually broached, and this news alarmed Lee and some of his colleagues. As leaders of a large organization whose members relied upon their steady judgment, they were taking a huge chance. Movement into Nigeria was a response to grassroots initiatives they did not control. Was that responsible? "Most of the Twelve" shared these concerns, Lee claimed. Did they really know that God wanted Williams to proceed? Lee did not think so. Perhaps Williams's "long delay in getting a permanent visa" was "evidence that the Lord is not ready to have this work done." Ezra Taft Benson, Mark E. Petersen, and Gordon B.

14. DOMD, June 3, 15, 24, Aug. 25, 1965.

Hinckley underscored Lee's concerns, adding that the establishment of black congregations in Nigeria might reduce South African authorities' support of the church. Tanner answered questions that his colleagues raised and reminded them that Williams was acting with the First Presidency's united approval.[15]

For over four years, McKay had wrestled with the conviction that the church must do all it responsibly could to extend saving ordinances to Nigerian converts without exposing the church to pressure from the NAACP to alter its racial policies, potential extortion by authorities, or adverse publicity. In 1961 when Lee had raised similar concerns, Brown had countered them. The following year in another meeting McKay had dismissed Lee's concerns, demonstrating his readiness to act upon his spiritual convictions. A word from McKay, even a mild insinuation that he knew God's will in the matter, would have silenced his associates; they sustained him wholeheartedly as prophet. Now he said nothing in defense of Williams's mission or his previous judgments. He sat on the horns of a dilemma whereby the spiritual progress of Nigerians who desired baptism might jeopardize the church's standing in South Africa and draw unwelcome attention to the church's politically unpopular priesthood and temple ban. When Petersen moved that Williams be ordered home, Delbert Stapley seconded the motion, and the body unanimously sustained it. Williams was called home, without ever being told the reasons his mission had been canceled. After hearing Williams's report of his abbreviated mission following his return and asking him questions about converts' possible demands for priesthood ordination, possible resentment of white church leadership, and converts' possible desires to immigrate or intermarry, the First Presidency excused Williams from the meeting, reviewed the minutes of the previous week's council meeting, and unanimously agreed that "we should postpone any attempt to carry out a program in Nigeria." Thirteen years would pass before the church would again send missionaries to Nigeria.[16]

While McKay's prospects for establishing the church firmly in India and West Africa faltered, he did achieve his broader vision of making the church's crowning ordinances available to members in Europe and the Pacific. Making the temple ordinances available to Saints beyond the United States and Canada was the most important legacy McKay bequeathed to Latter-day Saints living abroad.

Having traveled the world as an apostle, McKay understood the isolation of international church members, and he determined to visit as many of the church's far-flung missions as possible. His first international trip occurred in 1952, barely a year after he was sustained. Ray suppressed her fear of transoceanic flights and accompanied him. It was their first trip to Europe since their

15. DOMD, Apr. 21, 1965.

16. DOMD, July 1, 1961, Mar. 1, 1962, Nov. 4, 10, 1965; Allen, "Would-Be Saints," 236; Prince and Wright, *David O. McKay*, 93–94.

mission presidency in 1922–24. Church membership in Europe had fallen from 31,000 in 1939 to under 29,000 in 1950 because of wartime disruptions, deaths, and emigration to America. About 6,000 members of record lived in the British Isles in 1950; 12,000 lived in East and West Germany; about 4,900 lived in Scandinavia; and over 3,000 resided in the Netherlands, with an additional 1,000 in Switzerland and 1,500 in Belgium, France, Austria, and Czechoslovakia combined. For six action-packed weeks in June and July, David and Ray traversed Europe, holding conferences, answering questions with dozens of reporters, conversing with members and missionaries, sightseeing, and visiting dignitaries including Queen Juliana of the Netherlands and President Juko Paasikivi of Finland.[17]

The prophet loved interacting with and learning from the missionaries and members. His non-stop schedule in Europe worried Lawrence, who urged him to slow down, but he refused. When he agreed to visit and bless a missionary in the hospital late at night following a whirlwind of meetings and entertainment, he brushed off his family's concerns, quipping, "This is what I'm here for [even] if they have to carry me out on a slab." At a dinner party with missionaries in the Netherlands, McKay entertained the crowd by demonstrating how he had attracted audiences during street meetings as a missionary. He sang three hymns for them, each to the tune of "Israel, Israel God is Calling," and brought down the house with laughter when he quipped that the repetition of the tune made no difference "because we didn't have the same audience at the conclusion that we had at the beginning." The prophet was deeply touched by the sacrifices made by several dozen member missionaries from communist East Germany who attended a testimony meeting in Berlin. The men proselytized in the evenings after working all day at their jobs; they could not even afford to buy copies of the Book of Mormon and had few other printed materials to use in teaching. McKay's observations of the members' privations, combined with the devastation of the Russian sector of Berlin in contrast to the impressive rebuilding efforts in the French, British, and American zones of Germany, reinforced his contempt for communism and convinced him that a "terrible conflict" between communism and democracy was inevitable. "We are facing Satan himself," he warned his fellow apostles following his return, because communism was "anti-Christ."[18]

17. DOMD, May 27, 1952; McKay, *My Father*, 216–37; Van Orden, *Building Zion*, 161–62.

18. McKay, *My Father*, 221, 226; "President McKay's Report Council Meeting," in DOMD, Aug. 26, 1952. In 1955 McKay opined that there might be a providentially designed silver lining in the Communist control of eastern European nations. He said that "it came to him that [Communists] have in reality performed a helpful service for us in breaking down the old Greek [Orthodox]-Catholic power over there, which power would have to be broken down before we could carry the Gospel to those people." Spencer W. Kimball, journal, Mar. 17, 1955. In 1957 McKay told Senator John F. Kennedy that he believed the Soviet Union would eventually collapse because "there is no freedom and people will rise against it.... It is a fundamental principle of civilization that men will be free." McKay, *Confidence amid Change*, 199.

Looking back upon his trip, the prophet said he believed his tour "awakened a sense of belonging" on the part of European members. They realized more keenly that "they are not detached entities but are in reality part of the Church as a whole."[19]

McKay traveled to Europe intent upon selecting two temple sites. In 1951, Stayner Richards, president of the British Mission and Stephen L Richards's brother, had visited Salt Lake City for his son's funeral. While he was in town, he lobbied McKay for a temple in Britain. McKay responded positively, so when Richards returned to England, he began identifying potential building sites. In November, he proposed that the church buy 4.75 acres on the outskirts of London near Croydon, and without committing itself to that site, the First Presidency decided that "Great Britain should have the first temple in Europe." Barely a month later, McKay determined that the equally valiant and more numerous German-speaking Saints in Europe also deserved a temple. He recommended building one in Switzerland, "it being probably the safest country in Europe, and more accessible than England to most of the other European countries." The Quorum of the Twelve ratified his decision the following April. McKay envisioned small temples in Europe that could be erected for roughly the same price as a meetinghouse. In these structures, the endowment ritual, which was performed theatrically in a succession of ordinance rooms in the church's temples, could be consolidated for presentation in a single room using modern audio-visual technology. When the architectural plans for the temple were released the following year, the estimated price tag was $350,000, roughly twice the cost of a new stake center.[20]

On his European visit, McKay inspected temple sites in both Britain and Switzerland. He visited several locations identified by Richards and chose a thirty-two-acre estate about twenty-four miles south of London, even though the purchase could not yet be finalized. Selecting a temple site in Switzerland proved more difficult. The selection process reveals McKay's confidence in God's immanence and overriding influence, adaptability in the face of reversals and disappointments, and willingness to admit personal limitations in recognizing inspiration. McKay searched for spiritual impressions and followed those impressions as he perceived them, cautiously hopeful but open to the possibility that some impressions might be flawed.

Leaving England on June 10, 1952, McKay made a quick, unplanned trip to Switzerland to inspect several possible temple sites, believing that time was of the essence. After praying for divine guidance, he and his party, including Mission President Samuel Bringhurst, visited several sites near Bern, but each

19. David O. McKay, address of Oct. 3, 1952, *Conference Reports*, 9.

20. McKay, *My Father*, 223; DOMD, Nov. 30, 1951, Jan. 3, Feb. 13, Apr. 17, 1952, Apr. 3, 1953; "President Stephen L Richards Will Conduct Rites," *Millard County Chronicle*, May 1, 1952, 1.

seemed unsuitable. McKay was "very much discouraged" until they arrived at what seemed to be "the choicest place in Switzerland" for the temple, an easily accessible knoll at the end of a streetcar line. When McKay left for Holland that evening, he was confident they had selected the right site, but a few days later he learned the land was no longer available; the city government "had just" expropriated it for municipal use. Certain that a temple should be built in Switzerland, McKay reconciled himself to the disappointing news. After he returned to Switzerland on July 3 for his formerly scheduled visit, he inspected six more sites, including a five-acre plot "just opposite the ground they had hoped to buy." A widow owned the land, and Bringhurst had approached her even though the land was not on the market, "almost by ... inspiration," to ask if she would sell. The widow agreed to sell—at a high price—but a large number of other heirs would have to consent for the sale to proceed. Most quickly agreed, but two dithered. Shortly before boarding his return flight to the United States, the prophet joyfully announced that the church had acquired land for a temple in Switzerland—even though the two heirs had yet to agree to the contract. He made no mention of a temple near London.[21]

Back in Salt Lake, McKay almost breezily informed his counselors that "he was clear in his mind regarding the site" for the Swiss temple, but he admitted later in council meeting that he "felt uneasy" that some heirs had not yet agreed to sell. After he learned nearly four months later that the sale had fallen through, McKay told President Bringhurst that he was "disappointed" but "not surprised." Before he left Europe, he recalled, he "had a deep impression that opposing forces," perhaps another church, would "prevent our obtaining that site."[22]

McKay retained his faith that "the Lord will overrule," but he struggled to discern God's will in the matter of the temple site. He questioned his former judgment, wondering if he had been impervious to inspiration. When he inquired about another site they had considered and rejected on their visit, the mission president informed him that it was no longer for sale. "We should have followed our impression on that," McKay remarked, as if to chasten himself. "It is always best to follow the impression that comes to us." Bringhurst assured McKay he had found an even better site than the one McKay mentioned. It stood atop a hill, and McKay had seen it from the train station when they arrived in Bern. Indeed, the prophet had inquired about it during his visit, Bringhurst reminded him. It had not been for sale at the time but was now available. Trying to remember the site, McKay asked, "You think the property is

21. David O. McKay to Stephen L Richards, J. Reuben Clark Jr., and members of the Quorum of the Twelve, June 13, 1952; McKay to Richards, Clark, and members of the Quorum of the Twelve, July 5, 1952; "Report Made by President McKay to the First Presidency," Jul. 28, 1952; "President McKay's Report, Council Meeting," Aug. 28, 1952, all filed under the dates listed above in DOMD; McKay, *My Father*, 222–24; "Pres. McKay in N.Y. on Way Home," *Deseret News*, Jul. 23, 1952, 1.

22. DOMD, July 28, Nov. 18, 19, 1952.

better?" "It is considerably better—more accessible—more public," Bringhurst replied. "They are putting in the sewer and water lines. There will be no industry allowed—it is to be for churches and residences." Later that day, McKay recommended to his counselors that the church purchase the site even though he had not personally inspected it and was unsure if he even remembered it. Three days later, Bringhurst obtained the tract on behalf of the church at an excellent price. When he sent McKay some snapshots of the property, he wrote, "We gratefully acknowledge the help of the Lord in this transaction.... Our entire group of missionaries fasted and prayed after this property became available. We are greatly releaved [sic] and so thankful."[23]

The following year in June, the church finally announced that a temple would be built near London. That month McKay returned to Europe to dedicate the London and Swiss temple sites. In a message directed to the residents of Bern, McKay conveyed his "greetings and a prayerful wish that the Church and its objectives may be properly understood, that prejudice may be removed and the light of the Gospel enter the hearts of all." Prior to dedicating each site, McKay explained the purpose of temples in the context of the church's doctrine of proxy ordinances on behalf of the dead. Before returning to Utah he made a personal trip to Scotland to visit his father's birthplace. Ray and Llewelyn accompanied him, and Llewelyn reported for the *Church News*, "Do you know how a little boy feels with a new toy he has always wanted? That is the way Father reacted as soon as we entered Scotland."[24]

On December 29, 1953, just six months after the dedication of the European temple sites, President and Sister McKay departed on their next international mission, a fifty-day trip to Africa and Latin America, with stops along the way in London and Lisbon. Because of his age, Ray's precarious health, and the length of the trip, McKay deemed it "in many respects the most strenuous that [they had] ever taken." The experience taught him to "never attempt visiting [that] many missions again on one trip." Hamer Reiser, a friend and associate who was presiding over the British Mission, accompanied the McKays to Africa and was struck by the prophet's "ardor for living," reflected in his last-minute request to see the wildlife in Kruger National Park, time permitting. Unfortunately, the press of church business and official visits made a wildlife excursion impossible. Although McKay had contemplated visiting South Africa on his world tour in 1921, he had dropped it from his itinerary because of time and distance. Now he

23. Transcripts of telephone conversations between David O. McKay and Samuel E. Bringhurst, Nov. 18, 1952, McKay to Bringhurst, Nov. 19, 1952, Bringhurst to McKay, Nov. 21, 1952, all in DOMD under dates listed; Prince and Wright, *David O. McKay*, 262.

24. Gibbons, *David O. McKay*, 321; Henry A. Smith, "London and Berne Temple Sites Dedicated," *Deseret News Church News Section*, Aug. 8, 1953, 1; "Purpose of Temple Explained in Dedicatory Address," *Deseret News Church News Section*, Aug. 15, 1953, 2; Llewelyn R. McKay, "Day-to-Day Report on Temple Trip," Aug. 11, 1953, in DOMD.

was finally visiting the country, a land no general authority had ever seen, with its 1,800 Latter-day Saints, most of whom were white or of mixed racial descent. He explained to reporters, "We have confined our [missionary] activity to Europeans [in South Africa.] Otherwise, we should be faced with the same problems as your Dr. Malan [the South African prime minister] has in segregation." Nevertheless, people of black African descent had joined the church, and he wanted to observe firsthand the local impact of the church's ban on ordaining anyone with possible black ancestry. The ban was hampering church growth, the previous mission president, Evan Wright, had complained in several lengthy letters.[25]

Like most Latter-day Saints of his era, McKay did not question that the priesthood ban originated with God, notwithstanding the determined work of many African Americans for racial equality in all facets of life in the decades following World War II. Citing the first chapter of the Book of Abraham, which indicated that the Egyptian Pharaoh, a grandson of Ham, was "of that lineage by which he could not have the right of the Priesthood," McKay told an assembly of South African missionaries, "Now there's a nobleman Pharaoh, righteous, fair in his judgment, seeking earnestly to guide the people according to the Priesthood which was given to Adam,—[a] man who seems to have been worthy in every respect not only in regard to <u>nobility of character</u> but also in regard to ability in leadership, but he could not <u>receive the Priesthood</u>. Such is the order regarding his descendants of the Church today." McKay opined that "there is an explanation for this racial discrimination dating back to the pre-existent state." As he and George Albert Smith had written in 1949 to the South African mission president, "The position of the Church regarding the Negro may be understood when another doctrine of the Church is kept in mind, namely, the conduct of spirits in the pre-mortal existence has some determining effect upon the conditions and circumstances under which these spirits take on mortality." Regardless of the reasons for the ban, McKay felt duty bound, as had his immediate predecessors, to adhere to the policy "until the Lord gives us another revelation changing this practice established anciently." He did so, acknowledging that at least two African Americans had been ordained to the priesthood in the days of Joseph Smith and Brigham Young. He was convinced that the ban was not eternal. "The time will come when the Negro will receive . . . the Priesthood," he foretold, but he did not know when that time would come. Thus, he instructed the South African missionaries to inform all "men of Negro ancestry" that the blessing of membership open to them "include[ed] partaking of the sacrament" but did not extend to priesthood ordination.[26]

25. DOMD, Dec. 29, 1953; copy of A. Hamer Reiser diary, Jan. 11, 1954, in DOMD; copy of Robert R. McKay diary, Jan. 25, Feb. 8, 1954, in DOMD; "McKay Explains LDS Attitude on African Natives," *Provo Daily Herald*, Jan. 14, 1954, 16; Prince and Wright, *David O. McKay*, 76.

26. "Minutes of Special Meeting by President David O. McKay," in DOMD, Jan. 17, 1954; Wright, *South African Mission*, 427; Prince and Wright, *David O. McKay*, 495.

McKay was willing to set aside policies that had been devised as corollaries to the priesthood and temple ban, but that was as far as he was willing to go. In South Africa, unlike elsewhere, even male converts who passed as white were required to trace their ancestry out of Africa before they could be ordained. This strict requirement was crippling the church, McKay learned. "If the present policy were continued for another twenty-five years, it is doubtful whether the Church would have sufficient men to carry on the work of the branches," he concluded. Moreover, many men who were "worthy" and "capable" and who appeared to be white had been denied ordination. McKay modified the policy; those with white complexions could be ordained without having to trace their ancestry beyond the continent, he ruled. "I should ... much rather make a mistake in one case and if it is found out afterward suspend his activity in the priesthood than to deprive ten worthy men of the priesthood," McKay advised missionaries and church leaders. It was a moderate reform motivated largely by expediency but reflecting a measure of compassion as well. By announcing this policy shift, McKay acknowledged that men who passed as white but who descended from black African ancestry would be ordained to the priesthood in South Africa, and he implicitly acknowledged this was already almost certainly occurring elsewhere in the world. God would not hold priesthood leaders accountable for ignorantly contravening the priesthood and temple ban.[27]

The prophet's visit to South Africa was memorable not only because of the modest reform he initiated but also because he raised the possibility of building a temple there. He told a congregation assembled in Johannesburg that he looked forward to the day when a temple would be accessible to the Saints there. "In Europe, the first one is now under construction and plans are for another one in Great Britain. Why should not the members of the Church, faithful

27. "Minutes of Special Meeting," Jan. 17, 1954; McKay to Stephen L Richards and J. Reuben Clark Jr., Jan. 19, 1954, in DOMD. After his experience in South Africa McKay was also willing to extend the same policy to light-skinned members elsewhere. In 1957 two exemplary Latter-day Saints from Fillmore, Utah, Paul Anderson and Joyce Marshall, became engaged. Anderson easily secured a temple recommend, but Marshall ran up against the temple ban by virtue of her maternal grandmother, Dorcas Faulk's, dark complexion and alleged African ancestry. In 1880 Faulk's race was listed as "mulatto" on the census in Alabama. Although she passed as white on the 1910 and 1920 censuses in Utah, the 1930 census identified her as Black. Faulk died in 1938, but her rumored ancestry impeded her descendants. In 1944 Joyce's mother appealed unsuccessfully to a visiting general authority to ordain her two sons to the Aaronic priesthood. Lowell Bennion, the director of the institute of religion adjacent to the University of Utah, became a friend and mentor to one of the Marshall boys and called McKay's attention to the young couple's plight in 1957. When McKay investigated, he learned that no one in Fillmore possessed "absolute proof" of Joyce's alleged racial identity, although some recalled that her grandmother's skin was dark. McKay instructed the stake president that he was "going to give Miss Marshall the benefit of the doubt." The stake president was overjoyed. "We haven't any better people than the Marshall family," he assured McKay. Transcripts of telephone conversations regarding the Joyce Marshall case in DOMD, June 13, 1957; Greenwell, "Struggle with Racism," 155–80.

and true and loyal as we have met this morning and last evening, have greater opportunities than them?" he asked rhetorically. "May God hasten the day!" [28]

The prophet suffered severe back pain throughout his African tour, and the night before he departed, his legs became badly swollen from inflamed veins. Nevertheless, Ray noted, she and her husband felt he had accomplished an "incalculable amount of good." Members came forward to "shake his hand and rush away crying. Many have said to me, 'You have no idea what your coming here has done for us.' Over and over they say that." One South African Latter-day Saint wrote, "We felt that indeed we had lived to see the dawning of a great day to have had the supreme honour of meeting President David O. McKay in person."[29]

From Africa, the McKays traveled to Latin America, where their son Bob, who had served his mission in Argentina, joined them. They stopped first in Brazil, where the glaring summer sun and high humidity made Ray "grouchy." As had been the case in Africa, when they landed in São Paulo, and later in Montevideo and Buenos Aires, members thronged the tarmac singing "We Thank Thee, O God, for a Prophet." Seeing a living prophet was an electrifying once-in-a-lifetime experience for some members. One commented after meeting McKay, "What a beautiful prophet!" That night she slept "as I have never slept before—just like sleeping with the angels." McKay gratefully basked in the adulation. "Truly we deeply appreciate the true fellowship, friendship and genuine love manifest by these loyal friends," he recorded.[30]

The travelers met with members and missionaries in São Paulo, including several dozen Saints from Campinas who had traveled one hundred miles to sing for the prophet and to listen through translation to his message. In Uruguay, where the church had grown in six years to 850 members, a reporter, reflecting a common and natural perception of the church as an American entity, asked McKay if he was the spiritual advisor to President Dwight D. Eisenhower. McKay met the American ambassador and was interviewed for a ten-minute spot on the radio. On Sunday in Montevideo he laid the cornerstone for the church's first modern chapel and recreation hall in South America. His appointment with Uruguay's president, Andrés Trueba, had to be canceled due to Trueba's illness, but in Argentina McKay presented President Juan Perón with leather-bound, embossed copies of the Book of Mormon, Doctrine and Covenants, and Pearl of Great Price. Two years later after Perón undercut the Roman Catholic Church's privileged position, McKay wrote to the dictator thanking him for his "commendable efforts to liberate Argentina from church domination."[31]

28. Wright, *South African Mission*, 246.
29. McKay, *My Father*, 245; Wright, *South African Mission*, 250.
30. McKay, *My Father*, 243, 245; Robert R. McKay diary, Jan. 21, 1954, in DOMD.
31. "Buenos Aires Welcomes Pres. McKay," *Salt Lake Tribune*, Feb. 2, 1954, 15.

With well over 1,500 members and 25 branches, the LDS Church had a greater presence in Argentina than in any other South American nation. The prophet's party traveled to Rosario to hold a conference, visited several smaller branches, and met back in Buenos Aires on Sunday in the Teatro Nacional Cervantes (Cervantes National Theater), a spacious venue arranged by Perón as a goodwill gesture. In the capital city McKay also addressed an interdenominational congregation at an American Methodist church, extolling America's heritage of liberty and prosperity and calling upon the United States and its citizens to cooperate with Latin American republics in promoting peace and goodwill.[32]

From Argentina the party traveled to Santiago, Chile, to meet with Billie Fotheringham, an expatriate employed by the Eastman Kodak Company, and his wife, Yolanda, the only members of record in the country. Stopping in Lima, Peru, they met with a handful of North American families who regularly held Sunday school and made plans for a branch to be established. Next the McKays flew to Central America, where a large group of Latter-day Saints stationed in the Panama Canal Zone turned out at 3:00 a.m. to greet them. In Panama the McKays attended the baptism of a Cuna couple, Juan and Irene Andreve Colman, natives of the San Blas Islands and some of the first Panamanians to join the church. In Guatemala, where the first converts had been baptized in 1947, an impressive crowd of 235 attended Sunday services. The McKays planned to travel from there to Mexico, but their flight was canceled. They were "somewhat fatigued," and rather than wait forty-eight hours for another plane to Mexico, they chose to abbreviate their journey and fly directly to Los Angeles.[33]

President McKay returned from Latin America impressed with the church's prospects in Argentina, Uruguay, and Brazil and optimistic that a mission could be established in Peru. He contrasted his experiences on his 1921 world tour, where "[they] met prejudice and suspicion everywhere" with the tolerance and goodwill they experienced in 1954. The ecumenical zeitgeist of the 1950s benefited minority sects like the Latter-day Saints. Most of the non-Mormons he met seemed uninterested in exploring creedal differences but hungry for "more brotherhood and practical, everyday religion." He noted the diminished isolation of nations in an era of air travel and global mass communications. Latin Americans strongly resented US intervention and "the arrogant attitude of superiority on the part of North Americans, both tourists and government officials." When he was in Guatemala City, where the US Central Intelligence Agency and Department of State were conspiring to overthrow President

---

32. "Leader Visits Missions on Two Continents," *Deseret News Church Section*, Feb. 6, 1954, 5; "Pres. McKay in South America," *Deseret News Church Section*, Feb. 13, 1954, 2–4; McKay, *My Father*, 245–46.

33. McKay, *My Father*, 244; "Pres. McKay Cites Church's Future Abroad," *Deseret News*, Feb. 10, 1954, 1; "Pres. McKay in South America," *Deseret News Church Section*, Feb. 20, 1954, 4

Jacobo Árbenz, anti-American protests rocked the streets. Frequently criticized in the American press, Juan Perón was an affable host. McKay had "never been so warmly welcomed" as by the dictator. By their ethnocentrism, he concluded, North Americans inadvertently bolstered the appeal of Marxism and leftists like Árbenz in Latin America and thwarted productive inter-American relations. Americans needed to exercise restraint and promote a "better understanding" through soft diplomacy. McKay's trip to South Africa, where he interacted with a largely white membership, had not induced him to question the priesthood and temple ban. In reporting his trip to the Quorum of the Twelve, he informed them that the priesthood ban would remain in force "until a new revelation comes." It was a ban, he said, "established anciently and adopted in our day." Within two months of his return he did convene an apostolic committee chaired by Adam S. Bennion to compile a record of all previous deliberations in meetings of the First Presidency and the Quorum of the Twelve regarding the priesthood ban. Bennion reportedly informed one group that the committee's work was part of "a careful reevaluation of our doctrine."[34]

By the end of 1954, less than a year after they returned from Latin America, the McKays were sufficiently rejuvenated to embark on another major international tour, this time to the South Pacific. It would be McKay's first visit there since his 1921 world tour. Frank Murdock, an employee of the Missionary Department who worked closely with McKay, accompanied them. The prophet identified two objectives for his tour: to "tell the story . . . of the glories of the Restored Gospel" and to assure members in the Pacific that "we are all one—members of the Divine Church; children of our Father in Heaven." The prophet hoped his visit would enable the members of far-flung branches to feel closer to him and more connected to the worldwide church. He also intended to select the site for a soon-to-be-announced temple in New Zealand, a nation with nearly 15,000 Latter-day Saints—the largest population of Saints in any nation outside North America. He had decided three years earlier to build a temple there for Saints in the South Pacific and Australia.[35]

The party's first stop was Fiji, where a hurricane grounded them over Sunday. On his world tour McKay had been unimpressed with Fiji and the Melanesian people. Now, recognizing Fiji's centrality as a transportation and communication hub for the South Pacific, he interpreted the storm-induced delay as a sign that God was riveting his attention on the island country and inviting him to reconsider his negative preconceptions. To their surprise, while

34. Henry A. Smith, "Pres. McKay Finds All Missions Growing Rapidly," *Deseret News Church Section*, Feb. 20, 1954, 5, 10; Jack M. Reed, "LDS President Returns, Satisfied with Journey," *Salt Lake Tribune*, Feb. 22, 1954, 15, 22; DOMD, Feb. 25, 1954; Keen and Wasserman, *Short History*, 439; Harris, *Second Class Saints*, 56–58.

35. Statement made by David O. McKay upon arrival in Tahiti, Jan. 18, 1955, in DOMD; DOMD, Feb. 20, 1953, Jan. 13, 18, 1955; Newton, *Tiki and Temple*, 257.

walking through the streets of Suva, the McKays met two young missionaries who informed them of a small group of church members there. The prophet had been unaware that the church had any presence in Suva. McKay met with the group of twenty-eight in a hastily called gathering at the home of Branch President Cecil B. Smith, a Tongan immigrant, and told them the event was "of historical importance." "Surely God has had a hand in changing our schedule so that we can be with you," he exulted. Given the priesthood and temple ban, McKay was encouraged by Smith's perception that the dark-skinned Fijians were not of African descent. He ruled that unless they had known African ancestry, Fijian men could be ordained to the priesthood. "The race problem [for the church] would be no worse than in South Africa or Brazil," McKay assured his colleagues following his return.[36]

The party proceeded by boat from Fiji to Tonga, where the prophet met Crown Prince Tāufaʻāhau Tungī and invited him to visit Salt Lake later that year. One of the men standing at the gangplank when he disembarked had sailed 140 miles to shake the prophet's hand. McKay's entourage feasted and drank kava in a welcoming ceremony and inspected the church's Liahona College. They marveled that the Tongan Mission had quadrupled in size since McKay's first visit; it now boasted nearly 4,000 members in 45 branches. En route from Tonga to Samoa McKay and his party planned to visit members on Niue, a raised coral atoll where the church had only recently gained a tiny foothold, but the captain forbade them from landing due to the rough seas. Knowing how much his visit meant to the members and that anti-Mormon sentiment on the island was strong, McKay fretted that his inability to land might "set back … the work." He sent his assurances that "the authorities are interested in your welfare and pray regularly that our Father in Heaven will protect you from the evils of the world."[37]

The McKays traveled next to Samoa, a land with nearly 7,000 members, 4,000 more than when McKay had last visited. Ray was smitten by the beauty of Pago Pago, describing it as "the most beautiful harbor I have ever seen, miles and miles of harbor with hills and rocks in the ocean crowned with beautiful verdure." A church band playing hymns greeted them as they arrived, and the women and children were arrayed in white for the occasion. Unitedly they sang "We Thank Thee, O God, for a Prophet," and even some prominent non-members witnessing the scene acknowledged, "Surely, he is a real man of God," one member, Lafi Toelupe, recalled. "It was a beautiful picture," Ray wrote. Going

36. Reports given by McKay in council meetings, Feb. 17, 24, 1955, DOMD; Franklin J. Murdock, "Day by Day with President McKay," *Deseret News Church Section*, Jan. 29, 1955, 1–4.

37. Franklin J. Murdock, journal, Jan. 12, 13, 1955, DOMD; McKay handwritten diary of trip to South Pacific missions, Jan. 13, 1955, DOMD; McKay to the elders and members of the church in Niue, Jan. 13, 1955, DOMD; Britsch, *Unto the Islands*, 438, 469.

ashore, they found "a touch of America, with derricks, pile drivers, good roads, good buildings representing much money spent during the war." McKay inspected the site for a new church school at Mapusaga, the gathering place he had visited in 1921. As an educator he found the architectural design for the school unacceptable and ordered that the plans be revised. At the mission headquarters on Upolu the McKays spent hours shaking hands; Ray nearly collapsed from the strain. Toelupe recalled, "President McKay so loved his Father in Heaven's children in this far end of the earth, that he forgot his health and shook hands with over 2,000 people that Sunday evening." McKay "did not miss anyone who wanted to touch the Lord's Prophet." When McKay shook his hand, Toelupe "felt the warm of his clean hand touching my weak hand. The tone of his voice when he said to me 'Talofa' was full of love." Eugene England, a missionary, recalled that McKay "remembered Samoan phrases and protocol from his first visit, thirty-five years before. He participated with impressive self-assurance and graciousness" in the formal kava ceremony, "deftly perform[ing] the ceremonial flourish of first dribbling a few drops on the ground" before drinking "the mouth-numbing drink right down." Seated cross-legged for hours on woven mats, he listened to the chiefs' orations and responded to them by "admiring the chiefs' ornate costumes and praising their traditions." He then "reminded them there was one thing greater—their shared Christian faith and various callings in that faith." As Murdock recalled, the experience of being in McKay's presence that day was momentous for members. "I don't believe the Savior could have made a much greater impression. People were thrilled just to touch his coat or his briefcase. And of course he shook hands with everyone.... He had a long hand, long fingers, but a very soft, long hand. It was so warm." One woman who had traveled from another island took the prophet's hand with a silk handkerchief wrapped around her own. She was confident that if the prophet touched the handkerchief and she carried it to her husband, the touch would "cure him." Twenty-five miles inland at Sauniatu, where he been moved to tears in 1921 by the faith and generosity of the Saints and had pronounced an impromptu apostolic blessing, McKay found a white obelisk and a plaque commemorating the blessing. A large sign near the footbridge leading into the community proclaimed, "Welcome to Sauniatu Pres. McKay." The clean, well-landscaped homes and striking setting "was so perfect as to bring the assurance that here are the people of God," Murdock recorded. Hundreds had come by bus and car to witness their prophet's dedication of the new school there.[38]

38. Britsch, *Unto the Islands*, 388, 407; McKay, *My Father*, 249–50; Franklin J. Murdock, "Day by Day with President McKay," *Deseret News Church Section*, Jan. 29, 1955, 3–4; David O. McKay, handwritten diary, Jan. 14, 16, 1955, DOMD; Franklin J. Murdock, interview by Gordon Irving, Mar. 28–30, 1973, 28; Lafi Toelupe, "Tribute to President David O. McKay," in "President David O. McKay," 52–53; Eugene England, "The Place of David O. McKay in Mormon Culture," *Sunstone*, Feb. 2000, 19; Harris, *Samoa Apia Mission History*, 177; Woodger, *David O. McKay*, 211.

Traveling by seaplane, the McKays stopped briefly in the Cook Islands, where the prophet met with a group of sixty, many of whom had traveled far to hear his voice and shake his hand. Next they touched down in Tahiti and spent the night at the mission home. Missionary work had proceeded more slowly there than elsewhere in Polynesia; about 2,000 members were scattered across French Polynesia, only about 400 more than when McKay had visited on his world tour, but the mission president had recently begun concentrating efforts on the main island, a strategy McKay had urged decades earlier that was beginning to bear fruit. On the morning of the group's departure members thronged the dock to place flower and shell necklaces over the travelers' heads. Soon the weight of the necklaces became too great for their shoulders to bear, so the members piled more on their outstretched arms.[39]

After leaving Tahiti, the McKays returned briefly to Fiji and then went on to New Zealand, where they toured a new chapel in Auckland, spoke to congregations in many of the places McKay had visited in 1921, met with the missionaries in a six-hour testimony meeting, and inspected buildings under construction at the Church College of New Zealand in Hamilton. In Auckland, where they shook hands with an estimated 2,000 people and rubbed noses with others, "our hearts overflowed," Ray recorded. "People kissed his hand, would look into his face or mine, and burst into tears." As the president's party drove through the countryside, members who were unable to attend larger gatherings lined the roadways for a glimpse of the prophet. In some places, McKay asked the driver to stop so that he could "greet each one," the mission secretary, LuDene Fresh, reported. At gatherings across the land, members reverently greeted McKay. Members of the Te Hauke Branch, dressed in their Sunday best, lined both sides of the walkway leading from the road to the chapel with flowers in their hands. As he passed, the children reached out and touched his white suit coat.[40]

The high and low points of McKay's visit to New Zealand involved temple and missionary work. He was disturbed to learn that most missionaries were spending only four hours a day proselytizing, and he found the mission wanting in leadership and vision. Conditions were "deplorable." The president, Sidney Ottley, was worn out after serving for over three years, and his replacement from Utah had been named only a few days before McKay arrived. McKay did what he could to encourage the missionaries to be more actively engaged. McKay arrived in New Zealand intent upon designating a temple site. Wendell

39. Franklin J. Murdock, journal, Jan. 18, 20, 1955, included in DOMD; Britsch, *Unto the Islands*, 68.

40. McKay, *My Father*, 250; LuDene Fresh, record of David O. McKay's travels in New Zealand, Jan. 23–31, 1955, copy in DOMD; Franklin J. Murdock, "Day by Day with President McKay," *Deseret News Church Section*, Feb. 5, 1955, 6.

Mendenhall, soon-to-be-appointed head of the Church Building Committee, had preceded the prophet to New Zealand with the confidential assignment of working with President Ottley to scout out possible temple sites. They had settled upon a dairy farm adjacent to the new church college. As he walked over the farm, McKay drew Mendenhall aside from the rest of the group. Pointing to a hill, the prophet asked him, "What do you think?" "What do *you* think?" Mendenhall responded. "This is the place to build the House of the Lord," McKay declared, confirming Mendenhall and Ottley's thoughts. Four days later McKay again visited the site to verify his impressions. After a few seconds he stated, "I am now satisfied. This is the place." Because the Quorum of the Twelve had not ratified the decision, McKay chose not to announce it until after he returned to Salt Lake and met with them.[41]

Following the farewell ceremony at the airport in New Zealand, where a prayer for his safety pronounced by a well-known member, James Elkington, was broadcast throughout the airport, McKay boarded a plane to Australia, where church membership would soon surpass 4,000. As had been the case elsewhere, joyful members celebrated his visit. Philip Mitchell, a member from Tasmania, recalled, "The media were baffled; they couldn't understand why people who had not seen the prophet before cried when he alighted from the plane." For Mitchell the answer was simple: "This was the Prophet, and the Spirit was bearing witness to the Saints." At the cornerstone laying ceremony for a new chapel in Ipswich, Australia, McKay hinted that a temple might be built soon in the region. Advising members against making the expensive trip to the United States, he said he hoped a temple would be built in the South Pacific and counseled, "Let a temple be built nearer to you." The prophet paid courtesy calls to government leaders, including Governor Dallas Brooks of Victoria; spoke with the press; and met with missionaries and members in Brisbane, Adelaide, Melbourne, and Sydney. The lack of "courtesy and refinement" among some missionaries dismayed him, and without revealing his displeasure he advised them to cultivate pure living. On a hill overlooking the Chermside Valley in Queensland, McKay urged Mission President Charles Liljenquist to send missionaries there, impressed that the valley was "ripe and ready for [spiritual] harvest." Liljenquist complied, and within two years a thriving branch of one hundred had been built up.[42]

En route home, McKay met with members and missionaries in Hawai'i, stopping on Moloka'i, Lanai, and the Big Island. At the village of Pulehu on

41. DOMD, Feb. 4, 17, 1955; Wendell B. Mendenhall, "Daily Diary Report of David O. McKay's Visit to New Zealand," Jan. 25, 29, 1955, in DOMD; Newton, *Tiki and Temple*, 249; "Church Will Build New Zealand Temple," *Deseret News Church Section*, Feb. 19, 1955, 12.

42. Franklin J. Murdock, "Day by Day with President McKay," *Deseret News Church Section*, Feb. 12, 1955, 1–4; DOMD, Feb. 4, 1955; Newton, *Southern Cross Saints*, 190; Britsch, *Unto the Islands*, 231–32.

Maui, where he and his traveling companions in 1921 had sensed the presence of two deceased early missionaries, George Q. Cannon and Joseph F. Smith, he reverently recounted the experience for his traveling companions. In Hilo, where he was scheduled to plant a tree for the chamber of commerce, torrential rains fell for much of the day, and his companions expected him to cancel the appointment. But he proceeded to the site, and the rain ceased. "Always remember this," he advised Murdock. "Man's extremity is God's opportunity." On O'ahu the prophet broke ground for a new college on the north shore near the temple in Laie. "God has had a hand over this entire valley," he proclaimed. "This land is a choice land."[43]

McKay returned to Utah in mid-February after an absence of one and a half months, in good spirits and basically healthy. Despite the frequent, lavish feasts held in his honor, he had lost two pounds from the strain and lack of sleep. He had delivered seventy-two talks in formal meetings, with congregations ranging in size from nine missionaries in Tahiti to over two thousand members and friends at a school dedication in Samoa. He had answered questions about the church at twenty-six press conferences and enhanced the church's status in the public square by visiting with "crown princes, premiers, deputy premiers, cabinet officers, members of parliaments, governors, governor generals, mayors, high chiefs, and chiefs." Of greatest consequence for the church, he had selected the site for its first temple in the South Pacific, and he had been inspired to set aside his prejudice against the dark skin of Fijians and nurture the church in Melanesia.[44]

Seven months later, the McKays were ready to venture abroad again to extend the church's international footprint. This time they would cross the Atlantic so McKay could dedicate the Swiss Temple and break ground for one in London. McKay was amused to read the report of a journalist who toured the Swiss Temple during the open house. On the exterior, the building looked "like a church," the reporter wrote, but inside it had "more the appearance of a club or picture show house." The tour had been so bland that the journalist came away knowing "no more about" what went on in the temple than he had known when he entered. Turning more somber, McKay reflected, "Some good members of the Church can say the same thing." On the other hand, some of

43. Franklin J. Murdock, "Day by Day with President McKay," *Deseret News Church Section*, Feb. 19, 1955, 3–4; Franklin J. Murdock interview by Gordon Irving, Mar. 28–30, 1973, 46–74; Britsch, *Unto the Islands*, 181. McKay enjoined Latter-day Saints to embrace a metaphor he attributed to Murdock: "You brethren in the Church will come against the wall. It seems to be across your path. It may be morally. You cannot overcome it, or you cannot get through it, you cannot see. You can walk from here to that wall, having faith that God will give you a ladder, or show you a hidden ladder or an opening, and he will do it, if you will walk just as far as you can in the performance of your duty." David O. McKay, address of Oct. 10, 1959, *Conference Reports*, 90.

44. DOMD, Feb. 17, 1955; Franklin J. Murdock, "Day by Day with President McKay," *Deseret News Church Section*, Feb. 19, 1955, 3–4.

the faithful glimpsed heaven within the temple. As McKay entered the room to dedicate the temple, Marjorie Hinckley recalled, it seemed "as though Moses had arrived." To the prophet himself, "it seemed that an unseen audience had joined in," including his long-deceased parents. He felt "deeply impressed that former Presidents of the Church" were present in spirit, including Joseph Smith and Joseph F. Smith, who had "prophesied forty-nine years ago in the city of Bern that 'temples would be built in divers countries of the world.'" The experience of witnessing the elation of "young husbands and wives with their families" in the temple gave Gordon B. Hinckley, who was there by assignment to prepare the temple for ordinance work, "a certainty even beyond what I had known before that [McKay] was inspired and directed of the Lord" to erect a temple in Europe.[45]

By design, the trip coincided with the Tabernacle Choir's European tour, and McKay attended many of their performances, pushing himself to do as much as was physically possible. His mere presence at a concert in London deeply impressed Bill Bates, a recent convert who knew little about the prophet. Bates had arrived early at the Royal Albert Hall and was seated alone in the balcony listening to the choir rehearse when McKay entered the hall. The choir stopped and stood until he took his seat in the largely vacant auditorium. Decades later Bates recounted, "As I looked the atmosphere that came from him radiated and made me vibrate right through. I was overwhelmed by the Spirit that came from him." The experience "really converted" Bates to the church and left him "absolutely certain" that McKay was "a man of God." After spending his entire day in the Swiss Temple, McKay traveled six hours round trip to attend another of the choir's concerts and didn't return to his hotel until 3:00 a.m. A key objective of the choir tour was promoting goodwill and enhancing the church's reputation, and through his easy banter and diplomacy McKay advanced that objective. At a dinner in the American embassy in London, a fellow guest asked McKay if the church intended by the choir's tour to "explode the common idea that polygamy and Mormonism are synonymous." McKay denied this was the intent but added, "let us hope that it may be one of the resulting accomplishments." Perhaps with that question in mind he began a press conference in Glasgow with a good-natured, disarming introduction: "I would like to introduce you to my wife. My only wife."[46]

Less than a month after they returned from Europe, the McKays traveled to Arizona, where they spoke at the Lamanite conference to over 400 Spanish-speaking members from Mexico and the southwestern states. As a counselor in the First Presidency, McKay had attended the inaugural conference. His visit

45. DOMD, Sep. 11. 1955; Dew, *Go Forward with Faith*, 182–83.

46. DOMD, Sep. 29, Aug. 23, 1955; Bill Bates, excerpts from interview by Greg Prince, Oct. 5, 1999, box 22, folder 13, Prince Papers; McKay, *My Father*, 253.

as prophet and church president further legitimized and dignified the annual gathering. Reminding the congregation of the first Lamanite conference a decade earlier, when the first Spanish-speaking temple session was held, he praised the people for their desire to receive the ordinances of the temple in their own tongue. With the dedication of the temple in Switzerland, the endowment was now being offered in several languages. The Spanish-speaking people of this area had played an integral role in the internationalization of the church. "It was because of your faith and diligence that we were impressed to give to other people the opportunity of receiving these blessing in their own language."[47]

After taking a two-year break from international travel, the prophet embarked on multiple overseas trips in 1958. It was, McKay remembered, "one of the busiest and most eventful [years] of [his] life." He was now eighty-four, and his impaired vision due to cataracts complicated travel. Each trip celebrated the completion of key initiatives undertaken earlier in his presidency. The prophet traveled to New Zealand in mid-April, where he was greeted at the airport by hundreds of members and a brass band playing "We Thank Thee, O God, for a Prophet." Members from across the South Pacific had gathered to participate in the temple dedication. On the day prior to the dedication, over 5,000 participated in a celebration of Māori culture, including the haka, a traditional warrior dance that former American mission presidents had tried to suppress. James Elkington, a stalwart member who had attended to McKay on his world tour thirty-seven years previously, escorted the prophet to his seat for the festivities. McKay conducted eight dedicatory sessions over a four-day period so that all who had secured recommends and traveled to Hamilton for the occasion could participate. He regarded the temple's completion as a key component of the church's mission to carry the gospel to the "descendants of Father Lehi," the Book of Mormon patriarch. Following the last dedicatory session, ordinance workers labored around the clock to ensure that hundreds of Saints who had come from abroad could receive their temple blessings before traveling home. Meanwhile, McKay dedicated the campus of the adjacent Church College of New Zealand, which had cost seven million dollars to build, and a branch chapel in Auckland. He promised that many more chapels would be built soon.[48]

From New Zealand, the prophet and his entourage proceeded to Fiji, where he dedicated a chapel in a service attended by the governor. This, too, was an important initiative of McKay's presidency and a fulfillment of his promise, made three years previously, that "someday there will be a thriving branch of

47. Eduardo Balderas and Nina Nixon Bowman, "Pres. McKay Speaks About Temple Work," *Deseret News Church Section*, Oct. 29, 1955, 22.

48. DOMD, Dec. 31, 1958, Apr. 17, 20–24, 27, 1958; Gibbons, *David O. McKay*, 361, 364; Newton, *Tiki and Temple*, 259–60; "Dedicatory Prayer Delivered by Pres. McKay at New Zealand Temple," *Deseret News Church Section*, May 10, 1958, 2.

the Church here with their own little chapel." Far from the modest chapel architects had originally designed for the small branch, the building that McKay dedicated was, due to his insistence, an imposing structure nearly the size of a stake center with decorative white coral stones embedded in cement exteriors, a symbol that the church intended to stay and was building for the future. This handsome chapel fulfilled strong impressions that had come to McKay on his previous visit. In his dedicatory sermon McKay told the assembled crowd that the church had no political or economic motives in its ambitious international building program—only the New Testament imperative to "teach all nations." From New Zealand McKay traveled to Hawai'i, where he spoke in a devotional at the new Church College of Hawaii, still under construction, another initiative of his presidency.[49]

Despite cataract surgery in June 1958, which caused "a great shock to his system," the loss of thirty pounds due to exhaustion and stress, an automobile accident, and Ray's hospitalization twice that summer, the prophet insisted on traveling to London early in September to dedicate the temple. No construction project undertaken in his presidency meant more to him personally than this one because of his years as a missionary and mission president in Britain. He deeply regretted that Ray was unable to accompany him on this significant trip. Instead he traveled with his assistant Hamer Reiser. Fighting jet lag on the day he arrived, McKay gave a less than sterling performance in a press conference. "I was fatigued, and I'm sure my answers to the reporters' questions indicated my weariness," he reflected after the ordeal was over. His interlocutors had peppered him with difficult questions. He justified the church's ban on priesthood ordination for people of African descent by referring to the Pearl of Great Price and stated the ban was temporary but could be lifted only by divine revelation. When one reporter asked why the church repeatedly selected Americans rather than British Saints to superintend its mission in England, he feebly responded that Brigham Young, an early missionary and prophet, had English ancestry. Joseph Fielding Smith clarified that some former mission presidents had indeed been from Britain. Smith followed up that it was "custom" to select mission presidents who lived near the church's headquarters but that there was no ironclad rule to that effect. Marring McKay's trip were reports he received of water leakage in the Swiss Temple, an architectural "defect" that McKay hoped could be fixed before it became common knowledge; a flood in the London Temple basement produced by heavy rains; and appalling evidence of widespread apostasy in the French Mission that came to light through interviews and hearings in the days leading up to the dedication. Publicity given to the teachings of former church leaders regarding polygamy galvanized the

49. DOMD, May 4, 6–7, 15, 1958; Jacob and Lesuma, "Latter-day Saints in Fiji," in *Pioneers in the Pacific*, 241–63.

latter crisis, shook the spiritual moorings of as many as one-third of the 130 elders and sisters in the mission, and culminated in the excommunication of nine missionaries who refused to sustain McKay as prophet. McKay himself did not interview the missionaries, but the news of their views regarding plural marriage grieved him. "They are misled. They should get clearly in mind the thought that the principle of that great revelation (D&C 132) is the eternity of the marriage covenant," he stated.[50]

The temple dedication proceeded on Sunday, Monday, and Tuesday, with McKay conducting the sessions, which accommodated nearly seven thousand attendees. Prior to the first dedicatory session, McKay retreated to a private room for "a few minutes in secret prayer and sweet communion." In his dedicatory prayer McKay reflected Cold War priorities as he expressed gratitude for the individual rights that were vouchsafed in the signing of the Magna Carta in Surrey County, where the temple was located, and as he prayed that governments of Great Britain, the United States, and "freedom-loving countries everywhere" would "make communistic governments … so universally reprehensible as to be discarded forever by liberty-loving peoples." Reflecting his familiarity with Scottish history, he quoted George Wishart, a sixteenth-century Scottish Protestant reformer who was burned at the stake: "We thank Thee that … Thou didst permit George Wishart to glimpse that 'This realm shall be illuminated with the light of Christ's evangel, as clearly as ever was any realm since the days of the apostles. The house of God shall be builded in it; yea it shall not lack the very copestone.'" He prayed that "any with gloomy forebodings or heavy hearts" who entered the temple would "depart with their burdens lightened and their faith increased" and that all who entered the grounds or glimpsed the temple "from afar" might "lift their eyes from the groveling things of sordid life and look up to Thee and acknowledge Thy providence." The day following the dedication, McKay met with the missionaries who had attended the dedication in a lengthy, memorable testimony meeting. Following quick trips to Stonehenge and his mother's birthplace in Wales, the prophet returned to London for some shopping and appointments before boarding the homebound plane on Sunday afternoon after Sunday school.[51]

After returning home, the prophet underwent eye surgery for cataracts. He had "a difficult time" regaining strength following the operation but had sufficiently recovered by December 15 to travel to O'ahu, where he dedicated the Church College of Hawaii, which had been operating in makeshift quarters

50. DOMD, June 19, July 9, Aug. 7, 28, Sep. 2, 4–5, 1958; Dew, *Go Forward with Faith*, 202; Mehr, "French Mission," 27–45.

51. DOMD handwritten entry, Sep. 7, 1958; "Church Leader Makes Ardent Appeal for Peace," *Deseret News Church Section*, Sep. 13, 1958, 3; A. Hamer Reiser diary typescript, Sep. 2–15, 1958, in DOMD.

since 1954. McKay had lobbied unsuccessfully for a modern school on the island ever since his 1921 visit when he witnessed a flag-raising ceremony at a small school there operated by missionaries. As church president he finally possessed the latitude to achieve his vision, and he pursued it assiduously. He regarded the dedication of the twenty new buildings of the church college, erected at the cost of $3.5 million, as the long-delayed fulfillment of his dreams and hopes. Watching a procession of children around a flagpole brought back memories of his world tour. "There are emotions that cannot be expressed in words. I have experienced some of those emotions today, particularly with the activity around the flagpole and the lane of flower-laden children," he stated.[52]

McKay intended to continue his international ministry the following summer by visiting members and missionaries in the Far East, a region where the church held barely a toehold. The church owned only a handful of properties there, including mission homes in Tokyo and Hong Kong and a few small homes that housed missionaries and served as meeting places in Japan. Several thousand members were listed on the rolls in Japan with an additional 1,500 in Hong Kong and smaller numbers in Taiwan and Korea, but activity rates were low. A visit from the prophet would have meant much to the members and missionaries, but McKay had to acknowledge his physical limitations. Near the end of 1958, he noted that his strength was spent after "about two hours of work here at the office." "I can no longer keep up the pace I have been going the past few months," he admitted in May. Serious problems in the Northern and Southern Far East Missions, including a program of investment in commercial enterprises designed to provide employment for the Saints that was hemorrhaging money, required resolution, though, so he sent Apostle Mark E. Petersen in his stead.[53]

Great Britain seemed a safer prospect for international travel, and McKay felt he had promises to keep there, so he crossed the Atlantic once again in 1961 at the age of eighty-seven, this time with Ray. There he dedicated the Hyde Park Chapel, an edifice built in one of the most prestigious districts of the city. The building, with its fabulous organ, bespoke the church's stature and wealth. In a press conference McKay contrasted the modern chapel with the rented halls in which church members met when he was a young missionary. "The Church is now building chapels and spending money," he proclaimed. "Each branch is given its own chapel." The quality of meeting spaces where members could "feel more at home" was "a contributing factor to the Church's growth" in Great Britain and elsewhere. When a journalist asked incredulously how the 20,000 members in Britain could afford to build such a stately structure, McKay

---

52. DOMD, Nov. 23, 1958, Feb. 8, 23, 1921; Nielson, *To the Peripheries*, 40–41; Britsch, *Unto the Islands*, 180; DOMD, Oct. 17, 1952, Dec. 20, 27, 1958.

53. DOMD, Dec. 30, 1958, May 11, 18, June 12, 1959; Britsch, *From the East*, 86, 96, 101–2, 109, 239–40, 248–51.

explained the law of tithing and the fact that many members donated labor in carpentry, plastering, and pouring cement for the temple. The mission president added that church headquarters had supplied 80 percent of the building cost. McKay rejoiced in modern chapels and temples that attested to the church's "numerical strength," and he recognized the importance of facilities in making conversion respectable. Still, he focused on a different theme in addressing a group of young missionaries; it was "not the surroundings" alone that would attract converts but their "personalities" if they were genuinely righteous. In Scotland, where a journalist asked McKay if missionaries were baptizing minors without the consent of their parents, a practice dubbed "baseball baptisms" that mission presidents and some general authorities including President Moyle had championed, the prophet inveighed against the practice and asked missionaries to raise their hands and explain if they had done so. Four confessed. Before returning to the United States, the prophet broke ground for a chapel in Merthyr Tydfil, the Welsh town where his mother had been born, and gambled against old age by promising to return for the dedication.[54]

In 1962 McKay made a five-day trip to Scotland to organize the first stake there. He visited the renowned Scottish poet Robert Burns's birthplace, where an enthusiastic tour guide provided inspiration for his conference address the next day. The guide's deep knowledge and enthusiasm were infectious. With equal fervor members should share their knowledge of the gospel with their neighbors, McKay advised. He marveled that the church's membership in Scotland now numbered in the thousands. "It is like a dream come true.... A wish of long-standing" had been "fulfilled."[55]

McKay defied old age and feeble health to cross the Atlantic to England for the last time in 1963, shortly before his ninetieth birthday. In Wales he dedicated the Merthyr Tydfil chapel; forty-six more were under construction elsewhere in Britain, with construction scheduled to begin on thirty-nine more by the end of the year. He marveled that there were thousands of members in attendance and exulted that it "was one of the greatest trips I ever made."[56]

54. "Trip to London, England, Scotland and Wales, Feb. 22, 1961 to Mar. 4, 1961," in DOMD, Feb. 1961; Henry A. Smith, "Pres. McKay Dedicates Hyde Park Chapel at London Session," *Deseret News Church Section*, Mar. 4, 1961, 3, 15; "Pres. McKay to Keep Promise," *Deseret News Church Section*, Aug. 17, 1963, 3.

55. "Trip to Scotland to Organize Glasgow Stake," DOMD, Aug. 23–27, 1962.

56. George Scott, "Pres. McKay Returns to Salt Lake from 'One of Greatest Trips,'" *Deseret News*, Aug. 28, 1963, 1, 4; "Pres. McKay Returns Home After Wales Visit," *Deseret News Church Section*, Aug. 31, 1963, 3. Leaders and members from across Britain made significant sacrifices because the building committee had committed to complete the structure by McKay's mother's birthday, August 28. Bill Bates of the Manchester Stake presidency learned about the structure when the building committee transferred construction supplies and building missionaries from his stake center's construction site. "They started diverting our materials. They were charging them to our building but diverting them to Merthyr Tydfil. And our building missionaries were taken away and

The church's stature abroad had markedly improved over McKay's lifetime. The prophet had been cordially welcomed by heads of state, including the Argentine and Finnish presidents, the Tongan king, and the Dutch queen. He had made a concerted effort through these visits to project a breadth of mind and an image of wholesomeness and diplomacy to enhance the church's status and respectability as a bona fide world religion rather than an eccentric cult. Despite the progress he facilitated, in most centers of political and cultural power beyond the United States, the church still possessed minimal political capital and commanded limited recognition. Early in his administration, Queen Elizabeth was oblivious to McKay's attendance at an eagerly anticipated, ticketed reception at Buckingham Palace. Hoping for a "formal reception by her Majesty," McKay instead stood in a drenching rain with 5,000 other guests, straining for a glimpse of the queen in 1952. The event betokened rough sailing as the church fought for an equal footing with other religions following the construction of the London Temple.[57]

In 1958, a local official in Surrey levied a tax on the new temple. Selvoy Boyer, the temple president, had chaired the property tax division of the Utah State Tax Commission, and based on that experience he urged the church to appeal the levy to a local tax tribunal. Houses of public worship were exempt from taxation under England's Rating and Valuation Act of 1955, but the government contended that the temple was taxable because it was not open for public worship. As a reporter for the *Daily Mail* noted after attending the temple open house, it was "the strangest church" she had "ever visited" because from the day of its dedication onward "it is closed for ever to the general public." McKay dispatched President Stephen L Richards, an attorney, to England in the spring of 1959 to try to sort out matters. Richards and others engaged a barrister to argue its case before a tax tribunal. In 1961, a lower court magistrate ruled in the church's favor, a ruling that elicited criticism in the British press and caused the local government to appeal the decision. This time McKay dispatched Henry D. Moyle, also an attorney, to England, where he along with McKay's son Lawrence, also an attorney, met with the church's legal counsel. In arguments before the appeals court in July 1962, the government's representative pointed out that only a subset of church members possessing recommends signed by their leaders could enter the temple. The Queen's counsel conceded that if all church members were permitted to enter and worship, the temple could be classed as a

sent to Merthyr Tydfil.... Then all of a sudden a call went out, 'We need all the help we can get from the British Mission to finish this by the 28th of August.' ... That meant we all had to go down there and even stay there, you know, make accommodations somehow. We had like ants swarming over the place, working night and day to finish it for August 28th. Sure enough, we got it finished. Hundreds of us were down there, where they had about a dozen members in the Branch." Bill and Irene Bates, excerpts from interview by Greg Prince, Oct. 5, 1999, box 22, folder 26, Prince Papers.

57. DOMD, June 17, 1952.

public place of worship, but such was not the case. The church's attorney cited judicial precedent for recognizing even private homes to which unrelated individuals were invited as places of public worship, but the court ruled that the precedent had no application in revenue cases and upheld a tax of 2,080 British pounds per year, the equivalent of 48,000 American dollars in 2023. Lord Alfred Thomson "Tom" Denning, the second-highest-ranking judge in England, ruled, "this temple is not a church hall, chapel hall nor a similar building. It is not in the least on the same footing as a church hall or chapel hall. It was a very sacred sanctuary, quite different from a building of that category."[58]

After phoning his father with the news, Lawrence opined that "the facts are against us" but thought they might justifiably appeal to the highest court of the land, the Law Lords within the House of Lords, even though the prospects for success were low. McKay's ire overflowed. He vowed impetuously, "If we have to pay taxes, that will cost too much. We will tear it down, and leave them without a Temple!... We will not pay such high taxes year after year for the next hundred years. We will not do it!" When Moyle came to the phone, McKay reiterated, "We shall take it [our appeal] to the House of Lords, and if they go against us, we can tear the Temple down, and leave them without a Temple." Moyle counseled unsuccessfully against filing an appeal because of the cost involved and the adverse publicity for the church that could follow.[59] When he returned to Utah, Moyle warned McKay that if the tax were upheld, the local government could legally raise the amount eight-fold from £3,000 pounds to £25,000, the equivalent of an increase from $70,000 to $580,000 in modern dollars. Moyle suggested that the church might be able to circumvent the ruling by opening the chapel on the ground floor to the public. Temple patrons would enter the building through a back door or annex and proceed to the upper floors for temple worship. It was possible the government might still levy a tax on the upper floors of the temple, but Moyle thought this was unlikely. McKay remained convinced the church should appeal before opening the ground floor of the temple to the public. If the appeal failed, he again threatened, the church might convert the entire edifice into a meetinghouse and "build another temple [instead] in Sweden" on land the church owned there.[60]

The church engaged one of the best lawyers in Britain, Edward Gardner, to argue its case before the Law Lords, and McKay dispatched Moyle and Lawrence

58. DOMD, Jan. 16, 1961, June 4, 1963; McKay, *Confidence amid Change*, 277; Rhona Churchill, "The Strangest Church I've Ever Visited," *London Daily Mail*, Sep. 9, 1958, 6; "Church Wins Temple Tax Case," *Church News*, Jan. 21, 1961, 3; "News Notes at Home and Abroad," *Church News*, July 14, 1962, 2; "Church of Jesus Christ of Latter-day Saints v. Henning (Valuation Officer): CA 1962," swarb.co.uk.

59. DOMD, July 10, 1962 (telephone conversation with Lawrence McKay, Henry D. Moyle, and David O. McKay).

60. DOMD, Aug. 9, Sep. 28, 1962.

to England, where they worked closely with Gardner in shaping the case. McKay expressed his faith that "there is a higher power working for us on this case" and favorably viewed the appeal as an opportunity to "present to the House of Lords the real purpose of Mormonism" for the first time in the church's history.[61]

Five judges heard the case in the spring of 1963. Gardner argued that the temple was a place of public worship in the sense that unrelated individuals came together to worship there, as opposed to a public place of worship, and that therefore it should be exempt from taxation. The judges set aside that technical distinction and on May 30 unanimously upheld the lower court's ruling. Lord Edward Pearce noted that tax exemptions were intended "to benefit those activities which are for the good of the general public." Although one might make the distinction between private worship in the home and public worship involving people who came together from various locales, it was "impossible" to conclude that the temple was a public house of worship "since the public was excluded." Lord Raymond Evershed read what Moyle called "a very learned and thoughtful statement" exploring the nuances of public versus private worship but ultimately agreed with his associates' opinion.[62]

Following the ruling, Moyle asked the church's attorneys if they thought the church could avoid the tax by opening the ground floor of the temple. All three opined that the tax would only be waived for that portion of the building. They explored other options, including petitioning the county for relief, but President Boyer doubted the officials would make any concession, noting that the feeling in the area toward the church had become "very bitter" as the appeal proceeded. The annual assessed tax amounted to \$5,350—the equivalent of \$53,344 in 2023. The rate was over five times as high as the taxes on the Alberta and Arizona temple properties but only slightly lower than the tax on the Los Angeles Temple property, including the mission president's home and the mission office there. After reflection Moyle became reconciled to the ruling. "After I had had twenty-four hours to contemplate," he wrote in his diary, "I had a satisfaction come over me that was very gratifying. I had a feeling that the tax which we would be required to pay would be as good an investment as we could make toward establishing a better feeling on the part of everybody towards us in Surrey." Back in Utah, McKay was less easily reconciled. When he learned of the adverse ruling, McKay asked Lawrence to work with the church's attorney in Frankfurt to determine whether the Swedish government would exempt a temple from taxation there. He was still toying with the idea of shifting temple work from England to Sweden.[63]

61. DOMD, Jan. 31, 1963; Andrew Roth, "Sir Edward Gardner" (obituary), *Guardian*, Aug. 31, 2001.

62. DOMD, June 4, 1963; "Henning v. Church of Jesus Christ of Latter-day Saints," vLex Justis, vlex.co.uk.

63. Poll, *Divine Miracle*, 217; DOMD, June 4, 1963.

After Boyer informed an acquaintance of McKay's threat to close the temple in London, the word spread quickly. Within a few months an Australian member reported hearing that the prophet had threatened to "demolish the Temple in England and erect it brick by brick in another land since the tax hearing went against the Church." Boyer was reprimanded for disclosing privileged information and "advised not to repeat it" again. McKay would only acknowledge that "my son, Lawrence, at my request had written to Sweden to learn if there would be any tax on a temple if one is built there."[64]

By early 1964, church leaders had learned that a temple in Sweden would likely be taxed too. The church continued to consider opening the temple chapel in England for weekly sacrament meetings and investigated the possibility of appealing the rating authority's levy on the grounds that the church as a charity was entitled to at least a 50 percent reduction in taxes under English law. But such an appeal, if it were to go to the House of the Lords, could cost over $13,000, and the likelihood of success was limited. Ultimately, McKay reconciled himself to the disappointing outcome that countered his faithful expectation. He buried the hatchet, and the church paid the tax. In order to function abroad, the church would need to follow the Christian injunction to "render therefore unto Caesar the things which are Caesar's" (Matthew 22:21). The church continues to pay taxes on its London Temple property.[65]

The church's inability to secure a tax exemption underscored its limited clout in the United Kingdom, where its membership of record comprised less than 0.15 percent of the population. And in every other European nation, members comprised an even smaller percentage of the total population. By 1965, in only two nations across the globe, Tonga and Samoa, did Latter-day Saints comprise over 10 percent of the population.[66]

Despite its minority status, the church's numerical growth during McKay's presidency was unprecedented, as was the construction of temples, chapels, and schools around the world. Moreover, McKay as prophet had visited more nations and continents and met with more Latter-day Saints than any of his predecessors, promoting a sense of belonging and connection to the global community of Saints and the institutional church. A key message he had taken to members everywhere was "we are all one—members of the Divine Church; children of our Father in Heaven." The church itself was largely North American in both its general and mission leadership and its membership, and McKay openly proclaimed his patriotism and pride in the American way. But he had demonstrated a cultural flexibility in honoring indigenous traditions that some conservative Mormons disparaged, such as the Samoan kava ceremony

64. DOMD, Oct. 29, 1963.

65. DOMD, Feb. 7, 1964, Aug. 25, Nov. 16, 1965.

66. Plewe, *Mapping Mormonism*, 230, 239.

and Polynesian dancing, and in extolling Juan Perón, the Argentine populist strongman, at a time when he was widely distrusted in the United States. At the London Temple dedication McKay had adapted his remarks to his British audience, referring to the Magna Carta and quoting the Scottish reformer and martyr George Wishart. Before becoming prophet he had encouraged and participated in Lamanite conferences for Spanish-speaking members of the church from Mexico and the US Southwest, and he dignified the gathering by attending as prophet and church president in 1955. In Fiji he abandoned his prejudice against dark skin in response to what he took to be a divine sign that the gospel should be preached there, and he laid plans to baptize black Africans and establish congregations among them, a prospect that frightened many of his fellow apostles. Still, there were limits to his openness to cultural and racial diversity. He strongly opposed interracial marriages, even those in which the race-based temple ban did not apply, pulled back from plans to establish the church in India due to concerns about decentralization and assimilation, and accepted and justified the traditional view of black skin as a divine curse.[67]

67. Statement made by David O. McKay upon arrival in Tahiti, Jan. 18, 1955, in DOMD; Eduardo Balderas and Nina Nixon Bowman, "Pres. McKay Speaks About Temple Work," *Deseret News Church Section*, Oct. 29, 1955, 22.

13: God's Mouthpiece

David O. McKay's administrative decisions and globalizing priorities as church president are his most enduring institutional legacies. Thousands treasured the memory of shaking his hand or receiving his counsel or blessing. Yet he endeared himself to far more Latter-day Saints through his uplifting spiritual instruction and encouragement. "Every time he gave a conference talk, it was on some human value, or some human relationship which, to me, was very important and significant," Robert Simpson reflected. Decades after McKay's death, his book *Gospel Ideals* remained one of retired businessman Donald Rasmussen's favorites. "I've got it underlined and underlined," he remarked in 1995. "The virtues of the laws, the virtues of the principles, and agency, and the simplicity of it, and how it all works together."[1]

As a prophet, seer, and revelator, McKay devoted the better part of his life to moral instruction, inspirational preaching, and testifying of spiritual realities. McKay believed that "proclaiming the divinity of the mission of our Lord and Savior, Jesus Christ" was of paramount importance, a duty for which he and his peers, by virtue of their apostolic calling, were uniquely qualified. Three years into his prophetic service, in a meeting of the apostles, he contrasted what he perceived to be some religious leaders' doubts regarding Jesus's "divine Sonship" and their "sense [of] … inadequacy to represent our Lord" with the solid "testimony" of Jesus and the "mighty … responsibility that [the apostles] possess." In 1955, he admonished his associates, "This is the Church of Jesus Christ, and it is our obligation to preach to the world that he is the Son of God, our Redeemer and Savior, not just a great teacher, but in reality the Son of our Father in Heaven, and the Redeemer of the world." In a meeting with civic leaders not of his faith in New Zealand, McKay forthrightly owned that testimony. When one official observed that "generally the leading scientists and leading men of the world" regarded religious people as naïve and unintelligent, McKay countered, "We take the opposite view.… The most intelligent people in the world … accept Jesus, if not as a divine personage as we do, at least as the greatest man that ever lived on earth." When the official clarified that he

1. Robert L. Simpson, excerpts from interview by Greg Prince, Jun. 2, 1995, box 22, folder 13, Prince Papers; Donald H. Rasmussen, excerpts from interview by Greg Prince, Jun. 6, 1995, box 22, folder 13, Prince Papers.

intended his remark as a compliment to the church for constructing schools despite the secularizing impact of education, McKay thanked the man, stating that his comment enabled him to "place our stand and belief in the divinity of the Savior before the audience."[2]

The prophet's spiritual certitude was keen, particularly as he expressed it away from the limelight. He was reticent to mention his most sacred experiences in public. Years before his appointment as church president he remarked that although he had received "many" sacred experiences, "I seldom speak of manifestations that have come to me." He reiterated, "I do not like to speak of some things which are most sacred to me." In 1961, John Cook, a feature writer for a Sacramento newspaper, asked McKay to answer a personal question, not intended for publication: had he seen Jesus? According to Salt Lake City business and civic leader Edwin Q. "Ted" Cannon, the prophet replied he had never seen Christ but added that he had often felt his presence and influence and heard his voice many times. "That is quite a testimony I have given you," Cannon reported him as saying. "I do not know when I have given this before." Publicly, McKay testified in 1966, "With all my soul I know that death is conquered by Jesus Christ.... I bear you witness that he does live. I know it." In 1967 while meeting with the apostles in the Salt Lake Temple he observed, "We meet today as the Savior and His Apostles met in the upper room. This morning we have the privilege to be near Him ... and He is near us." Confident in that presence, he urged his colleagues to join him in praying for deeper cognizance of it: "We have the right to say to Him with all our hearts: 'We love you. We ask Thy blessing, and may we feel Thy presence near us this morning as we have never felt it before.... We need Thy presence, and we need to feel near to Thee.'" The following year Middlemiss summarized McKay's comment to a church employee that he "felt the presence of Heaven near him all the time. In fact it was so close that he felt like he could speak to [God] anytime that he desired."[3]

McKay felt close to other heavenly spirits as well. "Heavenly beings were real from my babyhood on," he reflected in a 1951 general conference. He continued, "I like to feel that President Heber J. Grant is near us, ready to help and especially pleased to see the Church is growing." Five years later as he dedicated the Los Angeles Temple in 1956, McKay remarked, "It is easy for me to feel that there are others we cannot see who are joining with us in this temple dedication.... You who have lost loved ones, be comforted; they are not far away from you." In the following days attendees at the dedication privately shared corroborating impressions with McKay. In 1959, he taught that "the veil is thin

2. David O. McKay, address of Apr. 4, 1953, *Conference Reports*, 14; DOMD, July 1, 1954, Jan. 25, 1955; McKay, *Confidence amid Change*, 124.

3. David O. McKay, address of Oct. 5, 1919, *Conference Reports*, 180; David O. McKay, address of Apr. 9, 1966, *Conference Reports*, 59; DOMD, Jan. 5, 1961, Feb. 2, 1967, Jan. 16, 1968.

between those who hold the priesthood and divine messengers on the other side of the veil."[4]

McKay believed in the active influence of evil supernatural beings as well as heavenly ones. In 1955 he cited recent evidence that "the Adversary is at work," including challenges the church had encountered in securing permission and land to build a temple in Switzerland, negative publicity in a Catholic-owned Argentine newspaper, and proselytizing by fundamentalist Mormon apostates. "As long as the Adversary to truth is free to exercise dominion in this world, we are going to have attacks," he warned.[5]

The prophet perceived spiritual insights more often in the wee hours of the morning than at other times. Plagued by insomnia, he was often awake by 3:00 a.m. and almost always awake by 5:30 a.m. He was more likely, he said in a temple meeting, to receive spiritual impressions soon after he awakened, when he was "relaxed and thinking about the duties of the day." The impressions came, the minute taker recorded, "as if he were to hear a voice," but only if he was not distracted by worry or unkind feelings. "The operation of the Spirit of the Lord upon our spirit is as real as when we pick up the telephone," he stated, but when those impressions come "we must be brave enough to take the suggested action."[6]

Not all spiritual impressions were soothing; some came as warnings or premonitions through a process he called pre-vision. In 1957 McKay fretted about a dark feeling that engulfed him as he was dedicating a small chapel on the church's vast cattle ranch in Florida. He began the dedicatory prayer with a hopeful feeling, but midway through the prayer, that cheery "vision of the future seemed to leave him." The change in feelings might have only been the result of late-afternoon exhaustion or the isolation of the building, he admitted, but he was quite "certain the spirit of prophecy came to him." In reporting the foreboding sentiment later to the apostles, he said that he "hope[d] that it has no significance as to the future of that place." Nearly six years later, his friend and counselor Henry D. Moyle would be overcome with pain and fatigue while speaking in that same chapel—warning signs of a heart problem that would take his life within two days.[7]

After four local church leaders from Chico, California, died in a private plane crash while traveling home from a solemn assembly in the newly dedicated Los Angeles Temple, McKay reflected on the accident, which "deeply concerned" him. As they were making a surprise landing to visit a friend, the men apparently lost control of the plane and crashed. McKay reflected that the

---

4. David O. McKay, address of Oct. 6, 1953, *Conference Reports*, 183; DOMD, Mar. 8, 12, 16, 1956; David O. McKay, address of Oct. 9, 1959, *Conference Reports*, 8.

5. David O. McKay, address of Oct. 1, 1955, *Conference Reports*, 89–90.

6. DOMD, Oct. 3, 1957, June 14, 1956.

7. DOMD, June 20, Dec. 5, 1957; Poll, *Divine Miracle*, 218–19.

accident should not have occurred without an advance warning. "I think warning comes to a man holding the Melchizedek Priesthood," he told the apostles, and he wondered if the men had received any impression that it would be unwise for them to travel by plane or to make the surprise visit. When he heard that the wife of one of the men had dreamed of a plane crash the night before it occurred and remonstrated herself for not warning her husband, he reflected, "I know the Lord will protect us if we will just watch and heed that spirit [of warning]." He rather thought "that those men were warned, but they did not heed the warning."[8]

Eager for a more intimate, inside view of their prophet's clairvoyance, some church members naively circulated reports of purported special revelations and warnings; the origins were usually murky. Perhaps someone who knew or worked with the prophet allegedly heard him make a statement and relayed that privileged information to a friend, who then passed it on. The 1950s Cold War was a time ripe for apocalyptic thinking. Voicing a common sentiment among Latter-day Saints, one member wrote, "I think the last days are surely here, for all the things the prophets foretold are coming to pass now." The nuclear arms race and the civil defense program's advice to Americans to store food apparently fueled one apocalyptic rumor in the mid-1950s that McKay had predicted an imminent food shortage; soon the shelves of grocery stores and warehouses would be empty, and those who had not stored food would suffer. Many in McKay's local congregation heard of the purported vision, and some fanatically considered borrowing money to purchase packaged cartons of emergency foodstuffs from commercial distributors. At a ward dinner where the commercially packaged food was being served and marketed, McKay displayed his characteristic practicality and quashed the rumor. He denied receiving a vision or issuing a warning and advised members not to go into debt to store food. The church's advice to store foodstuffs had "been in existence at least since [he] was a boy," he told the gathering, and it remained in place, but there was no cause for haste or alarm. McKay advised his neighbors that when he received a revelation, it would be disseminated through "proper channels" rather than through a whispering campaign.[9]

McKay's teachings were grounded in his spiritual convictions. But distilling those convictions and impressions into motivational language required effort. Inspiration did not necessarily come on demand. In 1954 he informed conference-goers that he had been "physically and mentally fatigued" and unable to focus his "mind on anything definite" as he searched one day for a topic for his general priesthood meeting address. He went to bed that night uneasy about

8. DOMD, June 20, 1957.

9. Suzanne Black to Pete Black, Sep. 30, 1955, original letter in author's possession; DOMD, Feb. 20, 22, 28, 1957.

what to say. In the morning he glanced at a bookshelf in his room and saw a quote book he had compiled. The thought came to him to build his address around some of the quotations. Sometimes he recycled portions of previous addresses. For instance, one of his conference addresses in 1956 closely resembled an address he delivered in October 1951. His April 1960 opening conference address quoted verbatim from large chunks of his April 1907 conference talk, and two of his addresses in the October 1960 conference reprised talks he had given in 1912 and 1948.[10]

Middlemiss wrote in 1963 that when McKay "takes his place at the pulpit, wherever it may be, a ripple of emotion seizes those present." When he spoke, "they catch his glow, his love of life and of humanity." In speeches early in his prophetic administration, his voice rose and fell in volume as he emphasized key points. He paused for effect and emphasis. As Richard Armstrong concluded in his scholarly study of the prophet's rhetoric, McKay's voice was "firm, but far from overbearing or pressing." The cadence of his speech was "slow," and became slower as he aged. Armstrong categorized McKay's rhetorical approach using rhetorician Herbert W. Simons's typology as a "moderate" who "'adapts to the listener's needs, wants and values; speaks his language, adjusts to his frame of reference." The faithful sensed a connection to deity when he spoke; as Mark E. Petersen observed, they regarded him as "the Lord's mouthpiece on earth—a prophet and a seer," and those gifts were extraordinary. Referring to McKay's gift as a seer, one general church authority, Robert L. Simpson, described the clairvoyance Saints attributed to him: "A modern-day prophet can look into the eyes of a fellow church member and search his very soul without as much as a question being asked." No wonder the faithful wanted him to continue speaking to them as long as he lived.[11]

---

10. David O. McKay, address of Oct. 2, 1954, *Conference Reports*, 82–83; Armstrong, *Rhetoric of McKay*, 51. McKay's recycling of sections from his conference addresses, including the ones referenced above, is readily apparent using the search function in Liddle and Galbraith, *Scripture Citation Index*, version 3.5.0, scriptures.byu.edu.

11. Clare Middlemiss and Robert L. Simpson, "Tributes to President David O. McKay," *Improvement Era*, Sep. 1963, 764, 778; Armstrong, *Rhetoric of McKay*, 116; Mark E. Petersen, "preface," in *Man May Know*, vii. Simpson spoke from personal experience. While employed as a telephone company executive in California, Simpson traveled to New Zealand, where he had served a mission, to attend the temple dedication. In the temple, he stepped into a room and was surprised to see the McKays seated alone. "He reached out his big right hand and he pulled me in really close. He put his left hand on my shoulder, and he proceeded to look into my eyes. He looked and he looked. It must have been the better part of a minute, maybe 45 or 50 seconds. Then, he made his first gesture. He gave my hand a shake, my shoulder a squeeze, and said, 'Brother Simpson, I'm pleased to know you.'" That was all there was to the interchange, but several weeks later McKay called Simpson to preside over the New Zealand Mission, based, he said, "on our personal interview in the New Zealand Temple." Simpson stated, "The term Seer took new significant [sic] on that day, because I thought he was actually able to look into my heart and soul and know what was there." Robert L. Simpson, excerpts from interview by Greg Prince, Jun. 2, 1995, box 22, folder 13, Prince Papers.

Over the course of his prophetic service President McKay appealed to a broad audience in his talks by quoting liberally from articulate writers and observers beyond the Latter-day Saint population. More than one-fifth of his opening address in the April 1952 conference (over 560 words), was taken from a speech by Fred G. Clark, a prominent conservative businessman and radio personality who founded and chaired the American Economic Foundation, on the dangers of atheistic communism. In one address he quoted Thomas Carlyle, Ralph Waldo Emerson, Henry David Thoreau, Katharine Lee Bates, and James R. Lowell, among others. In another talk he illustrated the corrosive effects of "evil passions" by quoting from Charles Dickens's *Oliver Twist* and Nathaniel Hawthorne's *The Great Stone Face*. He often quoted the British playwright and author Beverley Nichols on the human capacity for positive change with Christ's help. His most frequently cited literary works outside of the scriptures were literary critic Stopford Brooke's paraphrase of Robert Browning's epic poem *Paracelsus* ("Live all things outside yourself by love, and you will have joy")and Ella Wheeler Wilcox's "The Man Worth While" ("It is easy enough to be pleasant / When life flows by like a song / But the man worth while is one who will smile / When everything goes dead wrong"). Not surprisingly he quoted liberally from scriptures, primarily the New Testament and the Doctrine and Covenants. In his general conference addresses McKay quoted a passage from the Book of Moses in the Pearl of Great Price fourteen times—more than any other passage. The passage summarized the Latter-day Saint understanding of God's design for humans: "For behold, this is my work and my glory—to bring to pass the immortality and eternal life of man." Thirteen times McKay quoted Acts 4:12: "For there is none other name under heaven given among men, whereby we must be saved."[12]

McKay peppered his addresses with memorable, engaging anecdotes. To illustrate his point that "a true Latter-day Saint is kind to animals [and] … every created thing," he recounted his conversation with a hired man on his farm who claimed to have killed a porcupine "just for fun." McKay later found the animal very much alive and writhing in misery, its "head beaten." "What fun can there be in treating dumb animals in that cruel way?" he asked the congregation. One anecdote, related in a Scottish brogue, of a Scotsman named Jock's conversation with his neighbor following the death of Jock's wife, brought the house down with laughter: the neighbor commented that the wife had been thoughtful of others, neighborly, and a good wife. Jock replied, "Aye, Tamas, Janet was a guid

12. David O. McKay, address of Apr. 4, 1952, *Conference Reports*, 14; McKay, *My Young Friends*, 26–33; David O. McKay, address of Oct. 5, 1951, *Conference Reports*, 7; Armstrong, *Rhetoric of McKay*, 29–30, 42–43; Stopford A. Brooke, *The Poetry of Robert Browning*, 135. Nichols was referenced in McKay's October 1944 and 1958 addresses and in his April 1948 and 1954 addresses. Over his entire career as both an apostle and prophet, McKay quoted Acts 4:12 twenty times and Moses 1:39 eighteen times in general conferences.

woman, a guid neighbor as you say; she was a' you say an' mair. She was aye a guid, true wifey tae me, and I *cam' near tellin'* her sae aince or twice." Thrice in general conferences he shared the story of a party that searched for three-year-old Alfred Cornell who wandered barefooted from his home in the North Dakota Badlands in 1933. Two hundred fifty residents lined up a few feet apart from each other and committed to search "every square inch." After a day of searching, they found the boy "badly bruised and inflamed" but alive. McKay used the story to encourage teachers and church workers to search "for young boys and girls who are in the Bad Lands of immoral influence that surround us." Several times he told a story about a group of young people floating down a river who refused to heed dire warnings from the shore about rapids and falls ahead. When it was too late, "with all the power at their command they failed to turn their boat upstream." So "shrieking and cursing, over they went." Depending upon the occasion, McKay employed the story to illustrate the urgency of heeding advice from one's teachers and leaders or the need for leaders who were willing to "row into the stream" to try to, "by companionship, by persuasion, by legitimate force, when necessary, turn the boat from the rapids."[13]

In the face of doomsday scenarios, the prophet remained hopeful and conveyed that optimism to his listeners. Not a Pollyanna, he acknowledged that the Saints had "cause for apprehension." Secularism was sweeping the western world, and modern weaponry possessed unprecedented destructive power. "Today civilized nations are sitting on a mountain of explosives, accumulated in defiance of Christ's teaching," he warned during the nuclear arms race. "Let the heat of hatred, suspicion, and greed become a little more intense, and there will be . . . an international explosion." But, he insisted, the faithful need not fear because God had decreed that "the human race will continue, and the kingdom of God be established." "I feel this morning with all my soul, that the sun of hope is rising," McKay told conference-goers in 1953. Not only divine purpose but also the human capacity to change inspired McKay's optimism. A key purpose of Jesus Christ and his church, he taught, was "to change people's lives."[14]

In his role as truth teller, McKay called out wrongdoing among church members, although the tenor of his addresses was more often encouraging than condemnatory. In one stiff rebuke he disparaged the "absolutely inexcusable"

---

13. David O. McKay, address of Oct. 6, 1951, *Conference Reports*, 181; David O. McKay, address of Oct. 9, 1960, *Conference Reports*, 115; David O. McKay, address of Apr. 6, 1955, *Conference Reports*, 125; David O. McKay, address of Apr. 4, 1965, *Conference Reports*, 6; David O. McKay, address of Oct. 6, 1946, *Conference Reports*, 114; David O. McKay, address of Apr. 4, 1964, *Conference Reports*, 4–5; David O. McKay, address of Apr. 6, 1949, *Conference Reports*, 180.

14. David O. McKay, address of Apr. 4, 1952, *Conference Reports*, 13; David O. McKay, address of Oct. 9, 1959, *Conference Reports*, 6; David O. McKay, address of Oct. 2, 1953, *Conference Reports*, 8–9; David O. McKay, address delivered at the dedication of the Hyde Park Chapel, Feb. 26, 1961, in Lampropoulos, *A Vision Splendid* 58.

behavior of a husband who cursed his wife and "in a mad fit of anger overturn[ed] a table spread with dishes." The man was "a creature in the form of a man harboring the nature of an animal!" In another address he censured "some sadist young boys who have been going around with '22's shooting, just for mere sport, the starving deer." In 1953 he urged members to refrain from slander and quoted a recent convert to the church who expressed "surprise to hear how many people talk against the Authorities here in Salt Lake City." In 1956 he expressed gratitude to church members who were "contributing their time and means" to the church. This included "wealthy men and women," millionaires, who donated their time. Although he did not name them in this address, they included Leo Ellsworth, who was managing the church's ranch in Florida; President Ernest Wilkinson at BYU; and the head of the Church Building Committee, Wendell Mendenhall, who had been derided by some as an opportunist and climber. He alluded specifically to Mendenhall's contributions: "it means something to leave your vocation, cross the ocean, and render service in the building of schools and temples." "Some of you seem to condemn them," McKay chastened, an observation that applied to some church employees and authorities. As often as not, though, McKay emphasized encouraging examples rather than flaws. He shared praise from the "head of a national Drug Store chain," whom he met on a plane. The man said that he was eager to hire "young Mormon boy[s]" to manage his drug stores because of their integrity. "I have many of them in my employ," he reported. McKay encouraged ward teachers (similar to later home teachers and ministering brothers) by describing the service of a duo who accompanied an elderly woman to the dedication of the Los Angeles Temple. "What a beautiful example of watching over the church always.... They were her ward teachers and they knew her needs." He shared the success of one priesthood quorum in fellowshipping and activating lapsed church members. Forty in their quorum had been reclaimed and ordained to the office of elder in the priesthood. One of them had overcome addictions, returned to college, and was now serving as president of the quorum.[15]

In nearly one-third of his conference speeches as prophet, McKay addressed the physical and spiritual duality of humans, building upon Paul's epistle to the Galatians in which the ancient apostle contrasted the "works of the flesh" with the "fruit of the spirit." "Man is a dual being— he is physical, has his appetites, passions, desires, just as any animal has," McKay told one audience, "but his is also a spiritual being." "Animal instincts" which "permit you to crush your

15. David O. McKay, address of Apr. 4, 1958, *Conference Reports*, 5; David O. McKay, address of Apr. 4, 1952, *Conference Reports*, 13; David O. McKay, address of Apr. 4, 1953, *Conference Reports*, 59–60; David O. McKay, address of Oct. 7. 1956, general conference digital video collection, catalog.churchofjesuschrist.org; David O. McKay, address of Oct. 11, 1958, *Conference Reports*, 86; David O. McKay, address of Apr. 7, 1956, *Conference Reports*, 87; David O. McKay, address of Apr. 2, 1960, *Conference Reports*, 22–23.

neighbor that you yourself might rise" ignited rivalry and even war, whereas spiritual beings sought "the good of [one's] fellowman and the glory of God." He counseled that "the body's pleasures, its appetites, its desires, its passions" for food, sex, alcohol, tobacco, and self-absorption must be subordinated to the eternal spirit, which was "the real man." The intended outcome of self-denial, he taught, was "spirituality," which he defined as "the consciousness of victory over self, the consciousness of being above the passions" and ultimately the realization of being in "communion with Deity." McKay inveighed against the sexual revolution of the 1960s as the acme of animal urges run amok, branding "unchastity" as "a dominant evil of the world today" and warning that if sexual license ran unchecked, it could "wreck present-day civilization." Employing traditional tropes, he spoke of a woman's virtue as "that which is most precious in life" and likened women to flowers. Some were like the wild roses he had often passed on the canyon road near his boyhood home, "covered by the dust of every traveler and by the men who hauled lumber down that old street." How much fairer were the roses blooming in a meadow far from the road, "kissed only by the morning dew, unsullied by the dust of every traveler passing by." He vigorously derided the sexual double standard that licensed men's sexual dalliance. He blacklisted boys and men who rationalized fornication as "contemptible" and men who abandoned pregnant partners as "human rats."[16]

McKay advised that genuine happiness or joy, as opposed to pleasure, resulted from self-abnegation. "Do not worry about these teachers who say something about inhibitions" or "repression," he counseled. McKay differentiated between joy, or happiness, and pleasure. "Things which pertain to the physical nature are so easily obtained and the pleasures so immediate that many spend most of their time seeking them and neglecting the permanent joys of the spirit," he told BYU graduates. Sexual license might bestow momentary pleasure and gratification at the price of lasting joy. "Happiness leaves no regrets. Happiness is always sweet to recall... and that happiness is what the Church offers you," he guaranteed. He promised additional benefits to those who elevated their actions. Adherence to "the ideals of the gospel of Jesus Christ... will make you handsomer young men, more beautiful young women—because your thoughts modify your features." Righteous self-discipline would "make [adherents] more clever students, more faithful lovers, more desirable companions, more loyal friends, more helpful members of society, more worthy mothers and fathers of future families.[17]

16. David O. McKay, address of Oct. 11, 1959, *Conference Reports*, 122; Middlemiss, *Man May Know*, 420–23; David O. McKay, address of Apr. 6, 1960, *Conference Reports*, 122; David O. McKay, address of Apr. 4, 1969, *Conference Reports*, 6; David O. McKay, address of Apr. 9, 1966, *Conference Reports*, 6; McKay, *My Young Friends,* 44, 70, 73; McKay, "Two Contending Forces."

17. McKay, *My Young Friends,* 8–9, 50, 64, 72; "Pres. McKay Warns All Cherish Ideals," *Deseret News Church Section*, June 4, 1951, 1, 4; "'Cherish the Soul,' Y. Rites Told," *Salt Lake Tribune*, June 4, 1951, 3.

Those who sought spirituality would also cultivate reverence, McKay advised. Reverence commenced with an appreciation for the earth, for beauty, and for life. "The earth is drenched with the blood of innocent women and children, and choice young manhood lies mangled and torn," he taught "because there has gone out of the heart of man the spirit of reverence." Reverence for sacred things, including others' feelings and rights, was the "fundamental virtue in religion," while irreverence "was the lowest state in which a man can live in the world." In the late 1960s, McKay's teachings regarding reverence for life took on new hues, seemingly reflecting the widening social consciousness that also helped to galvanize the War on Poverty and Civil Rights legislation. His April 1968 conference speech, which Lawrence read after reviewing and editing it with his father, eloquently advocated "increased tolerance of racial and religious differences, increased respect for those of... lower social and economic levels" and "a greater sense of social responsibility for the less fortunate in our society."[18]

McKay advocated reverence for the human body too. Addictive substances such as tobacco and alcohol that compromised the health and agency of their consumers particularly aroused his ire. "The voice of the Church will ever be raised against the increasing tendency among men and women to stain their lives with nicotine," he proclaimed. It was "an insidious enemy of health and morals," and its consumption by women who were indulging in "one of man's vices" was repugnant. In the 1960s McKay broadened his warnings to include drug abuse; he expressed "alarm" at the "prevalent use" of marijuana "and other vicious drugs" by high school and university students.[19]

The prophet envisioned the dualism between the physical and the spiritual as one among many permutations of a broader Manichean tension between related dualisms: Christ and Satan, service and selfishness, individual liberty/agency and state domination/communism. By this logic, communism was pure evil. In 1966, long after the nation's preoccupation with the communist threat in the early 1950s, he continued to single out communism as "the greatest satanical threat to peace, prosperity, and the spread of God's work among men that exists on the face of the earth." It was the foremost modern manifestation of the anti-Christ. "Either Christ is a reality, and communism is wrong; or Christ is a theory and communism is right," he preached. The two were incompatible because "fundamental in the belief and promulgation of communism is the denial of the existence of God, and the desire to substitute for this belief confidence

18. McKay, *My Young Friends,* 30–31; David O. McKay, address of Oct. 1, 1955, *Conference Reports*, 91; David O. McKay, address of Oct. 5, 1956, *Conference Reports*, 6; David O. McKay, address of Apr. 6, 1968, *Conference Reports*, 93.

19. David O. McKay, address of Apr. 5, 1959, *Conference Reports*, 74; David O. McKay, address of Apr. 5, 1968, *Conference Reports*, 8.

in the state." Communism was also evil because it restricted freedom and resorted to force, a method linked to the pre-mortal war in heaven, as described in Joseph Smith's revelations, and that "emanates from Lucifer himself." By contrast, "God intends the individual to be free," McKay preached. McKay held up the American ideal as vouchsafed in the Constitution and Declaration of Independence as "the antithesis of communism and fascism." He patriotically declared, "The government of the United States as given to us by our fathers is the real government under which individuals may exercise free agency." McKay frequently quoted pundits who decried totalitarian ideologies and the erosion of freedom, including Sir Percy Spender, Australia's ambassador to the United States, who charged that communism posed a "deadly challenge" to "political, economic, and individual freedom." Like the devil, communists relied upon deception. He cited army psychiatrist William E. Mayer's allegations of communist "brainwashing" in Korea. Repeatedly he charged that communists propagandized youth by removing them from their households and "making them members of the state instead of leaving them with their mothers and fathers." Even more than the Chinese and Soviet military arsenal, McKay feared "the sowing of false ideals by the enemy" and "misrepresentation" of legitimate governments. Communists also trafficked in hatred, a Satanic passion. Following his European tour in 1952, he reflected on communist leaders' "hatred" of America and of Christianity. The Iron Curtain symbolized their determination not only to "keep Western influence out" but also to "inculcate hatred in the hearts of the youth." China, Russia, and Cuba were governed by "the spirit of hate," he believed. Quoting from an Associated Press article in 1965, he read that Mao Tse-tung was animated by "hatred for the United States, hatred for rich landlords, for counter-revolutionaries, for Chiang Kai-Shek." Occasionally, McKay seemed to endow capitalism as well as democracy with a quasi-divine status. He taught that "the right of private property is sacred and inviolable," condemned compulsory unionism as a violation of agency, criticized state interference in agricultural production, and warned that British socialists were laying the foundation of "a totalitarian state." Nationalization of industries in Britain was a step toward "planned economy [and] control of all productive power, including persons and property."[20]

20. McKay, "Two Contending Forces"; David O. McKay, address of Apr. 9, 1966, *Conference Reports*, 109; Middlemiss, *Man May Know*, 312, 374, 373, 377, 402, 448; McKay, *My Young Friends*, 29, 37; David O. McKay, address of Oct. 7, 1951, *Conference Reports*, 161; David O. McKay, address of Oct. 5, 1962, *Conference Reports*, 6–7; David O. McKay, address of Apr. 5, 1959, *Conference Reports*, 72; David O. McKay, address of Apr. 9, 1961, *Conference Reports*, 132; David O. McKay, address of Apr. 5, 1951, *Conference Reports*, 96; David O. McKay, address of Oct. 3, 1952, *Conference Reports*, 11; David O. McKay, address of Oct. 1, 1965, *Conference Reports*, 9; David O. McKay, address of Sep. 29, 1961, *Conference Reports*, 7; David O. McKay, address of Apr. 4, 1952, *Conference Reports*, 15; David O. McKay, address of Apr. 6, 1950, *Conference Reports*, 35.

Strident and impassioned in his principled denunciation of communism, McKay never acquired the extremist reputation of Ezra Taft Benson. The contrast between the two men is instructive. Unlike McKay, Benson courted controversy in his implication of Dwight D. Eisenhower as a communist, his lavish endorsement of the John Birch Society and close association with the society's cofounder Robert Welch, and his condemnation of Martin Luther King as a "communist or communist tool." McKay reserved his ad hominem attacks for internationally prominent ideologues and revolutionaries like Stalin, Lenin, and Mao.[21]

In his prophetic capacity McKay emphasized the importance of religion in government. In the 1950s his words resonated with a nation caught in the throes of the Cold War and eager to demonstrate its moral superiority to godless communism. When McKay in 1952 quoted American Economic Foundation chair Fred G. Clark's warning that "every collectivist from Karl Marx to Stalin has agreed that faith in God must be destroyed before socialism can take over," he was voicing widely shared views. In the mid-1950s Congress shored up the state's official recognition of divine sovereignty by adding the words "under God" to the Pledge of Allegiance and adopting "In God We Trust" as the nation's motto. To illustrate the centrality of God to good government and diplomacy, McKay frequently recounted an anecdote taken from a chapter by Robert Speer that appeared in the 1924 book *Christianity and Modern Thought*. Speer, secretary of the Presbyterian Board of Foreign Missions, recounted a Japanese student's reaction to an address, "The Moral Values Which Unite the Nations," delivered by Lord Alfred Balfour at the University of Edinburgh in 1909. Balfour highlighted common knowledge, shared commercial interests, diplomatic intercourse, and human friendship as the ties linking the nations of the world. Following the address, the student asked, "'But Mr. Balfour, what about Jesus Christ?" According to Speer, "everyone felt at once the justice of the rebuke," a rebuke that also stirred McKay's believing listeners. By the 1960s secularism appeared to McKay to be resurging, a trend that he, along with other revered evangelists like Billy Graham, condemned. McKay's views placed him well within the Christian mainstream. After the Warren Court in 1961 overturned a Maryland law requiring public officials to affirm belief in God, the prophet expressed his "grief" and "shock" in a conference address. "Without Jesus of Nazareth . . . the traits of the jungle will hold the human family in bondage," he warned. In October 1964, two months after Congress had approved the Gulf of Tonkin Resolution authorizing the president to escalate American military action in Vietnam to achieve peace and security in Southeast Asia, McKay warned that peace was possible only through Christian regeneration:

21. Harris, *Watchman on the Tower*, 56–59, 64–65, 76–78.

"Men may yearn for peace, cry for peace, and work for peace, but there will be no peace until they follow the path pointed out by the Living Christ."[22]

Another hallmark of McKay's prophetic teaching was a focus upon family, an additional theme that responded to and dovetailed with the trends and sensibilities of the era. McKay's administration spanned the 1950s, the ostensible golden age of the misleadingly labeled "traditional family"—a self-contained, nuclear household with a working father, stay-at-home mother, and children. In that decade, couples married relatively young, birthrates were high, and divorce rates were low. McKay's tenure also spanned the 1960s, with the sexual revolution's assault on sexual containment and the women's movement's questioning of rigid, gender-based roles in the home and workplace. Although acceptance of premarital sexual activity rose significantly over the 1960s, McKay's frequent teachings about marriage, family, and fidelity resonated with much of the American mainstream in the 1950s and also with a vast cross section of Americans in the 1960s, the "silent majority" courted by Richard Nixon in the campaign of 1968. President McKay's frequent emphasis upon family flowed from the twin convictions that "putting in order our homes, and keeping them in order" was an important "function of the Church" and a central means of combating Communism.[23]

McKay extolled marriage as "a divine institution" and regarded the home as "the foundation of the state, especially of a republic." He promulgated a utilitarian view of marriage and sexuality: "Marriage is for the purpose of rearing a family" and not for "sexual indulgence," he advised. "If we do not put the proper value on parenthood, we are not emotionally or socially ready for marriage," he counseled. The prophet counseled children to obey their parents, even if they appeared old-fashioned, and he instructed parents not to "put business or pleasure above [the] home," advising that "no other success can compensate for failure in the home." Common consideration and courtesy were vital in spousal relations. "Do not forget—when difficulties arise, when debts begin to pile up and taxes have to be paid, when babies require coddling and perhaps feeding at night—courtesy after marriage is a contributing factor toward harmony and peace in the home." He advised husbands to respect their wives' bodily autonomy and encouraged family members to avoid profanity and vulgarity and to speak politely, using phrases such as "if you please" and

22. David O. McKay, address of Apr. 4, 1952, *Conference Reports*, 14; Kruse, *One Nation Under God*; David O. McKay, address of Apr. 4, 1958, *Conference Reports*, 8; David O. McKay, address of Oct. 1, 1965, *Conference Reports*, 11; David O. McKay, address of Sep. 29, 1961, *Conference Reports*, 8; David O. McKay, address of Oct. 2, 1964, *Conference Reports*, 5.

23. David O. McKay, address of Apr. 4, 1953, *Conference Reports*, 14; David O. McKay, address of Apr. 4, 1952, 15–16; Cannon and Long, "Behavior in the Sixties," 36–49; Finer, "Trends in Premarital Sex," 73–78.

"excuse me." "During courtship, keep your eyes wide open, but after marriage, keep them half shut," he quipped.[24]

Piercing the veneer of suburban contentment in the 1950s, McKay diagnosed that many households were misshapen, unhappy, and in need of redemption. Letters he received disclosed the strife under which some existed. "The stability of the family life is crumbling," he warned in 1952. Alcohol and tobacco were sources of "unhappiness" in what might "otherwise [be] happy homes." In 1958 the divorce rate began to rise modestly after having fallen for over a decade. The rate accelerated in the 1960s. McKay blamed men for much of the increase. In 1959 he warned men against neglecting their wives: "We have too many divorces in the church, and men, I think we are to blame for most of them, not all, but most of them." In 1964 he warned against "the increasing number of divorces and the tendency to look upon marriage as a mere contract that may be severed at the first difficulty or misunderstanding that may arise." He acknowledged, though, that in "extreme cases," including unfaithfulness, "habitual drunkenness, physical violence [or] long imprisonment" of one spouse for serious lawbreaking, divorce was warranted.[25]

McKay tracked reports of rising juvenile delinquency in the postwar decades and the tendency of teens to date younger and to date only one partner. He counseled that "going steady too early in life is fraught with handicaps" because "it gives to the young man a sense of familiarity or ownership and, to the young girl, a feeling of belonging, a rapturous state to be consummated only by marriage vows." He taught that the foundation for successful marriages was laid long before "the marriage altar" in chastity and in loyalty to parents. In 1957 he referenced statistics from the sheriff's department showing that nearly two-thirds of juvenile delinquents in Salt Lake County came from homes broken by death or divorce. McKay viewed the church as a potent substitute for dysfunctional families. "If we can get some of the boys under the influence of the bishoprics, boys who perhaps have unfortunately come from broken homes, or more unfortunately, homes in which God does not dwell, we shall save souls here at home," he opined.[26]

---

24. McKay, *My Young Friends,* 46, 52, 60, 62; David O. McKay, address of Oct. 2, 1955, *Conference Reports*, 129; David O. McKay, address of Apr. 4, 1964, *Conference Reports*, 5; David O. McKay, address of Apr. 5, 1952, *Conference Reports*, 86; David O. McKay, address of Apr. 3, 1955, *Conference Reports*, 26; Middlemiss, *Cherished Experiences* (1976), 194. Few members knew how deeply disgusted McKay was with parents whose children misbehaved. "He thought parents were terrible to not have well-behaved children, and he used to say, 'Never give a child … an order unless you expect it to be carried out. Don't tell your child to stop doing that and then let him do it,'" his granddaughter Midene recalled. Midene Anderson, excerpts from interview by Greg Prince, Oct. 1, 1996, box 22, folder 13, Prince Papers.

25. McKay, *My Young Friends,* 61, 77; David O. McKay, address of Oct. 10, 1959, *Conference Reports*, 89; David O. McKay, address of Apr. 4, 1964, *Conference Reports*, 5.

26. McKay, *My Young Friends,* 59–60; David O. McKay, address of Apr. 6, 1956, *Conference*

Some Latter-day Saints, particularly those coming of age in the cultural ferment of the 1960s, "respected the kindly David O. McKay" but complained that "he never spoke out on the major contemporary issues," including racism, poverty, the Vietnam War, environmental pollution, and sexism. They felt his focus on family relations, kindness in the home, fatherhood, and motherhood were "'skirting the real issues'" of their era. Others insisted that the prophet's focus on the family was timely. The root causes of poverty and violence were "the lack of Christ-like character," Joseph Murin told students at the institute of religion adjacent to Stanford University. McKay's focus on the family was apt because the family was "the vehicle by which personalities and attitudes can be changed."[27]

One of McKay's most oft-quoted aphorisms was "every member a missionary." As a mission president in Great Britain he had employed the phrase to encourage members to introduce their friends to the church. He renewed that call in October 1958, observing, "It is generally understood that every member of the Church should be a missionary." His focus in that address was primarily upon members' setting a sterling example and teaching through action. But he returned to the theme six months later, emphasizing, "*Every member*—a million and a half—a *missionary!*" He encouraged prospective missionaries attending high school or college to enroll in language classes to be better prepared to preach the gospel abroad. In 1968 in an address read by his son, he reminded listeners that "the responsibility has been given to us to convey the gospel to our fellowmen." Rather than "wait[ing] until some special opportunity is given," he advised Latter-day Saints to "proclaim it in [their] acts." But there was more. "Everywhere that we mingle with men we have the responsibility resting upon us to give the good news to the people of the world."[28]

In addition to teaching and counseling, McKay almost always closed his conference addresses with a petition to God to bless those who listened to conference. Occasionally he concluded with more direct prophetic benedictions, pronounced with "all my heart," or "all my soul," in Jesus's name or "with all the power the Lord has given his servants." Through these blessings, McKay exercised his prophetic calling on behalf of the faithful, linking believers he might never meet to heaven. He blessed believers with "peace and love and kindness" and "happiness" in their hearts and homes. On other occasions he offered spiritual assurance or testimony. "I bless you with increased testimony of God's existence, increased testimony of the divinity of Christ's mission, his life, his death, his establishing the gospel," McKay announced on one occasion, also

Reports, 6; David O. McKay, address of Apr. 6, 1957, *Conference Reports*, 92–93; David O. McKay, address of Oct. 7, 1951, *Conference Reports*, 159.

27. Joseph C. Muren, "When Spirit Speaks to Spirit," in "President David O. McKay," 52–53.

28. David O. McKay, address of Apr. 6, 1959, *Conference Reports*, 122; David O. McKay, address of Apr. 4, 1953, *Conference Reports*, 59; David O. McKay, address of Apr. 7, 1968, *Conference Reports*, 145.

bestowing an "increased testimony of the value of the individual." In another conference he pronounced an inspiring, salvific blessing upon the congregation, empowering them to "attain that testimony, that high spiritual state" requisite "to enter through the veil into the presence of God." Some listeners paid scant attention to these benedictions, but for others they conveyed heavenly blessings and power from the man they revered as God's mouthpiece and regent.[29]

29. David O. McKay, address of Oct. 4, 1963, *Conference Reports*, 124; David O. McKay, address of Oct. 7, 1962, *Conference Reports*, 120; David O. McKay, address of Oct. 6, 1951, *Conference Reports*, 183; David O. McKay, address of Oct. 11, 1959, *Conference Reports*, 124; David O. McKay, address of Apr. 7, 1957, *Conference Reports*, 131.

14: Age, Debility, and the Levers of Power

Called to the apostleship at age thirty-two, McKay dedicated his energies to the Church of Jesus Christ of Latter-day Saints. His decades of experience in church service prepared him well intellectually and spiritually to lead the church, but they also took a toll on his body. In his last decade in office that toll became increasingly evident as his physical strength and stamina ebbed, making that decade much different for him than the 1950s. Aside from a prostatectomy in 1951 shortly after being sustained as church president, cataract surgeries in 1958, frequent insomnia, and periodic chest pains due to overwork, the 1950s were years of decent health, considering his age (he turned eighty in September 1953). Repeatedly over the decade, his cardiologist, Louis Viko, encouraged him to work fewer days, take vacations, and cancel evening appointments, but McKay complained his schedule was unmanageable and his responsibilities inescapable. "I wish you had been here for the last two hours," he reportedly told Viko at a checkup in 1957. "One thing after another … things that were not planned today.… They are things I cannot delegate.… These things come on and I cannot avoid them." He felt he could not afford the luxury of taking more extended breaks because if he did, the press of matters that had accumulated in the interim would be crushing when he returned. He also was driven by the conviction that "when you stop, you die."[1]

McKay's strength began to wane perceptibly as early as 1958. In June, Clark remarked that the prophet's health was "failing" and opined that he "could pass on any time." As we have seen, McKay canceled his anticipated trip to the Far East the following year due to health difficulties. Reminders of physical decline surrounded him; his best friend and first counselor President Richards died suddenly of a heart attack in 1959. The news came as "a terrible shock." Richards was "a true and loyal friend" and "as dear to me as a brother," McKay observed. Richards reciprocated his love. His son told the prophet that excepting Richards's wife, Irene, "father loved you more than anyone on this earth." McKay sorely missed his friend's "brilliant intellect," his "clear and sound judgment" and his "loving heart." He would appoint a succession of dedicated counselors

1. DOMD, Sep. 13, 1957. See also DOMD, Aug. 17, 1951, July 6, 1956; Richard and Vivan McKay, excerpts from interview by Greg Prince, May 21, 1996, box 22, folder 13, Prince Papers.

over the next nine years, but none sufficiently gained his confidence to fill the void left by Richards.[2]

Shortly after Richards's death, President Clark also began to absent himself from the office and First Presidency meetings due to his inability to climb stairs and a general weakness in his legs. With difficulty, Clark managed to attend the October 1959 general conference, where he was sustained as McKay's first counselor, but by November his legs could scarcely bear his weight. One year later, he delivered his last conference address. In December 1960, McKay lamented, "I fear President Clark has given up. It has been months since he has been to the office."[3]

McKay's new counselor following Richards's death, Henry D. Moyle, did what he could to assist under these difficult circumstances. Indeed, because of Clark's and McKay's health challenges, much of the First Presidency's daily administrative work devolved upon Moyle, as it had upon McKay when he entered the First Presidency in 1934. As severe exhaustion, continued insomnia, and swelling in his legs plagued McKay, he relied more heavily than ever upon Moyle. In September Moyle confidentially informed Ernest Wilkinson that McKay's mental acuity was declining too; in a recent First Presidency meeting, McKay had insisted "with his customary pride" that he fully understood a discussion item, but Moyle did not believe he did.[4]

The year 1960 was also unkind to Ray. Early in the year she suffered a stroke that left her temporarily unable to speak or use her left arm. She spent several weeks in the hospital—a time that wore McKay out with worry. For a short time after she returned home, she seemed to improve, but then she suffered a succession of ministrokes and blackouts over the next few months. By afternoon on many days, she was drowsy and sometimes even unresponsive. Although a night nurse was on duty in the house to care for her, the nighttime attacks kept McKay awake with worry. Ray's speech was garbled, and her hand movements were limited.[5]

Near the end of 1960, McKay was torpedoed by new evidence of the church's rising indebtedness. Late in the 1950s, the church had embarked upon what the *Church News* termed "the largest building program in the history of the Church" under the direction of Wendell Mendenhall, head of the Church Building Committee. Although the church had ended 1958 with a surplus of $7 million, that was wiped out, and expenditures exceeded income by $8

2. Ernest L. Wilkinson, diary, June 2, 1958, UA 1000 series 1, sub-series 9, Ernest L. Wilkinson Papers hereafter cited as Wilkinson Papers; DOMD, May 11, 19, 21, 1959; Gibbons, *David O. McKay*, 401–16.

3. Quinn, *Elder Statesman*, 172; DOMD, Nov. 18, 1959, Oct. 9, Dec. 1, 1960.

4. DOMD, Aug. 26, 1960; Wilkinson, diary, Sep. 6, 1960, UA 1000 series 1, sub-series 9, Wilkinson Papers.

5. DOMD, Feb. 25, Mar. 10, 19, 25, Apr. 9, May 9, 10, June 14, July 17, 1960, Apr. 18, June 5, 1961.

million in 1959. The heavy expenditures continued in 1960. The *Church News* reported in July that by the end of the year, 800 chapels would be in design, under construction, or awaiting dedication. At the same time, the church was expanding its educational footprint with expensive new buildings at BYU and in the Pacific Islands, where Mendenhall also chaired the church's Pacific Board of Education. In October 1960, McKay advised Mendenhall to "move slowly on some of these important Church buildings which are causing a vast expenditure of money." The outlay of funds "had caused much concern in [his] mind," McKay reportedly stated. In December as he reviewed budgets for the new year, McKay learned that the proposed expenditures for 1961 exceeded anticipated revenues by a whopping $25 million. Belt-tightening decisions, including deferring construction of three new buildings at BYU, brought the expected deficit down to $9 million, but cash flow problems persisted. The church had ample assets to cover its expected expenditures but not without liquidating some of its properties. Accustomed to taking business risks, Moyle championed expansion despite the financial gamble. As Alan Blodgett, an employee in the financial department, later recalled, "deficit spending did not concern President Moyle as long as the church had the resources and so long as needed facilities were being constructed." Moyle was convinced that the new buildings would attract converts—a central objective of a church commissioned to take the gospel to the world—and that over time tithing revenues would rise. McKay supported this view in the 1950s. Clark, who had previously warned against extravagant expenditures, was too weak and depressed by ill health to continue his criticisms. He had been eclipsed by the more energetic Moyle. As Hugh B. Brown recalled, because Clark "could not attend many of the meetings of the First Presidency," the prophet "was making a number of decisions without referring to him in any way."[6]

The following June, McKay called Brown, who had been an apostle for only three years, as an additional counselor in the First Presidency. Brown recorded that he felt "overwhelmed" but trusted that he "had but one course to take and that was to humbly accept the responsibility." Much later, he remembered being called as "a counselor *to*, not *in*, the First Presidency," a distinction he would later try to apply to subsequent third and fourth counselors. To his way of thinking, a counselor to the presidency would be an advisor rather than a full-fledged presidency member. But McKay's public announcement of the call actually designated Brown as "a counselor in the First Presidency of the Church." Concerned for Clark's self-esteem, Brown drove to Clark's home immediately after

6. Poll, *Divine Miracle*, 189; "800 Chapels To Be Built By Church In '60," *Deseret News Church Section*, July 23, 1960, 3; McKay, *Confidence amid Change*, 343, 350; Wilkinson, diary, Jan. 13, 1961, UA 1000 series 1, sub-series 9, Wilkinson Papers; Brown, *Abundant Life*, 131; Bill and Irene Bates, excerpts from interview by Greg Prince, Oct. 5, 1999, box 22, folder 6, Prince Papers.

receiving the call to assure him that he had not sought it. Clark "seemed to feel very good about it," Brown recalled, although "he wept like the dickens" at his physical inability to continue serving as he would like.[7]

On September 23, 1961, McKay visited Clark for the last time. They enjoyed reminiscing about their school days at the University of Utah and their association in the First Presidency stretching back to the Great Depression. A study in contrasts, their relationship and relative power had seesawed over the years, but their affection for each other was genuine. Seeing his counselor in such a weakened state pained McKay; he left the house "with a heavy heart." Clark died two weeks later on October 6, and then McKay named Brown as his new second counselor. Moyle and Brown "worked together with considerable harmony" and "were very fond of each other," Brown recalled, although at times Brown suspected that Moyle "felt that [he] was somewhat of an upstart," even though he was five years older than Moyle.[8]

At the end of 1961, the proposed budget for the coming year once again outstripped estimated income, this time by $20 million. The financial burden was compounded by the fact that the church in the 1950s had purchased and begun developing over 300,000 acres of rangeland in Florida and Georgia at the cost (by 1963) of $24 million, and development and operating costs for the property, including property taxes, exceeded revenues. McKay hoped to resettle landless families from farm country in Utah and refugees from Berlin on some of the land, but that would require additional expensive development. In order to meet the church's growing financial needs, McKay, Moyle, and Brown needed to emphasize tithe paying in stake conferences. They anticipated that members would rise to the challenge and make amends, but it would take time, and until income increased, they deferred construction of an archives building, a new church office building, and a visitor center on Temple Square.[9]

While the prophet's intellect was intact and at times acute in 1962, he did

7. Campbell and Poll, *Hugh B. Brown*, 239; Brown, *Abundant Life*, 131–32; Henry A. Smith, "Hugh B. Brown Named to First Presidency," *Deseret News Church Section*, June 24. 1961, 3.

8. DOMD, Sep. 23, 1961; Brown, *Abundant Life*, 132.

9. McKay, *Confidence amid Change*, 388, 400; Poll, *Divine Miracle*, 134, 136, 140; Prince and Wright, *David O. McKay*, 213; DOMD, Jan 25, Nov 20, 1950, Nov. 21–Dec. 4, 1957, Jun. 28, 1963. In 1963 the church received a $35 million lifeline in the form of a loan, mortgaging the Florida land as collateral, but interest payments were high, and the farm continued to lose money. In the first five months of 1965, for instance, income on the Florida ranch was only $420,000 while expenses totaled $1.3 million. The church advertised the entire property for sale in 1966 and 1967. Late in 1968, the Gulf America Land Corporation offered to buy the Florida property for $80,000,000, and the church agreed. But the company was unable to place the requisite funds in escrow, and in 1970 the contract was canceled. By that date McKay had passed away, and the church, in a much better financial situation, decided to retain the property, eventually expanding its landholdings there. DOMD, Oct. 6, 1965, Feb. 3, Apr. 12, Jul. 6, 1966, Jul. 27, 1967, Apr. 8, Dec. 30, 1968; Ellsworth, *History of Deseret Ranches*.

"not have quite the quick perception he once had," Ernest Wilkinson judged. Ray's health also continued to be poor. In the spring she suffered several additional ministrokes. Then she fell at the cabin in Huntsville and broke several vertebrae. The accident confined her to bed for several weeks. After she got back on her feet she suffered continued ministrokes, fainting spells, and stomach pains. One bad night the prophet awakened to groaning, trembling, and crying, as was typical of Ray's "spells." She was unusually disoriented and desperate. David got her into the kitchen and gave her some aspirin, and in about an hour she calmed down. Two days after Christmas, while performing a wedding in the Logan Temple, McKay became dizzy, and his body began shaking uncontrollably. He managed to complete the ceremony, but the symptoms naturally worried him. At age eighty-nine, he simply could not accomplish what he had once done, and he sensed that his grasp on administrative matters was slipping as his counselors of necessity took up the slack. After McKay returned from a ten-day absence in California, Middlemiss reported that he "was concerned over [the] number of decisions" that had been made by his counselors or employees in the Church Administration Building "without [his] knowledge."[10]

In May 1963 on a day trip to Huntsville with Llewelyn, McKay decided to ride his horse Sonny Boy—a fateful decision. McKay was holding the rope as Llewelyn lifted the saddle into place when the saddle blanket slipped to the ground, spooking Sonny Boy. Llewelyn managed to step clear, but McKay was dragged by the horse for nearly a block. When the horse finally stopped, McKay regained his footing. Although he did not immediately realize it, the mishap had badly strained his body. Over the following week, his stamina dwindled noticeably. A few days after the accident, he returned home from work so exhausted that he ran a hot bath to soothe his aching limbs, promptly fell asleep, and awoke in the middle of the night in a tub of cold water. On June 13, he arrived at work "so nervous that [he] could not sign [his] name," he told Middlemiss. Two weeks later, when he arrived home from the office, "he could hardly talk." When he left work on July 3 after a morning of meetings, he was quaking so violently that he could barely walk. By September he was experiencing increased weakness in his legs and difficulty in speaking, warning signs of neurological or circulatory problems. Upon the advice of his doctors, he canceled a planned trip to Liberty, Missouri, to dedicate a church historic site. Shortly after, yet another counselor, Moyle, passed away unexpectedly while on a church assignment in Florida.[11]

Following President Moyle's death, McKay brought Brown's nephew, N. Eldon Tanner, a financial wizard, into his inner circle as Moyle's replacement in

10. Wilkinson, diary, June 12, 1962, UA 1000 series 1, sub-series 9, Wilkinson Papers; DOMD, Apr. 8, 11, May 16, June 15, Oct. 30, Dec. 27, 1962, Feb. 26, 1963.

11. DOMD, May 7, 15, June 27, July 3, Sep. 12–14, 1963; Poll, *Divine Miracle*, 216–18.

the First Presidency. Brown told his son Charles that McKay was flooded with recommendations regarding whom he should appoint. He retreated to the temple to "find out whom the Lord wants." When McKay returned, he confidently informed Brown, "The Lord wants N. Eldon Tanner." McKay tasked Tanner with placing the church on a firm financial footing. After receiving the call, Tanner was "in a state of shock all day," but he accepted, telling McKay "that [he had] rededicated [his] life to this service and that all that [he had would] be dedicated to the work." McKay's selection of Brown and Tanner marked a new pattern for him whereby he bypassed seasoned members of the Quorum of the Twelve such as Harold B. Lee and selected men with little or no previous apostolic experience as his counselors, much as Heber J. Grant had done when he tapped J. Reuben Clark. As Tanner noted, "I have been a member of the Twelve for just one year, and during the two years that I was an Assistant to the Twelve, I spent only one month with the president and the other members of the General Authorities here in Salt Lake City." Ironically, McKay's confidence in relative rookies, which he demonstrated in bringing both Tanner and Brown into his inner circle, would ultimately frustrate them. But that was still in the future.[12]

Following Tanner's sustaining, McKay's health continued to worsen. A few days after the October general conference, Middlemiss found him even "more hesitant in his speech and more halting in his walking." About midnight on November 9, 1963, McKay awakened feeling gravely ill. In the morning when he tried to dress, he could not button his shirt. "I think I've had a stroke," he told Lou Jean. Dr. Viko confirmed that he had suffered a mild stroke, likely not his first. Viko confided to President Brown that the stroke "really worried" him but told Lou Jean that the strength of her father's grip meant the stroke had been mild. McKay remained under observation in the hospital for nine days. A few days after coming home he complained of a persistent "numbness in [his] arm and leg." Brown fretted that McKay might not recover sufficiently to resume his "active administration" of the church, but by early December he was walking haltingly with a cane, and by Christmas he was climbing stairs. Viko said the progress was encouraging, although it was not as rapid as McKay hoped it would be. At dinner on Christmas he struggled mightily to wrap his fingers around a fork and carry a morsel of food to his mouth. He would never be the same again.[13]

In his diminished condition, McKay met with Brown and Tanner on most days in his hotel suite, and they tried to consult with him on administrative problems, advising him of new developments. They "were among the few who

---

12. Prince and Wright, *David O. McKay*, 25; McKay, *Confidence amid Change*, 515; Durham, *N. Eldon Tanner*, 198–200.

13. DOMD, Oct. 18, Nov. 9, Dec. 20, 1963, Sep. 29, 1968; McKay, *Confidence amid Change*, 503–4, 507; Wilkinson, diary, Nov. 27, 1963, UA 1000 series 1, sub-series 9, Wilkinson Papers.

realized the extent of his problem," Lawrence wrote. On January 9, 1964, two months after his stroke, McKay attended his first council meeting in the temple since the mishap. In the meeting he insisted he had "not suffered a real stroke" but admitted that "something [was] wrong." He was "weak on [his] right side" but reported he could hold a pen and haltingly sign his name. He did not divulge that he was seeing a neurologist, Madison Thomas, who was treating minor tremors associated with Parkinson's disease with belladonna alkaloids. On January 22, he felt strong enough to walk from the hotel to his office next door for the first time since his stroke, enjoying the crisp January air, but the next day he felt too weak to attend the council meeting and admitted that he had overexerted himself. Notwithstanding McKay's weakness and slurred speech, when President Lyndon Johnson phoned to invite him to a private lunch at the White House in late January, he accepted. He flew out on a Thursday accompanied by President Tanner and Lawrence and met Johnson in the White House on Friday. A shrewd politician, Johnson may have viewed the meeting as a means of currying favor with Latter-day Saint voters, but he also seemed to genuinely admire McKay's charisma and spiritual fervor. Over lunch, Johnson asked McKay for his advice on how to strengthen "the spiritual and moral fiber of [the] country." McKay cut through any hypocrisy on the president's part and advised him to "let the people know" that the nation's spiritual and moral strength was a priority and to "lead out in it, and let the people follow." McKay's inability to enunciate clearly in his conference with Johnson and in other settings embarrassed him. In February he told Middlemiss he felt "angry" at his slow progress and the dragging of his feet. A little over a week before the April general conference, he requested a priesthood blessing for health. Acting as voice, President Brown blessed him with "strength, vitality and lift to strengthen your leg, your arm, [and] your voice."[14]

As he prepared for the conference, McKay asked Darcey Wright, the superintendent in the Church Administration Building who often served as his driver, to take him to the temple. He needed divine aid. Wright assisted the prophet in mounting the steep stairs leading from the Celestial Room to the Holy of Holies and then waited outside while McKay meditated and prayed for strength. On the following day McKay seemed much stronger. He conducted the first session of conference, standing at the pulpit for over thirty minutes. His voice was "fairly strong with just a trace of a tremor," Middlemiss exulted. The strain of the conference took a toll on his aged body, though, and his blood pressure rose alarmingly later that month. In mid-May he complained of a "weakness that [had] come over [him] which [he did] not understand" and

14. McKay, *My Father*, 262; McKay, *Confidence amid Change*, 511, 516–17, 524–26; DOMD, Jan. 9, 22, 23, Feb. 20, 1964; Prince and Wright, *David O. McKay*, 386; Madison Thomas, excerpts from interview by Greg Prince, May 22, 1996, box 22, folder 17, Prince Papers.

of "a defiant leg and a partially defiant right arm." New ailments compounded his discomfort—a pain in his ear caused by a hearing aid, a sore mouth from poorly fitting dentures, a recurrent sore throat, and stiff muscles. "His fluency of speech was gone," Lawrence recalled, along with "the wit and sparkle of his conversation." He was forced to repeat his words several times to make his meaning clear. "He would kind of hold onto you and just look into your eyes and just will you to understand what he was trying to say," his granddaughter Midene recalled. "'But you would have to ask questions, 'Did you mean this? Did you mean this?'"[15]

On August 6, 1964, McKay landed in the hospital, delirious from a viral infection and a 103-degree fever. In his weakened condition he suffered "a serious stroke that left him weak [and] barely able to stand," Lawrence recalled. In a private conversation with an associate, Brown frankly described the extent of McKay's incapacity. Fiercely loyal to her boss and already suspicious of Brown because of his liberal racial views and political leanings, Middlemiss misinterpreted his candid "unfavorable remarks" as evidence of disloyalty to her boss.[16]

McKay returned home from the hospital on August 12 but was readmitted a week later. When Middlemiss visited McKay on his tenth day in the hospital, a Saturday, McKay was agitated about competing "personalities" among his associates and fretted that "things are not just right." His recent stroke likely compounded his agitation. If Middlemiss intimated to the prophet that she distrusted Brown, that could have bolstered his unease. To promote healing and unity, he requested a special fast and blessing to be held in just two days, on Monday. When Middlemiss suggested it would be more convenient for the apostles, many of whom were out of town on conference assignments, to meet later in the week, McKay insisted that the meeting must take place on Monday and involve all general authorities and that they should prepare for the occasion by fasting. Because his hospital room was too small to accommodate them all, most would hold a prayer meeting led by Harold B. Lee in the Church Administration Building. Meanwhile, at the same time in the hospital, Brown and Tanner, with Joseph Fielding Smith representing the Twelve, would anoint McKay with consecrated oil and pronounce a healing blessing. The prophet had spoken, and his staff and colleagues responded with impressive alacrity. With Lee's assistance, Middlemiss and the church's telephone operator, Clarissa Sims, worked over the next twenty-four hours contacting the general authorities, several of whom were out of state and two of whom were abroad on conference assignments. Travel plans were adjusted, and Middlemiss was impressed by each

15. DOMD, Apr. 3, 4, May 12, June 25, Aug. 3, 1964; McKay, *Confidence amid Change*, 528, 530, 534; McKay, *My Father*, 262; Prince and Wright, *David O. McKay*, 386; Midene Anderson, excerpts from interview by Greg Prince, Oct. 1, 1996, box 22, folder 17, Prince Papers.

16. McKay, *Confidence amid Change*, 537; McKay, *My Father*, 262; DOMD, Aug. 26, 1964.

person's "spirituality, love and desire to fast and pray" for McKay. On Monday afternoon following the meeting and blessing, McKay told Middlemiss that his "prayers had been answered," not in a "spectacular" way but in that the blessing pronounced upon him had been "so inspired." A few days later, he told his counselors that he had "never felt closer to the Lord" than during the blessing. Even if he was not immediately healed, he had been spiritually succored as his associates united on his behalf. It was an endearing testament to the general authorities' reverence for him as God's representative. "We sincerely hope that he will be restored sufficiently to take care of the conference which is only a little over a month away," wrote Spencer W. Kimball in his journal.[17]

McKay was able to return home just four days after the blessing and resumed short meetings with his counselors, but Viko warned that he was too fragile to attend general conference. He and Ray watched instead by television from their hotel suite. By mid-October, though, McKay was going stir-crazy, having not left the apartment since returning from the hospital early in September. Although he was still weak and unsteady on his feet, he claimed he had no aches or pains and insisted on being driven to Huntsville for a brief excursion. On October 22, McKay attended his first council meeting in nearly four months. The following week he told his associates he "had come a long way" since they administered to him in the hospital but acknowledged that his continued stuttering worried him.[18]

Early in November, with the assurances of the healing blessing he had received in August in mind, McKay announced to everyone's amazement that he would attend the Oakland Temple dedication, where he planned to speak and read the entire dedicatory prayer. His doctors were dubious about the proposition, and his children feared his speech was too garbled to be intelligible. Miraculously, he defied their expectations. After traveling to Oakland, he stood unassisted at the pulpit for an hour to deliver his speech and the dedicatory prayer in the first session. "I welcome, as unseen, but I believe a real audience, among whom are former Presidents and Apostles of the Church, headed by the Prophet Joseph," McKay proclaimed. Lawrence was awestruck that his father's articulation was "as clear as it was ten years ago." He observed, "We've just seen a miracle.'" McKay's health held as he spoke at each of the six sessions and read the prayer at four of the sessions over a three-day period. "I am grateful to the Lord that my health has held up," he exulted. His strength continued for the rest of the month. On December 1, he reflected aloud to Middlemiss that he was "still thinking about the dedicatory services." Describing how he stood in the temple shortly before the dedication, he told her, "I wondered if I would be

17. McKay, *Confidence amid Change*, 540–41.

18. DOMD, Sep. 29, Oct. 17, 29, 1964; McKay, *Confidence amid Change*, 546–48; Spencer W. Kimball, journal, Aug. 31, 1964.

able to go through with standing there for over an hour to give the address and prayer, and then there came to my soul the assurance that I could go through with it; I had no doubt, and I was able to give an address at each session and to read the dedicatory prayer so that everyone could hear them!"[19]

Notwithstanding the thrilling experiences of November, McKay's stamina ebbed as Christmas approached. Early in December he fell, cracking his rib, and his energy plummeted. "I can only take about one-half a day of work when weakness comes upon me," he admitted on December 10. As he again declined, tensions beset his inner circle of advisors, who disagreed regarding managerial and personnel matters.[20]

Late in 1964, Tanner called for a 50 percent cut in the building committee's projected budget for 1965 and tighter accounting of the committee's expenditures. In his first few months in the presidency, Tanner had uncovered many abuses. Local church leaders had successfully lobbied for unnecessary features or extravagant building materials in new chapels. Buildings constructed under Mendenhall's watch were larger than necessary, and features such as air conditioning were included in places where the climate did not justify the investment. Some church leaders and employees had doubted Mendenhall's judgment and distrusted him ever since he was appointed as director of the building committee in 1955. Some resented his unfettered access to McKay, which seemed to give him carte blanche in spending money, and his brash, domineering temperament. Paul Dunn, who investigated Mendenhall's activities in the summer of 1965, explained, "He had sole power to determine who got a building, where it was going and what kind it would be. That was a source of real irritation." Some blamed primarily Mendenhall for the church's spendthrift course, but Tanner had developed a good working relationship with him and felt confident that together they would implement the necessary changes. On December 10, 1964, McKay approved the draconian cuts Tanner recommended, "if necessary," but the church president was no longer relying primarily upon his counselor for advice regarding the building committee. His reasons for turning elsewhere are unclear. They had nothing to do with Tanner's impeccable financial management. Perhaps McKay had already come to believe what he stated three years later: that Mendenhall was one of a number of church employees who were "doing work for the Church for their own personal gain; having only a selfish interest and not working for the cause of Zion" and that he could not count upon Tanner to oust Mendenhall.[21]

19. McKay, *Confidence amid Change*, 556–60; DOMD, Nov. 6, 12, 17, 1964; McKay, *My Father*, 263–64.

20. DOMD, Dec. 7, 1964; Prince and Wright, *David O. McKay*, 220.

21. McKay, *Confidence amid Change*, 547, 558–60, 564; Wilkinson, diary, Aug. 12, 1959, UA 1000 series 1, sub-series 9, Wilkinson Papers; DOMD, Nov. 30, 1967; Howard B. Anderson, excerpts from interview by Stephen L. Prince, Feb. 7, 1997, box 22, folder 6, Prince Papers; Paul H Dunn, excerpts from interview by Greg Prince, Mar. 27, 1997, box 22, folder 6, Prince Papers.

But it may have also been related to McKay's fear that in his diminished physical and cognitive state he was losing control of administrative matters. Family members saw increasing signs of what they called possible geriatric paranoia. Although Brown and Tanner, and Moyle before them, sought to honor McKay's stated wishes, they made necessary decisions in regularly scheduled meetings McKay was physically unable to attend. He was painfully aware of being the odd man out when, in the summer of 1964, he showed up for an expenditures committee meeting, the first he had been able to attend for some time due to illness, only to learn that it had been canceled. McKay fretted that Tanner sometimes "had confidential conversations with men … independent of" him.[22]

Early in 1964, only a couple of months after Tanner's call as counselor, McKay began consulting frequently with Thorpe Isaacson, whom he had designated as an assistant to the Quorum of the Twelve in 1961. Historian Dennis Lythgoe characterized Isaacson in the political realm as "politically aware" and "self-serving," based upon his review of Isaacson's "grandiose" and "effusive" correspondence with Utah Governor J. Bracken Lee. Despite Isaacson's firm religious commitment, some of the same tendencies he exhibited in civic matters may have colored his church service. In March of 1964, McKay moved Isaacson into J. Reuben Clark's former office, just down the hall from his own, a sign of McKay's exceptional esteem for the man. McKay had reason to appreciate Isaacson based upon their previous associations. As a member of the board of regents of the state agricultural college and the University of Utah in the 1940s and 1950s, after McKay was summarily dropped from the board for political reasons, Isaacson shared insider information with him. He also enabled McKay to continue influencing the board as he conveyed McKay's views to key administrators and board members. Moreover, in his fifteen years of service as a counselor in the Presiding Bishopric, Isaacson had earned McKay's respect as he did much to manage the church's temporal affairs, particularly after the presiding bishop, Joseph L. Wirthlin, suffered a stroke in 1954. Thereafter, Isaacson's son Richard recalled, his father and McKay became "very close." In 1961, shortly after Isaacson was named as an assistant to the Quorum of the Twelve, President Moyle reportedly commented that Isaacson "seemed to have the President in the palm of his hand."[23]

Tensions involving Isaacson and Tanner, both of whom were intensely loyal

22. DOMD, July 28, 1964, Jan. 4, 1965; Howard B. Anderson, excerpts from interview by Greg Prince, Oct. 4, 1999, box 22, folder 24, Prince Papers.

23. Lythgoe, *Let 'Em Holler*, 23, 91–93; Bergera, "Tensions," 197; DOMD, Aug. 10, Oct. 16, 1944, Feb. 7, 1947, May 22, 1950, Apr. 16, Dec. 2, 1952; Wilkinson, diary, May 11, 1961, UA 1000 series 1, sub-series 9, Wilkinson Papers; Richard Isaacson, excerpts from interview by Greg Prince and William Robert Wright, Mar. 20, 1995, box 22, folder 22, Prince Papers. McKay had been dropped from the board of regents by Governor Maw, who was upset that church leaders had not supported him in his gubernatorial bid in 1940.

to McKay and the church but whose temperaments and perspectives clashed, coalesced in the fall of 1964, within weeks of the Oakland Temple dedication, as the two men began working at cross purposes. A relatively small matter, the construction of a chapel in Saratoga, California, ignited the fuse, although the problems in California were symptoms of systemic mismanagement. Alan Blodgett, who worked at the time as an auditor in the financial department, later described some of the managerial problems. "Rather than using standard plans, local architects were often used, buildings were very expensive, and often not as efficient for church needs as a standard plan building would have been." In October McKay received a letter from Louis Latimer, president of the San Jose West Stake, regarding construction of an imposing, expensive stake center and detailing serious interpersonal conflicts and problematic purchases of construction materials. Local church leaders and building missionaries had clashed with full-time employees of the Church Building Department. Some were so upset that they threatened to take legal action. The misunderstandings typified broader problems in the church's building program. As historian Richard Poll has written, "Some Building Committee personnel were perceived as arrogant and inflexible. A few project supervisors fell short in diplomacy and/or deportment.... Many of the chapels seemed too big for immediate needs." Alan Blodgett elaborated, "The Church Building Committee [CBC] would select a project supervisor who would report to a CBC manager. Conflicts arose when a stake president or bishop felt the supervisor was inadequate or unresponsive, dishonest, or caused problems with local members with respect to donated labor. Some locals felt the CBC was too heavy handed." Either through his service on the church's personnel committee or his acquaintances in California, Isaacson became aware of the problems and looked into them. After McKay read the letter from Latimer, he called Isaacson, who had already spoken with church leaders in San Jose. Isaacson furnished "a very clear and definite report of the unpleasant conditions pertaining to the project in San Jose."[24]

Tanner had been aware of the problems for two months before McKay learned of them, and he had already taken matters in hand, apparently without informing McKay of his actions. At Tanner's request, Mendenhall had gone to San Jose to investigate, and Tanner had invited an aggrieved bishop to travel to Salt Lake to visit with him, so he was taken aback when he learned from Mendenhall in October that McKay had recently deputized Isaacson to "make a thorough investigation." Having been badgered by Isaacson in an interview, Mendenhall reported to Tanner that "he was in a state of mind that he felt that he could not carry on any longer; that there was so much criticism and fault-finding." Tanner sympathized with him. Later that evening, Isaacson

24. Poll, *Divine Miracle*, 198; McKay, *Confidence amid Change*, 548–60; DOMD, Jan. 17, 1963; Alan Blodgett to Gregory A. Prince, Oct. 19, 1999, Nov. 5, 1999, box 22, folder 6, Prince Papers.

phoned Mendenhall and reprimanded him for involving Tanner. President Tanner forthrightly visited McKay the next day and told him that "he did not understand how Brother Isaacson got the information that Brother Mendenhall had met with him in his office." He added that he was not sure that Isaacson was the best person to investigate, given his animus toward Mendenhall, but if McKay wanted him to do so, Tanner recommended that at least Isaacson and Mendenhall should meet with the First Presidency before Isaacson left for California. Perhaps McKay misunderstood Tanner's recommendation, but if not, he ignored it. Instead, he immediately picked up the phone and confirmed to Isaacson that he should travel to San Jose as soon as possible.[25]

McKay relied increasingly upon Isaacson in financial as well as personnel matters following a crucial conversation with Isaacson that occurred following his return from a business trip to New York. Decades after the conversation, Isaacson's son Richard recalled that the conversation took place in late November or early December 1964. According to Richard, on that trip his father visited at a reception with Walter Wriston, a high-ranking official in Citibank, the bank that had opened a $20 million line of credit to the financially strapped LDS Church in 1962. Wriston observed that the church had been "borrowing heavily" and appeared to be headed toward bankruptcy. David M. Kennedy, a Latter-day Saint and the president of Continental Illinois National Bank and Trust Company based in Chicago, one of the top ten banks in the nation, heard similar reports "from sources in New York and others" that the church was "in serious financial difficulties." Isaacson was shocked; he left immediately, boarded a redeye flight, and returned to Salt Lake early the next morning, where his son met him and drove him immediately to McKay's home. There Isaacson and McKay discussed the church's financial plight for several hours. They may have also discussed Isaacson's findings from his investigations in San Jose.[26]

Later in December, without first consulting with his counselors, McKay appointed Delbert Stapley, LeGrand Richards, and Howard Hunter of the Quorum of Twelve Apostles to work with Isaacson on a committee to "substantially curtail the expenditures in the Church Building Department in light of conditions that have arisen in all parts of the world in regard to extravagance, waste, etc." They were to work toward "the reorganization of the Church Building Committee." From Tanner's perspective, all of the appointees were

25. McKay, *Confidence amid Change*, 548–50.

26. Richard Isaacson, notes from interview by Greg Prince, Mar. 20, 1995, box 22, folder 24, Prince Papers. Richard's memory that Wriston's comments shocked his father because they were "entirely foreign to what he assumed the financial status of the Church to be," might fit late 1963 or early 1964 better than late 1964. Due to his investigations of matters pertaining to the Church Building Department in October, Isaacson may have been aware of the church's indebtedness prior to late November or early December 1964. David M. Kennedy, interview by Gordon Irving, Dec. 13, 1982, OH 968.

"prejudiced against the building committee" and appeared to have been handpicked by Isaacson. A few days later, Isaacson returned to McKay's office and pressed the president to fire Mendenhall. Isaacson criticized Tanner's handling of matters related to the building committee and charged that he could not be relied upon to rein in Mendenhall because, as he later commented, the two were as closely linked as intertwined fingers. When McKay replied that firing Mendenhall would "be a rather difficult thing to bring about," Isaacson emphasized that his committee could not proceed unless they knew Mendenhall would be replaced. To facilitate the change, he said the committee would provide McKay with "three or four names to consider" for Mendenhall's replacement.[27]

After Tanner returned from Christmas break and learned of the new committee and Isaacson's efforts to fire Mendenhall, he was dismayed. He wanted to serve McKay and the church to the best of his ability, and he felt stymied: "I cannot serve you nearly as well with the conditions as they are as I could if I knew what was going on," he told McKay. Tanner bore down hard, convinced it was his role to reprove sharply and counsel boldly. "I came in here twice last year and recommended to you that we set up a committee to work with the Building Committee. Nothing was done about it. Isaacson comes in and recommends we set up a committee and you set it up immediately," he complained. McKay seemed baffled by Tanner's claim. "I do not know of a thing that affects the Church without bringing it to you two men [Tanner and Brown]," he maintained. At another point he stated he was "not listening to" Isaacson." Plagued by lapses in memory in his old age, perhaps that morning McKay did not recall the extent to which he had acted unilaterally. Unless he consulted a written record, he often forgot conversations and decisions and had "great difficulty in talking and conveying his thoughts," according to Ernest Wilkinson. Tanner pressed his case, enumerating decisions McKay had made with Isaacson. Isaacson came to see McKay "alone all the time," he claimed. Tanner accurately warned that Isaacson's committee was "only set up to get rid of Mendenhall and reorganize the Building Committee." He protested that McKay had kept his two counselors in the dark, and he felt that was improper. He had more experience "in economics, in business administration, of things pertaining to this" than Isaacson. He reiterated his loyalty to McKay, assuring him, "There isn't a man more loyal to you than I am, I do not care who he is." It appeared to him that McKay was "being hurt" and "abused" by Isaacson's counsel. He warned accurately, "Nobody ... has the confidence of the General Authorities less than the man you are listening to." After Brown stated that he had "sweat under" similar concerns for "two or three years," McKay summarized their position aptly, having broken from his shocked stupor. "What you are saying is that I have a third counselor in Brother Isaacson." He told the two men that the intensity

27. DOMD, Dec. 15, 21, 1964, Jan. 5, 1965.

of their resentment came as "quite a shock" and assured them any offenses had been "unintentional." Remarkably, in the face of such strident criticism that wounded his ego, McKay maintained his composure and acknowledged his flaws. "You give me ... quite an insight into my own weaknesses.... I thought I was giving you everything." The meeting broke up without a resolution. "You had better go to your meeting now," McKay remarked as he dismissed the two counselors. When she read the minutes, Middlemiss, who could brook no criticism of the prophet, was flabbergasted. A comment she attributed to McKay and recorded in a notebook two months after the incident was written in her own voice, referring to the prophet in the third person: "When I think I had to sit and listen to a counselor rebuke a President of the Church ... I cannot get over it." Two years later, the memory of Tanner's frankness still stung. Middlemiss quoted McKay's comment to her: "No man either out or in the Church has ever talked to a President of this Church as I had been talked to." Having unburdened himself so candidly, Tanner came away from the meeting suspecting "he might possibly be released" because of his candor. He confided to his secretary, LaRue Sneff, "I don't think I'm going to have a job here very long."[28]

McKay valued Tanner too much to release him but not enough to disregard Isaacson. Indeed, Isaacson reflected McKay's own increasing distrust of Mendenhall's management. As Tanner predicted, Isaacson's committee recommended that McKay fire Mendenhall. "There has been great concern all over the Church regarding the extravagance, waste, high salaries, maintenance, costs of supervisors, travel, hotel, telephone, excessive building costs and other expenses, also domineering, in connection with the Church Building Committee.... Faithful members of the Church are deeply concerned, upset, and disillusioned; and ward, stake and mission leaders are questioning our laxity handling so serious a problem," Isaacson's committee charged. To avoid future interpersonal tempests and extravagances like the one in San Jose, they recommended that ward and stake leaders should play a greater role in supervising building construction and acquiring construction materials so that "buildings will be of better quality construction and costs much cheaper." Three months after receiving their recommendation, McKay removed Mendenhall from his post.[29]

Shortly after his shocking interchange with Tanner, McKay retreated to Laguna Beach to recuperate from health challenges and the stresses of the office. At sea level, away from the pressures of the office, he could walk short distances without using either a cane or walker and could breathe easily. When he returned to Salt Lake, however, he again struggled to breathe and landed in the

28. Wilkinson, diary, July 7, Aug. 4, 1965, UA 1000 series 1, sub-series 9, Wilkinson Papers; DOMD, Jan. 5, 1965; McKay, *Confidence amid Change*, 672–73; Durham, *N. Eldon Tanner*, 215; LaRue Sneff, excerpts from interview by Greg Prince, Aug. 3, 2000, box 22, folder 23, Prince Papers.

29. McKay, *Confidence amid Change*, 580–81.

hospital for eleven days, where he required supplemental oxygen. Sufficiently recovered, he returned home from the hospital in good humor, announcing playfully to Ray as he entered the apartment, "Mrs. McKay, David O. McKay is calling on you!" He remained fragile, though. Lawrence and Ed warned Middlemiss not to raise "any matters with the President that would worry him" and "have an effect upon his heart." That strategy further insulated McKay from church operations. He wanted to be kept informed, but discussing thorny problems elevated his blood pressure and weakened him.[30]

A month after his release from the hospital early in 1965, seeing little progress physically, he told Middlemiss he was "very tired and discouraged." He confided to Brown and Tanner that he wished God would "take" him if he was "not going to get well." McKay dragged himself to all but two of the April conference sessions. His opening address, read by his son Bob, closely replicated much of an October 1946 address but with references, gathered and added by Middlemiss with his approval, to a recent Gallup poll and quotations from a speech by J. Edgar Hoover. Few knew the extent of his weakness, and McKay did his best to satisfy the Saints' expectations. "I'm not as weak as it seems," he told the congregation on the third day of the conference. "I wish I had freer use of this old tongue that wants to wrap itself around my teeth." In the priesthood session, when the congregation spontaneously rose at a signal from the chorister and sang "We Thank Thee, O God, for a Prophet," he wept at the outpouring of love and respect.[31]

A few weeks after conference, Isaacson again engaged in the type of behind-the-scenes maneuvering that so vexed Brown and Tanner. In a First Presidency meeting in mid-May, Tanner and Brown recommended Howard Dunn, the building committee's project development director, as Mendenhall's interim replacement. McKay concurred and announced he would present the recommendation the following day to the Quorum of the Twelve in council meeting. However, McKay awoke the next morning feeling too ill to attend the meeting. Learning that McKay would not attend, Isaacson visited him in his apartment to discuss "some important matters" while the council was in session in the temple. After conversing with Isaacson, McKay asked Middlemiss to "find Brother Mark B. Garff and have him come right up to my apartment." Garff, unlike Dunn, was one of the four men whom Isaacson and Stapley had recommended to replace Mendenhall. He was the founder and senior partner in a major construction company in Salt Lake City that had built several buildings for the

30. DOMD, Jan. 22, Feb. 4, 25, 1965; Doctrine and Covenants 121:43. See also McKay, *Confidence amid Change*, 573.

31. DOMD, Mar. 24, 1965; McKay, *Confidence amid Change*, 577, 579; David O. McKay, addresses of Apr. 4, 5, 1965, *Conference Reports*, 5–9, 137–38; David O. McKay, address of Oct. 6, 1946, *Conference Reports*, 111–17; David O. McKay, address of Apr. 6, 1953, *Conference Reports*, 135–38.

church and BYU. McKay visited with Garff, who was on his way out of town, about his possibly assuming "the chairmanship of the Building Committee" and made a follow-up appointment for Sunday. Meanwhile, in McKay's absence Tanner and Brown were presenting Dunn's name to the council for ratification, as had been agreed upon the previous day in their meeting with the prophet. The quorum unanimously approved Dunn's appointment. Somehow, Isaacson learned the news that afternoon and relayed it to McKay. Contradicting the minutes of the First Presidency meeting for the previous day, the prophet now reportedly stated that Dunn's name "never should have been presented to the Twelve." The following day in their First Presidency meeting, Brown informed the prophet that the council had unanimously approved Dunn's appointment as McKay had directed. Although he was not a counselor, Isaacson was present as a guest at McKay's request and argued against Dunn's appointment because of his "close association" with Mendenhall. Tanner and Brown "both indicated that they were greatly pleased" with Dunn's work and expressed concerns about Garff's impetuosity. McKay cut short the discussion, stating that they would resume it after the weekend. Meanwhile, he met with Garff for a second time on Sunday. On the following Wednesday McKay privately confirmed Garff's appointment as chair of the building committee. The next day, while Tanner was out of town, McKay asked Brown to ratify the appointment. Brown reminded McKay of Tanner's objections but said he accepted the president's decision and assured him that Tanner would likewise loyally "support" the appointment. Soon after he took over the reins of the building committee, Garff dismissed nine holdovers from the Mendenhall era on the building committee, including Dunn. By June, with rumors rife that Mendenhall had been excommunicated for misappropriating funds, Tanner recommended that the First Presidency squelch the rumor. McKay, by this point deeply resentful of Mendenhall's expenditures, ignored the recommendation. He also refused three months' severance pay, which the counselors had approved, for Mendenhall's associates.[32]

Although the firings of Mendenhall and his associates seemed callous to Brown and Tanner, Garff proved to be an able administrator, fulfilling McKay's and Isaacson's expectations. Under Garff's lead, more cuts were made to the building program. Due to those cuts and increased tithing revenues, church receipts exceeded expenditures by $21 million in 1965. By the beginning of 1967, Garff reported to McKay, he had reduced the number of employees in the building department by 75 percent, had drastically scaled back the budget, and had reduced the cost of new church buildings by an average of $50,000. He was particularly proud that he had slashed international spending, pointing out that "too much of our money appropriated for buildings had been spent in the geographical regions outside the United States, and membership in these areas

32. DOMD, May 12, 13, 20, 1965; McKay, *Confidence amid Change*, 592–96, 599, 602.

only account for 10.7 percent of the total church membership." For his part, shortly after his dismissal Dunn was appointed project engineer for construction of a new civic auditorium in Salt Lake, the Salt Palace, on land the church had furnished. In 1970 shortly after McKay's death, Dunn was appointed president of Zions Securities Corporation, the church's investment and property management arm, where he worked closely with Tanner.[33]

In the summer of 1965, following Garff's appointment, McKay was "under the weather" for much of the time. He was "always embarrassed because of his immobility and speech," Spencer W. Kimball recorded. He spent much of August in Huntsville. The weather was cooler there, and the mountain air was invigorating. Most importantly for his ecclesiastical role, when he returned home from Huntsville he felt spiritually renewed. In September he informed the council that "the Lord [had] been very close in [his] work at home"; in fact, he had "never felt nearer to Him than [he did] during [his] recent illness." McKay returned to Salt Lake a few weeks before general conference stronger and able to work again from his office in the Church Administration Building. His health was much better during the October conference than it had been six months earlier. After praying privately prior to the opening session for strength and guidance, he stood for forty minutes at the podium delivering his opening address, and he also preached at two subsequent sessions. Later that month he and Ray attended a performance of *Brigadoon*. As McKay stepped from his car into a crowd of onlookers he quipped, "I might be staggering but it is not from strong drink."[34]

After the October 1965 conference, McKay appointed Isaacson as an additional counselor in the First Presidency. In so doing, he addressed Tanner's criticisms about Isaacson's ad hoc advisory role, although not in the way Tanner had hoped. When McKay issued the call, Isaacson wept freely and pledged his life and strength. Three days later McKay informed Joseph Fielding Smith of Isaacson's new calling and then asked Smith to serve alongside Isaacson as a fourth counselor in the presidency. Smith would continue acting as president of the Quorum of the Twelve but also serve in the First Presidency. Smith was taken aback by the unconventional dual assignment but loyally pledged to "do

33. "Auditorium Board 'Invites' Engineer," *Salt Lake Tribune*, July 21, 1965, 21; McKay, *Confidence amid Change*, 649, 682; DOMD, Apr. 25, 1967; obituary for James Howard Dunn, *Deseret News*, Oct. 26, 2008. Garff relied upon contractors to construct buildings rather than on the volunteer labor of building missionaries. From Alan Blodgett's perspective, "The change helped to clean out a lot of poor practices followed in the Mendenhall years, but it also led to the transition to an impersonal contracting program. Local members [became] isolated from the construction of their meetinghouses, and as a consequence were denied the degree of the attachment members felt under the older programs." Blodgett to Gregory A. Prince, Nov. 5, 1999, box 21, folder 6, Prince Papers.

34. McKay, *Confidence amid Change*, 608–9, 616; Spencer W. Kimball, journal, Aug. 19, 1965; DOMD, Sep. 3, Oct. 3, 1965; James Wilson, "Y Senior Spends Time With President McKay," *Daily Universe*, Nov. 5, 1965, 11.

anything you ask me to do." When McKay informed his associates of the calls, he said he had called the men to "relieve" Brown and Tanner of the added burden they bore because he was so frail. He needed more help, he believed, than Brown and Tanner could supply. Tanner asked McKay to clarify the nature of the appointments—were they counselors *to* the First Presidency or counselors *in* the First Presidency? McKay indicated that they were being called as full-fledged members of the presidency and not merely as advisors. When the prophet presented Isaacson's name to the general authorities, a few raised their hands only tentatively to sustain the call; at least one abstained. Later that day, at McKay's request, Tanner humbly set aside his concerns about Isaacson and set him apart as a counselor. Brown, who was not present in the meeting, was more resistant. When Tanner phoned his uncle, who was out of the country on an assignment, to inform him of Isaacson's calling, Brown was "completely stunned." Although Brown felt duty bound to publicly support McKay's decision, it rankled so much that, a few weeks later, he privately shared some reservations with the prophet. McKay, who was feeling poorly and expected cooperation from his counselors, responded, "We should have harmony," and dismissed Brown, stating that he lacked the energy to discuss the matter further.[35]

The optimism that Isaacson's call engendered in McKay was short-lived. The new counselor served in the presidency for only three and a half months before a severe stroke incapacitated him. News of the stroke was "one of the biggest disappointments of [his] life," McKay informed Middlemiss. With Isaacson at his side he had "felt relaxed and secure," confident that Isaacson would keep him informed. It was a view Middlemiss shared. Now that Isaacson was incapacitated, "we are in a bad way," he commented, not only because Isaacson was incapacitated but also because Brown was temporarily ill. The next day McKay reported he had been unable to sleep because both Isaacson and Brown were "ill and unable to do anything."[36]

McKay managed to attend a few council meetings that winter. His comments showed that he remained spiritually attuned and capable of exercising his prophetic gifts on many occasions. In one meeting a few weeks after Isaacson's stroke, he reminisced about his associates on the council over the previous six decades. All who had attended his first council meeting as a new apostle were now in the "Celestial world." But, he said confidently, "they are close to us whenever we meet here." He expressed "gratitude for the privilege of being together in the spirit of love and unity"—virtues he valued more keenly than ever after the misunderstandings of the previous year—"and to join [in spirit]

35. McKay, *Confidence amid Change*, 616–622, 629; Paul H. Dunn, excerpts from interview by Greg Prince, box 21, folder 6, Prince Papers; Bergera, "Tensions," 206–7.

36. McKay, *Confidence amid Change*, 638, 672–73; DOMD, Feb. 14, 15, 1966. Brown had been absent from his office with a severe lung infection for four weeks.

with those who have long since passed into the Spirit world." Feeling their influence so keenly, he announced, "I send my greetings to them." In March he was thrilled to be well enough to be driven to Huntsville, where he and Ray were cared for by a nurse for two and a half weeks. Following his return, he spoke to a pre-conference gathering of general authorities, telling them that he had "never felt nearer to the Lord" than during the previous weeks. He wanted to be taken home to God and did "not know why He is keeping me here," but he assumed that "there must be a reason." The day before his scheduled conference talk, he informed Middlemiss, "I am going to give my talk no matter what anyone says." Speak he did, delivering a resplendent, powerful oration on the resurrection. "With all my soul I know that death is conquered by Jesus Christ," he concluded, "and because our Redeemer lives, so shall we. I bear you witness that he does live. I know it." His associates in the presidency, Middlemiss, and the Saints rejoiced in his strength.[37]

In May 1966, a few weeks following the conference, McKay conferred with Alvin Dyer, an assistant to the Quorum of the Twelve, regarding historic lands in Missouri that Dyer hoped the church would purchase. With Dyer's encouragement, McKay decided to fly there to inspect the property, fulfilling his longtime desire to visit church history sites in the nation's heartland. Physically frail but enthusiastic, the prophet boarded a plane on June 1, accompanied by Dyer and his counselor Joseph Fielding Smith, who had served for decades as church historian. Dyer had arranged a first-class tour. They were met in Kansas City by Truman Laudie, a high councilor in a local stake and a convert to the church, who chauffeured them in his Cadillac to sites in Independence, Liberty, Far West, and Adam-ondi-Ahman. Dyer, who had carefully studied church history while serving as mission president in Missouri, expertly narrated the tour, sharing relevant passages from the scriptures and quotations from historical documents. At Tower Hill overlooking the Valley of Adam-ondi-Ahman, after inspecting the lands available for purchase, McKay commented that the tract was "most important and a very sacred place." He was particularly touched by Dyer's narrative of the events that transpired at Far West and was impressed by the temple site, a "place designated by the Lord as most holy" with an "important future." McKay's brief trip thrilled him. Dyer had helped him fulfill a long-standing dream at a time when others, hoping to safeguard his health, were discouraging travel. According to Middlemiss, following the trip McKay enthused that Dyer "knew more about the future of the Church as it would center in the days of the final gathering of the Lord's chosen than any other man."[38]

37. DOMD, Mar. 3, Apr. 5, 1966; David O. McKay, address of April 9, 1966, *Conference Reports*, 59.

38. McKay, *Confidence amid Change*, 656–57; DOMD, June 1, 1966, Feb. 14, 1967.

In his weakened condition in the months surrounding his visit to Missouri, McKay's natural proclivity for second-guessing himself and reversing his judgment was aggravated. Repeatedly in 1966 he was lobbied, cajoled, and pressured as individuals extracted contradictory decisions and concessions from him. Each associate likely believed they were acting in the best interests of the church and the nation, but their perspectives clashed. For instance, in February, Ezra Taft Benson requested and received permission to print McKay's photograph on the cover of *American Opinion*, the John Birch Society's magazine. A few weeks later, concerned that the photograph might be interpreted as an endorsement of the society, Elder Mark E. Petersen persuaded McKay to reverse course and "stop" the printing of his photo. The next day, Benson appealed the reversal, and McKay told him to "go ahead" as originally planned with publication. Two weeks later in a Huntsville meeting that Lawrence had arranged, Petersen, Tanner, and Joseph Fielding Smith came to see McKay with Lawrence, whose contempt for the John Birch Society was intense. Their visit ended with Lawrence peremptorily dialing Benson's number and handing the phone to his father, who instructed Benson not to publish the photo. "At the present time I think it would be unwise because the members of the Church would conclude … that I belonged to this [society] and was in favor of their ideals," McKay informed Benson. Then, he qualified his last statement, revealing how torn he felt: "I do [favor their ideals] as far as opposing communism [is concerned]."[39]

Following the April 1966 conference, Lawrence and Middlemiss again lobbied McKay, who seesawed in response to their conflicting perspectives, trying to please both of them. In the general conference priesthood session, following his reading of McKay's talk, Robert McKay read a statement on communism at his father's request. The statement was given "that there may be no misunderstandings by bishops, stake presidents, and others regarding members of the Church participating in non-church meetings to study and become informed on the Constitution of the United States, Communism, etc." The document consisted of messages that Middlemiss under McKay's direction had been sending out in response to inquiries from local church leaders. The statement faithfully reflected McKay's views, although Middlemiss, a strong anti-communist and Birch society supporter, may have committed some of those views to writing, as she often did in preparing responses to letters McKay received. Brown suspected Benson had written the part of the document that commended "every person and every group who is sincerely seeking to study Constitutional principles and awaken a sleeping and apathetic people to the alarming conditions that are rapidly advancing about us." When McKay learned, apparently through Middlemiss, that the *Church News* section of the *Deseret News* did not plan

39. McKay, *Confidence amid Change*, 639, 643–45; DOMD, Mar. 6, 1956.

to print the statement alongside his talk, he instructed editor Henry Smith to print it. Earl Hawkes, the general manager of the newspaper, contacted Tanner and Brown, knowing they were concerned the statement would be viewed as an indirect endorsement of the Birch society. When the statement appeared minus the endorsement of anti-communist groups, Smith informed Middlemiss that McKay had "deleted the paragraphs." When Middlemiss approached her boss, he indicated that "Lawrence ... at the request of the counselors" had urged him to remove the passages but that in retrospect "he did not want those paragraphs taken out." Upset by the deletion, Middlemiss brought in a sheaf of letters from members requesting that the *News* publish the entire statement. Persuaded by his secretary, McKay called Hawkes and instructed him to print the entire statement in the next issue. When McKay phoned Lawrence to inform him of his instructions to the manager, Lawrence insisted, "I must see you about it." That afternoon Lawrence and Middlemiss faced off in the office, with Lawrence arguing that the Birch society might use the statement as a recruiting tool and thereby "do a lot of harm to the Church" and Middlemiss downplaying the threat and insisting that the Birch society had been instructed "not to distribute it." Middlemiss reported that Lawrence became "so upset" as he visited with McKay that he induced his father to reverse himself and call off the reprinting. The debate between Lawrence and Middlemiss illustrated how little confidence either had in the prophet's ability to judge independent of their reasoning.[40]

A few months after the brouhaha over McKay's statement on communism, his health worsened, and his daughters suggested that he and Ray spend several weeks in their care at Laguna Beach. The trip was essential, Lou Jean told Middlemiss, because her father's numerous appointments made it impossible for him to recuperate, and without a break she feared he could not endure the strain "much longer." This time the seaside air did not work its magic. Instead, McKay contracted a viral infection on the coast that sapped his energy. It seemed he had "never [before] been so sick," he complained.[41]

One Saturday morning in August, after he returned from California, McKay called Middlemiss at her home in a disoriented panic. After repeatedly phoning the office and not getting an answer, he had insisted that his nurse call her. When he reached her, McKay demanded, "What is going on? Aren't there a lot of letters for me to sign?" His deep-seated desire to be kept informed and his concern that he was out of touch with administrative matters were evident.

40. David O. McKay, "Statement on the Position of the Church on Communism," address of Apr. 9, 1966, *Conference Reports*, 109; David O. McKay, address of Apr. 6, 1966, *Conference Reports*, 6; McKay, *Confidence amid Change*, 649–54; DOMD, Apr. 11, 1969; Prince and Wright, *David O. McKay*, 314.

41. McKay, *Confidence amid Change*, 664; DOMD, July 14, 30, Aug. 4, 17, 1966.

Although Middlemiss explained that it was Saturday, he persisted, "Can you come right over?" With considerable finesse she persuaded him that all was well. Despite bouts of confusion such as the one that occasioned his August phone conversation with Middlemiss, McKay's mental energy and clarity rebounded, and he delivered a full address at the opening session of October general conference while seated on a stool at the podium. Remarkably, McKay spoke enthusiastically as if he had no ailments. "I love life!" he exclaimed. "Every morning as I view from my window the mountains to the east and greet the sun as it ushers in these unexcelled autumn days, I feel the joy and privilege of life and appreciate God's goodness." Unfortunately, his strength subsided within a few weeks. On October 20 he fell for the second time in a month, and a week later he reported that he had "never felt weaker."[42]

In January 1967, McKay informed Middlemiss that he intended to call a new counselor to replace Isaacson, who had never recovered from his paralysis. Her participation in the calling process was unprecedented and reflected McKay's immense confidence in his secretary, independent of priesthood channels; she had worked with him more closely than any of the apostles. According to Middlemiss, he closed his eyes, leaned back in his chair as he was wont to do when seeking inspiration, and asked her to read the names of the general authorities. After she finished reading the apostles' names, he commented that he was looking for someone else, someone "like President Isaacson." She then began reading the names of the assistants to the Quorum of the Twelve. When she read Dyer's name, he brightened and opened his eyes. Dyer had created opportunities for him, escorting him to Missouri when his children, physician, and associates tried to preserve his strength by keeping him at home. "That's the one. I like him," Middlemiss recorded him as saying. "He is the one I have been thinking of; he is a man of good judgment and dependability." McKay appeared confident that he had received the divine confirmation he sought. Seven months later, McKay met alone with Dyer and Middlemiss and announced, "I am calling you to be one of my assistants." Dyer was shocked. When he turned to Middlemiss and asked, "What did he say?" Middlemiss clarified, "He meant just what he said—he is calling you to be one of his assistants, or counselors."[43]

McKay's search for a new counselor occurred against a backdrop of frustrating frailty. Physical weakness prevented him from addressing the congregation in the April 1967 conference, although he managed to preside in the morning sessions. As had occurred during his illness in 1965, Middlemiss had helped him compile statements and sentiments from previous addresses, and she had gathered illustrative evidence for the topics he wished to address in his conference

42. McKay, *Confidence amid Change*, 665, 668; DOMD, Sep. 27, 30, Oct. 28, 1966; David O. McKay, address of Sep. 30, 1966, *Conference Reports*, 4.

43. McKay, *Confidence amid Change*, 686–88, 702.

talks. After McKay reviewed and edited the script, his son Bob read it. Middlemiss later insisted that "there was never a word written [for McKay's general conference talks] that was not President McKay's own thought." But the line was growing thin because McKay's care in reviewing the material hinged upon his oscillating mental acuity. As he grew weaker in the months following the conference, McKay periodically appeared confused in his consultations with his counselors. In August, the day after he told Dyer he was calling him as his assistant, McKay met with Ernest Wilkinson, Tanner, Brown, and David B. Haight. Wilkinson reported that the prophet was uncharacteristically "without a smile" and did not greet any of the attendees. During the meeting he appeared badly disoriented to Wilkinson.[44]

A few days prior to the October 1967 conference, McKay met, as was customary, with all the general authorities in preparation for the conference. At one point he fumbled in his suit pocket for a piece of paper. Brown and Tanner assumed he was looking for his list of the order in which he wished the general authorities to deliver their addresses. Spencer W. Kimball reported that they "all were eagerly waiting to know when they would speak in the coming Conference." While McKay rummaged for the paper, Brown pressed, "Here, President, are the sheets with the names. Would you like me to read the names?" McKay jocularly quipped, "Don't you think I can read?" Then Brown inquired, "What is on the paper you are trying to locate?" From Dyer's vantage point, it appeared the counselors' well-meaning attempts to assist the president betrayed their lack of confidence in him. According to Dyer's record, at last

> President McKay had the note he was looking for. The President then said he desired to present the name of a man worthy to be ordained to the Apostleship, but not to be a member of the Quorum of the Twelve. At this point, President Brown evidently thought President McKay was confused and pressed again for the names. President Tanner joined in the effort to have the names announced. President McKay —"No I want to present another matter." Then glancing at the notes on his paper he said, "I present for your sustaining vote the name of Alvin R. Dyer; that man as worthy to be an Apostle, but not to be a member of the Quorum of the Twelve."

The announcement stunned the counselors and the other apostles. "There was total silence," recorded Spencer W. Kimball. "It was evident that neither the counselors nor the other authorities (unless it might be Bro. Dyer) knew

---

44. Armstrong, *Rhetoric of McKay*, 36; DOMD, Mar. 17, Apr. 6, Sep. 21, Nov. 7, 1967; Wilkinson, diary, Aug. 18, 1967, UA 1000 series 1, sub-series 9, Wilkinson Papers; David O. McKay, addresses of Apr. 6, 8, 1967, *Conference Reports*, 4–6, 84–88. In the spring of 1967, the prophet was strong enough to review supporting statistics and quotations collected by Middlemiss to update his talk and then send her back to the drawing board to revise. In preparation for subsequent conferences, a son who had been selected to deliver the address reviewed the text line by line with his father, and together they adjusted words and phrases. DOMD, Mar. 17, 1967, Apr. 5, 1969.

or suspected what the President intended to do." Paul Dunn sensed a "real negative … feeling" following the announcement. As Kimball wrote, they were "almost numbed—it was so different tha[n] the usual calling of the top leaders has been in our experience and knowledge." According to Dunn, when Dyer's name was presented for a sustaining vote, Harold B. Lee abstained. In a subsequent conversation with Lee, Tanner commented that it appeared Dyer's informal role was being formalized: "He has already been running ends directly to the President alone and without [the first and second counselors]."[45]

The next day in council meeting, Ezra Taft Benson commended McKay for "show[ing]" in the previous day's meeting "that you are the President and Prophet of this Church." McKay reportedly replied, "While I am the President, I should like to follow my impressions in directing this Church." In their meeting three days before conference, McKay told Brown and Tanner that Dyer would be sustained as an apostle, separate from the Quorum of the Twelve, and that he would not be sustained as were the other apostles as a "Prophet, Seer, and Revelator." According to Middlemiss, in a separate, later meeting with her, McKay reversed course, perhaps influenced by her reasoning, and determined that Dyer would be "ordained by me as a Prophet, Seer, and Revelator." Dyer was sustained separately as an apostle on the first day of the conference, and the next day, McKay, joined by Brown and Tanner, ordained him "an apostle of the Church" without any reference to his being a prophet, seer, revelator, or counselor.[46]

Middlemiss's record indicates that McKay privately instructed Dyer to "attend every meeting that I hold with my Counselors, including those held in the Temple." He was also to "stay close to me and keep me advised of all matters that the President of the Church should know about." When the presidency met on October 12, Tanner, Brown, and Dyer pressed McKay to clarify the new apostle's role. Dyer indicated it was his "understanding that to be called as an assistant was tantamount to being called as a counselor," but Brown and Tanner "took strong exception." They believed that as McKay's assistant, Dyer should attend meetings of the First Presidency and the Quorum of the Twelve only when the prophet was present. McKay inadvertently muddied the waters by first stating that Dyer was to attend presidency meetings "as a Counselor" and later stating that "[he would] be an assistant to the President." It seemed to Dyer that McKay did not fully appreciate in the moment the semantic difference that meant so much to

45. McKay, *Confidence amid Change*, 706; report by Alvin R. Dyer of meeting held Sep. 21 in DOMD, Sep. 21, 1967; Kimball, journal, Sep. 21, 30, 1967; Paul H. Dunn, excerpts from interview by Greg Prince, Jan. 15, 1996, box 22, folder 18, Prince Papers. Several months later Middlemiss told McKay she had heard that some had accused her of playing an inordinate role in Dyer's appointment. When she asked McKay if she "[had] to take these accusations," McKay reportedly replied, "Yes, the Lord will take care of it." DOMD, Feb. 20, 1968.

46. McKay, *Confidence amid Change*, 707–8, 711; Henry A. Smith, "An Eventful Conference," *Deseret News Church Section*, Oct. 7, 1967, 3.

his counselors. Dyer came away from the meeting feeling that "a more direct statement, as well as a formal announcement by the President is needed to bring this status into reality." When the First Presidency met a week later with the physically frail prophet in Huntsville, Dyer anticipated that McKay would clarify his status and was frustrated when Brown raised another matter. Although Dyer suspected Brown was trying to forestall discussion of his appointment, the matter Brown raised was the reason the meeting had been called.[47]

McKay's diminished health and judgment occasioned discussion in a November 1967 council meeting in the prophet's absence. Brown observed, "President McKay is in a weakened condition. His bodily strength is waning. He is not as alert as he was." When Middlemiss reviewed the minutes, she took umbrage at the comment. Later she passed the minutes to McKay, as was customary, and he reportedly took issue with the statement. According to Middlemiss, he insisted, "I am alert; and I know what I am doing." When Middlemiss informed Brown that McKay wanted his comment about McKay's weakness stricken from the minutes, Brown suspected she had called the comment to the president's attention. She denied having done so, and he apologized to her the next day for jumping to conclusions. They parted "with good spirits and feelings," Middlemiss recorded.[48]

In the month leading up to the April 1968 conference, McKay's health was poor. On March 6, after checking McKay's blood pressure and heart rate, his physician Dr. Alan Macfarlane advised him not to attend council meeting. A few days later McKay felt so poorly that he did not arise until 11:00 a.m. and canceled all meetings because of heart problems. That same day, Ray fell as she arose from the couch, broke her hip, and was hospitalized for several days. Although he remained under the constant care of a nurse in his apartment, McKay was still able to meet briefly with his counselors and approve important decisions. They decided to call new presidents of the Salt Lake and London Temples, for instance, and selected Loren Dunn and Hartman Rector Jr., as members of the First Council of Seventy.[49]

As final preparations were being made for the April conference, Tanner, Brown, and the Quorum of the Twelve passed a resolution recommending that additional counselors beyond the first and second counselors in the First Presidency be sustained as counselors *to* the First Presidency rather than counselors *in* the Presidency. Joseph Fielding Smith, who was both president of the Quorum of the Twelve and a counselor to McKay, voted for the resolution. The leaders felt this distinction would ensure the church's compliance with the revelation recorded in D&C 107, which specified that "three Presiding High

47. McKay, *Confidence amid Change*, 708, 712–14; DOMD, Oct. 18, 1967.
48. DOMD, Nov. 7, 1967, Jan. 15, 1968; McKay, *Confidence amid Change*, 715–16.
49. DOMD, Mar. 6, 12, 24, 26–28, 1968.

Priests" constituted the First Presidency. Dyer, who opposed the resolution but had not been present for the vote, suspected Smith had voted for it because the nonagenarian apostle "did not understand" or appreciate the distinction the younger men were making. Six days later, in a meeting of the First Presidency, Tanner and Brown presented the unanimous resolution to McKay, who accepted it and ruled that Dyer should be sustained in the upcoming conference as a counselor *to* the presidency. Later that morning, as if he had not fully grasped the fine points of the discussion, McKay reportedly asked Dyer, "What was that all about this morning?" From the question, Dyer surmised McKay "did not fully understand the motions which the Counselors had brought up." Dyer also met with Smith to be sure he appreciated the distinction being made. The following day Dyer and Smith came to see McKay. The meeting ended with Dyer phoning Joseph Anderson, secretary to the First Presidency, so that McKay could direct Anderson to revise the sustaining document by replacing the word *to* with *in*. Anderson was reluctant to make the change and advised Dyer, "I am afraid you haven't heard the last of this." Anderson informed Brown of the change, but when Brown read the script for the sustaining ritual in the Saturday afternoon session, he departed from it, presenting Dyer as a counselor *to* the First Presidency, as McKay had originally directed in the full First Presidency meeting.[50]

On April 11, in a council meeting that McKay did not attend, Tanner pled for unity and then expressed his misgivings about Dyer's attempt to overturn McKay's original decision to sustain Dyer as a counselor *to* the First Presidency. Dyer, a relative newcomer, had acted out of turn in assuming "that the President did not understand a particular matter" on the day it was discussed "but did on the following day" after Dyer explained it to him. It was inappropriate for a counselor to seek an audience with the prophet independent of the rest of the presidency, Tanner advised. Dyer's actions had been "most unfair" to the presidency in "try[ing] to get [McKay] to change his decision" by "going to the President alone," particularly in the prophet's "present physical condition." Tanner said he offered the observation "without any ill feeling toward Brother Dyer." Dyer responded politely by defending his actions; McKay's question to him following the meeting—"what was that all about?"—suggested that he was not "fully aware, at that time of that which was agreed to." Dyer had merely responded to the prophet's inquiry. Ezra Taft Benson then recalled hearing McKay state when he had been "more vigorous" six months previously that Dyer and Smith were to be sustained as counselors *in* the Presidency. Dyer stated that "he understood protocol, and there is nothing he would like better than to follow it ... but he felt that there was an attempt made to keep him out of these callings that rightfully belonged to him, and that if he had to fight for his position,

50. McKay, *Confidence amid Change*, 755–59; DOMD (Dyer record), Apr. 3–4, 8, 10, 1968.

he felt he had a right to do it." Indeed, it was his "obligation" to "stand up" for the office to which the prophet had called him. Both sides believed they were representing the prophet's wishes. And although they struggled to obtain it, both Tanner and Dyer recognized that they needed unity. Perhaps recalling the lessons learned from such difficult and sometimes strained conversations in mind, Dyer closed his general conference address in 1971, more than a year after McKay's death, with these words: "The Lord has given this counsel by revelation, with which I close my remarks: '... I say unto you, be one; and if ye are not one ye are not mine.'"[51]

On April 16, Dyer reminded McKay that he had not yet been set apart as a counselor. The prophet instructed him to return that afternoon. Middlemiss prepared the wording McKay was to use, based upon previous settings apart of counselors, something that would not have been as necessary when McKay was younger. McKay reviewed the wording and edited it slightly, then asked Dyer to review it and then asked Joseph Anderson, secretary to the First Presidency, to read it. When everyone was satisfied, McKay reportedly stated that the more he read what Middlemiss had typed, the more he liked it. Middlemiss relished her integral involvement in the process, which was exceptional for any church employee not acting in a sustained church position and especially for a female employee. Her involvement may have been partly what she had in mind three years later when she wrote that she had "gone all the way to help [Dyer] get where he is." The prophet then read from the text, setting apart Dyer as a counselor "*in* the First Presidency" and adding that he was "to be a watchman over the Consecrated lands of Missouri." Dyer had been set apart as he and Middlemiss believed he should be, with Anderson as the witness, in Brown's and Tanner's absence. Once the setting apart had been effected, everyone loyally accepted it. Despite their differences, over time following the setting apart, the four counselors in the First Presidency, who often operated in McKay's absence, found common ground and improved their working relationship, although some suspicions remained. In their meetings they petitioned for divine aid, deliberated effectively, and planned ably. Following McKay's death, though, Dyer resumed his post as an assistant to the Quorum of the Twelve and was no longer sustained as an apostle.[52]

In the months surrounding Dyer's setting apart, the prophet was failing fast. His blood pressure and heart rate were alarming, and in February he contracted a mild case of pneumonia. Council meetings, which often lasted for three or more hours, exhausted him, and his doctors generally advised him to skip the meetings

51. DOMD, Apr. 11, 1968 (official minutes and Dyer's journal record); Alvin R. Dyer, address of Apr. 6, 1971, *Conference Reports*, 127.

52. McKay, *Confidence amid Change*, 760–61; Bergera, "Tensions," 236; DOMD, Oct. 4, 17, 30, Nov. 14, 1968.

or leave early to conserve his strength. As spring progressed, his exhaustion deepened. In May, Middlemiss entered his apartment to find him slumped in his chair, sleeping profoundly. Although he was dressed impeccably in a new blue suit, seemingly ready for the day, Middlemiss worried about "how he looked." A few days later, Dyer reported that the prophet continued "in ill health, seeming to lack vitality and strength" and that he had been in that condition for over three months. McKay's doctors ordered a hospital bed to facilitate his getting in and out of bed and recommended that only family and general authorities visit. In his isolated condition, McKay became lonely and depressed and fretted that he would never visit Huntsville again. He felt cut off from affairs at the Church Administration Building and worried that "all [was] not right."[53]

That summer when Lawrence and his doctors decided he lacked strength to meet with presidential candidates, McKay protested. "I am not sick, and I want to meet some of these men," Middlemiss sympathetically reported him saying. Howard W. Hunter arranged a visit from Ronald Reagan, a candidate whom McKay particularly wanted to meet, but at the last minute those responsible for his care canceled the appointment, fearing he was too weak. When associates came to visit, McKay pressed them to stay longer than doctors advised. Ezra Taft Benson described these entreaties as "almost a longing for closer association." The brief visits were largely limited to pleasantries, but even so McKay craved interpersonal contact. He continued to meet briefly with his counselors in his hotel office but at times seemed to not fully grasp the matters being discussed. In this weakened state, he continued to bend to those around him. After a brief conference with Mark Garff of the building committee, McKay dictated a letter opposing the appointment of Rowland Cannon to the executive committee of the Utah-Idaho Sugar Company. When McKay's son Lawrence learned of the letter, he persuaded his father to retract it. A few months later, Middlemiss fretted about McKay's double-mindedness. McKay's pattern of announcing a decision, committing it to writing, and then reversing it when counselors or others objected created an "undesirable image that is being given to the people."[54]

Despite that spreading image, there were still intermittent periods of undeniable lucidity. In February 1968, building supervisor Darcy Wright drove McKay to a meeting and reported to Middlemiss that the president's "mind seemed crystal clear." Later that same day, McKay commented that the nation was "in deep trouble in Vietnam," impressing Middlemiss by his familiarity with current events. McKay continued to weigh in decisively on some issues. In mid-April he said the church must do what it could "to prevent liquor by the drink." In late June, he confirmed his counselors' impression that the church should discourage fathers from declaring the lineage of their children in

53. DOMD, Feb. 9, Mar. 6, 12, Apr. 25, 29, May 24, 27–29, June 18, 1968.

54. DOMD, June 24, July 11–12, 19 (Dyer's record), Aug. 16, 20, Nov. 8, 1968.

patriarchal blessings. The following month, he counseled caution after Joseph Fielding Smith recommended that the University of Utah Professor Sterling McMurrin should be excommunicated for publicly criticizing the church's race-based priesthood restrictions. Although he had often granted Ezra Taft Benson's requests, that summer McKay consistently vetoed Benson's petitions for permission to run for vice president on the George Wallace ticket.[55]

In fall 1968, McKay developed an ulcerated sore on his spine from extended periods of sitting. Doctors prescribed time in Huntsville, where he could rest in bed and avoid sitting at his desk. As he began to feel better, he became more assertive. On September 24, he decided to attend a meeting in Salt Lake. When his nurse reminded him that he was under doctor's orders to remain in Huntsville, he reportedly advised his driver to "stand by, they are not the boss, and I shall let you know whether or not I shall have you drive me to Salt Lake to attend the meeting." His own carefree mood surfaced in meetings too. In one council meeting Brown, who had been hospitalized recently but was attending, was under doctor's orders to rest his voice. Perhaps unaware of the instruction, McKay asked Brown to address the council. When Tanner remonstrated that "his doctor says he is not to talk," McKay parried, "But his President is asking him to do so." Brown complied and "did very well," McKay felt. The prophet appeared "very weak and feeble in body" but "quite clear in his thinking," Elder Kimball noted. After that meeting, McKay was exhausted, and his doctor explained that he should not have attended.[56]

Despite his frailty, McKay managed to attend two sessions of the October 1968 conference, although he did not speak. Jets coming from a tank placed beneath his chair in the Tabernacle supplied supplemental oxygen. McKay's opening remarks, read by one of his sons, echoed many of the same phrases as his October 1966 address, including his exclamation "I love life!" and his reference to gazing from his windows to the mountains in the east and "greet[ing] the sun as it ushers in these unexcelled autumn days." The speech incorporated a new quotation from J. Edgar Hoover about crime, referenced a recent article on alcohol and cigarette consumption, and incorporated stories and warnings McKay had read in a 1949 conference address. His son Bob read his opening address but refused to read a statement McKay had issued previously advising voters to reject the upcoming liquor-by-the-drink referendum. Middlemiss had inserted the statement in his talk at the request of Gordon B. Hinckley, whom the First Presidency had appointed to coordinate church opposition to the referendum. Bob's reluctance to read the statement reflected his and his siblings' fears about the authenticity of verbiage that was being attributed to their father.

55. DOMD, Feb. 8, 1968; McKay, *Confidence amid Change*, 763, 767, 774–75.
56. DOMD, Sep. 24, 29, 1968; Kimball, journal, Sep. 25, 1968.

Bob finally read the statement the following evening in the priesthood session, the only session not broadcast by radio or television.[57]

Late in the year, McKay seemed to rally slightly. On October 23, a group of BYU students, recipients of the scholarship bearing his name, visited his apartment. One of them, George Ryskamp, a freshman from Oak Park, Michigan, suspected the reception was a staged photo op, an attempt to counter rumors of the president's incapacity. As Ryskamp entered the hotel suite, the prophet's appearance, propped up by pillows on a chair, seemingly confirmed his suspicion. But McKay's firm grasp of his hand and steady gaze into his eyes left Ryskamp spellbound. He walked from the room convinced that God was working through this physically frail but spiritually sensitive man. On a day in early November, Elder Benson found McKay "in wonderful spirits," looking "fine" and speaking "easily and deliberately." Middlemiss was thrilled the following week to find him "so much like his old self, without that worried, tired look in his face." In a First Presidency meeting in December 1968, McKay "was very determinate in his decisions and expressions and … took part in all that transpired in the meeting." He even insisted on reviewing and approving general authorities' travel plans, something he had not done for some time. Shortly before Christmas, when the apostles and counselors met with McKay in his apartment, Harold B. Lee was struck by the clarity of the prophet's speech.[58]

After Christmas 1968 a cold laid McKay low for weeks, but by February 10 he "seemed better" and was "quite perceptive," Dyer reported. Hoping that the mountain air and change of scenery would revive him, McKay and Ray spent two weeks in Huntsville in March but returned home with colds. A week before the general conference, McKay was "breathing heavily, was a gray color and would lapse off closing his eyes." Although his blood pressure was normal, he needed more oxygen and was suffering from excess fluid. When Middlemiss asked him if he wanted a priesthood blessing, he eagerly agreed. She summoned Dyer, who had never seen the prophet so ill. Dyer prayed fervently for inspiration and blessed McKay to "feel stronger and better" and "complete his work here upon the earth in accordance with the will of our Heavenly Father." He then blessed Ray, who was also ill, and "promised her that she would be made well." Following the blessing, the prophet leaned back in his chair and whispered, "Oh Lord, help us." A week later, his doctor warned him not to attend even one conference session. "Your condition is such that you might not hold up for an entire meeting, and you would dislike to have to be taken out of the

57. DOMD, Oct. 2, 4, 1968; McKay, *Confidence amid Change*, 776; Alan Macfarlane, excerpts from interview by Greg Prince, Feb. 19, 1995, box 22, folder 17, Prince Papers; David O. McKay, address of Oct. 4, 1968, *Conference Reports*, 6–8.

58. DOMD, Oct. 23, Nov. 8, Dec. 5, 1968; McKay, *Confidence amid Change*, 784; George Ryskamp, interview by author, Aug. 25, 2021, notes in author's possession.

meeting before a large Conference audience," Dr. Macfarlane warned. Middlemiss said that she had "never seen the President so tired and weak."[59]

Close to two-thirds of McKay's opening address in the April 1969 conference was taken from addresses he had delivered in 1943 and 1945. His concluding speech also incorporated material from previous speeches, including conference addresses delivered in 1958, 1963, and 1968. His advice to servicemen in Vietnam came verbatim from advice he had directed to soldiers in World War II in 1942. With a heightened level of specificity, his text mentioned a "particular time" when an "answer came as distinctly as though [his] Heavenly Father stood by [his] side and spoke the words." The text continued, "I feel as I have never felt before that God is my Father." McKay had probably spoken these words in a more intimate, reverential setting. Now with his father's apparent assent, Robert broadcast them over the airways.[60]

By the end of April, with the onset of warmer weather, McKay felt "much better," could converse "in a very clear and distinct manner," and no longer needed constant supplemental oxygen. Over the next few months, he received a brief visit from Vice President Spiro Agnew in his hotel suite, toured the new David O. McKay Hospital in Ogden, and attended the hospital dedication, fulfilling a promise he had made at the groundbreaking. His counselors continued to consult with him and seek his approval on proposed courses of action. In August, Elder Benson found him "in a somewhat weakened position" with labored breathing but reported that "his mind was clear and he was able to get out his sentences quite well."[61]

The following month Lawrence and Llewelyn met with their aging father to lobby him to consider reversing the priesthood ban, a policy that they strenuously opposed. They had recently read and been influenced by a draft article written by Stephen Taggart, a graduate student at Cornell, who argued that the ban arose from specific historical challenges the church faced in Missouri in the 1830s rather than revelation. Strangely, the sons invited Dyer, who was just leaving the room, to join their conversation. They asked their father "if this was not perhaps the time to announce that the Negro could be given the priesthood," asking, "what proof do we have that the Negroes are descendants of Cain?" After Dyer argued for the ban's doctrinal validity and maintained that it could be overturned only by divine revelation, the two brothers took their leave, asking their father to consider the matter further. After they departed, McKay held Dyer's hand "for quite some time" and told him that "he loved [him] and that he always had." Dyer surmised the expression of love might have been motivated by Dyer's remarks on the ban. Lawrence and Llewelyn returned

59. DOMD, Feb. 10, Mar. 24, 25, 1969; McKay, *Confidence amid Change*, 795.
60. David O. McKay, addresses of Apr. 4, 6, 1969, 4–9, 153.
61. DOMD, Apr. 30, May 8, 16, July 9, Aug. 27, 1969.

the following week to press their case. In this or a subsequent meeting they reportedly asked their father to approve the ordination of Monroe Fleming, a longtime African American member and employee at the Hotel Utah. It was a last-ditch, deliberate attempt to capitalize upon their father's affection, exert their utmost influence upon him in his feeble state, and secure a modern, prophetically sanctioned precedent for ordaining other members with African ancestry, thereby vitiating the ban. McKay had begun to "fail mentally" by that point according to his doctor: "Sometimes he would understand, and sometimes he wouldn't." It is unclear how fully he comprehended the implications of his sons' proposal. Moreover, Fleming was a problematic choice, almost certain to arouse opposition. He was beloved by several church leaders, including perhaps McKay, but distrusted by others. Indeed, a warning about his possible ties to the NAACP had set off alarms in the Quorum of the Twelve a few years earlier, helping to trigger the cancelation of plans to establish a mission and baptize converts in West Africa. According to Hugh B. Brown, McKay signaled his approval for the ordination—although Brown had several times exaggerated McKay's readiness to overturn the ban—but "some of the other brethren" learned of the approval and somehow quashed it. Unsurprisingly, in his frail condition McKay did not resist their opposition.[62]

McKay was too weak a few days later to attend any sessions of the October conference. In an attempt to heighten the currency of the prophet's opening speech, Middlemiss inserted news reports and an excerpt from the office journal she kept. Beginning with something McKay had said about the future of space travel back in 1957 amid the Cold War race to launch satellites, Middlemiss then drew from her record of McKay's conversation in 1963 with the astronaut Edward White. She quoted news reports describing the achievements of Apollo 8 and Apollo 11, including references to the scriptures the astronauts had beamed back to earth. The address then quoted at length from the Pearl of Great Price regarding the astronomical observations and knowledge of Moses and Abraham. Shifting to present-day moral calamities, the talk mixed the results of a Gallup poll and President Richard Nixon's condemnation of drug abuse with quotations from speeches McKay had delivered in 1956 and 1958. Backed into a corner by the perceived necessity of producing addresses for McKay's sons to read, she had done her best and compiled a speech that was perhaps as much Middlemiss as McKay.[63]

A week after the October conference, Dyer again administered to McKay, joined this time by Joseph Fielding Smith. Dyer was impressed that McKay warmly

62. DOMD, Sep. 10, 17, 1969. Harris, *Second-Class Saints*, 151. Harris's remarkable work cites Paul Salisbury's report of a September 29 conversation with Brown in Brown's office, box 172, folder 9, Eugene England Papers.

63. DOMD, Oct. 3, 1969; David O. McKay, address of Oct. 3, 1969, *Conference Reports*, 4–9; Alan Macfarlane, excerpts from interview by Greg Prince, Feb. 19, 1995, box 22, folder 17, Prince Papers.

greeted Smith with the words, "Oh, Joseph." But when Clare Middlemiss arrived in his apartment on October 24, McKay appeared "extremely tired," and his handshake was flaccid. He tried to focus but could not keep his eyes open. She left the apartment feeling "dejected." On November 3, Middlemiss again visited the prophet in his hotel and feared he did not recognize her. "You know your secretary, don't you?" she queried, to which he replied, "Of course I do."[64]

Following the October conference, Lawrence announced he would no longer read his father's "talks." He and his siblings objected to the process by which the talks were being cobbled together from his previous writings and statements even though they were reviewed with the prophet prior to being shared in conference. The practice had concerned Lawrence and his siblings for some time because no historical context was provided for the quotations, but now Lawrence felt certain "his father was not in a condition to give approval to what had been prepared to be read as representing the remarks of the President." McKay's children also objected to the reproduction of McKay's signature on correspondence and the updating and collating of their father's writings and speeches for republication in editorials as if they were current messages from the prophet. Middlemiss was confident she could channel McKay in responding to personal correspondence and claimed that McKay approved of what she had written. Over the years she had written letters for him about which he had said, "it was as though I had dictated those letters myself," but the family objected. Lawrence complained that Middlemiss had been "preparing the editorials" and had inserted "current matters" of her own accord. After conversing with Lawrence, Tanner asked him to poll his siblings. They all felt that "their father was not competent to serve as the President of the Church." According to Dyer, "considerable discussion ensued about the competency of the President," with Dyer "refus[ing] to yield on the point of mental incompetency" and Tanner agreeing that the minutes would refer "only to the President's incompetence," minus the defining adjective. Dyer noted that he and Tanner "disagreed as to the extent of the President's incompetence, but the matter was not belabored." They had learned to disagree without being disagreeable.[65]

The following day in the council meeting with the Quorum of the Twelve, Tanner reviewed the McKay family's concerns and shared a handwritten letter from Dr. Macfarlane, declaring him "mentally deficient." Elder Richard L. Evans fretted that if editorials over the prophet's name could no longer be printed in church magazines, the silence would be tantamount to "telling the people that the President cannot speak to them anymore." Apostles Marion G. Romney and Howard W. Hunter, both attorneys, had met with the church's legal counsel, Wilford Kirton. Tanner summarized their conclusion: in McKay's

64. DOMD, Oct. 13, Nov. 3, 1969.

65. DOMD, Mar. 25, Apr. 5, Aug. 14, Nov. 12 (Dyer record), 13, 1969.

weakened condition, "the First Presidency has to carry on as far as the Presidency of the Church is concerned as the administration" of the church. The counselors had determined, though, that "nothing [could] be done about giving or taking away the sealing power" while McKay was incapacitated. Harold B. Lee said that "he thought that none of us … can determine a new policy or new changes without the President of the Church until the Lord releases him." In a preliminary discussion of McKay's condition two weeks previously, the council had determined not to make the minutes of their discussion part of the official record. Now the council determined that the minutes of their current discussion should be "made and fully recorded."[66]

When the apostles met on December 4 and reviewed the minutes of their most recent council meeting, Dyer and Benson recommended excising the discussion of McKay's incompetence. Dyer feared that the discussion could be interpreted as "a stigma on the life of this great man." Hunter defended his use of the term mental incompetence, pointing out that the term was legally correct, that it "did not mean mental illness" but "merely meant that he was not able to give proper consideration to various matters that would come before him." Elder Romney recommended that the minutes as written be approved; Elder Stapley seconded the motion; and the majority voted in favor, although Dyer abstained, and it appeared to him that some hesitated in raising their hands. Tanner pledged that the counselors would continue to meet with the prophet "when he was able to give counsel and directions," which they did. On December 11, the prophet's nurse informed Middlemiss that his "toxic condition [was] getting steadily worse."[67]

On January 16, Dyer dreamed he saw McKay's corpse on a bed beside a "wreath of mourning" and "white streamers hung down over a long footage of white doors." That same day, as Middlemiss approached McKay, he was "coughing heavily," and his face was ashen. Still, he recognized his devoted aide and whispered, "You come over here any time. I want you to be here."[68]

Realizing that the end was near, the family summoned Lou Jean from Chicago and gathered in his bedroom. McKay struggled mightily for breath until he fell into a coma. His breathing slowed, and he passed before dawn on January 18, 1970, from congestive heart failure. The following Tuesday, Wednesday, and Thursday, McKay's body lay in state in the Church Administration Building. Over 40,000 people waited in line in the cold winter air to file past the coffin and pay their respects to their beloved leader.[69]

66. McKay, *Confidence amid Change*, 811–19; see also Dyer's record in DOMD, Nov. 13, 1969.

67. DOMD, Dec. 4 (Dyer record), 11, 1969.

68. Dyer notes in DOMD, Jan. 16, 1970; McKay, *Confidence amid Change*, 823.

69. McKay, *Confidence amid Change*, 824; DOMD, Jan. 20, 1970; Alan Macfarlane, excerpts from interview by Greg Prince, box 22, folder 17, Prince Papers.

15: Legacy

Tributes to David O. McKay flowed freely in the days following his death. Former Utah governor J. Bracken Lee, whose iconoclasm had sometimes placed him at odds with McKay, reflected appreciatively that "the man looked the part of a leader, acted the part and was a leader in the true sense of the word." BYU president Ernest Wilkinson, who had privately grumbled about McKay's tendency to reconsider and reverse administrative decisions, lauded his spiritual leadership: "He led the membership of the Church not by edict or command, but by the power of Christian example" and earned others' respect with his "love, neatness, kindness and courtesy." Right Reverend Richard S. Watson, who served as the Episcopal bishop of Utah during McKay's entire tenure as church president, expressed his "great and deep affection" for the man and for "his concern for people of every faith." Middlemiss, who probably knew McKay better than anyone aside from Ray, reflected, "No one could have worked for a man who was more thoughtful and sweeter to his employe[e]s." McKay was "always cheerful about his work and expected those around him to be cheerful also, because we were engaged in the work of the Lord."[1]

At his funeral top church leaders eulogized the prophet. Joseph Fielding Smith, soon to be sustained as church president, characterized McKay as "one of the greatest and most inspired leaders of this dispensation." Hugh B. Brown stated that McKay had "lived as nearly as it is humanly possible … a Christlike life." N. Eldon Tanner focused on the results of McKay's leadership, measured in the church's "unprecedented physical and spiritual growth," gauged by missionary efforts, conversions, and temple building. Senior apostle Harold B. Lee summarized McKay's impact upon individuals' spirituality. "As a special witness of our Lord Jesus Christ, he lighted lamps of faith of many by the intensity of the fire within his own soul."[2]

Shortly after McKay died, Eugene England and Wesley Johnson, the co-editors of *Dialogue: A Journal of Mormon Thought*, an independent quarterly journal based in California and pitched primarily at intellectually inclined

1. "General Authorities, Leaders Voice Sorrow," "Clergymen Mourn President," "Educators Sorrow for Pres. McKay," "Nixon, Johnson Among Leaders Mourning Death of President McKay," *Deseret News*, Jan. 19, 1970, M 2–3.

2. "President McKay Laid to Rest," *Deseret News Church Section*, Jan. 24, 1970, 4, 13–15.

Latter-day Saints, solicited the memories and feelings of readers "of various age and experience and place" who knew McKay. Most who shared their memories lived in the South Bay Area and knew the editors personally; the respondents included both women and men and represented a variety of educational backgrounds, ethnicities, ages, and political leanings. Their comments show some of the things that Latter-day Saints valued most in McKay near the end of his life. They viewed him as a spiritually magnetic personality who conveyed a sense of the divine to the Saints through his mere presence, his bearing, his words of greeting, and his teachings. Myra Thulin was a schoolteacher working in Huntsville in 1916 when she met McKay, the first apostle she ever met, at "a simple ward party." A half century later she cherished the memory of his "charm and magnetism and spirituality." Lafi Toelupe, who had interpreted for McKay during his visit to Samoa in 1955, remembered McKay's concern for Samoans; he was the first apostle and prophet to reach out to them personally by visiting their islands. Toelupe believed "no other man has done more for the Samoans spiritually than President McKay." His impact upon Toelupe himself was profound. Toelupe described his reaction when McKay took his hand and warmly greeted him: "He uplifted my heart and I felt a new life and a new strength, physically and spiritually." Scott Cameron, a student at Stanford University, recalled sitting in a sacrament meeting as a teenager while McKay spoke and suddenly "knowing that [he] was listening to a prophet." Eight years later, having served a mission and obtained a university degree, Cameron's "knowledge of the purpose of a prophet, seer and revelator" was far greater, but his conviction that "God does speak to men in this day" was still "primarily based" on that single "personal experience" that came to him "when the Church was little more than a habit in [his] life." Mona Jo Ellsworth marveled that McKay remained relevant as her spiritual needs evolved. As a young convert from Florida, she met McKay in 1954 while working for a summer in Salt Lake. He extended his hand and invited her into his office, and his gaze seemed to pierce her heart and mind. "He asked me how I was but before I answered I sensed he already knew my deep inner feelings," she recalled. A decade later, enmeshed in the cultural ferment of the 1960s and "no longer a young girl full of belief," she attended a session of the Oakland Temple dedication during which McKay offered the dedicatory prayer. She had come to the service "full of questions and so spiritually hungry that I hurt deep in my soul." As McKay prayed, she heard "as if for the first time, gratitude for our relationship to God, for the mission of Christ, and for the beautiful commandment to love one another." She departed having been spiritually "fed" and renewed. McKay's most important legacy for Joseph Muren, a teacher at the church's institute of religion in Palo Alto, was his example and teachings. Muren called McKay "the paradigmatic man of our dispensation in exemplifying, through the written and spoken word, the rewards of Christian living." Muren chafed when some criticized McKay for "never speak[ing] out on the major contemporary issues." For Muren, McKay's teachings about Christlike character "went straight to the very core of the problems of our society." Those teachings had been personally transformative, making him "a better man, a better husband, a better father."[3]

In the decades following the publication of *Dialogue*'s retrospective tribute, church members and leaders continued to credit McKay with playing a pivotal role in their spiritual conversion and development, illustrating his long-lasting legacy. Many who saw, heard, or met him in their childhood or youth recalled a mystical sensation of holiness and goodness radiating from his imposing face, his wavy white hair, and his striking physique. Alan Blodgett was a farm boy in eastern Oregon when he first saw McKay in person at a stake conference. "I was so awed by him that I carried the hymn book on the tractor while I was plowing and memorized all verses of 'We Thank Thee O God for a Prophet,'" he remembered. Pat Bronson Brower idolized McKay as a teenager growing up in Idaho. She was "impressed with his stately physical appearance," as demonstrated by his photos printed in church magazines, and the "warm manner" conveyed in his conference talks. For years she prayed to meet him. While staying at her grandmother's home in Utah, she attended a sacrament meeting where McKay was seated on the stand. Throughout the meeting she was "unable to take [her] eyes off that holy man." Afterward, she sensed "a flood of joy" as he grasped her hand and "smiled into [her] eyes, and gave full attention to [her] stammering words." Separated by an ocean and a language from McKay, Dieter Uchtdorf grew up in Germany. But much like Pat Brower, Uchtdorf "seemed to know him personally" from what he read and heard. Stories and feelings of the prophet's "love, kindness, and dignity ... gave [him] confidence and courage in [his] young life." In her childhood Sheri Slaughter met McKay briefly while shopping with her mother. Nearly forty years later she remembered thinking that his face was "the kindest, gentlest face [she] had ever seen." Similarly, Donald Hallstrom, who attended a stake conference in the Honolulu Tabernacle as a boy, recalled that he "felt something quite intense and very personal" through the "influence of the Holy Spirit" as he saw McKay standing at the pulpit "dressed in a cream-colored suit ... with his wavy white hair" and wearing a "triple-thick red carnation lei." When Piriko Valkama Petersen first glimpsed the prophet at a youth retreat near Finland, all she could see was "his majestic silhouette against the sun, the light against his beautiful white hair forming, it seemed, a shining halo around his head." Later when he took her hands in his, "a feeling of complete peace flowed from his hands into [her]." Bonnie Dansie Parkin was in her late teens or early twenties when she saw McKay descending the steps from

3. "President David O. McKay, 1873–1970," *Dialogue: A Journal of Mormon Thought* 4, no. 4 (Winter 1969): 47, 50–59.

the Church Administration Building one winter day. She recalled, "I could not take my eyes off him.... He said nothing as he passed me; he merely smiled gently and tipped his hat," but "the Spirit literally filled my being [and] I knew I had seen a prophet of God."[4]

While many remembered glimpsing McKay or shaking his hand, others carried the memory of meaningful conversations with him. Elaine Schwartz Dalton traveled with several fellow BYU students to visit the prophet and his wife in their apartment; she was struck by the McKays' joy and affection for each other. "Now, young women, I would like you to meet *my queen*," McKay said. His chivalrous regard for his frail wife taught Dalton about "what [she] now [calls] 'deep beauty'—the kind of beauty that shines from the *inside* out." David Burton was in his early teens when McKay paused to visit with him after calling on someone in his neighborhood. The prophet told Burton of his own encounter as a teenager with a former prophet, John Taylor, who "rolled up his shirtsleeve, and showed the evidence of the wounds he had sustained while he was with the Prophet Joseph Smith in Carthage Jail." Over five decades later, Burton vividly recalled "how strongly [he] felt the Spirit and the power of President McKay's prophetic calling" as he conversed with him. Rex and Phyllis Reeve were one of hundreds of couples who were married in the temple by McKay. McKay advised them "to never let the sun set on a misunderstanding," a strategy that the couple followed faithfully. The counsel shaped their relationship. Forty-one years later Reeve reflected, "I can say we've done that." Monroe McKay, who attended the temple wedding of his brother Gunn, recalled, "His performance of temple weddings was a thing of beauty. His commentaries were inspiring but not flamboyant.... He made marriage really feel like a true sacrament, not just a ritual."[5]

Others who learned from or met him at later stages in life when they had different roles and responsibilities also recalled his profound impact. Alan Moorehead was a convert to the church in his late twenties, serving as the coach for a ward basketball team in Maryland, when he met the prophet. He and the team had traveled to Utah to play in the all-church basketball tournament. Initially unimpressed by the old man he saw seated at a table when he entered McKay's office, Moorehead's impression soon changed. The coach remembered:

4. Alan Blodgett to Greg A. Prince, Nov. 9, 1999, box 22, folder 13, Prince Papers; Patricia L. Brower, "The Hand of a Prophet," *Ensign*, Mar. 1995; Sheri E. Slaughter, "Who Was That Man?," *Ensign,* Dec. 1997; Donald Hallstrom, "Converted to His Gospel through His Church," *Ensign*, May 2012; Piriko Petersen, "When the Sun Broke Through," *Ensign*, Aug. 1976; Bonnie D. Parkin, "An Anchor for Eternity—and Today," *Ensign*, May 1996; Dieter F. Uchtdorf, "The Global Church Blessed by the Voice of Prophets," *Ensign*, Nov. 2002.

5. Elaine S. Dalton, "Remember Who You Are!," *Ensign,* May 2010; H. David Burton, "Lessons from the New Testament: Quiet Stirrings of the Heart," *Ensign,* Apr. 2007; "Elder Rex C. Reeve," *Ensign*, May 1978; Monroe G. McKay, excerpts from interview by Greg Prince, Mar. 5, 1999, box 23, folder 1, Prince Papers.

"He took my hand and he shook it and said, 'You must be Brother Moorehead.' He looked at me a long time and I had this feeling, 'He knows everything I've ever done or even would like to have done.' I just said, 'Yes sir.'" After speaking to each boy on the team, he again took Moorehead's hand and offered riveting advice. As Moorehead remembered the advice decades later, McKay said, "Brother Moorehead, you have an interesting call here. You have an opportunity to change the lives of many people. You will be blessed to work with the youth of Zion, and you will make them stronger. I know you will do this. It is a big responsibility. I hope you live up to it." Tom Perry parented differently after hearing McKay's counsel that "the raising of a child is basically, fundamentally, and most exclusively a spiritual process." While presiding over a stake in California, David Haight hosted McKay in his home. His interaction with the prophet "gave [him] a new vision of the magnitude and the breadth and the importance of the mission that we have here upon the earth to fulfill." When McKay called Loren Dunn as a general authority, he charged Dunn "to carry out this calling in a way that would be pleasing to [his] own father." For Dunn, who revered his father, McKay's counsel provided "a challenge for a lifetime."[6]

Aside from the writings of prophets canonized in the church's standard works of scripture, the teachings of modern Latter-day Saint prophets lose much of their daily currency following their deaths, as new prophets assume their functions. A subset of McKay's teachings continued to resonate and be cited by church officers and authorities for decades. In the decades following his death, McKay has been referenced in an average of 5.4 conference talks per year. Only one of the other nine prophets who passed away in the twentieth century, Spencer W. Kimball, has been posthumously referenced by more speakers per year.[7]

Church leaders have cited and quoted McKay's teachings about the home and family more frequently than his messages regarding any other topic. The adage "no other success can compensate for failure in the home," a quotation he popularized from a 1924 book by sociologist James Edward McCulloch, has been quoted in over twenty-five general conference talks. Church leaders have also repeatedly quoted McKay's counsel to parents to "make home a bit of heaven," to express and demonstrate love, and to avoid angry or profane outbursts. The prophet's pithy phrase "every member a missionary" has been quoted in at least a dozen conference talks. McKay's teachings about self-control, the

6. Alan Moorehead, excerpts from interview by Greg Prince, Dec. 5, 1995, box 22, folder 13, Prince Papers; L. Tom Perry, "Train up a Child," *Ensign* May 1983; David B. Haight, "Prophets Are Inspired," *Ensign*, Nov. 1996; Loren C. Dunn, "Because My Father Sent Me," *Ensign*, May 2000.

7. The average number of references per year for each prophet was calculated from the Scripture Citation Index for the years between each prophet's death and 2024. They are: Lorenzo Snow, 0.71; Joseph F. Smith, 3.6; Heber J. Grant, 2.19; George Albert Smith, 1.6; David O. McKay, 5.4; Joseph Fielding Smith, 4.63; Harold B. Lee, 4.5; Spencer W. Kimball, 8.18; Ezra Taft Benson, 3.45; Howard W. Hunter, 1.9.

pliability of human nature, the importance of spirituality, Christlike ideals, obedience, gospel teaching, and agency have also been quoted periodically. McKay told many stories, and two have become particular favorites: his reminiscence about kneeling without immediate result beside a bush on a mountainside in his youth to seek a spiritual witness, only to receive the witness years later; and his memory of feeling chastened as a missionary when he saw the inscription in stone, "What e'er thou art act well thy part."[8]

With particular fondness, many urbane Saints have recalled McKay's optimism and openness. Although the church under his watch barred members with African ancestry from the priesthood and temple rites, Latter-day Saint academics rarely have faulted him for the ban's continuation, reasoning that he was a victim of circumstance and felt duty bound to maintain it. McKay was "charismatic and human, traditional and innovative," recalled English professor Eugene England in 2000. He was "clearly the most liberal of any LDS prophet in the twentieth century" in the classic definition of that term. Politically conservative, McKay nonetheless appealed to left-of-center church members with his "generosity and open-handedness," his high regard for individual autonomy and agency, and his "belief in progress [and] the essential goodness" of humanity. Scientists and humanists have especially appreciated McKay's openness to science in contrast to the strident anti-evolutionism of Joseph Fielding Smith and Bruce R. McConkie. University of Utah administrator and former institute teacher Lowell Bennion recalled that McKay leaned toward "the basic position" of science on the age of the earth but allowed other leaders, including Elder Smith, the liberty to voice their own opinions. Thereby the prophet exhibited "great tolerance and graciousness." BYU biology professor Duane Jeffery likewise praised McKay with regard to evolution as "a giant of tolerance" who "avoid[ed] any direct public statement" on the matter. McKay's merciful, expansive approach to religion has also impressed freethinkers. As McKay's son Llewelyn, a freethinking English professor, remarked, his father's religion was "concerned with large, all-embracing spiritual issues" and was inclusive rather than exclusive, unifying rather than dividing. Jack Newell, who later became a professor and leader at the University of Utah, joined the church as a young adult when McKay was its president. Newell remembered the prophet as "a remarkable speaker … who spoke to the essential values of Christianity and did so with style." McKay's approach "inspired" him and led him to take the church "seriously." Sterling McMurrin, a philosopher, dissident church member, and cultural gadfly whose freedom to speak his opinion unfettered by church discipline was defended by McKay, fondly remembered the prophet. He was "a man

8. McKay's teachings were analyzed by research assistant Jared Cluff using the Scripture Citation Index. Frederick Buchanan, excerpts from interview by Greg Prince, May 21, 1996, box 22, folder 21, Prince Papers.

of great and genuine love for others, a man of extraordinary compassion and love of humanity" who "believed very strongly in individual rights." McMurrin appreciated that McKay "functioned in a matrix of interpersonal relationships" rather than prioritizing policy and operating procedures. McKay was willing to take the risk of "driving out to some dissident's home [as he did for McMurrin] to discuss his heretical views in a friendly, positive way."[9]

In candid interviews, some family members and friends recall McKay's foibles and idiosyncrasies, which caused some to resent him. McKay's niece Flora, the oldest daughter of his brother Thomas, resented David's dominance in the extended family's financial concerns and complained that "he was not a very loving man" toward his nieces and nephews, with whom he had little contact. The fact that McKay denounced Flora's sister Fawn Brodie for her iconoclastic biography of Joseph Smith likely shaped Flora's resentment of her uncle. Another more distant relative, Gunn McKay, whose father grew up a stone's throw away from David, perceived him as "arrogant," "vain," and "a little bit of a showman." McKay's own children and grandchildren admired and adored him, but some also remember his imperious obsession with punctuality, which tried their patience. While living at the Hotel Utah later in life, McKay hosted Christmas Eve dinner in the President's Room. Granddaughter-in-law Vivian recalled that "it was very important to him to be punctual." As the owner of a jewelry store, Bob had a hard time getting away from his shop on Christmas Eve. His father would stand outside the door to the President's Room with his pocket watch until precisely 6:00 p.m. Then he would close the door and say, "Six o'clock, Bob's not here. We are going to eat anyway." Granddaughter Midene stayed in his home often when her parents were out of town. On one occasion she was busy finishing a task and delayed coming down to the dining room when she was called. She recalled, "The chairs were all turned around and they were all waiting for prayer, and I came down and scooted to my place, and he just looked at me and said, 'We have been waiting for you.' I was never late again." Those who worked with him in church settings also saw his obsession with punctuality. Paul Dunn recalled, "If a person walked into David O. McKay's meeting five minutes late, he'd only do that one time, I promise you. It wouldn't be a big chastisement, it would be because of the personality and what he expected, and you didn't fulfill it."[10]

9. England, "McKay in Mormon Culture"; 20–22; "President David O. McKay," 48; Jeffrey, "Seers, Savants and Evolution," 66, 67; McKay, *Home Memories*, 272; McMurrin and Newell, *Matters of Conscience*, 186, 201, 202.

10. Bringhurst, "Private versus Public," 28, 29. For McKay's relationship with Fawn McKay Brodie see Bringhurst, *Fawn McKay Brodie*, 84–85, 108–9, 113, 293; Vivian McKay, excerpts from interview by Greg Prince, May 21, 1996, box 22, folder 13, Prince Papers; Midene Anderson, excerpts from interview by Greg Prince, Oct. 1, 1996, box 22, folder 13, Prince Papers; Paul H. Dunn, excerpts from interview by Greg Prince, Mar. 20, 1997, box 22, folder 13, Prince Papers.

While individual members have framed their memories of McKay based upon personal experiences, in their general histories of the church, historians have concentrated upon McKay's institutional imprint and legacy, providing carefully reasoned judgments based upon their study of historical documents and broad historical patterns. Scholars have attributed McKay's long-lasting influence to both his temperament and his lengthy tenure, although they have disagreed about which factor was most important. "Much of McKay's influence was the product of sheer longevity," judges Terryl Givens. "No Mormon before him had served as long in the presiding councils of the church—sixty-four years." Conversely, J. B. Haws concludes that McKay's "influence had more to do with temperament than with tenure."[11]

Historians have given McKay high marks for his achievements, particularly as they relate to the church's reach. James Allen and Glen Leonard describe McKay as "the ideal leader for the Church in the postwar world" because of his extensive travels and his "broad understanding of the world around him." Leonard Arrington and Davis Bitton attribute the church's unprecedented, dramatic expansion following World War II to McKay's "forceful, internationally oriented leadership." McKay's commitment to building temples, church buildings, and schools abroad encouraged Latter-day Saints to sink deep spiritual roots into their homelands rather than emigrating to Utah and made Mormonism a global faith, J. B. Haws points out. Because he was "the most widely traveled President in the history of the Church" to that point, McKay was "the first living prophet most of the scattered Saints had ever seen," Richard Cowan observes.[12]

Historians have credited McKay with cultivating the church's unprecedented respectability and recognition in the middle decades of the twentieth century, citing not only his dapper dress and charisma but also his openness and outward reach. As the "most visible Mormon leader" of the twentieth century, McKay "led a public life," notes Matthew Bowman, and "intentionally cultivated an image as the embodiment of his faith: benevolent, fashionable, hardworking, and public-spirited." He appeared "an exemplary American to many." McKay "may have been the most humanistically inclined of the Mormon prophets," judges Terryl Givens, "renowned for his measured judgment, his political moderation and tolerance, and his gentleness of character." He built bridges across faith lines and cultivated friendships with politicians and industrialists who differed from him in their values and conduct. Indeed he "[encouraged] the church into new interpersonal and institutional connections," Haws writes, quoting a writer for *Time* magazine who opined that McKay "was perhaps the first Mormon president to treat non-Mormons as generously as members of

11. Givens, *Latter-day Saint Experience*, 283; Haws, *Mormon Image*, 20.

12. Arrington and Bitton, *Mormon Experience*, 286; Allen and Leonard, *Latter-day Saints*, 563; Haws, *Mormon Image*, 21–22; Cowan, *Twentieth Century*, 241–42.

his own faith." Likewise, Benjamin Park identifies McKay's "moderate voice" and "more cosmopolitan background" as characteristics that endeared him to the membership and positioned him to serve as a unifier and consensus builder—"an unflappable figure optimistic in outlook and determined in vision." He sketches a less favorable view of McKay as he aged in the 1960s, a leader "eager to please others" who became increasingly susceptible to lobbying and thus "[shifted] from one position to the other, torn between competing factions."[13]

Each person's recollection and retrospective appraisal captures a piece of David O. McKay's legacy. Collectively the collage of memories depicts a complex, powerful human being whose looks, actions, teachings, and decisions carried extraordinary weight by virtue of his position. He looked the part of a prophet, and both members and nonbelievers were captivated by his commanding appearance and charisma. His global vision and priorities accelerated and, in some respects, catalyzed the Church's international expansion and development.

Although it is natural to gravitate toward McKay's years as church president, when he exerted his greatest influence, in measuring the man, I hope I have shown in this book how the formative experiences of previous decades shaped McKay. Missionary service in Scotland transformed an intelligent young man who had never traveled beyond Utah into a Utahn with an international outlook. McKay's religious missionary experiences provided the bedrock for his lifelong faith and spiritual convictions, and his persistence in daunting missionary tasks from tracting to clerical work honed his work ethic and discipline. McKay returned from his mission with a newfound zest for preaching and a compassionate disposition, nurtured by his ministrations to others, that would become hallmarks of his subsequent ministry. Naturally drawn to others, McKay became adept at listening, counseling, and mediating disagreements.

Called as an apostle only six and a half years after returning from his mission, McKay's heavy workload intensified his disposition to work long hours—a health-compromising hallmark of his later tenure as church president. He traveled frequently to stakes and missions in the western United States, gaining a firsthand understanding of the strengths and weaknesses of the institutional church and its membership that would serve him and the church well when he was called to the First Presidency. On many of those travels, he accompanied more experienced general authorities, who shared counsel and perspectives about ecclesiastical matters, including the obligations of apostles to their quorum and to the church president. Steeled by his observations on his mission of the destructive impact of alcohol, he crusaded vigorously for prohibition, developing an uncompromising, hard-edged reformist tendency that would shape his approach as chair of Utah's centennial celebration. Although he

13. Bowman, *Mormon People*, 185–87, 245; Givens, *Latter-day Saint Experience*, 283; Haws, *Mormon Image*, 27; Park, *American Zion*, 253, 262, 282, 290.

would become famous for his admonition to members to prioritize home over other pursuits, his numerous church responsibilities often took him from the home, forcing Ray to shoulder most of the duties of parenting and maintaining their household.

In his late forties, McKay became the first apostle to travel around the world, and his tour broadened his perspective on the outlook and needs of the Saints in Asia, the Pacific, and the Middle East, increasing his understanding of cultural diversity and predisposing him to be more confident in the leadership abilities of converts, less dogmatic, and more open to different modes of thought and action than some of his associates. He also returned from his tour with a storehouse of memories of faith-promoting miracles and providential interventions, experiences that heightened his sense of God's immanence and daily relevance. McKay preached the transformative power of Jesus Christ and his teachings to reorient people's lives for the rest of his ministry. Called to preside over the European Mission less than nine months after completing his world tour, he gained a fine-grained, firsthand understanding of the church in Europe to complement the knowledge he had acquired of other regions on his world tour. Advocating member-missionary efforts, he blazed an approach to missionary work that would become a hallmark of his administration as church president. He returned from his service as mission president convinced that the church must establish a more substantial footprint abroad with respectable chapels, a concept that would blossom into the church's ambitious international building program in the 1950s. As mission president McKay experienced modest success in improving the church's image in Europe by defending and promoting the church and the gospel in editorials and correspondence and by visiting with government leaders and dignitaries. These efforts and successes provided precedents for McKay's and the church's approach to outreach and public relations during the 1950s and 1960s.

Called as a counselor in the First Presidency in his early sixties, McKay shouldered a disproportionate share of the presidency's administrative load, including overseeing the development and implementation of the Church Security Program, during the 1930s due to the extended absences of Presidents Grant and Clark. By serving in the presidency for decades, McKay became much more conversant with church finances, temple construction and operation, physical facilities, personnel, and public relations. By the time he was appointed church president in 1951, he had extensive firsthand knowledge of these matters. McKay also gained experience in counseling and dispensing advice related to major life decisions, an individually tailored ministry that required a blend of judgment, moral rectitude, respect for others' agency, and compassion. During the 1940s, after J. Reuben Clark limited his legal work, McKay's administrative scope narrowed as he concentrated primarily upon supervising the church's missionary efforts, including the opening of new nations to missionary work in Latin America and Asia. These responsibilities ideally positioned him to steer the church's international expansion as church president. Having served for over sixteen years in the First Presidency, a tenure exceeded by only four other men to that point in the church's history (J. Reuben Clark, George Q. Cannon, Joseph F. Smith, and Daniel H. Wells), McKay came into the church presidency with extensive knowledge of church operations.

Growth and international expansion, including the construction of schools, church buildings, and temples, were salient features of David O. McKay's tenure as prophet and church president. The international expansion was constrained in Africa and India by concerns about race and decentralization. McKay visited more nations and continents and met with more Latter-day Saints than any previous prophet, complementing his travels abroad with a demanding personal ministry to individuals. Members reciprocated his outreach and image with an intense and (in the twentieth century, at least) unprecedented veneration of him. Long before *belonging* became a buzzword, McKay used the term, stating that he hoped his world tours "awakened a sense of belonging." His eloquent teachings about the importance of the family, missionary work, and the duality of flesh and spirit resonated with many Latter-day Saints, although some wished for greater focus on pressing social justice issues such as sexism, civil rights, and poverty.

McKay's leadership style has been contrasted with that of J. Reuben Clark, his associate for decades in the First Presidency. In D. Michael Quinn's *Elder Statesman*, Clark and his protégé Harold B. Lee are portrayed as consummate organization men known for their inflexible, legalistic dogmatism; their racial conservatism; and their mastery of order, routinization, and correlation. McKay by contrast is portrayed as a flexible, pragmatic humanitarian who placed people ahead of policy, a leader who inspired others by his high ideals but exhibited fickle judgment and limited managerial skills.[14] The contrast is overdrawn, and it fails to account for change over time in McKay's leadership style as his physical strength and mental acuity waned. On moral matters, including political corruption, alcohol, tobacco, and moral misconduct of church leaders, McKay was decisive, even dogmatic, and uncompromising. He considered communism to be evil incarnate and viewed Roman Catholicism as its religious analog. Never manifesting a nuanced view of the Holy Land, he championed the Jews as God's chosen people, divinely destined to inherit Palestine. Generously solicitous of others' feelings in many situations, he still could prioritize principle over people, as he did in appointing counselors to the First Presidency in 1951 and the 1960s, regardless of the interpersonal implications. In some cases, including Wendell Mendenhall, when he became convinced that a confidant or

14. Quinn, *Elder Statesman*, 133–38.

employee was untrustworthy or self-serving, he summarily fired them. In other instances, when McKay disagreed with advisors, he enlarged his circle and privileged other voices, as he did by turning to Isaacson and Dyer.

By contrast, McKay's thinking on many matters was cautious and nuanced; McKay respected intellectual freedom and agency, countenanced a broad array of views on evolution, took lawbreakers ranging from some polygamists to juvenile delinquents under his wing and tried to help them reform, and mentored the mentally ill. He sympathetically recognized and regretted the injustice and shame endured by faithful Black Saints who could not hold the priesthood or marry in the temple, although he was too respectful of tradition and distrustful of his own sympathies to overturn preemptively or petition incessantly for a change of course. He admired elements and values of Hinduism and Confucianism and retreated from his initial hard line inclinations and substituted a conciliatory approach to Mexican Saints who broke away from the church. He cared enough about others' feelings and justice to rethink his decisions and reverse course, even when doing so might alienate close advisors. Such was the case when he vetoed the proposed relocation of Ricks College to Idaho Falls. In other instances, he reversed course when others advised him to do so, pulling back, for instance, from the church's contemplated expansion into West Africa.

As McKay aged he became less nuanced in his thinking, increasingly suspicious of his associates' agendas and priorities, and fearful that he was losing his grip on administering the church. Liberals and conservatives alike pressed the aging prophet to accommodate their own positions on matters including race, communism, and politics. The tug of war between more conservative advisors including Dyer, Benson, Lee, and Middlemiss and more liberal advisors including Brown, his sons Lawrence and Llewelyn, and (at times) Tanner placed McKay somewhere in the middle, encouraging him to vacillate and preventing him from moving too far in the direction of anti-communism and the John Birch Society on one side or relaxed restrictions on proselytizing and ordination of men with African ancestry on the other side.

Causes McKay championed, from his focus upon families to international expansion, assiduous proselytizing, and temple building, flourished beyond his death. Other causes such as anti-communism lost much of their currency, and his rhetoric about the tension between the physical and the spiritual has been seldom recalled or quoted. Two of McKay's key appointments were also discontinued. Called as an apostle and member of the First Presidency, Alvin R. Dyer returned to his post as an assistant to the Quorum of Twelve Apostles following McKay's death. Meanwhile McKay's employment of a woman as secretary to the church president was discontinued. D. Arthur Haycock replaced Middlemiss as personal secretary to the prophet, a position he held until 1986.[15]

15. Hazel S. Parkinson, "She'll Remember David O. McKay," *Salt Lake Tribune*, Aug. 23, 1970,

The institutional and personal imprint of every leader wanes as time passes. The same will be true of McKay as those of the baby boomer generation, the last to remember McKay personally, are replaced by younger generations and as the church engages a rapidly changing world. McKay helped to set the Church of Jesus Christ of Latter-day Saints on a trajectory of international expansion that continues to gather steam, though, and for the time being, memories of McKay and his ministry remain a taproot for the spiritual convictions and values of many members and leaders of the church.

4W; Gerry Avant, "Looking Back: What D. Arthur Haycock Learned as Secretary to Several Prophets and Apostles," *Deseret News Church Section*, Dec. 12, 2019; Kimball, journal, Jan. 19, 23, 1970. On January 19, Dyer attended a meeting of the apostles where McKay's funeral arrangements were discussed. Following that meeting, Spencer W. Kimball, Harold B. Lee, and Ezra Taft Benson, who had been appointed to plan the details of the funeral, met with Joseph Fielding Smith. Kimball records, "Elder Lee raised the question of whether Bro. Alvin R. Dyer, Counselor to the Presidency formerly, should be in attendance at the reorganization meeting [where the new prophet would be designated] … and President Smith indicated there was no reason why he shouldn't—that he was an Apostle. I interjected this question, 'But President Smith, he is not a member of the Council of the Twelve, and therefore would not have a voice. Would you want him to be present?' And the President changed his mind and suggested that that would probably not be necessary—perhaps he should not be there, and we left with that impression." On January 23, the day of the reorganization meeting, which Dyer did not attend, Kimball noted, "Elder Alvin R. Dyer was ordained an Apostle but never made a part of the Council of the Twelve so he would drop out of the highest councils unless recalled or re-appointed."

Bibliography

"1891 England, Scotland & Wales census." findmypast. 2012. http://www.findmypast. From GRO6/275, National Archives of the UK, Kew, Surrey, United Kingdom.

"391 Lance Corporal Hoani Te Okoro WiNeera aka John Jogles Naylor—Australian Imperial Forces." Porirua War Stories. Accessed Jan. 17, 2025. poriruawarstories.com.

Alder, Douglas D. Review of *David O. McKay and the Rise of Modern Mormonism*, by Gregory A. Prince and Wm. Robert Wright. *Utah Historical Quarterly* 73, no. 4 (Fall 2005): 387–90.

Alexander, Thomas G. *Mormonism in Transition: A History of the Latter-day Saints, 1890–1930.* Urbana: University of Illinois Press, 1986.

Allen, James B. "The Story of *The Truth, The Way, The Life*," in B. H. Roberts, *The Truth, The Way, The Life: An Elementary Treatise on Theology*, ed. John W. Welch (Provo: BYU Studies, 1994), clxxi–clxxxviii.

———. "Would-Be Saints: West Africa before the 1978 Priesthood Revelation." *Journal of Mormon History* 17 (1991): 207–47.

———, and Glen M. Leonard. *The Story of the Latter-day Saints*. 2nd ed. Salt Lake City: Deseret Book, 1992.

Anderson, Devery S., ed. *The Development of LDS Temple Worship*. Salt Lake City: Signature Books, 2010.

Anderson, Lavina Fielding. "Prayer under a Pepper Tree: Sixteen Accounts of a Spiritual Manifestation." *BYU Studies* 33, no. 1 (1993): 55–78.

Anderson, Paul L. "Mormon Moderne: Latter-day Saint Architecture, 1925–1945." *Journal of Mormon History* 9 (1982): 71–84.

Armstrong, Richard N. *The Rhetoric of David O. McKay*. New York: Peter Lang, 1993.

Arrington, Leonard J., and David Bitton. *The Mormon Experience: A History of the Latter-day Saints.* New York: Random House, 1980.

Arrington, Leonard J., and Wayne K. Hinton. "Origin of the Welfare Plan of the Church of Jesus Christ of Latter-day Saints." *BYU Studies* 5, no. 2 (1964): 67–85.

Bates, Irene M., and E. Gary Smith. *Lost Legacy: The Mormon Office of Presiding Patriarch.* Urbana: University of Chicago Press, 1996.

Beatty, Dylan. "The Devil in Our Pews: Locating Latter-day Saints in Colonial Samoa." Honors thesis, Rutgers University, 2012.

Belegenland (1878). Wikipedia. Wikimedia Foundation. Accessed Jan. 16, 2025, en.wikipedia.org.

Bergera, Gary James. "Tensions in David O. McKay's First Presidencies." *Journal of Mormon History* 33, no. 1 (Spring 2007): 179–246.

Bertha Clara Langton [Clarke], entry for. KWZ7-KZK. Family Search. Church of Jesus Christ of Latter-day Saints. Accessed Jan. 19, 2025. familysearch.org.

Black, Susan Easton [Ward]. Reminiscences of Susan Easton Black. Witnesses of the Book of Mormon. Interpreter Foundation, June 2021, witnessesofthebookofmormon.org.

Bowman, Matthew Burton. *The Mormon People: The Making of an American Faith*. New York: Random House, 2012.

Bradley, Martha Sonntag. *Kidnapped from that Land: The Government Raids on the Short Creek Polygamists*. Salt Lake City: University of Utah Press, 1993.

Bringhurst, Newell G. *Fawn McKay Brodie: A Biographer's Life*. Norman: University of Oklahoma Press, 1999.

———. "The Private versus the Public David O. McKay: Profile of a Complex Personality." *Dialogue: A Journal of Mormon Thought* 31, no. 3 (Fall 1998): 11–32.

———, and Frederick S. Buchanan. "The Forgotten Odyssey of Obadiah H. Riggs: Early Pioneer for Education Reform." *Utah Historical Quarterly* 66, no. 1 (Winter 1998): 48–64.

Britsch, R. Lanier. *From the East: The History of the Latter-day Saints in Asia*. Salt Lake City: Deseret Book, 1998.

———. *Unto the Islands of the Sea: A History of the Latter-day Saints in the Pacific*. Salt Lake City: Deseret Book, 1986.

Brooke, Stopford A. *The Poetry of Robert Browning*. New York: Thomas Y. Crowell, 1902.

Brown, Hugh B. *An Abundant Life: The Memoirs of Hugh B. Brown*. Edited by Edwin B. Firmage. Salt Lake City: Signature Books, 1988.

Buchanan, Frederick S. "Missionary Roots of Change." Review of *What E'er Thou Art, Act Well Thy Part: The Missionary Diaries of David O. Mckay*, edited by Stan Larson and Patricia Larson. *Dialogue: A Journal of Mormon Thought* 33, no. 2 (Summer 2000):193–96.

Buerger, David John. "The Development of the Mormon Temple Endowment Ceremony." *Dialogue: A Journal of Mormon Thought* 20, no. 4 (Winter 1987): 33–76.

Butler, Helen Julene. Interview by Becky B. Lloyd. Mar. 27, 2010. Everett L. Cooley Oral History Project. J. Willard Marriott Digital Library, University of Utah. Accessed Jan. 17, 2025. https://collections.lib.utah.edu/.

Campbell, Eugene E., and Richard D. Poll. *Hugh B. Brown: His Life and Thought*. Salt Lake City: Bookcraft, 1975.

Cannon, Brian Q. "'What a Power We Will Be in This Land': The LDS Church, the Church Security Program, and the New Deal." *Journal of the West* 43, no. 4 (Fall 2004): 66–75.

Cannon, Donald Q., and Richard O. Cowan. *Unto Every Nation: Gospel Light Reaches Every Land*. Salt Lake City: Deseret Book, 2003.

Cannon, Kenneth L., and Richard Long. "Premarital Behavior in the Sixties." *Journal of Marriage and Family* 33, no. 1 (February 1971): 36–49.

Carl Daniel Greenhalgh, entry for. KWZM-M1P. Family Search. Church of Jesus Christ of Latter-day Saints. Accessed Jan. 19, 2025. familysearch.org.

Chamberlin, Ralph V. *The University of Utah: A History of Its First Hundred Years, 1850 to 1950*. Salt Lake City: University of Utah Press, 1960.

"Charles Henry Owen." Davis County Cooperative Society. Accessed Jan. 17, 2025. dcc-society.org.

Charles Henry Owen, entry for. KWCD-LNS. Family Search. Church of Jesus Christ of Latter-day Saints. Accessed Jan. 19, 2025. familysearch.org.

Chicago Tribune. Chicago, IL, 1938.

"Church of Jesus Christ of Latter-day Saints v. Henning (Valuation Officer): CA 1962." 1 WLR 1091. Index of UK case law. David Swarbrick. Updated May 5, 2022. swarb.co.uk.

Church News. Salt Lake City, UT, 1953–1969.

Claire Jenny Whitehead, entry for. KWJC-2B4. Family Search. Church of Jesus Christ of Latter-day Saints. Accessed Jan. 18, 2025. familysearch.org.

Clark, J. Reuben. Papers. University Archives, L. Tom Perry Special Collections, Brigham Young University.

Condie, Spencer. *Russell M. Nelson: Father, Surgeon, Apostle*. Salt Lake City: Deseret Book, 2003.

Conference Reports of the Church of Jesus Christ of Latter-day Saints. 1897–2017. Semi-annual report containing speeches delivered at the church's semi-annual general conference. Salt Lake City: Church of Jesus Christ of Latter-day Saints.

Conway Alan Ashton, entry for. KWC6-GVD. Family Search. Church of Jesus Christ of Latter-day Saints. Accessed Jan. 19, 2025. familysearch.org.

Cowan, Richard O. *The Church in the Twentieth Century*. Salt Lake City: Bookcraft, 1985.

Cumbler, John T. *A Social History of Economic Decline: Business, Politics and Work in Trenton*. New Brunswick: Rutgers University Press, 1989.

Daily Universe. Provo, UT, 1965.

D'Arc, James V. "The Mormon as Vampire: A Comparative Study of Winifred Graham's *The Love Story of a Mormon*, the Film *Trapped by the Mormons*, and Bram Stoker's *Dracula*." *BYU Studies* 49, no. 2 (2007): 164–87.

Darowski, Joseph F. "The WPA Versus the Utah Church." In *Utah in the Twentieth Century*, edited by Brian Q. Cannon and Jessie L. Embry, 167–85. Logan: Utah State University Press, 2009.

Davis County Clipper. Woods Cross, UT, 1919.

Deseret News. Salt Lake City, UT, 1906, 1934–1968, 1994, 1998.

Dew, Sheri L. *Go Forward with Faith: The Biography of Gordon B. Hinckley*. Salt Lake City: Deseret Book, 1996.

Driggs, Ken. "After the Manifesto: Modern Polygamy and Fundamentalist Mormons." *Journal of Church and State* 32, no. 2 (1990): 367–89.

Durham, G. Homer. *N. Eldon Tanner: His Life and Service*. Salt Lake City: Deseret Book, 1982.

Eager, Ross, and Zelda Fish Eager. *Man of Faith, Perseverance, and Courage*. In entry for Ross Eager. KW8Z-3D8. Family Search. Church of Jesus Christ of Latter-day Saints. Posted May 3, 2014. familysearch.org.

Ellsworth, D. Delos. *History of Deseret Ranches, 1950–1989*. Provo: n.p., n.d., ca. 1990. Accessed at Harold B. Lee Library, Brigham Young University.

Embry, Jessie. "The Church Follows the Flag: US Foreign Aid, Utah Universities and the LDS Church in Iran, 1950–1964." *Journal of Mormon History* 32, no. 3 (2006): 141–79.

England, Eugene. Papers. ACCN 2426. Special Collections, J. Willard Marriott Library, University of Utah.

———. "The Place of David O. McKay in Mormon Culture." *Sunstone*, Feb. 2000, 20–22.

Ensign. Salt Lake City, UT, 1976–78, 1982, 1988, 1995–98, 2000, 2007, 2010, 2012, 2023.

Farnes, Edith Virginia Budd Jacobsen. "[Auto]biography of Edith Virginia Farnes part 2." Entry for Edith Virginia Budd. KWCJ-PGT. Family Search. Church of Jesus Christ of Latter-day Saints. Accessed Jan. 18, 2025. familysearch.org.

Finer, Lawrence B. "Trends in Premartial Sex in the United States, 1954–2003." *Public Health Reports* 122, no. 1 (Jan.-Feb. 2007): 73–78.

Francis Lorenzo Lund, entry for. KWCD-PL2. Family Search. Church of Jesus Christ of Latter-day Saints. Accessed Jan. 19, 2025. familysearch.org.

Garlitz, Richard. *A Mission for Development: Utah Universities and the Point Four Program in Iran*. Logan: Utah State University Press, 2018.

Geisner, Joseph. "Very Careless in His Utterances: Editing, Correcting, and Censoring Conference Addresses." *Sunstone Magazine Podcast*, Jan. 3, 2012. Audio and transcript. *Sunstone*. sunstone.org.

General conference digital video collection. AV 3500. Church History Catalog. Church of Jesus Christ of Latter-day Saints. Accessed Jan. 17, 2025. catalog.churchofjesuschrist.org.

Gertrude Victoria Kemp [Wineera], entry for. LKG6-MK4. Family Search. Church of Jesus Christ of Latter-day Saints. Accessed Jan. 19, 2025. familysearch.org.

———. *David O. McKay: Apostle to the World, Prophet of God*. Salt Lake City: Deseret Book, 1986.

Gibbons, Francis M. *George Albert Smith: Kind and Caring Christian, Prophet of God*. Salt Lake City: Deseret Book, 1990.

Givens, Terryl L. *The Latter-day Saint Experience in America*. Westport, CT: Greenwood Press, 2004.

"Glimpse into the Life of Gertrude Orth Shirra." Entry for Gertrude Orth. KWC4-15H. Family Search. Church of Jesus Christ of Latter-day Saints. Accessed Jan. 18, 2025. familysearch.org.

Global Histories. The Church of Jesus Christ of Latter-day Saints. history.churchofjesus-christ.org.

Goates, L. Brent. *Harold B. Lee: Prophet and Seer*. Salt Lake City: Bookcraft, 1985.

Goodwin's Weekly. Salt Lake City, UT, 1916.

Golden Haight, entry for. KWC8-SGL. Family Search. Church of Jesus Christ of Latter-day Saints. Accessed Jan. 19, 2025. familysearch.org.

Grant, Heber J. *The Diaries of Heber J. Grant, 1880–1945, Abridged.* Edited by Davis Bitton, Scott G. Kenney, and D. Michael Quinn. Salt Lake City: Privately published, 2010.

Greenwell, Robert. "One Devout Mormon Family's Struggle with Racism." *Dialogue: A Journal of Mormon Thought* 51, no. 3 (Fall 2018): 155–80.

Groome, Francis H., ed. *Ordnance Gazetteer of Scotland: A Survey of Scottish Topography, Statistical, Biographical, and Historical.* Edinburgh: Grange Publishing Works, 1882–1885. http://www.scottish-places.info.

The Guardian. England, 2001.

Gunther, John. *Inside U.S.A.* New York: Harper & Bros., 1947.

Harris, Carl. *Samoa Apia Mission History, 1888–1983.* Apia: Samoa Apia Mission, 1983.

Harris, Matthew L. *Second-Class Saints: Black Mormons and the Struggle for Racial Equality.* New York: Oxford University Press, 2024.

———. *Watchman on the Tower: Ezra Taft Benson and the Making of the Mormon Right.* Salt Lake City: University of Utah Press, 2020.

Haws, J. B. *The Mormon Image in the American Mind: Fifty Years of Public Perception.* New York: Oxford University Press, 2013.

Heber Chase Smith, Sr., entry for. KWCW-657. Family Search. Church of Jesus Christ of Latter-day Saints. Accessed Jan. 19, 2025. familysearch.org.

"Henning v. Church of Jesus Christ of Latter-day Saints," All E.R. 733 [1963], or [1963] UKHL J0530-1. vLex Justis. Accessed Jan. 17, 2025. vlex.co.uk.

Henry Hooper Blood, entry for. KWCW-K53. Family Search. Church of Jesus Christ of Latter-day Saints. Accessed Jan. 19, 2025. familysearch.org.

Hicks, Michael. *The Mormon Tabernacle Choir: A Biography.* Urbana: University of Illinois Press, 2015.

Holley, Val. *25th Street Confidential: Drama, Decadence, and Dissipation along Ogden's Rowdiest Road.* Salt Lake City: University of Utah Press, 2013.

Improvement Era. Salt Lake City, UT, 1936.

Intermountain-Republican. Salt Lake City, UT, 1909.

Jacob, W. James, and Meli U. Lesuma. "History of the Church of Jesus Christ of Latter-day Saints in Fiji." In *Pioneers in the Pacific*, edited by Grant Underwood. Provo: BYU Religious Studies Center, 2005.

James Gain, entry for. KWZV-8Q8. Family Search. Church of Jesus Christ of Latter-day Saints. Accessed Jan. 18, 2025. familysearch.org.

James Rongotoa Elkington, entry for. LTHW-8LS. Family Search. Church of Jesus Christ of Latter-day Saints. Accessed Jan. 18, 2025. familysearch.org.

Janet Chalmers [Leggat], entry for. KWZS-ZMZ. Family Search. Church of Jesus Christ of Latter-day Saints. Accessed Jan. 19, 2025. familysearch.org.

Jeffrey, Duane E. "Seers, Savants and Evolution: The Uncomfortable Interface," *Dialogue: A Journal of Mormon Thought* 8, no. 3–4 (Autumn-Winter 1973): 61–75.

"Joseph Henry Stimpson." In *Latter-day Saint Biographical Encyclopedia*. Vol. 4, edited by Andrew Jenson. Salt Lake City: Andrew Jenson Memorial Foundation, 1936, 71–72.

Joy Beck Van Wagoner, entry for. KWZG-6Y6. Family Search. Church of Jesus Christ of Latter-day Saints. Accessed Jan. 19, 2025. familysearch.org.

Kātene, Selwyn. *Turning the Hearts of the Children: Early Māori Leaders in the Mormon Church*. Wellington, NZ: Steele Roberts Aotearoa, 2014.

Keen, Benjamin, and Mark Wasserman. *A Short History of Latin America*. 2nd ed. Boston: Houghton Mifflin, 1984.

Kennedy, David M. Interview by Gordon Irving, 1981–1987. OH 968. Church History Library, Salt Lake City.

Kenney, Scott G. MS 2022. Research Materials. L. Tom Perry Special Collections, Harold B. Lee Library, Brigham Young University.

Kimball, Edward L., and Andrew E. Kimball Jr. *Spencer W. Kimball: Twelfth President of the Church of Jesus Christ of Latter-day Saints*. Salt Lake City: Bookcraft, 1977.

Kimball, Spencer W. Journals. MS 21541. Church History Library, Salt Lake City.

Kruse, Kevin M. *One Nation Under God: How Corporate America Invented Christian America*. New York: Basic Books, 2015.

Lampropoulos, Anne-Marie Wright, ed. *A Vision Splendid: The Discourses of David O. McKay*. Draper, UT: Greg Kofford Books, 2022.

Latter-day Saints' Millennial Star. England, 1907, 1922–1924.

"Lewis Betts Parkin's Mission to Tonga." Entry for Lewis Betts Parkin. KWCH-X53. Family Search. Church of Jesus Christ of Latter-day Saints. Accessed Jan. 18, 2025. familysearch.org.

Liahona. Salt Lake City, UT, 2014.

Liddle, Stephen W., and Richard C. Galbraith. *Scripture Citation Index*. Index of citations of LDS scripture.Version 3.5.0. Brigham Young University. Accessed Jan. 17, 2025. scriptures.byu.edu.

Lineham, Peter J. "Story: Meha, Stuart." *Dictionary of New Zealand Biography*. New Zealand Government. teara.gov.nz.

"Lloyd Oscar Ivie." Church History Biographical Database. Church of Jesus Christ of Latter-day Saints. Accessed Jan. 17, 2025. history.churchofjesuschrist.org.

Logan Republican. Logan, UT, 1911.

London, Brett. "My Highway Patrol Uncle Gave His Wife and President McKay Speeding Tickets." *London Edition*. londonedition.home.blog.

London Daily Mail. England, 1958.

Lucille Beardall Worthen, entry for. KW8J-X9D. Family Search. Church of Jesus Christ of Latter-day Saints. Accessed Jan. 19, 2025. familysearch.org

Lund, Anthon H. *Danish Apostle: The Diaries of Anthon H. Lund*. Edited by John P. Hatch. Salt Lake City: Signature Books, 2006.

Lythgoe, Dennis L. *Let 'Em Holler: A Political Biography of J. Bracken Lee.* Salt Lake City: Utah State Historical Society, 1982.

Mangum, Garth L., and Bruce D. Blumell. *The Mormons' War on Poverty: A History of LDS Welfare, 1830–1990.* Salt Lake City: University of Utah Press, 1993.

Manti Messenger. Manti, UT, 1955.

McBride, Heber R. Diary, 1876 February–July. MS 9867. Church History Library, Salt Lake City.

McKay, David Lawrence. *My Father, David O. McKay.* Edited by Lavina Fielding Anderson. Salt Lake City: Deseret Book, 1989.

McKay, David O. *Confidence amid Change: The Presidential Diaries of David O. McKay, 1951–1970.* Edited by Harvard S. Heath. Salt Lake City: Signature Books, 2019.

———. *Gospel Ideals: Selections from the Discourses of David O. McKay.* Salt Lake City: Improvement Era, 1953.

———. *My Young Friends: President McKay Speaks to Youth.* Compiled by Llewelyn R. McKay. Salt Lake City: Bookcraft, 1973.

———. *Pacific Apostle: The 1920–21 Diary of David O. McKay in the Latter-day Saint Island Missions.* Edited by Reid L. Neilson and Carson V. Teuscher. Urbana: University of Illinois Press, 2020.

———. Papers. MS 0668. Special Collections, J. Willard Marriott Library, University of Utah.

———. "Two Contending Forces." BYU devotional address, May 18, 1960. BYU Speeches. speeches.byu.edu.

———. *What E'er Thou Art Act Well Thy Part: The Missionary Diaries of David O. McKay.* Edited by Stan Larson and Patricia Larson. Salt Lake City: Blue Ribbon Books, 1999.

———, and Emma Ray McKay. *Heart Petals: The Personal Correspondence of David Oman McKay and Emma Ray McKay.* Edited by Mary Jane Woodger. Salt Lake City: University of Utah Press, 2005.

McKay, Llewelyn R. *Home Memories of President David O. McKay.* Salt Lake City: Deseret Book, 1956.

McMurrin, Sterling M., and L. Jackson Newell. *Matters of Conscience: Conversations with Sterling M. McMurrin on Philosophy, Education, and Religion.* Salt Lake City: Signature Books, 1996.

Mehr, Kahlile. "The Trial of the French Mission." *Dialogue* 21, no. 3 (Autumn 1988): 27–45.

Middlemiss, Clare, comp. *Cherished Experiences from the Writings of President David O. McKay.* Salt Lake City: Deseret Book, 1955.

———, comp. *Cherished Experiences from the Writings of President David O. McKay.* Salt Lake City: Deseret Book, 1971.

———, comp. *Cherished Experiences from the Writings of President David O. McKay.* Salt Lake City: Deseret Book, 1976.

———, comp. *Man May Know for Himself: Teachings of President David O. McKay.* Salt Lake City: Deseret Book, 1967.

Millard County Chronicle. Delta, UT, 1916.

Minson, Sara. *Autobiography of Sara Minson.* In entry for Sara Minson. KWZR-JH6. Family Search. Church of Jesus Christ of Latter-day Saints. 1996. familysearch.org.

Minutes of the Apostles of the Church of Jesus Christ of Latter-day Saints. 4 vols. Salt Lake City: privately published, 2010.

Morrell, Jeanette McKay. *Highlights in the Life of President David O. McKay.* Salt Lake City: Deseret Book, 1971.

Mt. Pleasant Pyramid. Mount Pleasant, UT, 1916.

Murdock, Franklin J. Interviews by Gordon Irving. March 28–30, 1973. OH 89. Church History Library, Salt Lake City.

Neilson, Reid L., ed. *To the Peripheries of Mormondom: The Apostolic Around-the-World Journey of David O. McKay, 1920–1921.* Salt Lake City: University of Utah Press, 2011.

Newton, Marjorie. *Southern Cross Saints: The Mormons in Australia.* Laie: Institute for Polynesian Studies, 1991.

Newton, Marjorie. *Tiki and Temple: The Mormon Mission in New Zealand, 1854–1958.* Salt Lake City: Greg Kofford Books, 2012.

New York Times. New York, 1970, 2022.

Nibley, Preston. "Portrait of David O. McKay." BYU devotional address, January 13, 1960. BYU Speeches. speeches.byu.edu.

Nielson, Clyde, and Alonzo F. Cole. *The Four Rejected Revelations.* Privately published, 1940.

Norcross, Liz. "Biographical Sketch of Jennette Evans McKay." Entry for Jennette Eveline Evans [McKay]. KWZZ-KQW. Family Search. Church of Jesus Christ of Latter-day Saints. Posted Mar. 20, 2014, familysearch.org.

Ogden Daily Standard. Ogden, UT, 1906, 1909–1918.

Ogden Evening Standard. Ogden, UT, 1911.

Ogden Junction. Ogden, UT, 1880.

Ogden Standard Examiner. Ogden, UT, 1920, 1921.

Ogletree, Mark D. *No Other Success: The Parenting Practices of David O. McKay.* Provo: BYU Religious Studies Center, 2017.

Olinger, Mark A. "U.S. Army Mobilization During the Korean War and Its Aftermath." Land Warfare Papers no. 70W. Institute of Land Warfare. n.p., 2008.

Park, Benjamin E. *American Zion: A New History of Mormonism.* New York: Norton, 2024.

Parkinson, Benson Y. *S. Dilworth Young: General Authority, Scouter, Poet.* American Fork, UT: Covenant Communications, 1994.

Parry, Darren. *The Bear River Massacre: A Shoshone History.* Salt Lake City: By Common Consent Press, 2019.

Petersen, Boyd J. Review of *David O. McKay and the Rise of Modern Mormonism,* by Gregory A. Prince and Wm. Robert Wright. *Journal of Mormon History* 32, no. 2 (Summer 20006): 267–72.

Petersen, Mark E. Preface. to *Man May Know for Himself: Teachings of President David O. McKay.* Compiled by Clare Middlemiss. Salt Lake City: Desert Book, 1967.

Peterson, Charles S., and Brian Q. Cannon. *The Awkward State of Utah: Coming of Age in the Nation, 1896–1945*. Salt Lake City: University of Utah Press, 2015.

Pleasant Grove Review, 1978.

Plewe, Brandon S., ed. *Mapping Mormonism: An Atlas of Latter-day Saint History*. Provo: BYU Press, 2012.

Poll, Richard D. *Working the Divine Miracle: The Life of Apostle Henry D. Moyle*. Edited by Stan Larson. Salt Lake City: Signature Books, 1999.

"President David O. McKay, 1873–1970." *Dialogue: A Journal of Mormon Thought* 4, no. 4 (Winter 1969): 47–62.

Prince, Gregory A. Papers. ACCN 1334. Special Collections, J. Willard Marriott Library, University of Utah.

———, and William Robert Wright. *David O. McKay and the Rise of Modern Mormonism*. Salt Lake City: University of Utah Press, 2005.

Provo Daily Herald. Provo, UT, 1922, 1954.

Pusey, Merlo J. *Builders of the Kingdom: George A. Smith, John Henry Smith, George Albert Smith*. Provo: BYU Press, 1981.

Quinn, D. Michael. *Elder Statesman: A Biography of J. Reuben Clark*. Salt Lake City: Signature Books, 2002.

———. *The Mormon Hierarchy: Wealth & Corporate Power*. Salt Lake City: Signature Books, 2017.

Relief Society Magazine. Salt Lake City, UT, 1967, 1969.

Roberts, B. H. *The Autobiography of B. H. Roberts*. Edited by Gary James Bergera. Salt Lake City: Signature Books, 1990.

Roosevelt Standard. Roosevelt, UT, 1934.

Rutherford, Taunalyn F. "The Internationalization of Mormonism: Indications from India." In *Out of Obscurity: Mormonism since 1945*, edited by Patrick Q. Mason and John G. Turner, 37–60. New York: Oxford University Press, 2016.

Salt Lake Herald. Salt Lake City, UT, 1896–1902.

Salt Lake Herald-Republican. Salt Lake City, UT, 1902.

Salt Lake Telegram. Salt Lake City, UT, 1922, 1938–1949.

Salt Lake Tribune. Salt Lake City, UT, 1873–1968.

San Juan Record. Monticello, UT, 1953.

Schluter, F. E. *A Convert's Tribute to President David O. McKay*. Salt Lake City: Deseret Book, 1964.

Sikahema, Vai. "Church Culture, Ethnic Culture and Education." BYU–Hawaii devotional address, BYU–Hawaii Speeches, August 26, 2014. speeches.byuh.edu.

Smoot, Reed. *In the World: The Diaries of Reed Smoot*. Edited by Harvard S. Heath. Salt Lake City: Signature Books, 1997.

"*SS City of Rome*, Anchor Line." Norway Heritage. Accessed Jan. 17, 2025. norwayheritage.com.

Stanford Magazine. Stanford, CA, 1998.

Stevenson, Russell W. *For the Cause of Righteousness: A Global History of Blacks and Mormonism, 1830–2013*. Salt Lake City: Greg Kofford Books, 2014.

Sunstone. Salt Lake City, UT, 1979.

Talmage, James E. *The Story of "Mormonism."* Liverpool: Millennial Star Office, 1907.

Taylor, Vivian. "Lester R. Taylor History." Compiled by Peggy Geddes. In entry for Lester Rogers Taylor, KWC8-PWC, Family Search. Church of Jesus Christ of Latter-day Saints. July 30, 2020. familysearch.org.

Terry, Keith. *David O. McKay: Prophet of Love*. Santa Barbara: Butterfly Publishing, 1980.

Thiruthuvadoss, S. Paul. "First Indian Convert's Testimony." *Dialogue: A Journal of Mormon Thought* 13, no. 3 (Spring 1980): 96–99.

Thomas, John C. "Apostolic Diplomacy: The 1923 European Mission of Senator Reed Smoot and Professor John A. Widtsoe." *Journal of Mormon History* 28, no. 2 (Spring 2002): 130–65.

Time Magazine. New York, NY, 1942, 1970.

Tullis, F. LaMond. "A Shepherd to Mexico's Saints: Arwell L. Pierce and the Third Convention." *BYU Studies* 87, no. 1(1997): 131, 156.

Turley, Richard E., Jr., and Clinton D. Christensen. *An Apostolic Journey: Stephen L Richards and the Expansion of Missionary Work in South America*. Provo: BYU Religious Studies Center, 2019.

University of California Register, 1955–1956, with Announcements for 1955–1956. Berkeley: University of California, 1956.

The University Chronicle. Salt Lake City, UT, 1894–1897.

"United States, Census, 1880." FamilySearch. Jan. 17, 2025. https://FamilySearch.org. From microfilm publication T9. National Archives and Records Administration, Washington, DC.

Van Orden, Bruce A. *Building Zion: The Latter-day Saints in Europe*. Salt Lake City: Deseret Book, 1996.

Walker, Ronald W. "'Going to Meeting' in Salt Lake City's Thirteenth Ward." In *New Views of Mormon History: Essays in Honor of Leonard J. Arrington*. edited by Davis Bitton and Maureen Ursenbach Beecher, 138–61. Salt Lake City: University of Utah Press, 1987.

Watson, Marianne. "The Fred E. Curtis Papers: LDS Church Surveillance of Fundamentalist Mormons, 1937–1954." Audio, *Sunstone* Salt Lake City 2001 Symposium, session 263. *Sunstone*. Posted Jan. 1, 2001. sunstone.org.

Weber College Signpost. Ogden, UT, 1952.

Whitney, Orson. F. *The Life of Orson F. Whitney: Historian, Poet, Apostle, As Recorded in His Daily Journals*. Edited by Dennis B. Horne. Springville, UT: Cedar Fort, 2014.

Wilkinson, Ernest L. Papers. University Archives, L. Tom Perry Special Collections, Brigham Young University.

William Robert Calderwood, entry for. KWJ8-VNT. Family Search. Church of Jesus Christ of Latter-day Saints. Accessed Jan. 19, 2025. familysearch.org.

Williams, Frederick Salem, and Frederick G. Williams. *From Acorn to Oak Tree: A Personal History of the Establishment and First Quarter Century Development of the South American Missions*. Fullerton: Et Cetera Graphics, 1987.

Willis McCracken Smith, entry for. KWD3-HZG. Family Search. Church of Jesus Christ of Latter-day Saints. Accessed Jan. 19, 2025. familysearch.org.

Woodger, Mary Jane. *Against the Odds: The Life of George Albert Smith*. American Fork, UT: Covenant Communications, 2011.

———. *David O. McKay: Beloved Prophet*. American Fork, UT: Covenant Communications, 2004.

———. "David O. McKay's Progressive Educational Ideas and Practices, 1899–1922." *Journal of Mormon History* 30, no. 2 (Fall 2004): 208–48.

Woodruff, Josephine D. Booth. Journals, 1899–1901. MS 16963. Church History Library, Salt Lake City. Wright, Evan P. *A History of the South African Mission, Period III, 1940–1970*. Privately published, 1987. Harold B. Lee Library, Brigham Young University.

Wright, Evan P. *A History of the South African Mission, Period III, 1940–1970*. Privately published, 1987. Harold B. Lee Library, Brigham Young University.

Index

M

N

About the Author

Brian Q. Cannon is the Lemuel Hardison Redd Jr. Professor of Western American History at Brigham Young University. He served as chair of the BYU history department for six years and directed the Charles Redd Center for Western Studies at BYU for fifteen years. A past president of the Mormon History Association and the Agricultural History Society, he is an honorary fellow of both the Utah State Historical Society and the Agricultural History Society. The Western History Association honored him with the Gordon M. Bakken Award of Merit in 2020. He is the author of four books, the coeditor of three more, and the author of more than forty articles and book chapters regarding rural history, Western American history, Latter-day Saint history, and social and cultural history.